The Bible Study
and
Prayer
Book

*Guidance and Insight for Understanding
the Bible and Growing Closer to God*

JAMES STUART BELL, TRACY SUMNER, RONALD HENNIES *and* SONIA WEISS

JG
PRESS

Published by World Publications Group, Inc.
140 Laurel Street
East Bridgewater, MA 02333
www.wrldpub.com

Originally published as *The Everything® Bible Study Book* and
The Everything® Prayer Book.

ISBN 10: 1-57215-748-8
ISBN 13: 978-1-57215-748-4

ISBN 10: 1-57215-750-X
ISBN 13: 978-1-57215-750-7

Printed and bound in the United States of America.

10 9 8 7 6 5 4 3 2 1

Contents

Bible Study

01 A Bible Study How-to / 15

02 Bible Reading and Study: What's in It for You? / 29

03 Taking It Personally / 39

04 Other Uses for the Bible / 51

Prayer

Bible Study

Top Ten Greatest Things about Studying the Bible

1. The Bible is not just God's way of speaking to you, but also His way of blessing you with every gift He wants you to have.

2. You learn what the Christian life is all about, what it looks like, and how you can practically live it out in every day and in every way.

3. When you read the Bible, you are reading the words and messages of God Himself.

4. It is something God encourages—even commands—His people to do.

5. It enables you to tell others about your faith because now you have a better idea of what you're talking about.

6. You hear and interact with God as you read His words.

7. You get all the things you're really seeking from God—love, comfort, forgiveness, wisdom, hope, security, and so on.

8. You learn the details of stories you may know the basics about now—for example, Noah and the ark, Jonah and the whale.

9. You can fully understand the Good News of the salvation message—that Jesus died for your sins and will give you eternal life.

10. There are hundreds of promises from God to you that you can count on if you believe and obey His Word.

Introduction

ONE OF THE MOST dominant themes in the Bible—Old Testament and New Testament alike—is the importance of reading, studying, memorizing, knowing, and meditating upon God's written Word. For example, God told Joshua, the man charged with the responsibility of leading the Jewish people into the Promised Land, "Be careful to obey all the instructions Moses gave you. Do not deviate from them, turning either to the right or to the left. Then you will be successful in everything you do. Study this Book of Instruction continually. Meditate on it day and night so you will be sure to obey everything written in it. Only then will you prosper and succeed in all you do" (Joshua 1:7–8).

There is a theme running throughout the Bible, and it's this: A huge part of being a believer is spending time reading, studying, meditating, and personally applying God's written Word. Still, the problem for many Christians is that they don't know how to approach reading and studying the Bible. Do they just start at Genesis and work their way through to the end of Revelation? Do they just start with a book whose name sounds good to them that day? Or do they just concentrate on the New Testament?

Answering these questions by providing ways you can easily follow to read and study the Bible is the reason for this book. As you read through it, you will learn some of the methods of reading and studying the Bible, some of the benefits of Bible study, some of the uses for Scripture, and, of course, some actual Bible studies.

As you learn to study the Bible for yourself, you will find that just making the effort can be quite challenging. But as you figure out what method works best for you, you will realize that reading the Bible is not just challenging (you should always feel challenged and even provoked when you read God's Word) but also enjoyable and enlightening.

One final thing we want you to understand about the Bible before you launch into your own personal study: When it comes to the big picture of the Bible, the following anonymous quotation sums up what the Bible is all about: "In the Old Testament we have Jesus predicted. In the Gospels we have Jesus revealed. In Acts we have Jesus preached. In the Epistles we have Jesus explained. In the Revelation we have Jesus expected."

From "In the beginning..." on, every word in the Bible points to the fulfillment of God's promise and plan to bring salvation to all humankind through His Son, Jesus Christ. So as you learn to study the Bible for yourself, keep in mind that every word you read—every promise, challenge, and story—between its covers is about Jesus and what he means to you.

The first four chapters provide a background to the Bible and how to study it. The bulk of this book, Chapters 5–21, presents what we consider to be among the most important sections of the entire Bible. If you want to study the Bible comprehensively you won't want to neglect these. We try to provide the background, meaning, and potential application to life that you will need to truly profit from what is important in Scripture.

So as you read this book, allow yourself to learn to read and study the Bible! As you do, you'll find out that it is in every way a great book—the greatest!

CHAPTER 1

A Bible Study How-to

Like just about anything else, if you want to effectively read and study the Bible and apply its principles to your own life, you're going to have to have a plan. In this chapter, you'll find some techniques for Bible reading and study—all of which are tried and true over the centuries—that will help make it easier for you to become better acquainted with what God's Word has to say to you personally.

The Importance of Studying the Bible Effectively

There once was a story of a man who needed to buy a new family car. Since he was a man of prayer who often went to the Bible when it was time to make big decisions, he opened his King James Bible at random and pointed to one verse on the page, hoping to find some kind of direction for his decision. That verse was Acts 1:14, which reads:

"These all continued with one *accord*..."

The very next day the man went to the local Honda dealership, where he purchased a brand new Honda Accord. Never mind the fact that he and his wife had four children—three of them teenagers—and that this particular car was much too small to meet their needs. As far as he was concerned, the Word of God had spoken to him very clearly.

While most believers know that God can certainly give direction by guiding people to specific passages of Scripture—and by other means— more often than not, the "open-and-point" method of Bible study isn't going to yield the kind of results, knowledge, or direction needed to make sound decisions. Taking that a step further, God wants each of us to be ready and willing to make a commitment when it comes to studying our Bibles.

The topic of this chapter is how the individual believer/reader can more effectively study the Bible. If you've been wondering about that in your own life, then it shows you are ready—or getting ready—to make the kind of commitment it takes to make Bible reading and study a regular, everyday part of your Christian life.

This chapter includes a list of things you'll need as well as some ways to use those things in order to learn and apply not just what the Bible has to say but also what it has to say to *you*. And you can bet that it's well worth the time and effort it will certainly take!

What You'll Need or at Least Find Useful

There are several items—all of which are readily available for purchase or download—that can help make Bible study both easier and more beneficial to the one who wishes to take the time to make studying the Bible a life priority. While some of these items are essential for good Bible study—for example, you can't very well study the Bible unless you have one—some of them aren't absolutely necessary but can be very helpful.

Here are the things you will need or will find helpful:

Study Bible

You can't very well study the Bible without your very own copy. Fortunately, there are hundreds of Bibles in dozens of translations available today. Some of them, those we refer to as "study Bibles," include mini concordances (lists of words) and dictionaries, and some include cross references so that you can better understand a verse or passage and put it in context with the entirety of the Bible.

discussion question

What is the best time of day to study the Bible?
There is no bad time of day to study the Bible, but the Bible itself implies that we should begin each day in God's Word. The practical element of starting the day that way is that it makes it easier to commit time to Bible study.

There are study Bibles for different age groups, different ministries, and different life stations, so if you take the time you can find a study Bible that best meets your needs.

If you can afford it, purchase more than one translation of the Bible. It would be useful to have a copy of the King James Version and a copy of a version that uses more modern English, such as the New American Standard, the New Living Translation, or the New International Version, just to name a few. The Scripture you'll find quoted in this book is from the New Living Translation.

Bible Concordance

Most of us aren't experts in the original Biblical languages—Hebrew, Greek, and Aramaic—so a good concordance is a great help to those of us who want to study the Bible in depth. A Biblical concordance is a published list of keywords in the Bible text, and it includes thumbnail definitions and the context in which all those words are used. A concordance is especially useful when it comes to finding keywords and phrases in the Bible.

There are several concordances in both printed and electronic form—some you can even use for free online. The best known are *Strong's Exhaustive Concordance* and *Young's Analytical Concordance to the Bible.*

symbolism

When you go to purchase a concordance, it is helpful to buy one that is compatible with the version of the Bible you are using. For example, *Strong's Exhaustive Concordance* is regarded as a companion to the King James Version of the Bible. A few minutes of research or shopping will help you to buy the right concordance

Bible Dictionary

Like concordances, there are many quality Bible dictionaries in both printed and electronic form, and most of them are readily available at your local bookstore or as downloads from the Internet. You can use some of them for free by simply going online. Try the Holman Bible Dictionary at *www.studylight.org/dic/hbd/* or the Smith Bible Dictionary at *www.study light.org/dic/sbdl.*

Bible dictionaries are different from concordances in that they cover topics, events, places, and people rather than keywords. For example, if you wanted to study personal salvation, the Bible dictionary would give you the scriptural basics on that subject, while the concordance would direct you to passages in the Bible where that word (or variations of it) is used.

Bible dictionaries are also important in that they give the reader easier access to the different contexts of what they are reading. For example, any Bible dictionary will tell the reader the time and historic context of the writings of the Old Testament prophets as well as the target audiences of the New Testament writings of the apostle Paul.

point of interest

There are several Bible commentaries available today that are considered classics in Christian literature. While these commentaries offer excellent insights to the Bible, some of them are, because of the outdated English used, difficult to understand for the modern reader. Read a sample of a commentary before you buy

Bible Commentary

Over the centuries, many men of God have taken the time to write detailed Bible commentaries, some of which have withstood the tests of time. Renowned Christian figures such as Martin Luther, John Calvin, Charles Spurgeon, Matthew Henry, and John Wesley have all penned Bible commentaries. While there may be differences between them in the interpretation and applications of specific texts, they all have valuable insights for those who make Bible study a part of their daily lives.

Dictionary and Thesaurus

If you're going to study anything in the English language, it is helpful to have a dictionary and thesaurus available. A thesaurus is especially helpful because the Bible text often uses different words to convey what is essentially the same thought or idea.

Writing Supplies

Remember what you did as you sat through class lectures during your high school or college years? If you're like most successful students, you took notes on the lecture of your teacher or professor. Doing that was helpful in two ways: First, it enabled you to go back to your notes so you could be reminded of what the instructor said. Second, it helped brand what he or she said on a particular day into your memory.

But what student has never taken a pen or colored highlighters and marked key passages in a textbook? Obviously, that is an excellent way to remember what is noteworthy and important in the class. The same techniques work when it comes to studying the Bible, and for that reason it is recommended that you have a pen, a notepad, and colored highlighters available when you study your Bible.

Some people are reluctant to mark up their new study Bible with colored pens, but those who are experienced at personal Bible study will tell you that this is an effective way to focus on the keywords in a text, thus giving the reader a leg up in understanding what God is saying through it. You can always keep a second Bible free of all markings if you are distracted by the colored highlighting.

Once you arm yourself with the items listed above, you'll be ready to start a systemized Bible study. The only question then is which method to use. There are many good ways to read and study the Bible, and some are detailed for you in the rest of this chapter.

Reading Through the Bible in a Year

The simplest way to read and study the Bible is to read it very much like you would a novel, meaning starting at "In the beginning" (Genesis 1:1) and ending with "The Grace of the Lord Jesus be with you all" (Revelation 22:21).

There are many excellent study Bibles on the market that can guide the reader through the entire Bible in a year. In addition, there are many outlines available that can take you through the Bible in 365 calendar days—some for sale in the local bookstore and some readily—and freely—available through Internet sources.

factum

Without a plan to get through the Bible in a year, it's nearly impossible to keep accurate track of your progress. That's why it's important if you begin reading through the Bible in a year to have a plan or outline and that you stick to it once you've started

Reading the Bible verse by verse from beginning to end in a year is a great way to get an overview of what the Book as a whole has to say, and it is something every believer should strive to do at least once. But there are more effective ways to take from the Bible the personal applications God wants each Christian to have. In order to help you achieve those goals, try one or more of the following tried and true methods of Bible study.

Deductive Bible Study

The deductive method of studying the Bible means picking a certain subject as your starting point, then going through the Bible and finding Scriptures that address it. In short, it is a topical approach to studying the Scriptures.

Most preachers and Bible teachers prepare their materials using the deductive method of study. For example, if a preacher or teacher wanted to give a sermon or teach on the subject of sin, he'd look throughout both the Old Testament and the New Testament to find passages or verses that best fit the point he wanted to make.

One of the advantages of the deductive approach to Bible study is that it gives the reader a good Biblical overview of a particular topic as well as more personal applications. That's because it takes the different things that are said in the Bible on a particular word or topic—all of which you'll find are in amazing harmony—and gives you the bigger picture look at what God has to say about those topics.

Inductive Bible Study

While the deductive method of Bible study involves studying the Bible topically, studying it inductively means taking a passage of Scripture and reading it, pondering it, and asking questions about it until you are able to draw conclusions about what that text is saying in and of itself.

If you wanted to do a deductive study on the word *love*, you would search your concordance for that word, as well as variations, and begin looking at the passages and verses that include it. But if you were to do an inductive study, say of 1 Corinthians 13, which has been called the Love Chapter, you would find out how important godly love is and what it looks like—all from reading just one chapter.

The first thing you should do when conducting an inductive Bible study is to simply read what the text says and think about what it means. Ask how this text applies to you and how you can practically and effectively apply this text to your life.

point of interest

When you use the deductive method of Bible study, you will absolutely, positively need a good concordance as well as a thesaurus. That will allow you to look at synonyms (words that mean the same as the ones you are looking at) as well as variations of particular words and phrases.

What you observe when you read and study the Bible is absolutely vital because your understanding and application of anything you see or read—including a text of Scripture—will be based upon what you hear it saying. That is why it is so important to take the time during an inductive Bible study to ask God to teach you what He wants you to learn through the particular passage you are looking at.

It is also important that you understand the context of the text you are looking at. Context means everything when it comes to studying anything, particularly the Bible. Without knowing the context, it is impossible to take your studies a step further and understand what a particular passage says in general and what it says to you individually.

When making sense of what a passage of Scripture means, it is always best to look for the obvious. Sometimes what the Bible appears to be saying is exactly what it is saying, and there is no need to read anything else into it. As you read the text, ask the following questions (as well as any others the text might bring to mind):

- Who wrote it, when did he write it, and to whom did he write it?
- Who are the main characters and what are the main events in the text?
- How are the people in the text similar or different from me?
- What is the meaning of the passage?
- What is God telling me and how is He encouraging and strengthening me through this passage?
- What promises can I see in this passage?
- What changes does this passage show me I need to make in my life and how does God want me to make them?
- What sins do I need to be rid of so that I can grow more and enjoy closer fellowship with God?
- What does God want me to share with someone?

symbolism

When you begin your study of the Bible—no matter what method you use—it is important that you ask God to speak to you through what you are reading and meditating on. So go to the source of all Scripture and ask Him to open your heart, your ears, and your eyes to what it is really saying.

When interpreting a passage in the Bible, ask such questions as how, who, what, when, and where. The answers provide the context and lead to deeper meaning. And in terms of applying the passage, this is where you propose to *do* what God has taught you through these questions and answers. It is through applying the principles you've learned that God changes your life. God enlightens our minds and we apply it with our wills, and the Spirit of God empowers us to carry out these choices.

As you ask yourself these questions, write them—as well as your answers—down in your notebook. Continued studies may change how you answer those questions later on, but that is a good thing. That just means you are gaining a deeper understanding of what the Bible really says.

factum

Many people grow up learning about the Bible, however, it is vital that you read it without any preconceived notions. In other words, don't focus on what you think the Bible says but instead let it speak for itself. It has done so just fine for thousands of years and will continue to do so for you

Devotional Study Method

While all Bible study should have an element of personal devotion to it—meaning that it is with the purpose of deepening one's personal relationship with God—there is one method that makes that aspect of Bible study its primary focus. It's called the devotional study method.

If you study the Bible using this method, you'll need a Bible as well as a notepad and writing utensil. With those items at the ready, go to the passage you wish to study and read it several times over, all the while making notes of observations and questions that come to mind about what you're reading. Then take the time to rewrite the passage in your own words while at the same time personalizing it.

For example, turn in your Bible to Psalm 1:1–3, which reads:

Oh, the joys of those who do not follow the advice of the wicked, or stand around with sinners, or join in with scoffers. But they delight in doing everything the LORD wants; day and night they think about his law. They are like trees planted along the riverbank, bearing fruit each season without fail. Their leaves never wither, and in all they do, they prosper.

After you've read this Psalm several times, rewrite it and personalize it. Your version might read something like this: *God gives me great joy because I choose not to follow the advice of evil people, or spend my time with sinners, or join in when I hear people ridicule or mock the words and ways of God.*

When you study the Bible using this method, its words and messages jump off the pages and become words and messages spoken to you personally. That makes it easier to apply these things to your own life, which in turn brings you closer to God Himself. That's because you're reading the Bible as if God wrote it as a personal letter to you and you alone.

Character, Event, and Place Studies

When God inspired and motivated the writers of the Scriptures to record the words and deeds of those whose names appear in the Bible, He did this so that we could learn from their examples—good and bad—and from how He instructed and responded to them. When you read the Bible and see a name, a place, or an event, you can know that it's in there for a reason. For example, when you study and get to know the story of an Old Testament prophet named Jonah, you find that it's more than a well-known children's Sunday school story of a guy who was swallowed by a fish but also an encouragement and a warning to listen to and obey God, knowing that there is blessing in obedience and folly in turning away from Him.

When you study Bible characters and events, look at the details—the things they said, the things they did, how God instructed and corrected them, the events that took place around them—and ask yourself what significance they all have when it comes to having a better understanding of God's Word and of God Himself. When you do that, you will be able to take personal instruction from things these men and women did and said, as well as the things God did for them.

Keyword Study

If you are adept in the use of modern-day computers, you know how useful it can be to use keywords. In the context of Bible study, keywords are those singular words—and their variations—that give a certain text life and meaning.

Keyword studies are an excellent way to find out what God has to say in the Bible about certain subjects, such as love, forgiveness, sin, and blessing—all of which are important in the believer's life. This is a fairly simple way to study the Bible, because all it involves is going to a concordance and finding out where particular words appear in Scripture.

For example, suppose you were struggling with the idea that God had truly forgiven you for every sin you had committed and confessed to Him. In looking for assurance that you were really forgiven, you would probably want to look up what the Bible has to say about the word *forgive*. You would start your search by looking up that particular word in your concordance, then moving on to variations of the word (*forgive, forgave, forgiving*, and so forth). Next, take out your thesaurus and look up synonyms (different words that mean the same thing) for the word you are studying. For example, one synonym for forgive is *pardon*.

point of interest

When you do keyword studies, make sure that you look at a word in context so that you aren't looking at a homonym, which is a word that is pronounced the same but means something different. For example, the word *light* can be an adjective meaning "not heavy" or a noun meaning "physical light."

Once you had done that word study, you would know what the Bible has to say about the forgiveness of God. You would know that God's forgiveness is:

- one of His character attributes (Daniel 9:9)
- conditional based on our willingness to forgive others (Matthew 6:14, 15)
- conditional based on our willingness to confess our sins to God (1 John 1:9)
- conditional based on our willingness to repent, or turn away from, our sins (2 Peter 3:9)
- something we can ask Him for (Matthew 6:12)
- available to us through the sacrifice of His Son, Jesus Christ (Ephesians 1:7)

These are just a few of the many Biblical passages dealing with God's forgiveness. And when you take the time to use variations of the word forgive, you will see the provision God has made to forgive sin and the conditions attached to that forgiveness.

A Final Note Before You Start

The Bible tells us that, "All Scripture is inspired by God and is useful to teach us what is true and to make us realize what is wrong in our lives. It straightens us out and teaches us to do what is right. It is God's way of preparing us in every way, fully equipped for every good thing God wants us to do" (2 Timothy 3:16–17).

This tells us that God didn't give us the Bible just so we could have something nice to read before we go to sleep. It means that our goals in studying the Bible are to learn God's truth, to find out what changes we need to make in our personal lives, and to be prepared to do the good things God wants us to do.

As you study the Bible, don't just do it with the goal of learning what might be called "head knowledge." Knowing the contents of the Bible is always a positive, but only if you take its messages and apply them to your life personally.

CHAPTER 2

Bible Reading and Study: What's in It for You?

One of the most important things you need to remember as you begin reading and studying the Bible is that God wants to use your reading and study as an avenue through which He can do good things in your life. God has given us the Bible so He can show us more about Himself and more about how He wants to relate to humanity as a whole and to individuals.

The Good That Comes from Bible Study

You don't have to attend church or take part in Christian fellowship for long before you hear at least a little something about the importance of reading and studying the Bible for yourself, and doing it daily. If you're in a group study or an accountability group, you may hear questions such as, "What is God showing you through His Word lately?" or "How has God blessed you through your Bible study?"

This is part of the Biblical encouragement for believers to encourage one another in their faith, and it brings up a practical question for the average Bible reader: What good does it *really* do us to read the Bible daily? Or to put it more personally, "What's in it for me?"

You won't have to read and study the Bible for long before you find out that the answer to that question is this: plenty! If you're trying to decide what kind of computer to buy or what to wear to tomorrow's big job interview, you probably won't find anything in the Bible concerning those kinds of decisions. But if you're looking for solid wisdom when it comes to fixing what is wrong in your life or just making your life better, or when you're trying to find out how to be a better person, parent, spouse, friend, or spiritual leader, then you'll find it in the pages of the Bible—*if* you take the time to look for it.

The rest of this chapter details some of the benefits you will most certainly receive if you make daily Bible reading and study a priority in your life. The following sections won't give you all the benefits of reading and studying the Bible—you may find that you come up with a few of those on your own—but they will give you an idea of how God wants to bless you as you place the study of His written Word at the top of your personal daily list of things to do.

Finding Out More about God Himself

If you want to get to know someone very well—if you wanted to find out what makes that person tick and what that person loves, hates, desires, and finds most important—there is no better way to find out than to talk to that person face to face or to read what that person has written himself or herself. That's exactly what happens as you read the Bible.

When you read the Bible, you learn about the person of God. You find out what makes Him tick—what He loves, what He hates, what pleases Him, what angers Him, and what motivated Him to reach out to a lost humanity who had nothing to offer Him in return.

point of interest

While reading extrabiblical materials about God can be helpful in your spiritual growth (and there are lots of that kind of material around to help you in your study), you should remember that absolutely *nothing* can take the place of reading the Bible itself.

One of the most important things new believers learn early about the Christian faith is that it is not just a set of rules or regulations. It's much more than that. It's a personal relationship—one where you become the friend, child, and servant of God—one that grows and changes over time, just as your relationship with a good friend or your spouse grows and changes.

The apostle Paul expressed the passion that should be within every believer—namely, to know Jesus Christ better and better every new day—when he wrote:

> *Yes, everything else is worthless when compared with the price-less gain of knowing Christ Jesus my Lord. I have discarded every-thing else, counting it all as garbage, so that I may have Christ and become one with him. I no longer count on my own goodness or my ability to obey God's law, but I trust Christ to save me. For God's way of making us right with Himself depends on faith. As a result, I can really know Christ. (Philippians 3:8–10)*

If your goal as a believer is, like Paul's, to know Christ personally, then Bible reading and study must be a consistent part of your daily life in him. When you read the Bible—Old Testament and New Testament alike—you will learn the purposes for Christ, the thoughts and ways of Christ, and the way to Christ. You will learn that God is more than our Creator, but also a loving heavenly Father who wants more than anything for us to draw close to Him in a personal, loving relationship. When you learn those things, you will make yourself ready to know Him in a deeper and more personal way.

Seeing the History of God's Interaction with People

From the creation story in Genesis 1–2 to the final words of Revelation, the Bible is all about God and His loving interaction with humankind. Scriptures tell us how God has blessed, cursed, loved, and redeemed and saved men and women in spite of their rebellion, and also all about how God brought into the world a Savior who could make that redemption and salvation possible.

But why exactly is it important to know the Biblical history of God's interaction with people? Because those accounts stand as examples—both negative and positive—for us today of how God responds to us as humankind in general and as individuals.

factum

Remembering is a big theme in the Bible. God wanted His people, the Israelites, to remember how He had brought them out of captivity in Egypt. He continually called them to remember that chapter in Jewish history because He wanted His people to remember His blessings and faithfulness as well as the consequences of their disobedience.

The apostle Paul wrote, "All these events happened to them as examples for us. They were written down to warn us, who live at the time when this age is drawing to a close" (1 Corinthians 10:11). These "events" Paul was writing about were the sins of the Jewish people who had left bondage and slavery in Egypt and were on their way to the Promised Land as well as the punishment they received because of their disobedience.

God wants us to know the history of His interaction with His people. He wants us to observe all the promises, warnings, blessings, and punishments they received and what led to those things. He wants us to observe these things and see what pleases Him, what angers Him, what grieves Him, and what moves Him to action on our behalf.

When we know those things, we get a better peek into the character of God, into what He expects and desires from those who follow Him in faith.

Getting Direction—Straight from the Top!

Anyone who has served in the military knows the importance of following orders. In that culture, it's absolutely essential that servicemen and service-women learn how to obey the orders of their superiors to the letter. That's because it's in heeding those orders that each serviceman and service-woman becomes part of an efficient and smooth-running fighting machine.

The same thing is essentially true of the Christian life. The Bible tells us that when we put our faith in Jesus Christ, we become part of his "body" (1 Corinthians 12), meaning that we have a part to play in making sure that body is healthy and growing. In order to effectively play that part, each of us needs to seek God's direction. And one of the most important ways we seek that direction is through diligently reading God's written Word.

In Psalm 119, the longest psalm among the 150 recorded in the Bible, the psalmist wrote: "How sweet are your words to my taste; they are sweeter than honey. Your commandments give me understanding; no wonder I hate every false way of life. Your word is a lamp for my feet and a light for my path" (Psalm 119:103–105).

If you read the entirety of this psalm, you will see that the psalmist thanks and praises God for His law, His commands, His decrees, and His words—all of which we can find recorded in the pages of the Bible. And as you study the Bible, you'll find that it contains God's directions in a variety of situations many of us find in day-to-day life.

Here are just a few examples of where you can find Biblical guidance for specific life situations:

- **marriage** (Proverbs 5:15–19, Matthew 19:5–6, 1 Corinthians 7:1–16, Ephesians 5:21–33, Colossians 3:18–19, 1 Peter 3:1–7, Hebrews 13:4)
- **parenting** (Deuteronomy 6:5–7; Proverbs 13:24, 19:18; Colossians 3:20–21; Ephesians 6:4)
- **when** others hurt or offend you (Matthew 6:12–15, Mark 11:25, Colossians 3:12–15, Romans 12:9–19)
- **work** (Ecclesiastes 5:18–20, Colossians 3:23, 1 Thessalonians 3:7–14)
- **patience** (Psalm 37:7–9, Galatians 5:22, Colossians 1:11, 1 Thessalonians 5:14, Hebrews 12:1, James 1:3–4)

Obviously, there are many more life situations addressed in the Bible. Also, there are more verses and passages that apply to the topics listed above. That tells us something wonderful about the Bible, specifically that it's a book chock full of directions for the Christian life and that each of us benefits greatly when we take the time to find and follow those directions.

In that respect, you can read the Bible as something of a field manual for the Christian life, which we are promised will be a battle in this world. And it's a field manual that will never fail us, simply because we know that God's Word can be trusted and depended upon in all things.

Gaining Practical Insights to the Christian Life

Those who aren't personally familiar with the Bible may not realize it, but it really is a very practical book. It gives us specific instructions and guidelines for every area of the Christian life, and it gives them in a way that we can understand—as long as we are committed to understanding.

As a practical handbook for the Christian life, the Bible tells us everything we need to know in order to live the life God wants us to live, and it also gives us instructions on how to do those things in every situation that faces us. It gives us instructions in what are known as spiritual disciplines, which is really just another way of saying that the Bible tells us how to do the things that are involved in a growing Christian life. For example, the Bible tells us how to:

- **Pray** (Matthew 6:9–13, 7:7–11, 18:19–20; Mark 11:24; John 14:13–14; James 5:15; 1 John 5:14–15)

- **Worship God** (Exodus 20:4–5, Psalm 150, Matthew 4:10, Mark 7:7, John 4:23–24, Romans 12:1)
- **Fast** (Leviticus 16:29, 23:32; Ezra 10:6; Isaiah 58:6; Matthew 6:16–18, 17:21; Acts 13:2–3)
- **Demonstrate Christian love to others** (Matthew 5:43–48, John 15:9–13, 1 Corinthians 13)
- **Fight temptation** (Psalm 95:8; Luke 22:40, 46; 1 Corinthians 10:13; James 1:2–12; 2 Peter 2:9)

Again, the list above is not a comprehensive one, and the Bible covers many other spiritual disciplines. There are also many other passages not listed here that deal with the subjects listed above. But these examples alone should show you that there isn't anything in the realm of your life with Jesus Christ that isn't covered in the Scriptures.

point of interest

If you want to read some really practical instructions on the Christian life from Jesus himself, read Matthew 5–7, which records what has come to be known as the Sermon on the Mount. In it, he tells us how to pray, how to give, how to love, and many other practical insights and instructions.

When you study specific areas of the life of faith, it's good to have your concordance and your Bible dictionary on hand. That way you can readily find the passages that deal with the area in question. Also, make sure you read the whole passage surrounding that issue and not just one verse. That will give you some context on that issue.

Growing Spiritually

You don't have to be an experienced parent to know that in order for children to grow they need nourishment—physical, emotional, and spiritual alike. Without proper care and feeding, a child will be stunted in his or her growth and never become what he or she could have been. But with those things, the child grows and becomes a healthy, mature grownup who can function in all ways as an adult.

The very same is true in the spiritual realm. In fact, the Bible uses the comparisons and contrasts between infancy, childhood, and adulthood in teaching us that after God saves us, He wants us to grow and mature spiritually. And it also lets us know that there is a matter of choice and commitment on our parts when it comes to that growth.

That is exactly what the apostle Paul was referring to when he wrote to a bunch of immature believers in a city called Corinth:

Dear brothers and sisters, when I was with you I couldn't talk to you as I would to mature Christians. I had to talk as though you belonged to this world or as though you were infants in the Christian life. I had to feed you with milk and not with solid food, because you couldn't handle anything stronger. And you still aren't ready, for you are still controlled by your own sinful desires. (1 Corinthians 3:1–3)

In short, Paul is saying, "It's time to start growing up!"

The New Testament is very clear that spiritual maturity is a process and that, though we will all reach a point of maturity, we should never stop growing as long we are on this earth. That was Paul's point when he wrote, "I keep working toward that day when I will finally be all that Christ Jesus saved me for and wants me to be. No, dear brothers and sisters, I am still not all I should be, but I am focusing all my energies on this one thing: Forgetting the past and looking forward to what lies ahead, I strain to reach the end of the race and receive the prize for which God, through Christ Jesus, is calling us up to heaven" (Philippians 3:12–14).

The Bible tells us there are several things we need in order to grow toward spiritual maturity, things such as fellowship with other Christians, prayer, and, of course, Bible reading and study. That was partly Paul's point when he told Timothy, "[Scripture] is God's way of preparing us in every way, fully equipped for every good thing God wants us to do" (2 Timothy 3:17).

There are any number of books, study guides, and multistep programs available for the purpose of helping the believer to spiritual maturity. And while some of them can be very good and helpful, all believers need to keep in mind that nothing can take the place of regular, personal Bible reading and study.

factum

> The apostle Peter, who walked with Jesus during his earthly ministry, wrote of this theme of spiritual growth, "Like newborn babies, you must crave pure spiritual milk so that you will grow into a full experience of salvation. Cry out for this nourishment, now that you have had a taste of the Lord's kindness" (1 Peter 2:2–3).

We also need to remember that maturity doesn't happen overnight, any more than a deep knowledge of the Bible happens overnight. It takes time, personal effort, and, yes, patience for the average believer to see the fruits of true spiritual maturity.

So as you read and study your Bible, remember that you're doing more than filling your mind with some good spiritual material. You're actually feeding the inner part of you that needs nourishment if you are to become a spiritually mature believer.

Having the Joy and Peace of Knowing and Living God's Word Daily

It may come as a surprise to those who haven't yet made Bible reading and study a key part of their lives, but there is a supernatural joy and peace that come from immersing ourselves in the Word of God through daily reading and study.

God's written Word is a source of joy and peace, of inspiration and instruction. When we read, study, and meditate on the words and message of the Bible, we find a joy like no possession or relationship can give and a peace deeper than anything the world has to offer.

When you are down, try reading some of the words of praise and worship recorded in the Psalms. When you need wise direction, try looking through the Proverbs, which give us some of the most profound wisdom ever written. When you need inspiration, try looking at the stories of great men and women whose faith have made them heroes of the Bible. (Start with Hebrews 12 and work backwards.) And when you need peace and joy, focus on the numerous verses and passages in the Bible that give assurance of God's love and compassion for those who call out to Him and ask for it.

When you do those things, when you make the words and messages contained in the Bible your source of comfort, you'll receive every blessing and every bit of wisdom, direction, and peace God has for those who make His written Word a priority in their lives. It's just that kind of book! And, as you will see in the next chapter, it's also the kind of book you can take personally.

CHAPTER 3

Taking It Personally

A cartoon that appeared in newspapers nationwide showed a preacher standing at the front door of his church sending his flock away for the week. As he shook hands with each of his departing parishioners, he said to each of them, "Nothing personal." That was some good religious humor, but it doesn't at all reflect the reality of what God says to us through the Bible. He *wants* us to take it personally; in fact, that's why He gave it to us in the first place.

The Bible: God's Message to You Personally

God has given His people the Bible so that they can be blessed, challenged, encouraged, warned, loved, enlightened, saved—the list goes on and on. But each of us finds that those things happen to us more profoundly and more powerfully when we take the Bible in our hands and think of it as God's message to us as individuals.

That, after all, is exactly the way God wants each of us to take His written Word.

It has been said that every believer should learn to read the Bible as if it was God's message to him or her personally, as if He had written it to them and them alone. When we do that, we receive personally every blessing He intended for those who love and trust Him.

As you read and study the Bible, learn to take it personally. Learn to see every principle, every promise, every caution, and every blessing as being meant for you personally. And you can do that because God has given not just us but *you* personally His written Word.

He's done that for several very good reasons, and that is what this chapter is about. As you read on, you'll see that the Bible was given as a means for you to know, to become, and to remain everything God wants you to be.

Knowing How to Properly Relate to God

If you know anything at all about the Bible, you know that it is the story of God's interaction with humankind—of the creation of humanity in an environment of perfection, of the fall of humanity into sin, of the consequences of that sin, and of God's plan to redeem and save us all. But perhaps even more important is the fact that the Bible is also a collection of stories of how God related to and interacted with men and women as individuals. That makes the Bible more than a collection of stories about people who somehow figured out what it took to relate to God; it's also a collection of stories that show us through example how to do it for ourselves.

There are many examples in the Bible of men and women who had an understanding of how to relate to God and who acted on that understanding. People like Abraham, Moses, Joshua, and King David stood out as people who, despite their own personal and spiritual flaws and warts, lived the lives and spoke the words that demonstrated their love for God.

symbolism

> The psalmist who wrote Psalm 119 underscored the importance of the Bible in helping people properly relate to God when he wrote, "I used to wander off until you disciplined me; but now I closely follow your word. You are good and do only good; teach me your decrees" (Psalm 119:67, 68).

If you want to read good examples of lives of devotion to God, read more about the people listed above. They were men whose love for and obedience to God guided them in their daily lives and whose love for God always brought them back around to Him when they failed.

But when you want to read of perfect devotion to God in every word and deed, read of the life, the deeds, and the words of Jesus Christ as they are recorded in the four Gospels—Matthew, Mark, Luke, and John. Most of the Bible is devoted to *telling* us how to properly relate to our Creator, but the life and words of Jesus were devoted to *showing* us how. And while we will never in this life attain perfection, we have his life as the perfect example of how to properly relate to God.

There are three parts to properly relating to God, and Jesus demonstrated them all perfectly. They are as follows:

- **love for God** (Exodus 20:6, Deuteronomy 6:5, Joshua 22:5, John 16:27, Romans 8:28, 1 Corinthians 8:3)
- **believe and trust in God** (Genesis 15:6, 2 Kings 18:5, Psalm 31:14, Daniel 6:23, John 14:1, Romans 15:13, 1 John 4:16)
- **obedience to God** (Genesis 26:5, Joshua 1:7, Job 36:11, Psalm 25:10, Luke 6:49, John 3:36, Philippians 2:12)

If you've taken the time to look up the above verses—which are just a few of the many verses and passages containing the messages of love, trust, and obedience to God—you'll see very clearly that we as believers are to love, trust, and obey God. But the question remains: How do we do those things? What actions should we take and words should we speak to show our love, faith, and obedience to God?

That is where personal Bible reading and study come in. It is only through reading God's Word—and especially looking to the example of Jesus Christ—that you'll learn to love Him, trust Him, and obey Him in the way that is due Him. It is only through reading the Bible that you'll find the specifics of what loving God, believing God, and obeying God entails.

Becoming More Like Jesus

In any area of life, it's good to set goals for yourself. Goals are what keep you moving forward simply because they give you something to strive for and attain.

In the New Testament, one of the recurring themes is that believers are to strive to become more and more like Jesus Christ in every area of their lives. For example, the apostle Paul wrote, "So all of us who have had that veil removed can see and reflect the glory of the Lord. And the Lord—who is the Spirit—makes us more and more like him as we are changed into his glorious image" (2 Corinthians 3:18).

"Changed into his glorious image" means we are transformed into something we weren't before, namely the image of Jesus Christ. This means that we are made to be just like him in how we think, talk, and act. This is what Christians call "Christlike," and it's something we are to strive to attain not just in the hereafter but also in the here and now.

We are to be imitators of Jesus Christ in our:

- **approach to temptation** (Matthew 4:1–11)
- **love** (John 13:34–35)
- **humility** (Philippians 2:2–8)
- **attitudes and actions toward others** (1 John 3:18)
- **purity** (1 Thessalonians 4:1–8)
- **compassion** (2 Corinthians 1:3–7)
- **doing good for others** (Matthew 5:16)

This list could go on and on simply because Jesus made himself the perfect example in every area of life.

We don't become like Jesus just by accident or by some sort of supernatural osmosis where we just sit back and let his character and ways be formed in us. If that were the case, then becoming a Christian would mean losing all our free will. And while God wants our wills and thoughts to be submitted to Him, He won't simply take them from us and force us to be like Jesus.

discussion question

According to Galatians 5:16–23, who or what is the driving force behind the believer becoming more like Christ?
The Holy Spirit, because it is only he who keeps us walking, talking, and living in the same way Jesus did. It is the Holy Spirit who guides us, directs us, and empowers us to live the way God wants us to live.

Being like Christ only happens when we make a conscious choice to seek and follow him, when we willfully and purposefully ask him to come in and change us from the inside out. It only happens through prayer, worship and praise, spending time in fellowship with other believers, and—you guessed it!—reading and studying the Bible.

But how can we know specifically what the life of Jesus Christ looked like? How can we know how he lived, talked, prayed, and walked? Well, the Bible contains a four-book biography of Jesus's time on earth, with an emphasis on the three-plus years of ministry leading up to the time of the Crucifixion.

As we read the Gospels we see that Jesus did far more than just talk a good game of faith and devotion to God, he played it out every moment of his life. And while we can't—at least in this life—live out those things as perfectly as he did, we can look to him as our perfect example of life, love, faith, and obedience.

Living Within the Family of God

As you read in the last chapter, Christianity is all about relationships, starting with a relationship with God Himself. But the Bible also teaches extensively on the subject of relating well to other people, particularly other believers.

As Jesus prepared to meet with his final earthly destination—the cross—he gave the disciples some final instructions. Among those was this: "This is my commandment: Love each other in the same way I have loved you. There is no greater love than to lay down one's life for one's friends" (John 15:12–13).

Jesus came to earth to live, teach, and die so that he could establish a family, and it's a family of believers who would be tied together by the same kind of love he demonstrated when he gave of himself in every way possible.

The Bible—in both the Old Testament and the New Testament—gives the reader many commands, guidelines, and wisdom on how to lovingly and selflessly operate within that family. Those specific commands can be summed up in the words of Jesus himself: "Love each other."

factum

The apostle Paul gave the church in Corinth an excellent outline for what Christian love should look like in 1 Corinthians 13. In verses 4 through 7 of that chapter, we are told that love is patient and kind and that it is not jealous, boastful, proud, rude, or selfish.

The word *love* as it is used most often in the Bible doesn't refer to feelings nearly as much as actions. When Jesus told his disciples to "love each other," he wasn't telling them to have warm feelings of friendship for one another. He was telling them to do for one another the things that built up and made each of them better servants of God and to avoid doing those things that could drag one another down and keep them from being all God had called them to be.

Much of the Bible gives instructions on how we are to love one another, but you'll find the most practical and easily applicable guidelines in the proverbs, in the teachings of Jesus (particularly Matthew 5–7), and in the epistles of the apostle Paul, which were more than anything letters of instruction for the operations of churches at that time.

Knowing the Dos and Don'ts of the Christian Life

It has been pointed out that the Christian faith isn't really a religion or a list of dos and don'ts. Instead it is a relationship—a personal, living, growing relationship—with the living God that we enter into through our faith in Jesus Christ.

Unfortunately, too many people view the Bible as a harsh book that does nothing but put limitations on people, that just tells them what they can and can't do. But knowing that our faith is based in a personal relationship, we also need to understand that this relationship—like any we'd have on earth—requires nurturing, care, and work to help it grow and thrive. Another way to put that is to say that there are things we need to do as well as things we need to avoid if we want to fully enjoy a faith-centered, growing relationship with God.

symbolism

When you are looking through your Bible to find guidelines for living, use your concordance to look for key verbs (action words, such as *give, love, pray*) or adjectives (descriptive words, such as *holy, righteous, blessed*) and it will lead you to some good dos and don'ts of the Christian life as they appear in the Bible.

Yes, that means there are things we should do and things we shouldn't do if we want our relationship with God to continue growing. And the Bible contains many warnings, commands, and bits of wisdom telling us what we should do and what we shouldn't, what we can do and what we can't.

For example, some of the *dos* the Bible tells us to follow are to...

- be filled with the Holy Spirit of God (Ephesians 5:18)
- remain in—or stick close to—Christ (John 15:1–11)
- tell others the message of salvation through Jesus (Matthew 28:18–20, Mark 16:15)
- rejoice in the Lord (Philippians 4:4)
- pray about everything (Philippians 4:6)
- resist the devil (James 4:7)

And, for example, the Bible says, *don't*...

- do good expecting your reward here on earth (Matthew 6:1–4)
- hang on to anger and bitterness (Matthew 5:22–23)
- steal (Leviticus 19:11, Ephesians 4:28)
- forget to spend time in fellowship with other believers (Hebrews 10:25)
- engage in drunkenness (Ephesians 5:18)

While the Bible contains a lot of instructions for living the Christian life—including some dos and don'ts—it also gives the rewards for doing what we should and the consequences for doing what we shouldn't. God has promised both blessings and protection for those who follow Him in obedience, for those who read what the Bible says and then act on it. (See James 1:22–25.)

Knowing What to Say and How to Say It

After Jesus's death and resurrection, he spent forty days on earth, appearing several times to disciples before he went back to heaven to be with his Father. It was during this time that he gave them some additional teaching and some final instructions.

Probably the most important message Jesus gave the disciples at that time was what has come to be known as the Great Commission, a command that goes like this: "Therefore, go and make disciples of all the nations, baptizing them in the name of the Father and the Son and the Holy Spirit. Teach these new disciples to obey all the commands I have given you" (Matthew 28:19–20).

It was because of the disciples' obedience to this command that Christianity spread throughout the world at that time and why it continues to be the dominant faith of the Western world today. The disciples who heard that command all played a part in taking the gospel to the world around them, and they were later joined by the apostle Paul, a former persecutor of Christians who became the most important and influential Christian missionary of all time.

factum

The apostle Paul, who wrote much of the New Testament, didn't begin his traveling ministry of preaching, teaching, and writing immediately after he became a Christian—though he did preach in the city of Jerusalem. In fact, he spent three years training in Arabia with Jesus Christ himself before he began his missionary journeys. (See Galatians 1:11–12, 15–18.)

Christians through the centuries have taken Jesus's command to his disciples of that time to apply to all believers, even those who don't go into what we would consider "fulltime ministry." In other words, believers today are charged with the responsibility of making new disciples.

But what does a believer need in order to win converts to Christianity? Obviously, he or she would need to know a little something about the Bible, particularly the works and teachings of Jesus Christ as well as the writings of the apostle Paul. Without that, ministry to others would be all but impossible.

If you're going to encourage fellow believers and influence nonbelievers, you're going to have a good grasp of what the Bible has to say about God, sin, forgiveness, and discipleship. You're going to have to know enough to be able to boldly encourage other Christians and confidently field questions—even objections—you may hear from those who don't yet understand the message of salvation through Christ.

That is what the apostle Peter meant when he wrote that we should always be ready to give an answer to those who ask about the hope we have within us and to do it gently and respectfully. (See 1 Peter 3:15.)

point of interest

If you want a good foundation of Biblical truth to present to those who aren't yet believers, a good place to start is the New Testament book of Romans. This book is often referred to as the Gospel according to Paul, and it contains a great overview of the message of salvation.

There are few things more damaging to the reputation of the Christian community than those well-meaning but ill-prepared believers who try to tackle the task of introducing people to Jesus Christ without a good knowledge and grasp of the message of salvation as it is laid out in the Bible. On the other hand, there is nothing more powerful than a believer who is equipped with a solid grasp of the fundamentals of the faith as they are presented in Scriptures.

There are a lot of great reasons to read, study, and know the Bible, one of the best of them being that it gives the believer the ability to present a clear, concise, and (most of all) Biblically accurate picture of the message of salvation through Jesus Christ.

Knowing What Comes Next

There is a common belief among people—even those with a basic knowledge of the Bible—that God will reward us in the afterlife for the good things that we do. And while the Bible is clear that our salvation has nothing to do with our own good works, it does tell us in several places that there are rewards for those who do good things for the right reasons.

Speaking through the apostle John, Jesus tells those who follow him, "Look, I am coming soon, bringing my reward with me to repay all people according to their deeds" (Revelation 22:12). This means that part of God's final judgment of individuals is assessing what their eternal rewards will be.

It's not popular in some Christian circles to talk about rewards as the results for faithfully serving God. And while the Bible indicates that our first priority in serving God is to do so out of love and obedience, Jesus himself talked about rewards for those who do so. In Matthew 5–7, in Jesus's famous Sermon on the Mount, he makes reference at least nine times to rewards for obedient living.

factum

Speaking of rewards, the apostle Paul wrote, "Salvation is not a reward for the good things we have done, so none of us can boast about it" (Ephesians 2:9). That is in keeping with the Biblical theme that our salvation is based on the work of God and nothing we can do ourselves.

Even in the Old Testament there are many references to rewards for obedient living. For example, in the book of Genesis we read how God promised Abraham a "great reward" if he would simply trust and obey (Genesis 15:1). Later, King David wrote, "The Lord rewarded me for doing right" (Psalm 18:20).

As you read and study the Bible, you will see that there are great rewards for personalizing what you see, for making the messages of God contained in the Good Book your very own. And, as the Bible itself tells us, the rewards will be both in this life and in the one to come!

CHAPTER 4

Other Uses for the Bible

To most people, the Bible is like other books in that it can be read, studied, learned, and even applied to their lives if they choose to do so. That, after all, is what the Bible is for. But there are several other ways to use the Bible to enhance and enrich one's life of faith. As you read through this chapter, take some personal mental notes on how you will use the Word of God to help you grow and flourish in your faith.

Taking It to Another Level

In an earlier chapter, you read about the different methods of studying the Bible. In this chapter you will find that there are just as many uses for what you study as there are methods of study, and that you can actually add layers to your Bible reading and study experience.

What you are about to read are simply things you can do with what you study or while you are studying the Bible. They are ways to make reading and studying the Good Book a more informative, useful, challenging, and personally rewarding experience.

Before you read on, a couple of notes. First, please understand that the material in this chapter moves Bible reading and study into a more spiritual direction. While simple reading and study of the Bible will touch your mind and spirit, the things in this chapter are meant to actually make the Word of God a part of you in a very real way.

Second, as you endeavor to make the things in this chapter a part of your spiritual life, it's important that you spend time in prayer. Ask God to illuminate to you personally what the Bible says and what it means to you today. Ask Him to indelibly imprint what you read, hear, and see upon you so that it actually becomes a part of who you are. Now, read on and you'll see how the words and messages in the Bible can come alive within you.

Memorizing the Bible

It's no exaggeration to say that memorizing Scripture is one of the most important things a believer can do. It's important for a number of reasons, and it's rewarding and enjoyable to boot.

Having a variety of Bible verses and passages committed to memory can be helpful in many ways. It can help you when you need to remember some good Biblical wisdom or instruction that applies to your own life situation. It can help you minister to other believers who need encouragement. And it can help you to tell others about what exactly the Bible has to say to them as people for whom Christ came to die.

The apostle Peter, who was with Jesus during the entirety of his earthly ministry, explained the importance of knowing Scripture by mind and by heart when he wrote, "And if you are asked about your Christian hope, always be ready to explain it" (1 Peter 3:15).

factum

> The writer of Psalm 119 strongly implied the importance of memorizing Scripture and making it a part of our thinking when he wrote, "I have hidden your word in my heart, that I might not sin against you" (Psalm 119:11). This tells us that memorizing Scripture is a help when it comes to battling temptation to sin.

If you're ever in a situation where someone asks you about your faith—and it's sure to happen eventually—you can more easily explain what you believe, why you believe it, and what it's done for you if you have some of the Bible memorized. But what steps should a Bible reader take to begin effective Bible memorization? Here are some tips and ideas that might help you make memorization a part of your Bible reading and study.

- *Pick a version of the Bible that works for you.* This may not sound like a huge part of Scripture memorization, but you might be surprised to find that the version of the Bible you memorize can make a big difference. Some people find that the more poetic tone of the King James Version is more easily memorable, while others like a more modern-sounding version such as the New King James or the New Living Translation. Pick one you are comfortable with, one whose style and language is easiest for you to connect with. That will help make Bible memorization easier and more comfortable for you.
- *Pick out the verse or verses you want to memorize.* You can do this by topic or by whatever portion of Scripture you are presently studying. (While studying the Bible, some people like to jot down specific verses for memorization.) Read it through several times—silently and aloud. Focus on the keywords in the verse and pay special attention to the meaning.

- *Write the verse down.* Write it in your study notes, on a note card—anywhere that makes it easy to review later. Many Bible readers are amazed to find out how writing a verse down word for word helps them to memorize it. They also find that writing verses down is helpful for review. If you write the verse on a note card, you can easily carry it with you so that you can look at it and reread it in those spare moments during the day. That goes a long way in helping you memorize particular verses or passages.

- *Don't try to memorize too much at a time.* There's an old saying about the best way to go about eating an elephant: one bite at a time. When you read your Bible, it can seem like a daunting task to memorize enough of it to make a difference. The key is to memorize it in amounts you are comfortable with. Start with three or four verses or passages a week and then see if you can take on more. Remember, different people have different abilities when it comes to memorization. Find your own pace and stick with it.

- *Work with a partner.* Like many other things in life, memorizing Scriptures goes better with teamwork. Memorizing Bible verses with a friend, spouse, roommate, classmate, or any other partner you can count on to consistently help you and challenge you gives you accountability as well as someone to quote Scriptures to when the opportunity presents itself. It's more effective and more fun, too!

symbolism

Remember learning to spell in grammar school? If you're like most schoolchildren, you used flashcards that contained not just the spelling of a particular word but a picture of it. You can use homemade flashcards to help you memorize Scripture. It's an effective way to help you memorize, especially if you are working with a partner.

Personalizing the Scriptures

The message of the Bible is one of God's love and compassion for a needy, sinful, undeserving world. But have you ever stopped to think that it's also a message God sent just for you?

There is something about taking the Scriptures and personalizing them that makes them come alive, that further opens lines of communication with God and that empowers us to live the way God wants us as believers to live. When we personalize Scriptures, we go from saying "That's a great message" to "That's a great message just for me."

As you study the Bible, take the time to personalize what it says. Take the message of "God so loved the world..." (John 3:16) and make it "God so loved *me*." Think of "...God...will supply all your needs from his glorious riches" (Philippians 4:18) as "God...will supply all *my* needs from his glorious riches."1

When you approach Bible reading and study that way, you will begin to feel more and more connected, not just with the messages in the Bible but also with God Himself.

Meditating on the Bible

In some Christian circles, the word *meditate* (as well as variations of the word) is often greeted with both misunderstanding and fear. That is often because the practice of meditation is associated with Eastern and other religions, many of whose practices are in conflict with sound Biblical teaching.

However, the Bible does teach the practice of meditation, even using that specific word in several places. For example, God told Joshua, the man who would take up the mantle of leadership following the death of Moses, "Study this Book of the Law continually. Meditate on it day and night so you may be sure to obey all that is written in it. Only then will you succeed" (Joshua 1:8).

Also, the book of Psalms, a collection of prayers and songs of praise, starts out with these words: "Blessed is the man who does not walk in the counsel of the wicked or stand in the way of sinners or sit in the seat of mockers. But his delight is in the law of the Lord, and on his law he meditates day and night. He is like a tree planted by streams of water, which yields its fruit in season and whose leaf does not wither. Whatever he does prospers" (Psalm 1:1–3).

point of interest

> When you meditate on the Bible, it's a good idea to do it at a time when you don't have to attend to any other business, particularly the kind that requires your full attention (for example, driving or working with heavy machinery). Meditation requires that you give all of yourself to pondering and dwelling in what you read.

That is just one of many references to the Biblical practice of meditation in the Psalms alone that tells us very clearly and strongly that this is a practice God wants us to take part in—even daily. In fact, the psalmist makes it very clear that there is great spiritual blessing in meditating on God's law.

But what exactly does it mean to meditate on the Word of God? If you were to look up the word *meditate* in your dictionary, you'd find that it means simply to reflect deeply upon something or to ponder it. It means to spend time clearing your mind of everything but what you are thinking about and to think about it from every possible angle. It means asking God to show you personally what He wants you to comprehend.

For example, you can bring to your mind a particular verse or passage, pray over it, and ask yourself the following questions (and others you may think of) about it:

- What was God saying to His people when this was written?
- What is He saying to Christians in general through it right now?
- What is He saying to me personally today?
- What kind of changes should I make in response to what this is saying to me?
- How can I personally and practically apply the message in this Scripture right now?

When you take this approach to the Bible, you will likely find something wonderful happening in your own mind and spirit. You may find that you see and understand things about God and His Word more clearly and from a new angle. You may hear what is to you a new message coming from verses and passages—even some you may have read or memorized before.

discussion question

When is the best time and where is the best place to meditate?
You don't have to get under a tree in the middle of a field, cross your legs, and mumble chants to meditate. You can do it just about anywhere you can get alone, clear your mind, and contemplate what God is saying through a certain passage.

This is why prayer is such an important part of Biblical meditation. When you bring your thoughts and contemplations to God and talk to Him about them, He very often will speak back to you, giving you new thoughts and insights. When that happens, you will have "heard" the voice of God.

Praying with the Bible

Earlier in this book you read how the Bible is all about God's interaction with His people. Part of that interaction is the prayers Biblical characters—even Jesus himself—have spoken to the heavenly Father. Probably the most famous of Biblical prayers is what has come to be known as the Lord's Prayer:

Our Father in heaven,
may your name be kept holy.
May your Kingdom come soon.
May your will be done on earth,
as it is in heaven.

Give us today the food we need,
and forgive us our sins,
as we have forgiven those who sin against us.
And don't let us yield to temptation,
but rescue us from the evil one.
—Matthew 6:9–13

The Bible contains many other model prayers, and it is a good practice to read, memorize, and even use these prayers in our own devotional lives. Here are some examples:

- Joshua's prayer for God's help (Joshua 7:6–13)
- David's prayer for blessing (2 Samuel 7:18–29)
- Solomon prays for wisdom (1 Kings 3:6–15)
- a prayer for prosperity (1 Chronicles 4:10)
- Jesus's prayers for himself, for his disciples, and for others who would believe (John 17)
- Jesus's prayers for deliverance and strength (Matthew 26:39, 42, 43)

These are just a few of the hundreds of prayers found in the pages of the Bible. And in addition to the prayers listed here, there are several different kinds of prayers in Psalms. As you read through them, take note of how the psalmists offered prayers of thanksgiving and praise, prayers for various blessings, prayers for forgiveness, and prayers of faith.

When you read an example of a prayer in either the Old Testament or the New Testament, pay close attention to the tone and the wording of the prayer, and also pay attention to the way God responded to those who prayed the prayers. That way you'll be able to model your prayers after the Biblical ones that were most effective.

Praying God's Word Back to Him

It's one thing to pray the prayers of the Bible or to use them as models, but it's a whole new level of interaction and communion with God to actually pray the words of the Bible to Him.

When you read through Psalms, you're reading some of the most heartfelt, urgent, and loving prayers humankind has ever uttered toward God. It is in Psalms that we read of the writers' love for God, their faith in God, and their questions about God. They even at times express disappointment with God, or at least their perceptions of Him during the time of the writings.

In a very real way the psalmists demonstrate for us a principle concerning the written Word of God, and it's this: God loves it when we pray the very words in the Bible back to Him.

It may sound like a strange thing to do, but the truth is that this is a very Scriptural and effective way to use the words in the Bible. It's a way to access and even claim for ourselves His promises, His encouragements, and His warnings.

What's more, we can know that He will always respond to that kind of prayer. And how do we know this? For one thing, the Bible tells us, "And we are confident that he hears us whenever we ask for anything that pleases him. And since we know he hears us when we make our requests, we also know that he will give us what we ask for" (1 John 5:14–15).

point of interest

When you pray God's Word back to Him, make sure you know what you're asking for. Realize that while He will always answer, you can't know for sure how He'll answer. For example, praying for more patience could mean facing a series of situations where your patience is tried and stretched. Pray that way, but be prepared!

In other words, when we pray and request what we know is God's will in a given situation, we can be absolutely certain He hears and responds. For example, if we ask Him to give us more love for our spouses, He's sure to provide an affirmative response only because that fits precisely with the commands in His Word. It may not come in the way we expected, but we can be sure it will come.

Now, knowing that God hears our prayers when we request what pleases Him, is there any source more reliable when it comes to questions of what

God wants for us than the Bible? When we read the Bible, we can understand that it contains the absolutely perfect will of God for us. And knowing that, we can pray the very words of the Scriptures to God knowing—not thinking and not hoping—that He'll hear us.

Earlier in this chapter you read about how you can personalize the words of the Bible, making them yours in a very tangible way. Now you can take that a step further, actually using those words as a basis for your very own communication with God Himself.

For example:

- When you feel doubt, you can pray, "Lord, your ways are perfect and you keep all of your promises. You are my shield because I look to you for protection" (based on Psalm 18:3).
- When you feel in need of peace, you can pray, "Lord, I have been made right in your sight by faith, so I have peace with you because of what my Lord Jesus Christ has done for me" (based on Romans 5:1).
- When you are tempted, you can pray, "Lord, the temptations in my life are no different from what others experience. And you are faithful. You will not allow the temptation to be more than I can stand. When I am tempted, you will show me a way out so that I can endure" (based on 1 Corinthians 10:12–13).

The Bible is a book filled not just with promises but promises made by the One who has the power and authority to fulfill all of them absolutely perfectly. You can make those promises a part of your life of faith, and you can also make them a part of your prayers.

The Word as a Weapon of Offense

Have you ever looked at your personal copy of the Bible and thought of it as a weapon? If not, then read on and you'll find out that the leather-covered book you carry with you to church and Bible studies—and, hopefully, that you take time to read on your own—is a devastating weapon when it's used correctly. The Bible is indeed a weapon, but it's a weapon in the kind of fight that a lot of people don't even know is going on right now: in the spiritual world.

symbolism

All of the steps of Bible reading and study listed in this chapter are important parts of being able to use God's Word as a weapon of offense against the devil. When you make all these things a part of your personal Bible reading and study, you'll be more than equipped to handle anything the devil throws at you.

Paul wrote to the church in a city called Ephesus and told the people that they were to put on what he called "all of God's armor" (Ephesians 6:11) with which they were to do spiritual battle not against humans or human institutions but against "evil rulers and authorities of the unseen world," "mighty powers of darkness who rule this world," and "wicked spirits in the heavenly realms" (Ephesians 6:12).

In that passage, Paul gives the readers a rundown of the armor of God, including the belt of truth and the body armor of God's righteousness (Ephesians 6:14), shoes of peace (Ephesians 6:15), the shield of faith (Ephesians 6:16), and others. The last piece of armor Paul lists isn't really armor at all but is in fact a weapon of offense. It's what he calls "the sword of the Spirit, which is the word of God" (Ephesians 6:17).

It's no accident that God has revealed His written Word as a weapon of offense against the work and wiles of the devil. In fact, that is very clearly demonstrated in accounts in the Gospels that tell us of Jesus himself facing down the temptations of Satan (see Matthew 4:1–11, Mark 1:12–13, and Luke 4:1–13).

In Matthew's account of this story, the devil throws three specific temptations at Jesus, all of which Christ answers with the words "It is written" followed by a direct quotation from the Old Testament. Finally, Jesus completely repels the devil's attacks by telling him, "Get out of here, Satan...For the Scriptures say, 'You must worship the Lord your God; serve only him'" (Matthew 4:10). With that said, the devil had no choice. He left the scene utterly and completely defeated.

factum

In the scene where Jesus faces down the devil and his temptations, it's interesting—and important—to note that the devil himself quoted Scripture to Jesus in order to tempt him. As believers, we need to keep in mind that the devil not only knows Scripture but also knows how to twist it to suit his purposes.

The Prince of Peace had successfully and decisively fought a spiritual battle against the one who was not just his spiritual enemy but also ours. And he'd done it using a weapon available to us all.

Paul's encouragement to the Ephesians as well as Jesus's victorious encounter with the devil demonstrates something all believers need to understand: When it comes to spiritual battle, when it comes to going toe to toe with the devil, there is no more powerful weapon at our disposal than the written Word of God.

As Christians, we face not only a spiritual enemy (the devil) who is in opposition to everything we do but also a world system that the Bible tells us is also an enemy (1 John 5:4–5). But we have a spiritual weapon that neither can stand against: the Word of God. For that reason we can answer every temptation, every trial, every discouragement, and every battle with the wisdom and truth of what God has already spoken.

- When the enemy says, "You're a miserable sinner," you can answer, "Yes, but I've been washed, sanctified, and justified in the name of the Lord Jesus Christ" (1 Corinthians 6:11).
- When the enemy says, "You're worthless and can't do anything!" you can answer, "On my own that might be true, but I can do everything through Christ who strengthens me" (Philippians 4:13).
- When the enemy says, "How could God love a miserable sinner like you?" you can answer, "While I was still a sinner, Christ died for me!" (Romans 5:8).

- When the enemy tempts you to sin, you can answer, "There isn't one temptation you can throw at me that people haven't seen before. Not only that, God is faithful to show me a way out of it before I give in" (1 Corinthians 10:13).
- And when the enemy starts whispering in your ear, trying to get you to worry, you can answer, "I won't be anxious about anything but instead I'll thank and praise God and pray to him about what I need" (Philippians 4:6).

It is true that our spiritual enemy has more ways to wage war against us than we, in our limited human understanding, can comprehend. But it is equally true that for every thing he can throw at us, we can have an answer, an answer from the very mouth of God.

CHAPTER 5

Genesis:
Abraham's Amazing Faith

From this chapter through the end of this book in an actual Bible study, we are covering the Bible from beginning to end. You will now need your favorite Bible alongside you in order to read the verses, chapters, and larger sections that we comment upon. Just reading the summary is inadequate in terms of accomplishing the study objectives previously set forth. You will also need your Bible to answer the study questions throughout these chapters.

The Beginning of Something Big

Even if you have only a rudimentary knowledge of the Bible, you probably know that it begins, "In the beginning…" (Genesis 1:1). The fact that the book of Genesis, the first book of the Bible, starts with those words is only fitting because Genesis is all about beginnings. In fact, the word *genesis* means "origins" or "beginnings."

This first book of the Bible tells the story of the beginning of our earth and cosmos and of humanity itself (Genesis 1–2), the beginning of human sin and its consequences (Genesis 3–9), and the beginning of human civilization (Genesis 10–11). But the most important beginning in Genesis is the beginning of the Jewish race, the people through whom God would bring salvation to the whole world.

This chapter provides a character study of Abraham, the father of the Jewish and Christian faiths. His story is told in the twelfth through twenty-fourth chapters of the book of Genesis.

Abraham wasn't by any means perfect, but he was a man of obedience to God, full of courage and generosity. He was a man of prayer and a man who, while he made his share of mistakes, was true to his God. Above all, he was a man of tremendous faith.

If you want to know your Bible well and fully understand how it ties itself together, it is important that you know and understand the events in the life of Abraham. That is because he is the man God Himself chose to be the physical father of the great nation of Israel and also the spiritual father of all who put their faith in the God of the Jewish and Christian people.

This book is not going to cover every aspect of Abraham's life—that you'll have to do in your own studies. But it does give you an overview of the events that led to Abraham's becoming the father of God's chosen people, the Jews.

As you read through this chapter—and through the Biblical chapters that tell the story of this great hero of the faith—take note of how Abraham responded to the commands and promises of God, how he related to those God brought into his life, and how God blessed him and those who would come after him.

Abraham's Early Life and God's Calling and Promises (Genesis 12)

Abraham was born around 1950 B.C. in a place called Ur of the Chaldees, which was located about 200 miles southeast of the modern city of Baghdad, Iraq. At birth he was named Abram, which means "God is exalted." Abraham spent his childhood as well as much of his adult life living in Ur. It was there that he married a woman named Sarai (later Sarah).

Later, Abraham traveled with his father, family, and household from Ur to a place called Haran, some 300 miles north of Ur. He lived in Haran until he was seventy-five years old. It was at that time that Abraham received his very special and unique calling from God.

factum

The book of Genesis doesn't say specifically why Abraham moved from Ur to Haran, but a New Testament reference says, "Our glorious God appeared to our ancestor Abraham in Mesopotamia before he moved to Haran. God told him, 'Leave your native land and your relatives, and come to the land that I will show you'" (Acts 7:2, 3).

After the death of his father Terah, Abraham received this call—and the promises that accompanied it—from God:

The Lord had said to Abram, "Leave your native country, your relatives, and your father's family, and go to the land that I will show you. I will make you into a great nation. I will bless you and make you famous, and you will be a blessing to others. I will bless those who bless you and curse those who treat you with contempt. All the families on earth will be blessed through you." (Genesis 12:1–3)

The Bible tells us that the land God promised Abraham's people would be Canaan, later known as Israel. It also shows us that God made Abraham the father of the great nation of Israel, through which he would bring a blessing to all nations and races in the form of Jesus Christ.

This promise was at the heart of the covenant (or contract) between God and His people, and it was carried through the centuries from Abraham through his descendants, starting with his son Isaac and his grandson Jacob.

Genesis goes on to give the account of the amazing life Abraham lived in service to his God. It wasn't without its stumbles and mistakes, but it was a life dominated by a faith and devotion to the God who called him to a high place in His kingdom and in human history.

Abraham did as God had called him to do, and he spent some time in Egypt before traveling to what would be God's land of promise, Canaan (Genesis 13). But that was just the beginning of an incredible story of Abraham's faith in and obedience to God.

Study Questions

○ What was Abraham's verbal response to God's command? What was his nonverbal response?

○ Read Hebrews 11:8. What did the writer of Hebrews say about Abraham's obedience to God's call to leave his home?

Reassurances and Promises for Abraham (Genesis 15)

Abraham had heard God clearly and believed, and he knew that God was going to make of him a great nation. But like so many believers who have chosen to follow God obediently, Abraham came to a point in his life when he needed some assurance.

First, the Lord gave Abraham what we might consider a general reassurance, telling him, "Do not be afraid, Abram, for I will protect you, and your reward will be great" (Genesis 15:1).

But Abraham needed something more specific, more concrete. "O Sovereign Lord, what good are all your blessings when I don't even have a son? Since I don't have a son, Eliezer of Damascus, a servant in my household, will inherit all my wealth. You have given me no children, so one of my servants will have to be my heir" (15:2–3).

God's answer to Abraham's specific question was itself direct and specific:

Then the Lord said to him, "No, your servant will not be your heir, for you will have a son of your own to inherit everything I am giving you." Then the Lord brought Abram outside beneath the night sky and told him, "Look up into the heavens and count the stars if you can. Your descendants will be like that—too many to count!" And Abram believed the Lord, and the Lord declared him righteous because of his faith. (Genesis 15:4–6)

Now God could have just told Abraham to just trust, obey, and wait for further instructions. But note as you read this passage that He gave Abraham exactly what he asked for, namely some specifics when it came to His promises. Also note that God gave him a concrete illustration of His promises: that his descendants would be more numerous than the stars shining in the nighttime sky.

After receiving such promises, you would think that Abraham would be willing to wait as long as it would take for God to move on his behalf. But as you will see in the next chapter of Genesis, Abraham made the mistake of moving out ahead of God.

Study Questions

○ Read Romans 4:1–22. What does this tell you about the basis of Abraham's relationship with God?

○ Read Galatians 3:7. Who does God count as the true descendants of Abraham (in other words, God's chosen people)?

Abraham's Big Mistake (Genesis 16)

Lest you believe that God only used the perfect—those who believed Him perfectly, obeyed Him perfectly, and lived their lives perfectly—to accomplish His purposes, just take a look at the actions of Abraham and his wife, Sarah, as they are recorded in Genesis 16.

factum

It is commonly believed that the descendants of Ishmael are the Arab nations, who over the centuries have been at odds with the people of Israel. That is why the Arab-Israeli conflict has been referred to as the world's oldest sibling rivalry.

God had twice already told Abraham that he would be blessed, that he would be the father of a great nation, but Abraham couldn't leave well enough alone. Instead of trusting in what God had told him, Abraham—as well as his wife—became impatient and attempted to move out ahead of God and do for themselves what He had promised to do for them.

This is the Bible's account of that big mistake:

Now Sarai, Abram's wife, had not been able to bear children for him. But she had an Egyptian servant named Hagar. So Sarai said to Abram, "The Lord has prevented me from having children. Go and sleep with my servant. Perhaps I can have children through her." And Abram agreed with Sarai's proposal. So Sarai, Abram's wife, took Hagar the Egyptian servant and gave her to Abram as a wife (Genesis 16:1–3)

Sarah meant no harm or dishonor to God when she attempted—successfully, it turned out—to persuade her husband to father a child for her through her servant. In her mind, God himself had kept her from having children, and it was up to her to do for herself what God hadn't done for her.

In purely human terms, it's hard to blame Sarah. After all, she was seventy-five years old, had been married for decades, and still had no children. Being in a childless marriage was at that time and in that culture no small matter of dishonor, and Sarah was determined to take care of the situation in the best way she knew how.

However, what Sarah and Abraham did in this case was a big mistake, if for no other reason than it was an act of unbelief. They went ahead of God and attempted to do for themselves what God had promised to do for them. One result was a son God didn't intend for Abraham to father: Ishmael. Another was the conflict that ensued between Sarah and her servant Hagar.

Study Questions

○ What was Abraham's biggest mistake in this account?

○ How were God's promises regarding Ishmael similar to those regarding Abraham's still-to-come child of promise?

A Confirmation and a Name Change (Genesis 17)

In the seventeenth chapter of Genesis, God establishes the Jewish rite of circumcision, but not before again assuring Abraham, by now all of ninety-nine years old, of his calling and promises:

> *This is my covenant with you: I will make you the father of a multitude of nations! What's more, I am changing your name. It will no longer be Abram. Instead, you will be called Abraham, for you will be the father of many nations. I will make you extremely fruitful. Your descendants will become many nations, and kings will be among them! (Genesis 17:4–6)*

God had made a promise, an agreement with Abraham and with all those who would come after him. Abraham's part in the deal was that he and all of his male descendants be circumcised, an act that would have great spiritual significance:

> *From generation to generation, every male child must be circumcised on the eighth day after his birth. This applies not only to members of your family but also to the servants born in your household and the foreign-born servants whom you have purchased. All must be circumcised. Your bodies will bear the mark of my everlasting covenant. Any male who fails to be circumcised will be cut off from the covenant family for breaking the covenant. (Genesis 17:12–14)*

In giving this command, God had appointed circumcision as a special symbol for His chosen people, a badge of their dedication and devotion to Him. And though Abraham was nearly a century old, he and his son Ishmael, who was thirteen years old at the time, were circumcised (Genesis 17:24–27).

point of interest

The change from the name *Abram* to *Abraham* for the father of the Jewish and Christian faith is very significant because the name *Abraham* means "the father of many" or "father of a multitude." That was in keeping with God's promise that his descendants would number in the millions.

Though there were still episodes ahead in Abraham's life (for example, his intercession for the cities of Sodom and Gomorrah and their destruction as recorded in Genesis 18–19), he would live to one day see the miraculous birth of the son God had promised him.

Study Questions

○ Read 1 Corinthians 7:17, Galatians 6:15, and Colossians 3:11. What is the New Testament approach to circumcision? What, if anything, has taken its place in the life and heart of the believer?

○ Read Genesis 18:23–33. What does this tell you about the importance of praying for others, even those who don't seem to deserve it?

The Long-Awaited Birth of Isaac (Genesis 20–21)

It had been more than twenty years since God had promised Abraham that he and Sarah would have a son, but in an example of how God's timing isn't always our timing, God gave this couple their long-awaited son: "The Lord kept his word and did for Sarah exactly what he had promised. She became pregnant, and she gave birth to a son for Abraham in his old age. This happened at just the time God had said it would. And Abraham named their son Isaac" (Genesis 21:1–3). It was as if God waited to fulfill His promise just because He wanted to show Abraham and Sarah His power and ability to do the miraculous.

factum

The name *Isaac* means "he laughs." That name has meaning in that it reflects the reaction of unbelief from his mother Sarah when she overheard it said that she was going to have a son in her old age (Genesis 18:10–15). At that time, Sarah was well past childbearing age.

As per God's instructions, Abraham had his son circumcised eight days after his birth. After Isaac was weaned, Abraham threw a huge party to celebrate. It was then that there were more conflicts between Sarah and Hagar, the mother of Ishmael. Sarah wanted to solve the problem by sending Hagar and Ishmael away. That is exactly what God told Abraham to do but with the assurance that Ishmael would be counted among his descendants and, therefore, would be the father of many descendants.

Later in Abraham's life he was confronted with the biggest test of his faith he would ever face, and it would involve his son Isaac. How he fared in that test would determine his place in God's plan to redeem humankind.

Study Questions

○ In what situations in your own life have you been tempted not to hold to your faith in God's promises but instead to run out ahead of God?

○ How do you respond when you read or hear of a promise of God that is a little hard to swallow?

Abraham's Big Test (Genesis 22)

In the Christian life we can talk all we want about our faith and how we are ready to trust God enough to obey His commands, even when they seem strange to us. But sooner or later we're going to have to put some action behind our faith. That is exactly what Abraham was challenged to do in Genesis 22.

After all Abraham had been through prior to receiving his promised son, Isaac, it must have been hard for him to understand what God had in mind when He gave him this command: "Take your son, your only son—yes, Isaac, whom you love so much—and go to the land of Moriah. Go and sacrifice him as a burnt offering on one of the mountains, which I will show you" (Genesis 22:2).

symbolism

The story of Abraham intending to sacrifice his own son before God is a stark Biblical example of what God wants from each of us: that we be willing to give up to Him anything we have, even those things we very clearly know He has promised us.

Didn't Abraham hear God say that he would have many descendants and that they would be a blessing to all the world? How could this be? How could God ask him to do such a thing? Although what God had commanded him to do probably didn't make a whole lot of sense—and seemed so distasteful—Abraham obeyed God's directions to the very letter.

Early the next morning, Abraham and Isaac set out for Mount Moriah, the place where it seemed God was about to take away what had been promised so long ago. Abraham set up an altar and built a fire, then he prepared to sacrifice his son. But at the very moment of truth, an angel of God stepped in and stopped him, telling him, "Abraham! Abraham!…Don't lay a hand on the boy!…Do not hurt him in any way, for now I know that you truly fear God. You have not withheld from me even your son, your only son" (Genesis 22:11, 12).

Then the angel of the Lord called again to Abraham from heaven. "This is what the Lord says: Because you have obeyed me and have not withheld even your son, your only son, I swear by my own name that I will certainly bless you. I will multiply your descendants beyond number, like the stars in the sky and the sand on the seashore. Your descendants will conquer the cities of their enemies. And through your descendants all the nations of the earth will be blessed—all because you have obeyed me." (Genesis 22:15–18)

From the very beginning this was a test for Abraham, a test to see if he would be faithful and obedient to God. Abraham needed to be tested in order to prove himself worthy to be the father of the people through whom God would bring salvation to all the world.

discussion question

According to the New Testament book of Hebrews, what did Abraham believe God would have done if he had actually gone through with sacrificing Isaac?
According to the writer of Hebrews, Abraham, so convinced that Isaac was the son he had been promised, believed that if he had actually slain his son, God would have raised him from the dead (Hebrews 11:17–19).

He passed that test, and because of that he stands as a Biblical example of faith, obedience, and faithfulness. That is also why his descendants were the foundation of the Jewish race and its calling, namely bringing the Savior into the world.

As you continue reading through Genesis, take a close look at the lives of Abraham's descendants, including his son Isaac, his grandchildren Jacob and Esau, and his great-grandchildren (those who would be the fathers of the twelve tribes of Israel), particularly Joseph.

Study Questions

○ How would you respond if God were to tell you to do something that just didn't make sense? How did Abraham respond?

○ What are some of the character qualities in Abraham that you want to emulate in your own life? What are some of his mistakes you want to avoid?

CHAPTER 6

Numbers:
Standing Out from the Crowd

One of the many great things about the Bible is that it tells the stories of some of the great men and women of faith— people who might not have been smarter or more talented than most of us today but who had the nerve to believe God and to act on what they knew. In this chapter you'll read about two early heroes of the faith, Caleb and Joshua, a couple of guys who refused to believe the negative but instead focused on what God had already said.

Standing Alone in Believing God

The book of Genesis closes with the story of Joseph, the fourth-generation patriarch of the Hebrew nation. Exodus, the second book of the Pentateuch (the books of Moses, the first five of the Bible), picks up with the people of Israel living in subjection and slavery to the nation of Egypt.

The books of Exodus, Leviticus, Numbers, and Deuteronomy tell the stories of the leadership of Moses during the Jewish people's flight from Egyptian captivity (known as the Exodus), the giving of the law of God, and the Israelites' journey toward the Promised Land.

This chapter covers a tragic event in the history of the Jewish people: their banishment to the wilderness for forty years due to their own unbelief and disobedience. This story, which is recorded in the thirteenth and fourteenth chapters of Numbers, tells how the people of Israel listened to the negative reports of ten faithless Jewish leaders and ignored the reports of two who dared to believe God and His promises. Worse than that, it's the story of a people who completely rebelled because they just couldn't persevere in believing in a God who keeps His promises.

However, there is a bright side to this story, and it's one we should pay careful attention to as well. It's the story of those two faithful spies, Caleb and Joshua, and the reward they would receive because they dared to continue believing in God despite what they saw.

God's Reconnaissance Mission (Numbers 13:1–24)

God had taken the people of Israel on an incredible journey. Now the time had come for them to claim the land He had promised them. The people were encamped in a place called Kadesh, which was to the south of Canaan, the Promised Land. All that remained for them to do was to follow God's lead, go into the land, and claim it for themselves.

As God prepared His people to enter into the land, He spoke to Moses and gave him these instructions: "'Send men to explore the land of Canaan, the land I am giving to Israel. Send one leader from each of the twelve ancestral tribes.' So Moses did as the Lord commanded him. He sent out twelve men, all tribal leaders of Israel, from their camp in the wilderness of Paran" (Numbers 13:1–3).

factum

This passage tells us that by the time Moses had sent the twelve spies to check out the land of Canaan, he had changed the name of one of the spies from Hoshea to Joshua (Numbers 13:16). The name *Hoshea* means "salvation," while the name *Joshua* means "the Lord is salvation."

This passage tells us that Moses did exactly as God had told him, sending twelve leaders—one from each tribe of Israel—to Canaan to check out the land. Moses told them to check out the land and the people who lived there. They were to find out if the land was fertile and to see how many people lived in the land and whether they were strong or weak. And while they were at it, they were to bring back samples of the produce that grew there (Numbers 13:17–20).

The twelve spies did as they were told, heading out on a forty-day trip around the land of Canaan. When that journey was finished, two of the men—Caleb of Judah and Joshua (or Hoshea) of Ephraim—would become symbols of faith, while the other ten would become living and dying lessons of the folly of unbelief and unfaithfulness to the commands and promises of God.

Study Questions

❍ Who were the twelve spies and what was their significance to the people of Israel?

❍ What were the specifics of Moses's instructions to the twelve spies?

It's All a Matter of Focus (Numbers 13:25–33)

When the twelve spies first returned to Kadesh to give their report, it must have appeared that they were about to give the go-ahead for the Israelites to go in and claim the land of Canaan. They brought with them a bundle of grapes so big that it took two of them to carry it, and they brought samples of the figs and pomegranates that grew there. However, they also brought with them a report for Moses that would, unfortunately, frighten and discourage the people of Israel to the point where they were ready to give up and go back to Egypt:

> We arrived in the land you sent us to see, and it is indeed a magnificent country—a land flowing with milk and honey. Here is some of its fruit as proof. But the people living there are powerful, and their cities and towns are fortified and very large. We also saw the descendants of Anak who are living there! The Amalekites live in the Negev, and the Hittites, Jebusites, and Amorites live in the hill country. The Canaanites live along the coast of the Mediterranean Sea and along the Jordan Valley. (Numbers 13:27–29)

The problem with this report isn't what the ten spies said about the land. These men freely acknowledged that there was a lot positive to be said about the land God had promised to give His people, that it was everything God said it would be and was a wonderful place to make a home for the people of Israel.

Focusing on the beauty of God's gift and on His ability to keep all His promises, the young spy named Caleb spoke with great confidence and boldness as he attempted to rally the troops for what he was sure would be a successful conquest of the land of Canaan: "We can certainly do it!" (Numbers 13:30).

symbolism

God had explicitly promised the people of Israel, through Moses, that He would drive the Canaanites out of the land so they could settle in it (Exodus 33:2), yet the ten cowardly spies said, "We can't do it!" Later, the psalmist wrote that the people actually hated the land because they couldn't believe God's promises (Psalm 106:24).

The majority in this group, however, didn't share Caleb's confidence. Instead of focusing on God's promises and on His power to do what seemed impossible, they focused on the giants, fighting men who they thought were unbeatable.

> But the other men who had explored the land with him answered, "We can't go up against them! They are stronger than we are!" So they spread discouraging reports about the land among the Israelites: "The land we explored will swallow up any who go to live there. All the people we saw were huge. We even saw giants there, the descendants of Anak. We felt like grasshoppers next to them, and that's what we looked like to them!" (Numbers 13:31–33)

Ten of the spies who had been sent to check out the Promised Land only saw the giants who stood in their way. But Caleb—as well as Joshua—saw the promises of God and His ability to keep those promises. For that reason, he was able to confidently encourage the people to go and take what God had promised them.

Sadly, however, it wasn't Caleb who had the people's ear. Instead of listening to Caleb, who was speaking the very words God wanted them to hear, they listened to the ten spies who were more than ready to give into their fears and stay right where they were—or worse, go back to the slavery and bondage in Egypt.

Study Questions

○ Who were the people that frightened the ten spies so badly that they discouraged the Israelites from entering the Promised Land?

○ What exactly were Caleb's words of encouragement to the people of Israel?

Our Latest Polling Data Shows…(Numbers 14:1–10)

The people of Israel had seen for themselves the miracles God had performed in bringing them out of Egyptian captivity and slavery. They had seen Him bring plagues upon the Egyptians because of Pharaoh's stubbornness, had crossed through the sea on dry land as Pharaoh's army descended upon them, had sung God's praises for their deliverance, had enjoyed His provision, and had heard His promises of a land flowing with milk and honey.

And yet, despite God's awesome demonstrations of love, power, and provision, they grumbled and complained—and rebelled—rather than simply accept and claim what God had already given them. All this because of some reports of giants in the land God had promised them. "We wish we had died in Egypt, or even here in the wilderness!" they wailed. "Why is the Lord taking us to this country only to have us die in battle? Our wives and little ones will be carried off as slaves! Let's get out of here and return to Egypt!" (Numbers 14:2–3).

factum

Kadesh-barnea, the name of the place where this rebellion took place, is believed to mean "the holy place of the desert of wandering." After this, it remained a camp during the Israelites' wanderings in the desert. This is also where Miriam, the sister of Moses, died and was buried shortly before the Israelites finally entered the Promised Land (Numbers 20:1).

This scene was more than one of people complaining and voicing their fears. It spun far beyond that and became one of open rebellion by the people against Moses and Aaron, the men God had called to lead them out of Egypt and into the Promised Land. In an effort to calm the people and bring them back to a place of trusting God, Caleb and Joshua pleaded with them, first telling them how wonderful the land really was, then begging them, "Do not rebel against the Lord, and don't be afraid of the people of the land. They are only helpless prey to us! They have no protection, but the Lord is with us. Don't be afraid of them!" (Numbers 14:9).

But it was too late to quell the rebellion. The people talked openly about stoning Caleb and Joshua to death, and the only thing that stopped them was an appearance of the glorious presence of the Lord before them.

The object lesson of the account in this passage of Scripture is that it is important for those who want to live a victorious life of faith in God to make sure they are focused on the right things. Sadly, the Israelites focused on the size of the giants in Canaan, not on the bigness and power and ability of their God to keep each and every one of His promises.

Study Questions
◯ What more than anything do you think caused the people of Israel to rebel and plot to turn back and return to slavery in Egypt?
◯ What qualities did Joshua display to the people of Israel when he pleaded with them not to rebel but to continue on and take what God had promised them?

What Really Offends God: It's Spelled U-N-B-E-L-I-E-F (Numbers 14:11–19)

This passage starts with a demonstration of what God looks and sounds like when He is angry with His people, and it shows us exactly what makes Him angry: "How long will these people reject me? Will they never believe me, even after all the miraculous signs I have done among them? I will disown them and destroy them with a plague. Then I will make you into a nation far greater and mightier than they are!" (Numbers 14:11, 12).

What had God really peeved with His people was their unbelief, which led to their open rebellion. After everything He had brought them through, they still refused to put their trust in Him and move on and claim what was already theirs. Instead, they wanted to go back to lives of bondage and slavery in Egypt.

But Moses had come too far with these people to give up on them. He earnestly pleaded for their lives, reminding God not of the worthiness of these rebellious, unbelieving Israelites but of the goodness and trustworthiness of His name and of His own love, patience, and mercy (Numbers 14:13–19). "Please pardon the sins of this people because of your magnificent unfailing love, just as you have forgiven them ever since they left Egypt" (Numbers 14:19).

In the end, God heard Moses's request and forgave the sins of the people of Israel. However, there would still be consequences for their unbelief and rebellion.

- According to Numbers 14:13–17, how did Moses plead with God not to destroy the rebellious people?
- Reread Numbers 14:18–19. According to that passage, what character attributes of God lead him to forgive the sins of those He calls His people?

Close but No Promised Land for the Rebellious Israelites (Numbers 14:20–38)

In one of the more tragic episodes in the Bible, and in the history of the Jewish people, a whole generation was lost in the wilderness simply because they couldn't obey God, which means they couldn't believe God and couldn't remember the things He had done for them previously. God had lost his patience with these wayward people, and it was only because Moses pleaded so ardently with Him that they didn't die on the spot (Numbers 14:13–19). And while God honored Moses's request and forgave these people their individual sins, there were still consequences for those sins:

> Then the Lord said, "I will pardon them as you have requested. But as surely as I live, and as surely as the earth is filled with the Lord's glory, not one of these people will ever enter that land. They have seen my glorious presence and the miraculous signs I performed both in Egypt and in the wilderness, but again and again they tested me by refusing to listen. They will never even see the land I swore to give their ancestors. None of those who have treated me with contempt will enter it." (Numbers 14:20–23)

Later on in this chapter, God tells Moses that no one over the age of twenty—except Caleb and Joshua, who believed God and pleaded with the people to do the same—would ever enter the Promised Land but would instead die in the wilderness. For the next forty years, every man, woman, and child who had left Egypt during the time of the Exodus would wander in the desert around Canaan but would never be allowed to possess it.

symbolism

While this passages tells us what was to become of all twelve spies—the two who believed and the ten who didn't, Joshua 14:6–15 tells us what eventually became of Caleb because of his faith. Caleb believed God and acted on what he believed, and for that reason he became an example of the kind of faith God honors.

Other than Joshua and Caleb, no one in that throng of millions—not even Moses and Aaron—would ever see the Promised Land. Even those ten spies who came back with a negative report died as a result of their unbelief (Numbers 14:36, 37). The others were sentenced to spending forty years in the wilderness.

Study Questions

○ God pardoned the sins of the people of Israel, yet they still suffered the consequences. What does this tell you about the nature of the sin of unbelief and about the vital importance of taking God at His word?

○ This passage demonstrates the importance of both having faith and putting action behind your faith. What has God challenged you to believe Him for, and what kind of action are you putting behind that faith?

Going It Alone, or Trying to Anyway (Numbers 4:39–45)

Some of the Israelites eventually saw the error of their ways—more or less. Sadly, though, it was too late for them as individuals to receive what God had promised His people. Still, they made plans to head into Canaan on their own. What's worse for them is that they didn't recognize that attempting to go into Canaan now was suicide. The reason? Moses explained to them:

But Moses said, "Why are you now disobeying the Lord's orders to return to the wilderness? It won't work. Do not go into the land now. You will only be crushed by your enemies because the Lord is not with you. When you face the Amalekites and Canaanites in battle, you will be slaughtered. The Lord will abandon you because you have abandoned the Lord." (Numbers 4:41–43)

God had kept these people under His protection, given them direction, and provided for them everything they needed to take and keep the Promised Land of Canaan. But in spite of all that, they listened to the voices of those who didn't represent the Lord, gave into their fears rather than trusting in God, and rebelled against God's appointed leaders (and, therefore, God Himself).

factum

Joshua, one of the two faithful spies who attempted to encourage the Israelites to take the Promised Land, later took the mantle of leadership for the people after the death of Moses. Before his death, Moses gave Joshua a public ceremony to name him leader. (See Deuteronomy 31:23.)

They had everything they could have wanted or needed, and they made the fatal mistake of not staying in that safe, secure place trusting and obeying the God who had proved himself far more than worthy of that trust and obedience. Consequently, not only would all of the adult Israelites who were present at Kadesh end up dying in the wilderness having never seen the Promised Land, but some of them would foolishly try to move into Canaan—despite what the Lord had told them. Again, they would pay a price for their disobedience, this time suffering a humiliating defeat at the hands of the people who presently lived in the land of Canaan.

While Caleb and Joshua would have to spend another forty years in the wilderness with their rebellious and faithless brothers and sisters, they would eventually be among the first of the nation of Israel to actually possess the Promised Land.

In fact, if you read and study the book of Joshua, you will see that he became one of the great spiritual and military leaders in the history of the people of Israel—and a man who holds his place in the faith Hall of Fame.

Study Questions

○ According to Moses's words to the Israelites who were planning to enter Canaan on their own, why was God no longer going to be with them in this endeavor?

○ What "giants" in your life are you focused on that keep you from obeying and enjoying what God has for you?

CHAPTER 7

Joshua: God Always Finishes What He Starts

One of the dominant themes in the Bible is faithfulness. God identifies Himself as being faithful in every way, and then He goes out time after time and proves it. And God also teaches in His Word that there is great reward in our being faithful, which means that we believe God and then act on what we believe. This chapter is the study of a man who believed God, acted on his faith, and then became one of the heroes of the Jewish and Christian faiths.

Time to Claim the Land

The book of Joshua tells the story of how the people of Israel—the people God had chosen to accomplish His plan of salvation for the whole world—at long last claimed and possessed the Promised Land that God had promised them centuries before.

Joshua (the man and book) picks up where Moses left off. At the end of Deuteronomy, Moses had died and been buried and "Now Joshua son of Nun was full of the spirit of wisdom, for Moses had laid his hands on him. So the people of Israel obeyed him, doing just as the Lord had commanded Moses" (Deuteronomy 34:9).

discussion question

Where does the name *Joshua* come from?
The name *Joshua* (originally Hoshea or Jehoshua) is a Hebrew name that means either "Jehovah is his help," "Jehovah the Savior," "the Lord is salvation," or "Jehovah is salvation." The name *Jesus* is a variant of Joshua.

Joshua was going to be God's faithful instrument in finishing what He had started through Moses. While Moses had led the people of Israel out of Egyptian captivity and slavery, Joshua was going to lead them into the Promised Land.

The book of Joshua is an amazing story of faith and obedience. But more than that, it is the story of how God always keeps His promises and how He finishes what He started. Though his people's disobedience, fear, and rebellion delayed their claiming of the Promised Land, God still kept His word. Though the people were forced to wander forty years in the wilderness, God still kept His word. And though their great leader, Moses, had died, God still kept His word.

Words of Encouragement (Joshua 1)

In the very first few verses of the book of Joshua, we see a theme that repeats itself throughout the book as God leads and guides and Joshua follows and obeys. Right away, God calls Joshua and tells him, "Moses my servant is dead. Therefore, the time has come for you to lead these people, the Israelites, across the Jordan River into the land I am giving them. I promise you what I promised Moses..." (Joshua 1:2–3).

And what had God promised to Moses but had been prevented from giving him because of his people's stubbornness? He goes on to tell Joshua:

- Wherever he walked, he would be on the land God had given him (Joshua 1:3).
- No one would be able to stand up against Joshua for as long as he lived (1:5).
- God Himself would be with Joshua and would never fail him or abandon him (1:5).
- He would be the one to lead the people of Israel as they possessed the land God had promised their ancestors (1:6).

There were, however, conditions to these promises, namely that Joshua be strong and filled with courage and that he obey everything God had commanded him and his people to do:

Be strong and very courageous. Be careful to obey all the instructions Moses gave you. Do not deviate from them, turning either to the right or to the left. Then you will be successful in everything you do. Study this Book of Instruction continually. Meditate on it day and night so you will be sure to obey everything written in it. Only then will you prosper and succeed in all you do. This is my command— be strong and courageous! Do not be afraid or discouraged. For the Lord your God is with you wherever you go. (Joshua 1:7–9)

Joshua wasted no time in getting the people ready to move out. First he called together the officers of Israel and told them to go through the camp and tell the people that they would be crossing the Jordan River in three days to take the land. Then he called together the tribes of Reuben, Gad, and the half-tribe of Manasseh and gave them words of encouragement and instruction.

The people didn't argue, question, or resist anything Joshua said. Instead, they enthusiastically told him, "We will do whatever you command us, and we will go wherever you send us" just as they had Moses.

With that, Joshua and the people made final preparations to do what their forefathers had been denied doing themselves because of their rebellion: Take the land God had promised them!

Study Questions

○ What precisely were Joshua's instructions for the people of Israel as he took the mantle of leadership in leading them at long last into the Promised Land?

○ How did the people of Israel respond to Joshua's leadership as he instructed them what to do next?

A Hero Named Rahab (Joshua 2)

One of the recurring themes of the Bible is God using the unlikeliest of people to do great things to further His kingdom and His causes. The second chapter of Joshua provides one of the best examples of this theme in all of Scripture as God gave a prostitute named Rahab a part in his plan to fulfill His promises.

Joshua 2 begins with Joshua doing something Moses had done years earlier: sending out spies (remember, Joshua himself was once a spy) and asking them to scout out the land on the opposite side of the Jordan River, especially around Jericho, which was considered the strongest fortress in the land of Canaan.

When the spies arrived in Jericho, they stayed at Rahab's home where, presumably, they would be safe. But when the king of Jericho was alerted that two men had come to spy on the land, he sent Rahab orders to bring the men out of her home and turn them over.

Rahab had hidden the spies in the house, but she told the king that, yes, they had been at her home earlier but that they had left and she didn't know where they had gone. If they hurried, she told the king's servants, they might be able to catch up with them.

With that threat taken care of, Rahab went to the hidden spies and told them, "I know the Lord has given you this land. We are all afraid of you. Everyone in the land is living in terror. For we have heard how the Lord made a dry path for you through the Red Sea when you left Egypt" (Joshua 2:9–10).

point of interest

Rahab's actions in saving the two Hebrew spies earned her mention in the New Testament—in the epistle to the Hebrews and the epistle of James. The writer of Hebrews pointed out that it was by faith that she did what she did (Hebrews 11:31), and James tells us that it was her actions that demonstrated that faith (James 2:25).

Rahab didn't mince words. She and her family and friends in Jericho were terrified because they knew that Joshua's God was supreme. But she then made one request, one the men were happy to grant since she had helped them out: "Now swear to me by the Lord that you will be kind to me and my family since I have helped you. Give me some guarantee that when Jericho is conquered, you will let me live, along with my father and mother, my brothers and sisters, and all their families" (Joshua 2:12–13).

The men swore to her that she and her family would be safe, and Rahab let them out of her home through the window—but only after hearing their terms for keeping her and her family safe. After that, they hid out and waited for three days, avoiding the search party that was looking for them to return. They then returned to the encampment and reported to Joshua what Rahab had told them.

Study Questions

○ What were the spies' conditions for making sure Rahab and her family would be safe when Israel took Jericho? (Read Joshua 2:17–20.)

○ How did the two spies know that the Lord had given the Israelites the land?

Crossing the Jordan (Joshua 3–4)

The people were encouraged by the reports the two spies had brought them, and almost immediately they were ready to cross the Jordan and take what God had said was theirs. The morning after the spies returned, they left their encampment at a place called Acacia Grove, traveled to the banks of the Jordan River, and set up came there.

Three days after setting up camp on the riverbank, the officers of the Israelites went through the camp and instructed the people to follow the priests carrying the Ark of the Covenant at a distance of about a half mile, making sure they didn't come any closer. Joshua also told the people to purify themselves in preparation for seeing God do great wonders among them the following morning (Joshua 3:3–5).

The next morning everyone did as they had been instructed, and as they headed out the Lord told Joshua, "Today I will begin to make you a great leader in the eyes of all the Israelites. They will know that I am with you, just as I was with Moses. Give this command to the priests who carry the Ark of the Covenant: 'When you reach the banks of the Jordan River, take a few steps into the river and stop there'" (Joshua 3:7–8).

symbolism

Joshua has been seen in Christianity as a foreshadowing of Jesus Christ (Hebrews 4:8–16). That is because their names mean essentially the same thing and because Joshua brought his people into the Promised Land as Jesus brings his followers into God's heavenly Kingdom. Also, as Joshua's leadership succeeded that of Moses, the gospel of Jesus Christ succeeds the Law of Moses.

Joshua passed along the instructions, including the promise that when the priests' feet touched the water, it would dry up and make a path for them to cross the river. It was the time of year when the Jordan was overflowing its banks, but when the priests dipped their feet in the water, the water was held back and the people crossed over near the town of Jericho as the priests stood in the middle of the riverbed waiting for them to pass by (Joshua 3:14–17).

With everybody having safely crossed the river, God instructed Joshua to have twelve men—one from each tribe of Israel—set up a memorial to remember the miracle of that day. They were to walk back to the middle of the Jordan River and gather twelve stones to build the memorial. Joshua told them, "In the future your children will ask you, 'What do these stones mean?' Then you can tell them, 'They remind us that the Jordan River stopped flowing when the Ark of the Lord's Covenant went across.' These stones will stand as a memorial among the people of Israel forever" (Joshua 4:6–7).

Having obeyed everything God had told them to do, the people of Israel were now ready to take the land of Canaan. The warriors from the tribes of Reuben, Gad, and the half-tribe of Manasseh were ready for battle. And that day, Joshua was seen in the eyes of the Israelites as every bit the great leader Moses had been.

Study Questions

○ What do you think was God's purpose in having the people of Israel cross the Jordan River in such a miraculous manner?

○ What was God's purpose in having the twelve-stone memorial built?

Taking Down the Walls of Jericho (Joshua 5–6)

What had just happened at the Jordan River crossing wasn't good news for a lot of the kings west of the river and in Canaan. In fact, it was such bad news, that many of them were paralyzed with fear (Joshua 5:1).

But God was about to do even greater things among the people of Israel. After taking the time to re-establish among the people some of the covenant ceremonies, God made the final preparations in the hearts of the people for them to take the land—starting with the city of Jericho.

The people who lived in the walled city of Jericho were terrified of the people of Israel, and all the gates of the city were tightly shut with no one allowed to come in or go out (Joshua 6:1). But walls and gates meant nothing, because God had told Joshua, "I have given you Jericho, its king, and all its strong warriors" (Joshua 6:2). In this passage of Scripture, it's not the fact that God continued to remind Joshua of His previous promises but the way He kept the promise about the fall of Jericho that grabs the reader's attention.

God didn't tell Joshua and his fighting men to just go in and clean up, but instead instructed them to march around Jericho once a day for six days. Seven priests, each carrying with him a ram's horn, were to walk ahead of the Ark of the Covenant. On the seventh day they were to march around the town seven times with the priests blowing the ram's horns. When the priests gave out a long blast on their horns, all the people were to shout as loudly as they could and the walls of Jericho would collapse, allowing the Israelites to charge straight into town (Joshua 6:3–5).

point of interest

The people of Israel were instructed specifically to not take anything from the city of Jericho except for the silver, gold, bronze, and iron— all of which were sacred to God and to be brought into the treasury (Joshua 6:18–19). The consequences of doing otherwise would bring trouble on the camp of Israel.

Again, Joshua didn't question God or try to provide what he thought of as a better plan. Instead, he did exactly as he was told and instructed the people precisely what God had told them to do. On the seventh day, the people of Israel got up at dawn and marched around the city as they had been doing all that week—except this time they went around it seven times. On that seventh lap, the priests sounded a long blast on their horns, the people gave out a shout, and the walls of Jericho came tumbling down. Every living thing in the city—human and nonhuman alike—was destroyed. Only Rahab the prostitute and her family were spared, as Joshua told them to go to her house and bring her out so that she and her loved ones would live. From then on, she lived with the Israelites (Joshua 6:22–25).

With the destruction of Jericho complete, Joshua invoked a curse on anyone who tried to rebuild the city (Joshua 6:26). God was with Joshua, and his reputation grew in the area.

- ○ Why do you believe God had the people of Israel defeat Jericho in such an unorthodox way?
- ○ Why do you think Joshua didn't question God when he was given the instructions for the defeat of the city of Jericho?

The Consequences of Not Following God's Instructions (Joshua 7–8)

After what had happened at the bank of the Jordan River and at the walls of Jericho, it seemed like nothing could stop the Israelites. All around the region, people heard what had been happening and they were terrified. But Israel's air of invincibility melted away as quickly as it was established as the Israelites were routed in a battle against Ai, a target the spies who checked it out believed wouldn't take more than a few thousand soldiers to take (Joshua 7:2–5).

factum

The name of the ancient Biblical city of Ai means "ruins." It was one of the royal cities of the inhabitants of Canaan (Genesis 12:8) prior to the invasion of Israel. After the conquest of Canaan was complete, the city of Ai was rebuilt and inhabited by the Benjamite tribe of Israel (Ezra 2:28, Nehemiah 7:32).

Joshua and the elders of Israel, of course, were distraught over what had happened, and Joshua fell on his face and cried out to God:

Oh, Sovereign Lord, why did you bring us across the Jordan River if you are going to let the Amorites kill us? If only we had been content to stay on the other side! Lord, what can I say now that Israel has fled from its enemies? For when the Canaanites and all the other

people living in the land hear about it, they will surround us and
wipe our name off the face of the earth. And then what will happen
to the honor of your great name? (Joshua 7:7–9)

The problem was spelled out in the first two verses of Joshua 7. A man named Achan had stolen and kept for himself some of the things God had said were to be set apart for Him alone. And because one man had violated God's commands, it was as if the entire nation of Israel had violated His commands.

God commanded Joshua to get up, then told him that the problem was that someone had broken His covenant by stealing and then lying about it (Joshua 7:11). God then told Joshua that in order to set things back on track, the people would have to purify themselves and make things right again.

After going through a process of elimination (Joshua 7:16–18), Joshua discovered that it was Achan who had caused the problems for the Israelites. He had stolen a beautiful robe, 200 silver coins, and a one-pound bar of gold and then hidden them under his tent.

symbolism

It is in the tenth chapter of Joshua that the city of Jerusalem is first mentioned in the Bible. That city would later become the hub of all Jewish religious activity, the seat of government for Israel, and a place of conflict between Jews and Muslims and Israelis and Palestinians.

Once the wrong had been righted, and once the people of Israel repented for what Achan had done, God instructed Joshua to send the fighting men of Israel back to Ai. When they did, they defeated Ai decisively. After that, the covenant God had made with the people of Israel was renewed (Joshua 8:30–35).

Study Questions

○ What connection can you draw between obedience and God's blessing in this passage?

○ What does the account of the Israelites defeat at the hands of Ai tell you about partial obedience to God?

The Conquest of the South and the North (Joshua 9–12)

With the victories of Jericho and Ai behind him, Joshua then turned his attention toward leading the Israelites in completing the conquests of the peoples who had occupied the Promised Land.

The fame and fear of the Israelite forces was spreading in the area, but in chapter 9 of Joshua we read of the Gibeonites playing a trick on the Israelites that resulted in a treaty between the two. Instead of defeating the Gibeonites, the Israelites were placed in a position of having to defend them.

Chapter 10 begins with Adonizedek, the king of Jerusalem, beginning an alliance of five kings of the Amorites (himself and the kings of Hebron, Jarmuth, Lachish, and Eglon) and attacking the Gibeonites because they see them as traitors. The Gibeonites appeal to Joshua for help, so he attacks the Amorites and eventually defeats their forces and kills the five kings.

Chapter 11 describes the last phase of the Israelites taking the Promised Land. In chapter 10 Joshua had led his forces in conquering the southern part of Canaan, but in chapter 11 he is leading the conquest of northern Canaan.

The northern kings had joined forces in an attempt to stand up to the conquering Israelites, but Joshua led his forces in routing them, leading to the conquest of the entire land of Canaan. For the first time the land would enjoy a rest from war (Joshua 11:23).

Finally, what God had long ago promised the ancestors of the people of Israel had happened. They enjoyed a time of rest and security in their own land. Now all that was left to do was divide the land among the twelve tribes, an event that is recorded in Joshua 13–24.

Study Questions

○ What has God begun in your life that you know He will complete?

○ What tasks has God put before you that you know you must complete before you can fully enjoy His rest?

CHAPTER 8

First and Second Samuel: The Life and Times of David

While the Bible is filled with great stories and lessons on faith in and obedience to God, it's also a great book of history—especially when it comes to the early part of the history of the Jewish race. The books of 1 and 2 Samuel provide a great historical account as well as lessons we should learn from it. That includes the history of a man named David, the man who would become Israel's model for leadership.

David: A Legacy-Leaving King

One of the best-known and most highly regarded Old Testament characters is David, who reigned as king of Israel for thirty-three years, led his people to many military victories, established Jerusalem as the seat of government for Israel, and wrote many of the psalms that are in our Bible today. David is still seen as the most righteous king in the history of Israel, but as you study his life, you will see that he was far from faultless. Despite his personal weaknesses, problems, and sins, he left behind a legacy that affects the Christian and Jewish faiths to this very day.

While this chapter is by no means a comprehensive study of the man, it guides the reader in a Biblical study of the highlights and key events in David's life, starting with his being chosen to take over for Saul as king of Israel.

David Chosen as Israel's Second King (1 Samuel 16)

The prophet Samuel has just been informed that the reign of Saul as Israel's first king is about to end because he had fallen out of favor with God. As 1 Samuel 15:35 reports: "The Lord was sorry he had ever made Saul king of Israel."

But God had already picked out a replacement for Saul, and He called Samuel to go to Bethlehem and anoint that man. Samuel followed God's instructions to the letter, traveling to Bethlehem and finding a man named Jesse, who had a son who would one day replace Saul.

Samuel met with Jesse's first seven sons, but God let him know that none of them was the one He had chosen to be Israel's second king. Samuel said to Jesse, "The Lord has not chosen any of these" (1 Samuel 16:10). But Jesse had one more son—his youngest—who was out tending his father's sheep and goats. When David arrived, the Lord told Samuel, "This is the one; anoint him" (16:12).

The stage was set for David to become Israel's second—and greatest—king. But before that would happen, David would serve in Saul's court as a musician. King Saul was tormented by a spirit, filling him with depression and fear. Some of his servants suggested that they find a good musician to play the harp so that he could be soothed.

Saul agreed, and his servants told him "One of Jesse's sons from Bethlehem is a talented harp player. Not only that—he is a brave warrior, a man of war, and has good judgment. He is also a fine-looking young man, and the Lord is with him" (1 Samuel 16:18).

symbolism

One important theme of the Bible—that God looks at the heart and not at outward appearance—is demonstrated in this story: "The Lord said to Samuel, 'Don't judge by his appearance or height, for I have rejected him. The Lord doesn't see things the way you see them. People judge by outward appearance, but the Lord looks at the heart'" (1 Samuel 16:7).

Saul agreed to have David come, and not only did he play the harp for Saul, he also became his armor bearer.

But in time, David would replace Saul in the minds of the people as their leader. That change would start as David faced down and defeated what appeared to be an impossible military challenge.

Study Questions

❍ Where was Samuel to find David, and how would he know who he was?

❍ Who did Samuel initially think would be David's replacement and what did God say about that man? (See 1 Samuel 16:6–7.)

David Prepares to Fight Goliath (1 Samuel 17:1–40)

Nearly everybody in our culture—especially those who like sports—knows what is meant by a David and Goliath story. That's when an individual or a team who is an impossibly huge underdog goes out and defeats an opponent they had no business beating.

The real-life David and Goliath story is found in the seventeenth chapter of 1 Samuel. It pits the boy-who-would-be-king, David, against a giant Philistine warrior, Goliath, who taunted the Israelites and King Saul, challenging them to send out a man to fight him.

The stakes in this fight were high, but there was no one to answer the challenge. Instead of sending someone out to fight, Saul and the people of Israel trembled in fear. It wasn't until David, only a youth at the time, arrived on the scene that anyone had the nerve to even think about fighting Goliath.

factum

The Philistines, first mentioned in the Bible in the book of Genesis, were spread over the area of Lebanon and the Jordan Valley as well as Crete and other Mediterranean islands. There were in Biblical times a seemingly endless string of conflicts between the Philistines and the people of Israel.

The Bible tells us that a man named Jesse sent David, his youngest son, to take some food to his older brothers, all of whom were fighting the Philistines. While near the scene of the battle, David heard the taunts of Goliath and saw how the armies of Israel ran from the giant. That was all he needed to hear.

"What will a man get for killing this Philistine and ending his defiance of Israel? Who is this pagan Philistine anyway, that he is allowed to defy the armies of the living God?" David asked the soldiers nearby (1 Samuel 17:26). After a conversation with his brother, David approached Saul and told him, "Don't worry about this Philistine. I'll go fight him!" (17:32).

Saul's response to David was as one might expect. He pointed out that David was only a boy and that Goliath was an experienced warrior. Therefore, there was no way he could go up against him. But David wouldn't take no for an answer. He pointed out that he had been caring for his father's sheep and goats and protecting them from the lions and bears that came to find a quick meal, sometimes even killing them with a club. "I have done this to both lions and bears," David said, "and I'll do it to this pagan Philistine, too, for he has defied the armies of the living God! The Lord who rescued me from the claws of the lion and the bear will rescue me from this Philistine!" (1 Samuel 17:36–37).

King Saul finally relented and gave the lad his own armor—a bronze helmet and a coat. But when David put them on, he realized they wouldn't work for him because he wasn't used to them. So he took off the armor, picked up five smooth stones from a nearby stream, and, armed with nothing more than the rocks, his shepherd's staff, and his sling, headed across the valley to fight Goliath the Philistine.

Study Questions

○ What does the Bible say about Goliath's appearance? How big was he? What kind of armor did he wear?

○ What was the response of David's brother when he heard that David was inquiring about killing Goliath?

David Kills Goliath (1 Samuel 17:41–57)

The description the writer of 1 Samuel paints of David's initial confrontation with Goliath is a frightening one indeed. As the young shepherd approached this battle-hardened giant, he looked at David with utter contempt as demonstrated in the account of what he said to David at that moment: "'Am I a dog,' he roared at David, 'that you come at me with a stick?' And he cursed David by the names of his gods. 'Come over here, and I'll give your flesh to the birds and wild animals!' Goliath yelled" (17:43–44).

The sight of a nearly 10-foot-tall giant sneering down at you promising to turn you into food for birds and animals would be, to put it mildly, intimidating. But David answered Goliath with incredible confidence—the kind of confidence that only comes from absolute faith that his God would give him the victory:

> You come to me with sword, spear, and javelin, but I come to you in the name of the Lord of Heaven's Armies—the God of the armies of Israel, whom you have defied. Today the Lord will conquer you, and I will kill you and cut off your head. And then I will give the dead

bodies of your men to the birds and wild animals, and the whole world will know that there is a God in Israel! And everyone assembled here will know that the Lord rescues his people, but not with sword and spear. This is the Lord's battle, and he will give you to us! (1 Samuel 17:45–47)

As you read this passage, note that David had absolute and complete faith in God, and because of that he was absolutely sure how this battle was going to turn out. When Goliath began closing in to attack, David ran to meet the giant head on. As he ran, he reached into his shepherd's bag and took out a stone, placed it in his sling, and hurled it at the giant hitting him directly in the forehead.

The stone from David's sling sank into the giant's head, and he stumbled and fell facedown on the ground. David then ran over to Goliath, pulled the sword out of the Philistine's sheath, and cut off his head (1 Samuel 17:48–50).

Goliath had been the champion fighter for the Philistine army, and when the soldiers saw that he was dead, they turned and ran from the army of Israel, which chased them far away, killing many of the Philistine soldiers.

Study Questions

○ What was Goliath's response when he saw the boy David coming at him?

○ What did David say in return after Goliath had finished taunting him?

David and Saul (1 Samuel 18–27)

After David's overwhelming defeat of Goliath the Philistine, King Saul took him into his service permanently. However, it was an uneasy relationship because Saul became jealous of the attention Israel's future king was receiving from the people. What made things worse in Saul's mind was the fact that David developed a very close friendship with Jonathan, Saul's own son (1 Samuel 18:1–4). Also, Saul's daughter Michal fell in love with David and married him (18:20–21).

In a short time, Saul's jealousy turned to hatred, then his hatred turned into attempted murder. Saul, overcome by a "tormenting spirit," twice attempted to kill David by throwing a spear at him (1 Samuel 18:10–13).

point of interest

The circumstances surrounding the election of Saul as Israel's first king are recorded in 1 Samuel 8–10. Like David, Saul had been anointed by the prophet Samuel and had received three signs confirming his call from God to be king. Saul received the Holy Spirit at that time, which made him "into a different person" (1 Samuel 10:6).

Crazy with fear, jealousy, and anger, Saul went on a campaign of persecution against David, even sending out his servants to find and kill him. David fled to a place called Ramah (1 Samuel 19:12–18), where he stayed for some time with the sons of the prophets. It wasn't long, however, before Saul found out where David had gone and tried to bring him back.

Jonathan, a loyal friend to David, tried in vain to change his father's mind toward David. When David found out that his friend had failed, he fled a greater distance from the king—first to Nob (1 Samuel 21:1–9) and then to Gath (21:10–15), a top Philistine city.

This was only the beginning of Saul's mad obsession with finding and killing David, who seemed only to grow in popularity with the people. Several times Saul seemed to have a bead on David only to have him escape. And on two occasions, David had the opportunity to kill Saul but spared him. "Surely the Lord will strike Saul down someday," David said, "or he will die of old age or in battle. The Lord forbid that I should kill the one he has anointed!" (1 Samuel 26:10–11).

Eventually, Saul's fall from grace led to his death—and the death of his son—at the hands of the Philistines (1 Samuel 31). It was the tragic end of what was once a very promising start for Israel's first king. David, on the other hand, was about to take his rightful place as the one God had anointed to be Israel's king.

Study Questions

○ What was Saul's response when he found out that his daughter had fallen in love with and married David?

○ Why do you think David spared Saul when he knew that Saul would have killed him in an instant if the situation were reversed?

David Takes the Throne of Israel (2 Samuel 1–5)

When David received news of the death of Saul and his son Jonathan—David's close friend—he was genuinely grieved: "David and his men tore their clothes in sorrow when they heard the news. They mourned and wept and fasted all day for Saul and his son Jonathan, and for the Lord's army and the nation of Israel, because they had died by the sword that day" (2 Samuel 1:11–12).

It was a short time later that David prayed and asked God for direction, which he received. God told him to go to Hebron, where he was anointed king of Judah at the age of thirty (2 Samuel 2:1–4). David's ascension to the throne was disputed, however, and that touched off a civil war in Israel. Once that war ended, David was anointed king over all twelve tribes of Israel (2 Samuel 5:1–12).

discussion question

What was the Ark of the Covenant?
The Ark of the Covenant was the gold-covered receptacle used to carry the two stone tablets that contained the Ten Commandments, which were seen as the testimony of God's covenant with the Hebrew people. You can find descriptions of the ark in Numbers 7, 10, 19, and 20.

From that time on, the kingdom of Israel, under the leadership of King David, went through a time of incredible expansion. David and his men captured the city of Jerusalem and made it Israel's new seat of government (2 Samuel 5:6–14), defeated the Philistines (5:17–25), and brought the Ark of the Covenant into Jerusalem.

Second Samuel 7 records God's promise to David, spoken through the prophet Nathan. That promise was that although David himself would one day die, his kingdom would, through his descendants, last forever (2 Samuel 7:1–17). After receiving that promise, David prayed a long and beautiful prayer of thanksgiving and praise (2 Samuel 7:18–29).

That was followed by a series of military victories that expanded and strengthened the kingdom of Israel (2 Samuel 8). God had promised David great blessings as Israel's king, and that promise certainly came to pass. However, there came a time when David's own indiscretions and sin could have sunk his monarchy.

Study Questions

O Why do you think David would mourn at the death of Saul, a man who was his sworn enemy?

O What was the tone of David's response to receiving God's promise of blessing?

David's Sin with Bathsheba (2 Samuel 11)

There are few Old Testament stories that make the kind of impact as that of David's sin with Bathsheba. In that story we see a man—a man God had called "righteous"—fall into sin so deep and ugly that it's easy to wonder how his name can still be mentioned in the Bible in any kind of positive light.

But the story of David's sin with Bathsheba—which included adultery, murder, and the lies and deceptions it took to try to cover those crimes—is not just one of a man who had fallen but also one of a man God picked up from a self-imposed pit of despair.

This tragic story begins as David, just up from an afternoon nap, looks out from the roof of his palace and spies the very beautiful—but very married—Bathsheba. Without even thinking about it, David sent for Bathsheba, who he is told is married to a warrior named Uriah who is away fighting at the time (2 Samuel 11:1–4).

Bathsheba did the only thing she could when the king of Israel sends for her—she went to him. A short time later she sent him word that she was pregnant. In an attempt to cover up his sin, David sends for Uriah and invites him to go home to his wife for the night before going back to the battlefield. Being a man of amazing integrity and loyalty, Uriah refuses to go home to his wife while his men are still out fighting (2 Samuel 11:5–12).

point of interest

The story of David's sin is described aptly by the apostle James, who wrote, "Temptation comes from our own desires, which entice us and drag us away. These desires give birth to sinful actions. And when sin is allowed to grow, it gives birth to death" (James 1:14–15).

Since David's plan to cover up his sin has failed, he goes to plan B: have Uriah killed in battle so that no one will be the wiser to what has happened. David sends word to have Uriah placed where the fighting is fiercest so that it will be more likely that he is killed. That is exactly what happens, and when Bathsheba receives word of it, she is sent into a period of mourning over the death of her husband (2 Samuel 11:14–27).

Study Questions

○ Read 2 Samuel 11:2. What do you think was David's first mistake when it came to being tempted to commit adultery with Bathsheba?

○ What character qualities of Uriah do you think helped lead to his death?

The Consequences of David's Sin (2 Samuel 12)

It's likely that once Uriah was out of the way David thought he had gotten away with something. But as you can see throughout the Bible, there is nothing that escapes God's notice, particularly when it comes to his servants falling into sin.

God sent Nathan, a prophet of Israel, to see David and to tell him the story of two men—one rich and one poor—who lived in a certain town. The rich man had all the sheep and cattle he could want, while the poor man had one lamb that he and his children treated like a member of the family. One day the rich man had a guest he wanted to feed, but instead of killing one of his many animals for dinner, he took the poor man's lamb, killed it, and cooked it for his guest (2 Samuel 12:1–4).

David was furious to hear of such an injustice and vowed to Nathan, "As surely as the Lord lives, any man who would do such a thing deserves to die! He must repay four lambs to the poor man for the one he stole and for having no pity" (2 Samuel 12:5–6).

factum

Psalm 51, one of many written by David, is his psalm of confession and penitence for what he had done in committing adultery with Bathsheba and murder against Uriah. The fourth verse of that psalm reads, "I have done what is evil in your sight. You will be proved right in what you say, and your judgment against me is just."

But what David didn't realize at that moment was that Nathan was talking about him and his sin against Uriah. "You are that man!" Nathan said. "The Lord, the God of Israel, says: I anointed you king of Israel and saved you from the power of Saul. I gave you your master's house and his wives and the kingdoms of Israel and Judah. And if that had not been enough, I would have given you much, much more. Why, then, have you despised the word of the Lord and done this horrible deed? For you have murdered Uriah the Hittite with the sword of the Ammonites and stolen his wife" (2 Samuel 12:7–9).

But this harsh word from God wasn't all King David would have to face because of his sin. In addition, he would face the following consequences:

- his family would "live by the sword" (2 Samuel 12:10)
- his household would rebel against him (12:11)
- his wives would be taken by another man (12:11)

- all of Israel would know about the consequences he faced because of his sin (12:12)

There was nothing else David could do but confess his guilt, which he did. And when he did that, Nathan assured him that God had forgiven him for his sin and that he wouldn't die. However, there was one additional consequence for David's sin—that the child he had fathered with Bathsheba would die. And though David begged God to spare the child, it died.

David then comforted Bathsheba, who was now his wife, and they slept together, again resulting in pregnancy. This time the child born to David would live and grow to be a healthy boy and the next king of Israel: Solomon (2 Samuel 12:24–25).

Study Questions

○ Have you ever committed what you thought was a harmless sin only to see its consequences mushroom?

○ What can you learn from Psalm 51 in terms of your attitude toward God and others in repentance?

CHAPTER 9

Job: With Suffering Comes Wisdom

The Bible contains a lot of teaching about suffering and adversity, and some of that teaching comes in the form of human examples. Probably the best-known of those examples is Job, a man who suffered in every conceivable way. This chapter is a study of Job, the man who suffered loss and physical pain but who at the end came out of it with more than he had before, including a more refined and deeper faith in God.

God's Kind of Man

If there is a character in the Bible known for dealing with suffering and adversity, it's Job. The Bible describes him like this: "He was blameless—a man of complete integrity. He feared God and stayed away from evil" (Job 1:1).

Not only was Job a blameless man of integrity who feared God, he was also an incredibly wealthy family man. He had seven sons and three daughters and owned 7,000 sheep, 3,000 camels, 500 teams of oxen, and 500 female donkeys. He was, as the Bible calls him, the richest man in the area where he lived.

That doesn't sound like a man who knows a lot about suffering and adversity. But that is just the beginning of the story—in fact, it's just three verses into the whole book of Job!

Job had it all going for him, and it appeared that nothing could touch him. But out of nowhere came some tests and trials the likes of which Job had never seen. He lost his children, his wealth, even his health. And worst of all, he couldn't for the life of him understand why these things were happening.

Before this story ends, however, Job will again be blessed. And perhaps the best blessing of all will be the wisdom and strength of mind he earns by enduring some of the worst suffering you'll ever read about.

The Testings of a Lifetime (Job 1–2)

The devil believed that Job was a man who lived right and believed right simply because God had given him so much. In short, he was content and had no reason to do anything evil. So the devil challenged God to "reach out and take away everything he has, and he will surely curse you to your face!" (Job 1:11).

God took Satan up on that challenge, allowing him to take from Job everything he had but his health. In short order Job was met with one message of disaster after another. Job lost nearly everything: his livestock, most of his servants, even his beloved children.

Still, Job wouldn't curse or blame God. Instead, he tore his robe in grief, shaved his head, and fell to the ground and worshipped God: "I came naked from my mother's womb, and I will be naked when I leave. The Lord gave me what I had, and the Lord has taken it away. Praise the name of the Lord!" (Job 1:21).

factum

Job is believed to be one of the oldest books of the Bible—if not the oldest. The authorship of this book is not certain (Jewish tradition credits Moses with writing it), but the story of Job is set during the times of the Jewish patriarchs—Abraham, Isaac, Jacob, and Joseph. The name *Job* means "persecuted."

Job had passed the first test, but the devil wasn't finished. Again he challenged God to let him touch Job's life, and again God allowed him to do it. This time the rules were a little different. Where before the devil wasn't allowed to touch Job's body in any way, this time the only limitation God put on the devil was that he could afflict Job's body but he couldn't kill the man.

Satan left the presence of God, sure that he was going to get Job to curse God. A case of boils covering a man from head to toe will do that to a man, the devil thought, and he was about to give this man of God his very worst.

Study Questions

○ What did God allow the devil to do to Job? What limitations were put in place?

○ How did Job respond to all that had happened to him?

With Friends Like These (Job 2–25)

The scene following Job's physical affliction is a disturbing and discomforting one At the beginning of his case of head-to-toe boils, Job sat in an ash heap, scraping his badly burning and itching skin with a piece of broken pottery. But if his physical agony weren't enough, he then has to deal with some well-meaning but ill-informed people who try to help him out in his misery but don't do much to lift his spirits. The first of those people was his own wife, who offered: "Are you still trying to maintain your integrity? Curse God and die" (Job 2:9).

But as miserable as Job was—and as much as it must have hurt him to have his own wife advise him to turn away from God—Job maintained his integrity and did not curse or blame God in any way. Instead, he continued praising God through everything. But the situation was about to get more difficult for him, and it was made worse because of the attempted help of some well-meaning friends.

When a man like Job is going through difficult times, it is sure to get people's attention. When three of Job's friends—Eliphaz the Temanite, Bildad the Shuhite, and Zophar the Naamathite, as the Bible identifies them—heard what had happened to him, they traveled from their homes to go and comfort and console him. When they saw him, they hardly recognized him. And when Job finally spoke, it was as if they were the words of a man none of his friends knew: "Let the day of my birth be erased," Job began, "and the night I was conceived. Let that day be turned to darkness. Let it be lost even to God on high, and let no light shine on it" (Job 3:3–4). Job had gone from a man who seemed to have it all—including his integrity and his relationship with God—to a man who not only lost all his financial holdings and his very family, but also his health.

What followed was a series of conversations between Job and his friends. In those conversations they consider and debate the possibility that it is Job's sin that has caused his affliction. They talk about how Job needs to return to his God so that he can be healed.

symbolism

Job's three friends assumed that Job's suffering was as a direct result of personal sin. Jesus put an end to the notion that all suffering was due to personal sin as he prepared his disciples to witness the healing of a blind man in the city of Jerusalem (John 9:1–5).

As the conversations and debates continue, Job's three friends prove to be little if any help to him. In fact, they are only making him feel worse—largely because they don't understand Job or his God enough to give comfort and sound advice to their miserably suffering friend.

What they end up doing is spouting a seemingly endless list of accusations concerning Job's life. Eliphaz tells Job that since God doesn't make mistakes, then Job must have done something to deserve this. Bildad says, "God is just, so just confess your sin!" And, finally, Zophar tells Job, "God knows you and he is dealing with you justly."

There was, however, a problem with what these men were saying. At least three times in the book of Job, we read that he was an upright man of integrity whose life pleased God. And because the three of them didn't understand Job, they came to some very wrong conclusions about God and about why He sometimes allows suffering.

Obviously, there was another lesson to be learned here. And before this ordeal is all over, Job will have to look someplace other than his three friends to figure out what it is.

Study Questions
○ How did Job respond to his wife's telling him to "curse God and die"?
○ What did Job's friends do with him when they arrived on the scene of his suffering?

The Prosecution Has Rested (Job 26–31)

Eliphaz, Bildad, and Zophar have spoken their last—at least as far as this portion of Job's life is concerned—and have stated in no uncertain terms that Job is at fault for his suffering, that there is some sin in the man's life that brought on all that has befallen him.

Job patiently listens to the accusations and recriminations before he finishes this emotionally charged debate by speaking a long monologue, starting with his thoughts about the nature and person of God. Job even sounds slightly optimistic as he talks about the power and understanding of God (Job 26), the unfailing justice of God (Job 27), and the unsearchable wisdom of God (Job 28).

But Job also seems deeply discouraged as he says, "I long for the years gone by when God took care of me, when he lighted the way before me and I walked safely through the darkness" (Job 29:2–3). Obviously, Job felt as if he'd been abandoned by God—or worse.

He continues on in chapter 30 talking about the misery that his life has become. He is discouraged, depressed, and believing that he has been abandoned to his misery:

And now my life seeps away. Depression haunts my days. At night my bones are filled with pain, which gnaws at me relentlessly. With a strong hand, God grabs my shirt. He grips me by the collar of my coat. He has thrown me into the mud. I'm nothing more than dust and ashes. (Job 30:16–19)

Job is sure that God no longer sees him or what he's going through, that he is completely alone, or that, worse yet, God is going out of His way to bring him more harm and misery. Finally, Job closes his monologue by taking a personal spiritual inventory (Job 31) in which he finds that he has indeed lived a life that is pleasing to God.

Yet Job is suffering. As far as he knows he's done nothing to deserve what is happening to him, yet he's in the worst place he could be and still be alive. Why is that? He's close to finding out.

Study Questions

○ Read chapters 26–28. Despite his own terrible suffering, what is Job's view of the person of God?

○ What part does Job believe God Himself plays in his suffering?

Elihu: Some Angry Words (Job 32–37)

With Job's three friends now reduced to silence—and Job still left wondering why he's being tormented—a younger voice speaks up to talk about the situation. Elihu, who is identified as the "son of Barakel the Buzite," is angry and he wants to have some words with Job.

Elihu challenges Job's notion that he is innocent of all sin and that God had counted him as an enemy. He speaks up and defends the justice, the goodness, the mercy, and the righteousness of God—all of which he believes that Job has wrongly maligned, and he tells Job that he has sinned by speaking ignorantly about God (Job 34:1–35:36).

symbolism

> Elihu pointed out something important to Job, namely that God could have been speaking through his suffering: "God speaks again and again, though people do not recognize it. He speaks in dreams, in visions of the night, when deep sleep falls on people as they lie in their beds. He whispers in their ears and terrifies them with warnings" (Job 33:14–16).

Elihu goes to great pains to proclaim the majesty and greatness of God (Job 36:24–37:24), and he encourages Job to, "stop and consider the wonderful miracles of God!" (Job 37:14). At the end of his speech, Elihu tells Job, "We cannot imagine the power of the Almighty, yet he is so just and merciful that he does not oppress us. No wonder people everywhere fear him. People who are truly wise show him reverence" (Job 37:23–24).

Elihu has verbally chastised Job, has tried to correct his notions of the goodness and justice of God, and has tried to remind him that God is a powerful, merciful Creator who doesn't try to harm or oppress His people. While Elihu, like Job's other three friends, wasn't perfect in his scrutiny of Job's situation, it may well be that he prepared Job to hear from the One who could give him the answers he needed—although they weren't necessarily the answers he would have sought.

Study Questions

○ Reread Job 32:3. What was wrong with the counsel Job's three friends had given him?

○ Read Job 33:8–33. How does Elihu believe Job should see his suffering?

Time for Ultimate Wisdom (Job 38–39)

For most of the book of Job, it seems as if God has stood back and silently eavesdropped on the conversations between Job and his wife, Job and his three friends, then Job and Elihu. After listening as others tried in vain to explain what He had allowed to happen to Job, God answered Job directly and in a spectacular fashion: out of a whirlwind. But God had some questions of His own to pose, questions designed to take Job to a place he couldn't have expected.

The first question God posed to Job is, "Where were you when I laid the foundations of the earth? Tell me, if you know so much" (Job 38:4). Over the next two chapters (Job 38–39), God poses one question after another, all of which lead Job to one conclusion: He's talking to his Creator, and He's a Creator filled with power and wisdom.

As the questioning continues, God asks Job some very pointed questions: "Have you ever commanded the morning to appear and caused the dawn to rise in the east?" (Job 38:12). "Have you explored the springs from which the seas come? Have you walked about and explored their depths?" (Job 38:16). "Can you hold back the movements of the stars?" (Job 38:31). "Can you shout to the clouds and make it rain?" (Job 38:34).

factum

For thirty-seven chapters we have read of the suffering of Job and of the questions that suffering brought to his mind. However, not one of those questions is answered. Instead of giving Job what he wanted and thought he needed—namely, answers to his questions—God gives Job a closeup explanation and look at His person and glory.

Job can only listen as God makes His point. Job can't answer—though he knows the answers to all those questions is "No!"—but he does come to an understanding of who he is talking to. God had reminded Job of some valuable pieces of information, all of which would benefit him over the remainder of his life:

- God is the Creator, and Job was the created one.
- God is in control, and Job is at the mercy of what happens around him.
- God is infinite in his wisdom, and Job cannot understand lofty things.
- God is all-powerful, and Job is limited in what he can do.

With the questioning concerning who was the Creator and who was the created finished, God poses the question: "Do you still want to argue with the Almighty? You are God's critic, but do you have the answers?" (Job 40:2). Of course, Job realized he had spoken out of turn—far out of turn: "I am nothing—how could I ever find the answers? I will cover my mouth with my hand. I have said too much already. I have nothing more to say" (Job 40:4–5).

Study Questions

○ What criticisms or questions have you had of God, and how did He use them to teach you more about Him and help you to know Him better?

○ What is your response when you are faced with a situation in which you feel out of control or that makes no sense?

Who God Is in the Midst of All Things (Job 40–42)

God then changes the direction of His questions, leading Job to an even deeper understanding of how big and powerful the Lord is and how small Job really is (Job 40–41).

Job can do nothing but acknowledge what God has been teaching him: "I know that you can do anything, and no one can stop you. You asked, 'Who is this that questions my wisdom with such ignorance?' It is I—and I was talking about things I knew nothing about, things far too wonderful for me" (Job 42:2–3).

Finally, God has taken Job where He wanted His servant to go. And while Job may still not understand the reasons or the purposes for his suffering, he knows and understands God as he hadn't before. Job can only respond: "I had only heard about you before, but now I have seen you with my own

eyes. I take back everything I said, and I sit in dust and ashes to show my repentance" (Job 42:5–6).

symbolism

Job is an Old Testament example of what God says in the New Testament about how he can use adversity and suffering: "And we know that God causes everything to work together for the good of those who love God and are called according to his purpose for them" (Romans 8:28). Job didn't deserve to suffer, but God used that suffering for his own good.

Job has learned what God wanted him to learn through his suffering. And because of that, he is a blessed man. In addition to even greater wisdom, Job was given back the fortune he had lost—twice over! (Job 42:10). Job lived 140 years after his afflictions before dying as an old man who had lived a good life (Job 42:17).

Study Questions

○ What do you think your prayers would sound like if you were angry and frustrated—maybe even at God Himself—at your own misfortune or suffering?

○ Do you believe it is ever right or appropriate to voice objections over your life situation to God?

CHAPTER 10

Isaiah: A Word Picture of Jesus

This may come as a surprise to a lot of people who don't know the Bible well, but references to Jesus Christ aren't limited to the New Testament. It was as far back as the book of Genesis that the Bible tells us of the coming Savior/ Messiah. Probably the richest Old Testament book when it comes to references to Jesus Christ is that of Isaiah, which contains more than one hundred prophecies foretelling everything from the circumstances surrounding his birth to the events leading up to his death on the cross.

Beautiful Reading and a Whole Lot More

In purely literary terms, the book of Isaiah—the twenty-third book in the Old Testament—is hard to beat. It is written poetically and contains many descriptions that are beautiful as well as bleak, frightening as well as encouraging, and gloomy as well as hopeful. It is a book that has been studied, mulled over, and taken apart word by word over the centuries.

But Isaiah's prophetic book is far more than simple literature; it is also a collection of messages about judgment and salvation—both of which come from the same God. The first thirty-nine chapters of Isaiah are filled with pronouncements of judgment on an immoral and idolatrous people, but the final twenty-seven chapters are the declaration of a message of hope and salvation, not just for the people of Judah but also for the whole world.

discussion question

What does the name *Isaiah* mean?
The name *Isaiah* literally means "salvation of Jehovah," and the dual themes of the book of Isaiah are the judgment of God on a wayward people and the salvation for those who would turn back to Him.

Isaiah carried out his prophetic ministry to the people of Judah over a period of at least forty years. It was during this time that he warned and encouraged, and he saw not just what was happening in the world around him but also how God would finally accomplish His plan of salvation for all humankind.

The book of Isaiah is the most quoted Old Testament book in the New Testament. That includes many references in the Gospels—Matthew, Mark, Luke, and John. Matthew's gospel contains many references to events in the life of Jesus Christ fulfilling what the prophet Isaiah had written some seven centuries before Jesus's birth.

Isaiah saw in the future a Messiah—a Savior—who would come both as a suffering servant and as a conquering king.

Jesus's Own Family Tree

The Old Testament contains other prophecies concerning the family tree of the Messiah and about his background, which God had foreordained. Included in that list are the following:

- He would be a descendant of King David (2 Samuel 7:16)
- He would be born of the "seed" of a woman (Genesis 3:15)
- He would be born in the city of Bethlehem (Micah 5:2)
- He would be God's own Son (Proverbs 30:4)
- He would be a prophet (Deuteronomy 18:15–19)
- Angels would worship him (Deuteronomy 32:43)

However, it is in the book of Isaiah where we find the greatest number—and the best known—of the prophecies of the coming of Jesus Christ.

Isaiah's prophecies include this passage, which has become a popular one to read around Christmastime: "All right then, the Lord himself will give you the sign. Look! The virgin will conceive a child! She will give birth to a son and will call him Immanuel" (Isaiah 7:14).

point of interest

Isaiah 9:1–2 tells us the wonderful news that the Jewish Messiah wouldn't be for the Jews only but also for Gentiles. "The people who walk in darkness will see a great light—a light that will shine on all who live in the land where death casts its shadow."

This verse foretells one of the events that is central to the Christian faith, namely that the Messiah—Jesus Christ—would be conceived in a miraculous way and that his mother would remain a physical virgin at the time of his birth. This event is recorded beautifully in the gospels of Matthew (1:18) and Luke (1:26–35).

Isaiah also recorded this prophecy, which we also associate with Christmas celebrations:

For a child is born to us, a son is given to us. The government will rest on his shoulders. And he will be called: Wonderful Counselor, Mighty God, Everlasting Father, Prince of Peace. His government and its peace will never end. He will rule with fairness and justice from the throne of his ancestor David for all eternity. The passionate commitment of the Lord of Heaven's Armies will make this happen! (Isaiah 9:6–7)

When you think of the some of the songs and poems we associate with Christmas or some of the names by which Jesus is known even today, think of the prophet Isaiah who foretold that Jesus Christ would come to earth to be for us.

Study Questions

❍ By what name is Jesus referred to in Isaiah 7:14?
❍ What are the names of Jesus Christ in Isaiah 9:6–7?

What Kind of Man Is This? (Isaiah 11)

The eleventh chapter of Isaiah begins, "Out of the stump of David's family will grow a shoot—yes, a new Branch bearing fruit from the old root" (Isaiah 11:1). This tells us that Jesus would be a descendant of King David, the fulfillment of which is found in the first chapter of Matthew.

But Isaiah didn't just write in this chapter about the events and circumstances having to do with the earthly ancestors, birth, and life of Jesus Christ. He also wrote about the kind of person he would be and the things he would do.

This passage tells us even more wonderful facts about the Jesus Christ that Isaiah saw centuries before his birth. Isaiah tells us that God's Spirit would rest on Jesus (Isaiah 11:2), that he would have exceptional wisdom and understanding and fear of God (11:2), that he would love obeying God the Father (11:3), and that he would be a righteous and fair judge (11:3–4).

symbolism

Each of the four Gospels look sat the life of Jesus from different perspectives and focuses on different aspects of his person. The Gospel of Mark presents Jesus as Isaiah did in Isaiah 42—as a humble servant of God and of those he came to save from their sin.

Later on, Isaiah presents a picture of the Messiah who comes to earth to serve God and to serve those who are so desperately in need of the works he was going to perform during his earthly ministry:

Look at my servant, whom I strengthen. He is my chosen one, who pleases me. I have put my Spirit upon him. He will bring justice to the nations. He will not shout or raise his voice in public. He will not crush the weakest reed or put out a flickering candle. He will bring justice to all who have been wronged. He will not falter or lose heart until justice prevails throughout the earth. Even distant lands beyond the sea will wait for his instruction. (Isaiah 42:1–4)

Jesus came to earth and taught a new and radical kind of justice, mercy, and grace, and all those things were in keeping with what God had said centuries before Christ's birth through the prophet Isaiah as well as others.

Study Questions
○ Reread Isaiah 11:1–5. What attributes of Jesus Christ did Isaiah recognize?
○ According to Isaiah 42:1–4, what works will the Messiah perform while on earth?

The Miracle-Working Messiah

If you've studied the life of Jesus as it is recorded in the Gospels, you know that Jesus was a miracle worker who performed great wonders such as turning water into wine (his first recorded miracle), feeding thousands of people with next to no food, calming storms, healing the sick, walking on water, and raising the dead.

Isaiah wrote of the coming Messiah: "And when he comes, he will open the eyes of the blind and unplug the ears of the deaf. The lame will leap like a deer, and those who cannot speak will sing for joy! Springs will gush forth in the wilderness, and streams will water the wasteland" (35:5–6).

discussion question

What are the benefits of studying Isaiah's prophecies about Jesus?
There are several, but let's concentrate on two here. First, you get to know who Jesus was and learn to know him better on a personal basis. Second, you build up your faith through knowing that all the things surrounding Jesus's life—including the things he did—had been promised centuries before.

This passage lists a few of the specifics of Jesus's ministry of miracle healing—giving sight to the blind, giving hearing to the deaf, and allowing the disabled to walk—and if you read the Gospels you'll see Jesus performing these miracles repeatedly. Here are a few references for you to look up when you have the time:

- healed people of leprosy (Matthew 8:2, Luke 17:11)
- healed people who were paralyzed (Mark 2:3)
- gave sight to the blind (Matthew 9:27, Luke 18:35, John 9:1)
- gave hearing to the deaf (Mark 7:31)
- raised people from the dead (Mark 5:22, 35; John 7:11, John 11:43)
- healed and freed the demon-possessed (Luke 8:26, Matthew 9:32, Luke 4:33, Matthew 12:22)

While this list is a good starting place to look at some of the miracles of Jesus and how they line up with the prophecies of Isaiah, realize that there are many more examples of Jesus's miracles recorded in the Gospels. In addition to the healing miracles, Jesus also demonstrated power over the weather, over nature, and over earthly events.

Study Questions

❍ Read John 10:25 and 14:11. What was the purpose of Jesus's miracles?
❍ Read John 2:13–19. How did the Jewish religious leadership approach miracles in that account?

The Rejected Messiah (Isaiah 49)

Jesus came to earth as everything the Jewish people had long waited for. From centuries past came the promises from Isaiah and other Old Testament prophets that a Messiah would come and deliver the people of Israel from oppression.

Yet when Jesus came, he was rejected. He performed great miracles, preached and spoke with incredible power, and demonstrated authority over all things spiritual and physical. And despite all that, his own people rejected him.

That, however, didn't just happen. The Old Testament prophecies tell us that the Messiah, among other things:

- would come at a time of unfit leaders in Israel (Zechariah 11:4–6)
- would not be believed by his own brothers (Psalm 69:8)
- would have national and religious leaders conspire against him (Psalm 22)

Isaiah himself foretold the rejection of the Messiah by his own people: "The Lord, the Redeemer and Holy One of Israel, says to the one who is despised and rejected by the nations, to the one who is the servant of rulers: 'Kings will stand at attention when you pass by. Princes will also bow low because of the Lord, the faithful one, the Holy One of Israel, who has chosen you" (Isaiah 49:7).

Jesus knew the truth of what Isaiah wrote hundreds of years earlier. He knew that part of his earthly mission was to be rejected by a world that wasn't willing or able to understand who he was and what he wanted from all of humanity. And while the Gospels tell us Jesus was welcomed into Jerusalem with a wild celebration just a week before his death, it was only a matter of time before he would face the ultimate rejection by humankind: death on a cross.

Study Questions

○ Why do you think the Jewish people rejected Jesus when he fulfilled so many prophecies of the coming Messiah?

○ According to Isaiah 49:7, what will be the world's ultimate response to the Messiah?

The Suffering and Death of the Messiah (Isaiah 50–53)

Isaiah chapters 50 through 53 refer to Jesus Christ as what has been called "the Suffering Messiah" or "the Suffering Servant." Indeed those four chapters are filled with references to the mistreatment and horrible death of Jesus Christ on a cross of wood.

You read in the last section of this chapter how Jesus's own countrymen rejected him as the Messiah. But there would be more to this story than the people's refusal to believe Jesus and who he claimed to be. This rejection would lead Jesus to his ultimate earthly mission: his sacrificial death.

What is most amazing about this portion of Isaiah's book is the details concerning the Crucifixion of Jesus Christ—details we can easily read of in the Gospels, all four of which give glimpses into the death of the Lord. From a purely human and physical standpoint, it is a brutal picture.

Isaiah 50:6 tells the account of a Messiah who would be brutally—yet willingly—beaten about the face and back, mocked and humiliated, have his beard pulled out, and spit upon: "I offered my back to those who beat me and my cheeks to those who pulled out my beard. I did not hide my face from mockery and spitting."

Later, in chapter 52, Isaiah records that the physical abuse and beating of the Messiah would be so severe that, "many were amazed when they saw him. His face was so disfigured he seemed hardly human, and from his appearance, one would scarcely know he was a man" (52:14).

factum

Although Isaiah paints a poignant picture of a suffering and dying Jesus Christ, one of the best Old Testament prophecies concerning the crucified Christ appears is Psalm 22, which tells us that the Messiah's hands and feet would be pierced (Psalm 22:16), that he would be mocked (Psalm 22:8), that he would cry out to God but be forsaken (Psalm 22:1).

Isaiah tells us that all these things would happen to the Messiah despite the fact that he was innocent of any crime (Isaiah 53:9), despite the fact that he said nothing to his accusers (53:7). He would suffer great sorrow and grief (53:3), would be oppressed and afflicted (53:7), and would be thought of as cursed by God (53:4).

But all of these things didn't happen to the Messiah Jesus Christ for nothing. Isaiah explains that these things happened so that each and every one of us who put our faith in him can be healed, saved, and forgiven:

Yet it was our weaknesses he carried; it was our sorrows that weighed him down. And we thought his troubles were a punishment from God, a punishment for his own sins! But he was pierced for our rebellion, crushed for our sins. He was beaten so we could be whole. He was whipped so we could be healed. All of us, like sheep, have strayed away. We have left God's paths to follow our own. Yet the Lord laid on him the sins of us all. (Isaiah 53:4–6)

This is the central message of the whole Bible: that God saw a human race so lost and weak and enslaved to sin and corruption that it was completely unable to do anything to improve itself, much less save itself. But because of the amazing love of God, "it was the Lord's good plan to crush him and cause him grief. Yet when his life is made an offering for sin, he will have many descendants" (Isaiah 53:10).

symbolism

Prophecies aren't really prophecies unless they come true. The incredibly accurate fulfillment of Isaiah's "Suffering Servant" prophecies is found in, among other places, Matthew 26:67 and 27:26, which describe the beatings and abuse Jesus endured.

The New Testament tells us that Jesus willingly gave himself up for our sins, and because of that we are able to find healing and forgiveness, enjoy fellowship with God the Father, and inherit an eternal home in heaven. That is the message Isaiah preached, and it's the message Jesus lived out in every way, including dying a horrible death for all of us on a cross.

Study Questions

○ Read John 3:16 then Isaiah 53:10. How would you describe God's attitude and heart in sending Jesus to live and die for all of us?

○ How does Isaiah's description of Jesus's abuse and death affect your view of sin, forgiveness, and salvation?

Isaiah's Risen Savior (Isaiah 25:8, 53:10)

Absolutely central to the Christian faith is the fact of the resurrection of Jesus from the dead on the third day after his crucifixion. As the apostle Paul wrote, "If Christ has not been raised, then all our preaching is useless, and your faith is useless" (1 Corinthians 15:14).

One of the reasons for Paul's assertion that Christ's resurrection is central to our faith is the fact that the Old Testament prophets foretold not just the death of the Messiah but also his being raised from the dead.

Isaiah 53 contains the predictions of Jesus's arrest and suffering on the Cross, and it also hints that his physical death wouldn't be his ultimate end: "Yet when his life is made an offering for sin, he will have many descendants. He will enjoy a long life, and the Lord's good plan will prosper in his hands" (Isaiah 53:10).

But Isaiah's prophecies concerning Jesus's resurrection go even further—even if they don't do it in chronological order. Back in chapter 25, Isaiah tells us that Jesus's death and resurrection will have the effect of defeating death once and for all for those who would put their faith in him: "He will swallow up death forever! The Sovereign Lord will wipe away all tears. He will remove forever all insults and mockery against his land and people. The Lord has spoken!" (Isaiah 25:8).

Isaiah tells us the same thing about the death of the Messiah that the Gospels tell us: That his death, while cruel and horrible and necessary for the salvation of humankind, wasn't the end—not by a long shot.

The Messiah was going to defeat death once and for all, and he sealed that victory when on the third day after his death he rose from the grave and presented himself to his followers so that they could spread the news of what had happened.

Study Questions

○ How does the fact that Jesus's resurrection was foretold hundreds of years before it happened affect your faith and your approach to telling others his message?

○ Read 1 Corinthians 15. How does the fact of Jesus's resurrection affect your outlook on the subject of physical death?

CHAPTER 11

Jonah: A Picture of Disobedience Then Obedience

If you attended children's church, you probably remember one of the most popular stories of Jonah, the Jewish prophet who spent three days in the belly of a fish (or whale according to the song; it's not certain which) when he refused to go preach in a city called Nineveh and warn the people that their city was about to be destroyed. This chapter is a more detailed study of what happened to Jonah when he refused to do what God had called him to do and what happened when he finally obeyed.

Jonah's Call from God

The easiest reading of the book of Jonah is that the prophet just didn't feel like going to Nineveh. After all, we don't read of Jonah arguing with God when he was sent, only that he just didn't go. But a closer reading of the history of the people of Israel sheds some more light on the story of Jonah, revealing that he was more than just a rebellious prophet who didn't want to go where God had sent him.

In plain speaking, the mission for which the Lord had sent Jonah was one that, in human thinking anyway, didn't make a lick of sense. God was, in essence, sending Jonah to preach to his enemies. God was sending Jonah to preach to a race of people who were mortal enemies of the Israelites. Jonah knew that the Ninevites were a bloodthirsty, vicious people who posed a very real threat to his own countrymen. On top of that, they were desperately wicked people that Jonah no doubt believed were deserving of God's judgment and wrath.

Jonah just couldn't understand why he should go to a place like Nineveh, and the thought of being called to go there must have galled him. But it didn't matter why he didn't want to go to Nineveh, only that he refused to do what God had told him to do, instead relying on his own human understanding and reasoning. The results of that refusal made a most interesting—and very entertaining—adventure!

You're Sending Me Where? (Jonah 1)

The prophet Jonah was the son of a man named Amittai of Gath-hepher, and his name meant "a dove." The most familiar Biblical story about Jonah begins with this command from God: "Get up and go to the great city of Nineveh. Announce my judgment against it because I have seen how wicked its people are" (Jonah 1:2).

This was a fairly unusual assignment for a prophet of God. Usually when God sent a prophet, it was to the people of Israel with a warning to repent and return to God. This time, however, it was a call to preach to people who, for all Jonah knew, could have killed him on the spot.

But God had a plan for Jonah, and it was a plan to bless him by allowing him to be the vessel through which a generation of people would be saved. It didn't make sense to Jonah; in fact, there was no way he could possibly have understood what God was up to. It wasn't a calling a prophet of God could have expected, but it was God's command—one He expected Jonah to obey.

discussion question

Where else is Jonah mentioned in the Old Testament?
Other than in the book that bears his name, the prophet Jonah is not mentioned extensively in the Old Testament. He was a prophet of Israel, and he predicted the restoration of the ancient boundaries of the kingdom (2 Kings 14:25–27). He ministered in the very early reign of King Jeroboam II.

Sadly, however, Jonah did exactly the opposite of what God had told him to do. Rather than head straight for Nineveh, Jonah hopped a boat and headed in the opposite direction. As the book of Jonah tells us: "But Jonah got up and went in the opposite direction to get away from the Lord. He went down to the port of Joppa, where he found a ship leaving for Tarshish. He bought a ticket and went on board, hoping to escape from the Lord by sailing to Tarshish" (Jonah 1:3).

Jonah hoped to get away from God and the very distasteful mission he'd been sent on, and he probably thought he had it made once he boarded the ship. But that was just one of the several missteps Jonah would make before he finally turned around and got his mind and life right. Jonah went nowhere but "down" when he ran from God: down to the port of Joppa (Jonah 1:3), down to the hold of the ship (1:5), down into the stormy sea (1:15), and down into the belly of a giant fish (1:17).

And, as you will see as you study this book, it was only when Jonah looked up that he was pulled up.

Study Questions

○ Why did God send Jonah to Nineveh in the first place?
○ What was Jonah's verbal response to God when he was told to go to Nineveh?

I Think I Know Why This Is Happening (Jonah 1)

There is no more miserable place in life for a Christian to be than running from God and the things He has called us to do. When you turn away from God there is no protection from the devil, there are no messages or comfort from God, there is no peace of mind, and there is no joy or strength from the Lord.

While Jonah probably thought he'd gotten away with something—and away from God—it wasn't long before his sin and rebellion caught up with him. He had purchased a ticket to a place called Tarshish and boarded the boat. He was sleeping soundly in the ship's hold when he was awakened by the terrified and panicked cry of the ship's captain: "How can you sleep at a time like this?' he shouted. 'Get up and pray to your god! Maybe he will pay attention to us and spare our lives'" (Jonah 1:6).

symbolism

Jonah really believed he could run from God, and he probably wondered if God knew where he was when he ended up in the belly of the fish. But David the psalmist wrote that it was impossible to hide from God: "I can never escape from your Spirit! I can never get away from your presence!" (Psalm 139:7).

This was no ordinary storm that had struck. It was a storm sent specifically from God (Jonah 1:4) so that He could pull His prophet back to a life of obedience, and it was so violent that it threatened to rip the ship in half. Even the weather-hardened, sea-wise sailors who ran the ship were so afraid they were going to die that they started tossing cargo overboard.

Jonah informed the ship's crew that he was a Hebrew who worshipped the true and living Creator God and that he was on the ship because he was running from God. That, he said, was why they were in the predicament they were in. When they asked Jonah what they should do, he told them very directly and simply: "Throw me overboard" (Jonah 1:12).

But instead of getting rid of the cargo that was causing the problem— Jonah himself—the sailors tried harder to get the ship under control and back to port. When they found that they were helpless against the storm's fury, they threw Jonah overboard and down into the sea.

Just as Jonah had said, the storm ceased immediately and the ship's crew was safe. Jonah, however, had another problem to deal with.

Study Questions

○ How did the sailors respond when Jonah told them that he was a Jewish prophet and probably responsible for what they were enduring?

○ What happened in the hearts of those sailors after they threw Jonah overboard?

A Really Nasty Place to Be (Jonah 1:17)

The Bible tells us that Jonah didn't drown after he was thrown overboard but was swallowed whole by "a great fish" (Jonah 1:17), which the Lord had prepared. While the language in which the book of Jonah was written leaves it open to debate just what kind of creature swallowed the prophet, it is clear that he stayed in the belly of that beast for three days and three nights.

It is difficult to imagine or to try to describe the foulness of such a place. Perhaps one good point of reference is what fishermen refer to as a chum bucket, an onboard receptacle for a mixture of fish heads, blood, and innards, all of which are dumped into the water to help attract fish and bring them closer to the boat so that fisherman can more easily get them to take their bait.

factum

While many people might look at the story of Jonah and think that it defies plausibility, there is some historic precedence for what the Bible says happened to him. There are several examples of sailors or other men being swallowed whole by sharks or whales and then being rescued hours later.

Being buried head to toe in a bucket of chum would likely be only slightly less unpleasant than being in the belly of the creature God sent to swallow the prophet Jonah. No doubt it was a soaking wet place in which Jonah could hardly move or breathe because it was so enclosed and because it stunk so badly.

But it was a place where a prophet of God, or anybody else, could do only one thing: pray for a way out. That is exactly what Jonah did.

Study Questions

○ What do you think the Bible meant when it said that "the Lord arranged for a great fish to swallow Jonah"?
○ What do you think is the spiritual significance of the unpleasantness of the place where Jonah spent three days?

A Prayer for Deliverance (Jonah 2)

There are a lot of ways God can redirect our focus and bring us back to obedience, but it's hard to imagine one more effective than sending someone to spend three days in the stomach of some kind of giant sea creature. And while Jonah must have wondered if this was how his life would end, he prayed for God's deliverance from the situation.

point of interest

Jesus Christ himself gave the story of Jonah historical authenticity as well as a spiritual application when he said, "For as Jonah was in the belly of the great fish for three days and three nights, so will the Son of Man be in the heart of the earth for three days and three nights" (Matthew 12:40).

Jonah's prayer starts out sounding very much like one of the psalms: "I cried out to the Lord in my great trouble, and he answered me. I called to you from the land of the dead, and Lord, you heard me! You threw me into the ocean depths, and I sank down to the heart of the sea. The mighty waters engulfed me; I was buried beneath your wild and stormy waves" (Jonah 2:2–3).

As Jonah continued praying, he seems to understand that he had run from God and that God had banished him from His presence because of it. Then he seems to turn back to God, telling him, "Yet I will look once more toward your holy Temple" (Jonah 2:4). Finally, he tells God, "But I will offer sacrifices to you with songs of praise, and I will fulfill all my vows. For my salvation comes from the Lord alone" (Jonah 2:9).

That, apparently, was what God wanted to hear. He removed Jonah from the unpleasantness he had brought on himself through his own disobedience and rebellion: "Then the Lord ordered the fish to spit Jonah out onto the beach" (Jonah 2:10).

But the story was far from finished. There was still that matter of Jonah actually doing what God had called him to do in the first place.

Study Questions

○ Read Psalm 18. How is this psalm similar to Jonah's prayer? How is it different?

○ Does Jonah's prayer sound more like a request for mercy and deliverance or the prayer of a man who knows he is about to die?

Are You Ready to Go Now? (Jonah 3)

While not everyone who spends three days in the stomach of a fish will use that time to get his mind and spirit right, that is exactly what the prophet Jonah did. Once he did that—and once God got him out of that fish's belly—he barely had time to get himself cleaned up when God spoke to him a second time, giving him the same command as before: "Get up and go to the great city of Nineveh, and deliver the message I have given you" (Jonah 3:2).

Jonah had learned his lesson. This time he didn't head "down," but instead he headed out, straight to Nineveh, a city so large that it took three days to see all of it. He still may not have had a clue as to why God had called him to preach to a people like the Ninevites—or why God had chose him to do it—but this time he did as he had been commanded.

And once Jonah was in Nineveh, he didn't pull any punches. He spoke the very message God had given him to deliver.

The book of Jonah doesn't tell us what specific sin or sins the people had committed to bring God's judgment down on themselves, but it does tell us that the situation was dire, so dire that on the very day Jonah entered the city he announced, "Forty days from now Nineveh will be destroyed!" (Jonah 3:4). It was a message Jonah believed with all his heart, and it was a message the Ninevites believed, too.

factum

Jonah was not the only prophet to foretell the doom and desolation of the city of Nineveh. The book of the prophet Nahum, which is set about a century after the time of Jonah, is taken up almost exclusively with the prophecies of the destruction of the city because of its great sin.

Jonah had spoken from the heart and with passion, because the people of Nineveh—including the king himself—listened and made the changes God had called them to make. Jonah, the reluctant—even rebellious—prophet of God had made a difference, preaching salvation to a people who until that time had been his mortal enemy.

Study Questions

○ What would you do if you knew God wanted you to do something that in your human reasoning just didn't make sense? Would you obey? Argue? Bargain?
○ Why do you think God persisted with Jonah instead of just sending someone else to do the preaching?

The Results of Obedience (Jonah 3,4)

Any doubts Jonah had about the people of Nineveh receiving his message were quickly dispelled. Right away the people of the city—from the most important to the least—heard what he was saying, took heed of the message, and repented.

But there was more. Even the king of Nineveh took Jonah's message seriously. He stepped down from his throne, took off his royal robes, and went into "sackcloth and ashes" repentance. Not only that, he and his nobles passed this decree for the city:

> *No one, not even the animals from your herds and flocks, may eat or drink anything at all. People and animals alike must wear garments of mourning, and everyone must pray earnestly to God. They must turn from their evil ways and stop all their violence. Who can tell? Perhaps even yet God will change his mind and hold back his fierce anger from destroying us. (Jonah 3:7–9)*

Because Jonah had obeyed God—after a three-day side trip—and because he preached the truth that God had given him to speak, the city of Nineveh was spared. God saw how the people had repented and changed their ways, and He changed His mind and didn't carry out the destruction He had earlier threatened.

symbolism

Jesus himself mentioned Jonah and actually likened Jonah's assigned mission to his own: "The people of Nineveh will stand up against this generation on judgment day and condemn it, for they repented of their sins at the preaching of Jonah. Now someone greater than Jonah is here—but you refuse to repent" (Matthew 28:41).

God had shown mercy, just as He had wanted to in the first place, but that only angered Jonah, who complained, "Didn't I say before I left home that you would do this, Lord? That is why I ran away to Tarshish! I knew that you are a merciful and compassionate God, slow to get angry and filled with unfailing love. You are eager to turn back from destroying people. Just kill me now, Lord! I'd rather be dead than alive if what I predicted will not happen" (Jonah 4:2–3).

This seems like a strange response to the mercy of God, who asks him, "Is it right for you to be angry about this?" (Jonah 4:4). Jonah then went out to the edge of the city and started pouting while he waited to see what would happen to it. Would God do as He had said?

Jonah seems angry that such a wicked city had been saved, that what God had said was going to happen didn't. It seems that he was more concerned that what he prophesied come true than have his warnings lead to the repentance and salvation of a huge city. Finally, God uses a series of miracles to demonstrate the rightness of his mercy on the people of Nineveh.

The book of Jonah ends abruptly, and God has the last word, saying to Jonah, "Nineveh has more than 120,000 people living in spiritual darkness, not to mention all the animals. Shouldn't I feel sorry for such a great city?" (Jonah 4:12).

In the end, it seems that this question is posed for the reader to ponder as there is no answer from Jonah. In fact, that question leaves us only to think about the immense compassion of God—even for those who were not his "chosen" people.

God cares about and loves all people, regardless of what country or race they belong to. The mission of Jonah was an example of that great love and compassion.

Study Questions

○ How would you answer the question that God poses at the end of the book of Jonah?

○ How would you respond if God used you or someone you know to lead someone you thought wasn't worthy to salvation?

CHAPTER 12

Matthew: Some Tough— and Practical—Teaching

One of the most recognizable sermons of all time came from the mouth of Jesus Christ at the shore of the Sea of Galilee and has come to be known as the Sermon on the Mount. In this sermon, Jesus spoke with a power and authority the likes of which no one had ever seen or heard. This chapter is a study of that sermon, what it meant to the people who heard it straight from Jesus's mouth, and what it means to us today.

Another Look at the Law of Moses

If you've ever read through the first five books of the Bible—known as the Pentateuch or the books of Moses—and wondered what they have to do with your Christian life today, then maybe you should take the time to read and study what has been called the greatest sermon ever preached. It is found in the fifth through seventh chapters of the Gospel of Matthew, and it has been commonly called the Sermon on the Mount. It was delivered by Jesus Christ to a multitude of his followers.

In preaching the Sermon on the Mount, Jesus took the common approach to the law of that time and turned it on its ear. Most of the Jewish religious leadership at that time held to a very black and white application of Jewish law, but Jesus taught a different approach. His was an approach to the law that stressed obedience from the heart and not from a sense of legalism.

Jesus delivered this sermon on a small hill on the shore of the Sea of Galilee. It was different from anything anyone on the scene had ever heard. For those who could hear and understand the message, it revolutionized their lives. The same can happen for those believers who make studying this passage and applying its truths a life priority.

God Blesses Those Who... (Matthew 5:3–16)

Jesus began the Sermon on the Mount by speaking what has come to be known as the Beatitudes, which were simply declarations of blessing to those who follow them. Each of the Beatitudes starts with the phrase "God blesses" (or "Blessed are," depending on what version of the Bible you are reading) and ends with the blessing itself. In the Beatitudes, Jesus tells us that God blesses:

- those who are poor and know how much they need him (Matthew 5:3)
- those who mourn because they will be comforted (5:4)
- those who are humble because they will inherit the whole earth (5:5)
- those who are hungry and thirsty for justice because they will be satisfied (5:6)

- those who show mercy because they will receive mercy (5:7)
- those who have pure hearts because they will see God (5:8)
- those who work for peace because they will be called God's children (5:9)
- those who are persecuted for doing what is right for God's kingdom is theirs (5:10).

Jesus followed this list by telling his followers, "God blesses you when people mock you and persecute you and lie about you and say all sorts of evil things against you because you are my followers. Be happy about it! Be very glad! For a great reward awaits you in heaven. And remember, the ancient prophets were persecuted in the same way" (Matthew 5:11–12).

point of interest

You can find a more abbreviated version of the Sermon on the Mount in Luke 6:20–49. In that version, there are fewer Beatitudes. Jesus's teaching on loving enemies and judging others is also included in that version.

Jesus went on to tell his followers that they were to be those things and receive those blessings for one reason: because they are the salt and light of the earth, meaning they were to bring the earth light and flavor. Salt is worthless, Jesus said, when it loses its flavor. Likewise, a lamp is useless when it is covered up. For that reason, those who follow Jesus are to do good things for the kingdom of God so that people will see those things and praise God.

Study Questions

◯ What did Jesus say it took to "inherit the earth"?
◯ Read Matthew 5:12. What are believers to do when people persecute or make fun of them because of their faith?

A New Approach to the Law (Matthew 5:17–47)

Jesus wanted to make sure that his followers didn't misunderstand why he had come and what his relationship to the Law of Moses was, so he told them, "Don't misunderstand why I have come. I did not come to abolish the law of Moses or the writings of the prophets. No, I came to accomplish their purpose. I tell you the truth, until heaven and earth disappear, not even the smallest detail of God's law will disappear until its purpose is achieved" (Matthew 5:17–18).

He went on to encourage them to keep the law, telling them that those who obeyed the law would be rewarded in the afterlife. Where Jesus differed most from the religious authorities and teachers of his day, however, was in his approach to what obeying the law really meant.

symbolism

Six times in the fifth chapter of Matthew, Jesus used the phrase "But I say," indicating that he wanted to make some changes in how the Jewish leadership of his time had taught and applied the Law of Moses. Five other times he used the phrase, "I tell you." Those are good verses to underline and remember as you study the Sermon on the Mount.

Jesus wanted his followers to understand that obeying God meant more than just doing the minimum and strictly adhering to a bunch of rules. In other words, it's the spirit of the law that mattered more than the letter of the law. That is why he taught such radical ideas about the following subjects:

- **Murder is from the heart** (Matthew 5:21–26). Jesus taught that sin started in the heart and then demonstrated itself in actions. That is why he said in the Sermon on the Mount concerning those who speak hateful words, do hateful deeds, and think hateful thoughts:

  You have heard that our ancestors were told, 'You must not murder. If you commit murder, you are subject to judgment.' But I say, if you are even angry with someone, you are subject to judgment! If you call someone an idiot, you are in danger of being brought before the court. And if you curse someone, you are in danger of the fires of hell. (Matthew 5:21–22)

Obviously, Jesus wanted his disciples—then and now—to deal properly with their anger at or with one another. That is reflected even more directly in the following verses, where Jesus told them to make sure that they are reconciled with one another before they bother to come to God (Matthew 5:24–25) and to settle their differences with one another before going to court (Matthew 5:25–26).

- **Adultery isn't just about the act** (Matthew 5:27–30). Jesus's teaching on adultery again reflected on the fact that he stressed to his followers the importance of focusing on what was in their hearts and minds. He cited the commandment against committing adultery, but then told the people that any man who looks lustfully at a woman who is not his own wife has already committed adultery with her in his heart.
- **Don't make promises you can't keep** (5:33–37). Jesus addressed the subject of making vows when he said, "I say, do not make any vows! Do not say, 'By heaven!' because heaven is God's throne…Just say a simple, 'Yes, I will,' or 'No, I won't.' Anything beyond this is from the evil one" (Matthew 5:34, 37). In other words, answer with a simple yes or no when someone asks you for something.
- **Revenge is a dish best served not at all** (Matthew 5:38–42). The Law of Moses held that someone who had been wronged or injured by another had the legal right to seek retribution ("an eye for an eye"). But Jesus taught that while people have that right, it is better not to use it.
- **Love your friends but also your enemies** (Matthew 5:43–48). The Law of Moses as outlined in the Old Testament stated that believers were to love their neighbors as themselves. But by the time Jesus arrived on the scene, the meaning of that commandment had become muddled. Jesus wanted his followers to do something really radical—love those who hated and persecuted them: "I say, love your enemies! Pray for those who persecute you! If you love only those who love you, what

reward is there for that? Even corrupt tax collectors do that much" (Matthew 5:44, 46).

○ What did Jesus come to do with the Law of Moses?
○ What was different about Jesus's teachings on adultery?

Doing Right for the Right Reasons (Matthew 6:1–18)

By the time Jesus arrived, the approach of most of the Jewish religious leadership in dealing with the law had become very literal. They had lost the spirit of what God had tried to teach them through His law, so they began doing the right things—things God had commanded them to do—but for the wrong reasons.

Jesus wanted to bring people back to doing good for others for the right reasons, which were because they loved God and loved their neighbors. That is why he taught that acts of charity such as giving to the needy, as well as religious acts such as fasting, needed to be done in such a way that only God knew what the believer was doing: "Watch out! Don't do your good deeds publicly, to be admired by others, for you will lose the reward from your Father in heaven. When you give to someone in need, don't do as the hypocrites do—blowing trumpets in the synagogues and streets to call attention to their acts of charity! I tell you the truth, they have received all the reward they will ever get" (Matthew 5:1–2).

He taught essentially the same lesson about prayer and fasting, telling his followers that their prayers should be offered to God in private, not out in the open for everyone to see (Matthew 6:5–6). Furthermore, when they prayed they weren't to just "babble on and on as people of other religions do" (Matthew 6:7), but instead they were to pray according to his words recorded in Matthew 6:9–14, or what is known as the Lord's Prayer (see Chapter 4).

Jesus taught that those who did the things he calls all of us to do—giving, praying, fasting—using the guidelines he gives will receive their reward from God in heaven. However, those who do them with the wrong motivation will receive their reward here on earth.

Study Questions
○ How should Jesus's command/encouragement to do our giving and other acts of charity in private affect how we do those things today?
○ What did Jesus intend when he taught his followers to pray "like this" then spoke what has come to be known as the Lord's Prayer?

A Heavenly Approach to Money and Wealth (Matthew 6:19–34)

Throughout his earthly ministry, Jesus gave some of his most direct teaching when it came to the subject of money. In the Sermon on the Mount, he didn't condemn having money or working to acquire wealth. What he did, in fact, was condemn making money and wealth one's life focus.

"Don't store up treasures here on earth," Jesus taught, "where moths eat them and rust destroys them, and where thieves break in and steal. Store your treasures in heaven, where moths and rust cannot destroy, and thieves do not break in and steal. Wherever your treasure is, there the desires of your heart will also be" (Matthew 6:19–21).

Jesus, who obviously understood the negatives of human nature (including greed), taught that it wasn't just difficult but impossible to serve God and money at the same time (Matthew 6:24). In fact, he went so far as to say that attempting to serve both will lead one to hate one or the other.

factum

The theme of God meeting the needs of every one of his people is prominent throughout the Bible. Probably the best known Scripture on that subject is found in Paul's epistle to the Philippians: "And this same God who takes care of me will supply all your needs from his glorious riches, which have been given to us in Christ Jesus" (Philippians 4:19).

Jesus also understood that his followers' concerns about money weren't always motivated by greed but simply out of concern for day-to-day living. That is why he encouraged them not to worry about the things they need for everyday life—food, drink, clothing, and the like—but instead to just rely on a God who will give them everything they needed. (Read carefully Jesus's beautiful and inspirational words in Matthew 6:26–30.)

Jesus told them (and us), "So don't worry about these things, saying, 'What will we eat? What will we drink? What will we wear?' These things dominate the thoughts of unbelievers, but your heavenly Father already knows all your needs" (Matthew 6:31–32).

The bottom line when it comes to money and possessions and wealth, Jesus told his followers, is this: "Seek the Kingdom of God above all else, and live righteously, and he will give you everything you need" (Matthew 6:33).

Jesus knew as well as anyone that living this life required certain items, many of which can only be obtained with money. But he also knew perfectly the importance of making God his Father our first focus—with everything and anything else a distant second.

Study Questions

○ In this passage, what does it sound like Jesus's approach to money really is?
○ How should this passage change the believer's approach to money and possessions?

Judging and the Golden Rule (Matthew 7:1–4, 12)

Many of Jesus's teachings—as well as others in the Bible—have become so ingrained into our culture that we know their meaning even if we don't know who said it or in what context. One excellent example of this is from Jesus's Sermon on the Mount and is what has come to be known as the Golden Rule. It goes like this: "Do to others whatever you would like them to do to you. This is the essence of all that is taught in the law and the prophets" (Matthew 7:12).

symbolism

> Jesus's famous Sermon on the Mount very likely wasn't a sermon in the sense that we think of sermons. In that culture, it was very common for teachers to gather their followers for informal question and answer teaching sessions and not preaching in the traditional sense.

On an individual basis, it's not hard to understand what the phrase "do to others whatever you would like them to do to you" means. All of us want to be treated fairly and justly—to be spoken to and treated in a respectful manner, to be paid equitably for our work, to be given what truly is due us. Jesus wanted his followers to understand the importance of treating other people in a manner each of them wants to be treated.

The Golden Rule can be seen as a summarization of the teaching that Jesus had given in the previous few sentences. He started this section by talking about judging others, making the point that we shouldn't judge others if we ourselves don't want to be judged equally as harshly. "Do not judge others, and you will not be judged," he said. "For you will be treated as you treat others. The standard you use in judging is the standard by which you will be judged" (Matthew 7:1–2).

Being the Son of God, Jesus knew better than anyone the frailties and imperfections in humanity, and he also knew that humans would be prone to judging and condemning one another for things as bad or worse as anything they themselves had done. That is partly why he went on to warn people not to worry about removing a "speck" from their friends' eyes while there is a "log" in their own (Matthew 7:3–4). In other words, don't judge or condemn or try to correct someone before you first deal with your own issues.

Study Questions

○ In light of Jesus's teaching not to judge others, what do you think is the appropriate way to respond to those whose lives you can see are out of order?

○ What kind of "logs" do you need to get out of your eye in order to be a better example of Christianity to those around you?

Praying Effectively and Persistently (Matthew 7:7–11)

Earlier in the Sermon on the Mount, Jesus taught what has come to be known as the Lord's Prayer, which is in essence a model prayer containing all the elements of effective prayer, the kind God likes to hear. Later on Jesus picked up again on the theme of prayer (a common theme in his earthly ministry) when he implied very strongly that prayer was a matter of persistence, hard work, and seeking an answer: "Keep on asking, and you will receive what you ask for. Keep on seeking, and you will find. Keep on knocking, and the door will be opened to you. For everyone who asks, receives. Everyone who seeks, finds. And to everyone who knocks, the door will be opened" (Matthew 7:7–8).

Jesus taught his followers that this ask-seek-knock form of prayer is effective because we have a heavenly Father who loves us far beyond what even the most doting mother and father could imagine. As Matthew 7:9–11 illustrates: "You parents—if your children ask for a loaf of bread, do you give them a stone instead? Or if they ask for a fish, do you give them a snake? Of course not! So if you sinful people know how to give good gifts to your children, how much more will your heavenly Father give good gifts to those who ask him."

point of interest

The writer of Hebrews echoed this theme of approaching God and asking with confidence and persistence when he wrote: "So let us come boldly to the throne of our gracious God. There we will receive his mercy, and we will find grace to help us when we need it most" (Hebrews 4:16).

Jesus wanted us to realize that God isn't some disinterested celestial personality but a loving heavenly Father who wants to bless those who will come to him and humbly ask for what they need.

Study Questions

○ What in your physical, personal, emotional, or spiritual life do you need to begin asking God to give you today?

○ How does Jesus's teaching that God's love compels him to give good gifts to those who persistently ask him compare with your own perceptions today?

The Narrow Gate and Strong Foundations (Matthew 7:13–28)

As Jesus drew his Sermon on the Mount to a close, he spoke very directly and clearly about who would inherit the kingdom of God and who would not. His teaching in this area—while it was filled with love and compassion—made it very clear that not everyone would be going to heaven, only those who entered by what he called "the narrow gate" in Matthew 7:13–14: "You can enter God's Kingdom only through the narrow gate. The highway to hell is broad, and its gate is wide for the many who choose that way. But the gateway to life is very narrow and the road is difficult, and only a few ever find it."

factum

The Bible presents a message of salvation to all and tells us repeatedly that there is only one way to see the kingdom of heaven and that is through the "narrow gate" of Jesus Christ, who said, "No one can come to the Father except through me" (John 14:6).

Jesus was teaching those in attendance that day that it was necessary for them to be freed from their sins if they wanted salvation and that they would have to be careful not to listen to those who would come after Jesus with messages to lead them astray: "Beware of false prophets who come disguised as harmless sheep but are really vicious wolves. You can identify them by their fruit, that is, by the way they act. Can you pick grapes from thornbushes, or figs from thistles? A good tree produces good fruit, and a bad tree produces bad fruit" (Matthew 7:15–17).

Jesus intended for his teaching that day—and every day after—to be taken by his followers as the foundational truths by which they would live their lives and by which they would inherit salvation and eternal life in heaven. That is why he said, "Anyone who listens to my teaching and follows it is wise, like a person who builds a house on solid rock" (Matthew 7:24).

He pointed out that a house built on rock won't collapse even in the worst of storms but that one built on sand is a catastrophe waiting to happen. Those who hear and obey his teaching, she said, were like those who built their houses on the solid rock. The ones who don't were building the houses of their lives on sand (Matthew 7:25–27).

Jesus had just preached the greatest sermon ever heard. And when he finished, the people who heard him that day were amazed both at what he had said and at how he had said it: with authority unlike anything the religious teachers of that time could muster (Matthew 7:28–29).

Study Questions

○ How does Jesus's teaching that the gate to heaven is narrow and the highway to hell wide affect your approach to telling others about your faith in Christ?

○ What do you think are some of the "good fruits" you can readily see in those who claim to know the truth about God and the way to get to him?

CHAPTER 13

John: The Apostle's Account of Holy Week

All four of the accounts of Jesus's time on earth—the Gospels of Matthew, Mark, Luke, and John—describe his final arrival into Jerusalem, his arrest, his trial, his crucifixion, and his resurrection. But John's gospel has a different take on these events, and it's one that emphasizes the identity of Jesus as the Son of God as well as the spiritual implications for those who would believe in him.

Fulfilling What He Had Predicted

For about three and a half years, Jesus Christ traveled by foot around the land of Palestine (now Israel and some surrounding areas) teaching, preaching, performing miracles, and announcing the arrival of the long-awaited Messiah. This was the portion of his life that has been referred to as his "earthly ministry," and it's the time leading up to what some Christians refer to as Holy Week.

discussion question

How is John's gospel different from the other three?
The Gospels of Matthew, Mark, and Luke are called the synoptic Gospels because they more or less follow the same chain of events in the life of Jesus. John's gospel is known for a more spiritual focus and for its emphasis on different events in Jesus's life from the other three.

This was the final week of Jesus's life on earth, and it included his final entry into the city of Jerusalem (John 12:12–19), his final teaching, his arrest and trial, his death on the cross, and his resurrection. These were all events he had told his disciples would come, and now that time had come. Jesus was about to fulfill the mission for which he had come to earth in the first place: his death on the cross and his resurrection from the dead.

John's gospel—which was written by the apostle John, who refers to himself in the gospel narrative as "the disciple Jesus loved"—is the last book of the Gospels and it contains several incidents surrounding Jesus's final hours before his death that don't appear in the other three.

A Triumphal Entry (John 12:12–19)

Like most good Jewish men, Jesus had already been to the city of Jerusalem on numerous occasions. It was at that time the custom for Jews in that area of the world to make a pilgrimage from their own homes to Jerusalem to celebrate the Passover.

But there was something different this time as Jesus entered the city. This time he was greeted by a throng of Passover visitors who welcomed him with these words of praise: "Praise God! Blessings on the one who comes in the name of the Lord! Hail to the King of Israel!" (John 12:13).

This scene—which is also recorded in Matthew 21:1–11, Mark 11:1–11, and Luke 19:29–44—was one of near pandemonium as Jesus entered the Holy City. But it was also one with some serious undertones. It was in Jerusalem that the Jewish religious leaders of that time had been plotting and planning to put an end to what Jesus had been doing for the past three years.

symbolism

If you want a good overview of some of the other things Jesus did and said during that last week prior to the Crucifixion, read Luke chapters 19–22. That will give you a more complete perspective of what Jesus was up against during that week and why it would end the way it did.

If you've read through the entire Gospel of John prior to doing this exercise, then you know that the teaching and deeds of Jesus were often very much in conflict with the religious establishment of that time and place. And while Jesus's arrival into Jerusalem looked like a huge party, it would only be a matter of time before the religious leaders would find a reason to do away with Jesus.

Study Questions

○ Read John 12:17–18. Why were many of the people coming out to greet Jesus as he entered Jerusalem?

○ Look at John 12:19, then Luke 19:39–40. How did the Pharisees—the Jewish religious leaders—respond to Jesus's arrival?

A Heart-Wrenching Scene (John 13)

Out of the four Gospels, John's tells us the least when it comes to the things Jesus did and said during his final week in Jerusalem. In fact, all that is really mentioned after he entered Jerusalem and prior to the eve of his crucifixion is a request by some Greek pilgrims to visit with Jesus personally and the sermon he delivered after hearing that request (John 12:20–50).

In the other gospel accounts, we can read of what has come to be known as the Lord's Supper or the Last Supper, but in John's gospel, the events on the eve of the Crucifixion were as follows: Jesus washes the disciples' feet (John 13:1–17), announces that one of the disciples will betray him (13:18–30), then gives the disciples what can best be described as parting words.

The foot-washing scene is an especially touching scene because it is Jesus—the leader, Lord, and Master of the twelve disciples over the previous three-plus years—who takes out the wash basin and towel and begins washing their feet. Of the twelve, only Peter has the nerve to speak up and say what the others were no doubt thinking. But Jesus met Peter's protests with a firm response: "Unless I wash you, you won't belong to me" (John 13:8). Peter, of course, changed his mind and allowed Jesus to wash his feet.

point of interest

While John wrote of Jesus washing the disciples' feet on the eve of his crucifixion, the other gospel writers record Jesus serving in another way: by presenting them with what has come to be known as the Lord's Supper. In it, the disciples ate the bread that represented Jesus's flesh and drank the wine that represented his blood.

The foot washing was followed by Jesus's very direct announcement to the disciples that one of them would betray him. Judas, who John wrote had been entered by the devil himself, then left the group and disappeared into the night, going to the Jewish religious leaders to betray Jesus.

The stage was now set. Jesus had deliberately and with great purpose put himself in harm's way by coming to Jerusalem. Judas was about to betray him, and that would lead to his arrest, trial, and death. But first, Jesus had some final words for the eleven remaining disciples—as well as what is probably the most amazing prayer recorded in the Bible.

Study Questions

○ How did Jesus demonstrate who his betrayer would be?

○ What did Jesus say Peter would do on the night before his arrest and crucifixion? (See John 13:36–38.)

Some Final Words to the Disciples (John 14–16)

In those final hours before Jesus's arrest, he preached an incredible sermon (this one just to the disciples) filled with words of comfort, promises, encouragements, and warnings. In this sermon, Jesus told the disciples:

- not to be troubled but to trust in him (John 14:1–4)
- that they were to have faith in him as the One sent from God (14:5–14)
- that they were to continue in obedience to him, with the help of the Holy Spirit (14:15–31)
- that they were to remain in him, even though he would be gone soon (15:1–8)
- that they were to love one another the same way he loved them (15:9–17)
- that the world would hate them (15:18–25)
- that he would soon send the Holy Spirit (15:26–16:16)
- that their sorrow and grief would one day be turned to joy (16:17–28)

This section of the Gospel of John is filled with incredible instruction and encouragement for the believer today. It encourages the discouraged, comforts the afflicted, instructs those who aren't sure what to do, and promises that no matter what we go through on this earth, if we remain in Christ we will one day experience joy—all because Jesus remains with us.

Jesus told the disciples that even though he would soon be physically gone, they were to "Remain in me, and I will remain in you" (John 15:4). Jesus wanted the disciples to understand that they had some incredibly difficult work ahead and that the only way they would be able to finish it successfully was to stick close to him. One of the reasons they would need to stick close to Jesus, he taught them, was that they would be going into a world that would hate them—just like it hated Jesus himself—despite the fact that they would be taking with them a positive message of salvation and forgiveness from God.

symbolism

It is absolutely crucial for a believer to understand that bearing fruit, as Jesus referred to doing positive things for God and for others in his name, can only happen when he or she sticks close to him (John 15:1–4). That theme runs throughout the Bible, Old Testament and New Testament alike.

All of the promises Jesus made in this passage are invaluable to the believer, but it can be argued that the most important of them was his promise to send the Holy Spirit. Jesus went to great lengths to explain to the disciples that the Holy Spirit would remind the world of its need for God's forgiveness and righteousness and would guide them and remind them daily of the things he had taught them while he was on earth with them.

Study Questions

○ What specific things can the believer do to ensure that he or she continues to remain in Christ?

○ Read Acts 2. How does the event in that passage connect with what Jesus told the disciples in this passage?

A Final Word to the Father (John 17)

Just before Jesus went to the olive grove where he was to be betrayed and arrested, he gave the disciples their final marching orders and offered a prayer to God, his Father. It was one of the most beautiful and emotional prayers recorded in the Bible. In this prayer, Jesus prayed for:

- **himself** (John 17:1–6), because the time had come for his divinely appointed death on the cross and he wanted to glorify his Father;
- **his disciples** (17:7–19), because their next few days were going to be filled with pain, disappointment, and disillusionment and because they would be facing the challenge of taking Jesus's message into an unreceptive, even dangerous world;
- **all those who would be believers because of his work and the work of the disciples** (17:20–26), because he wanted them to live in unity with the Father and the Son as well as one another.

As you read this prayer, you get a good idea of the level of commitment Jesus had—and still has—to glorify God in all he did and to the well-being and eternal destinies of those he called to serve God and of those he came to save.

Study Questions

○ According to Jesus's prayer, what is the one way to eternal life?
○ For what specifically did Jesus pray when it came to those who would believe in him?

Jesus's Arrest and Trial (John 18–19:15)

The Jewish religious leaders of Jesus's time didn't like his teaching and interpretations of the Scriptures and their religious traditions. For that reason, he represented a threat to their authority and long-held power structure.

The way they saw it, something had to be done and now the time was right to do it.

After Jesus had finished his final prayer—for himself, for his disciples, and for others who would believe in him—he took his disciples and headed for a nearby olive grove, which we know from other gospel accounts is the garden of Gethsemane.

It was here where Jesus was arrested and taken into custody. While the other three gospels include Jesus's prayers just before he was arrested, John tells us only that Judas showed up guiding some soldiers as well as some representatives sent by the religious leadership. Jesus was taken into custody after a small scuffle that resulted in the wounding of Malchus, a servant of the chief priest. (In Luke's gospel, Jesus healed Malchus.)

Jesus was first taken to a man named Annas, who interviewed him about the things he had been teaching. Jesus declined to defend himself or explain himself, instead only telling Annas that he had spoken and taught openly and that there should be plenty of witnesses to anything he said worthy of death.

factum

John's gospel is the only one to mention Jesus's meeting with Annas following his arrest. Annas was the former Jewish high priest and the father-in-law of Caiaphas, the high priest at the time of Jesus's arrest. The Roman government of that time had, for purely political reasons, removed Annas from office and replaced him with Caiaphas.

John tells us that Annas sent Jesus away, still bound, to Caiaphas the high priest who then sent him away to Pilate, the Roman governor of Judea. The idea was to accuse Jesus of subversion against the Roman government, a crime the Romans took very seriously and dealt with very harshly.

At first Pilate probably believed that Jesus was no different than a lot of the troublemakers he had faced in his position of authority. But some of the things Jesus said troubled Pilate, and he had a difficult time deciding what to do with him. In truth, Jesus hadn't done anything to deserve the death penalty, and he even said as much to the assembled crowd. In the end, however, after pleading with those who wanted Jesus dead, Pilate gave him over to be crucified.

Study Questions

O Read Luke's account of Jesus's trial. What additional information does Luke provide to this part of the story?

○ According to John's account, what happened to Peter while this scene was developing?

The Crucifixion (John 19:16–37)

With Jesus's trial finished, it was now time for his appointment with the cross. John tells us that Jesus was led away to a place called Golgotha, or Skull Hill, where he was crucified, or nailed by the hands and feet to a cross made of wood—a common as well as shockingly brutal form of capital punishment in the Roman world of that time.

factum

The four Gospels' accounts of Jesus's death record him saying different final words. John's account tells us that he said "It is finished!" before he died, while the Matthew and Mark versions record him praying, "My God, my God, why have you forsaken me?" Luke tells us that his last words were "Father, into your hands I commit my spirit."

All four Gospels tell us some of what happened at the Crucifixion scene, with some leaving out what others omit (and vice versa). As you study this passage of John's gospel, it's a good idea to also take a peek at what the other three writers had to say about this scene. When you do that, you will see the complete picture of the most profound act of love in all of human history.

Also notice that John several times points out that events at the Crucifixion scene were direct and specific fulfillments of Old Testament Scripture concerning the Messiah. For example, John 19:23–24 tells us that the soldiers' dividing and throwing of dice for Jesus's clothing fulfilled a prophecy from Psalm 22:28. That was just the first of several of John's references to fulfillments of Old Testament prophecies.

John 19:28–30 tells us that Jesus died only after he was offered a sour wine-soaked sponge to quench his thirst. His last words in this passage: "It is finished!"

Study Questions

○ Look up the Crucifixion accounts in Matthew 27:35–50, Mark 15:25–37, and Luke 23:22–46. What do the words Jesus spoke while on the cross say to you personally?

○ What is the importance to your own spiritual life of the fact that Jesus's crucifixion fulfills so many Old Testament prophecies?

The Resurrection (John 20–21)

The death of Jesus Christ by crucifixion had put the disciples in a deep funk. To them it seemed that everything they had worked for—all that time they had spent following Jesus—was for nothing. Their leader was dead and gone, and the movement they believed he was starting was finished.

point of interest

The Resurrection is also recorded in Matthew 28:2–15, Mark 16:1–9, and Luke 24:1–12. As you study this passage, look at those three scenes and notice the differences of viewpoint and emphasis in the accounts. For example, Luke gives an account of angels telling the women who followed Jesus what had happened and why.

But this story wasn't finished. Not by a long shot. In fact, on the third day after Jesus's death, God would perform his greatest miracle of all: raising Christ from the dead. John sets up his account of the Resurrection scene by telling about two members of the Jewish religious leadership—Joseph of Arimathea and Nicodemus—who saw to a proper burial of Jesus's body (John 19:38–40).

John tells us that on the morning of the first day of the week (which would have been Sunday according to our calendars), a woman named

Mary of Magdala, one of Jesus's followers, went to the tomb only to find that the stone had been removed from the entrance. Mary ran to get Peter and "the other disciple" (John), who both ran to the tomb. When Peter looked into the tomb, all he saw was strips of linen and the burial cloth that had been around Jesus's head.

Although they still didn't understand that the resurrection of Jesus was in keeping with Old Testament prophecies concerning the Messiah, Peter and John both knew something was up (John 20:6–9). They both returned to their homes, while Mary stayed behind grieving over what had apparently happened. It was then that Jesus appeared to her.

symbolism

The apostle Paul pointed out to the Corinthian church, which was battling some doubts, the centrality to the Christian faith of the literal bodily resurrection of Jesus Christ on the third day after his death when he wrote, "And if Christ has not been raised, then all our preaching is useless, and your faith is useless" (1 Corinthians 15:14).

John points out that Jesus later appeared to all the remaining disciples, including one named Thomas, who had plainly stated that unless he could touch Jesus physically, he wouldn't believe he was alive again.

Study Questions
○ How do you respond when it seems that what God had said would happen didn't happen—at least in the way you'd believed it would?
○ In what instances of your own life have you seen God fulfill a promise you had forgotten he'd made?

CHAPTER 14

Acts of the Apostles: Paul's Life and Ministry

Historians rank the apostle Paul as one of the most influential and important figures in European and American history. It's small wonder, too, because Paul was the man charged with taking the message of salvation through Jesus Christ to the non-Jewish (Gentile) world, including parts of Europe. This chapter is a study of the accounts of Paul's ministries as they are recorded in the book of Acts—including his call to ministry and all three of his missionary journeys.

Empowered from Above

"But you will receive power when the Holy Spirit comes upon you. And you will be my witnesses, telling people about me everywhere—in Jerusalem, throughout Judea, in Samaria, and to the ends of the earth" (Acts 1:8). These were Jesus's last recorded words before he ascended back to heaven, and they were words the fledgling church—at that point just a group of believers waiting for the arrival of the Holy Spirit—took seriously as it began to move out and spread around the area. One person who wasn't there when Jesus spoke these words was a man named Saul, who was miraculously and spectacularly called to preach the Good News of the message of Jesus Christ to the Gentile world (Greece and Europe) and given a new name as well: Paul the apostle.

The Acts of the Apostles—also known simply as Acts—was written by Luke the physician (who also penned the gospel that bears his name) and tells the stories of the start of the church and of the men who were charged with taking Christ's message of salvation to the world around them. That includes the work of the apostle Paul (Acts 13–28), who took three missionary journeys, all of which resulted in the formation of several new churches in various villages and cities.

Time for a Change in Direction (Acts 9)

Since you've gotten this far in your study of the Bible, you have probably noticed that God often uses the unlikeliest of characters to do His work—people you'd probably never hire to help run your company but that God saw fit to charge with being a part of His plan of salvation for all humankind. The man who would be the apostle Paul was just such a person. Paul was a devout Jew—an expert in Jewish law who at the time of his conversion to Christianity was doing everything he could to wipe out this heretical new movement. The Bible says that he went everywhere, dragging Christian men and women out of their homes and throwing them into prison (Acts 8:3).

His conversion took place as he was on his way to Damascus (in what is now Syria) to persecute Christians. As he approached the city, a bright light from heaven suddenly shone down around him, striking him blind. As he fell to the ground, he heard a voice from heaven say, "Saul! Saul! Why are you persecuting me?" (Acts 9:4).

point of interest

The first mention of Saul—later the apostle Paul—is in Acts 7, which gives the account of the stoning of a disciple of Jesus named Stephen. While Paul didn't directly participate in this man's death, he did stand by and keep watch over the murderers' garments and later gave approval to the stoning (Acts 7:58, 8:1).

Jesus told Saul that it was him he had been persecuting, then instructed him to get up and go to Damascus where he was to meet with a believer named Ananias, who God had instructed to minister to Saul when he arrived.

Saul remained in Damascus with the believers who lived there. His sight had been restored, and after just a few days he began preaching about Jesus in the synagogues, telling people that he was indeed the Son of God.

Saul's preaching was so powerful and persuasive that the Jewish religious leaders plotted to kill him. But after he found out about the plot, he fled the city and went to Jerusalem where he preached and where the other apostles welcomed him in.

Study Questions

○ What instructions did Jesus give Saul on the road to Damascus?
○ What was Ananias's response when he was instructed to minister to Saul when he arrived in Damascus?

Paul's First Missionary Journey (Acts 13:1–15:35)

The apostle Paul is known to have taken three missionary journeys during which he founded or planted many churches and ministered to many others. All of this took place following his post-conversion preaching, training, travel, and time in Antioch, Syria, which had become the center or base of the Christian church.

factum

In Acts 13:13, we read of a man named Mark leaving Paul during his first missionary journey. While that isn't a great way to start a life of ministry, Mark finished strong. It is believed that this is the same Mark who penned the gospel that bears his name.

Paul is referred to as the first missionary to the Gentiles, and the start of his first journey is recorded in Acts 13. This journey took place around A.D. 46–48 and was his shortest—both in time and in distance traveled. But it was this first journey that established Paul as a key figure in the spread of the gospel of Christ to the Gentile world. Acts gives this account of Paul and Barnabas's commissioning:

Among the prophets and teachers of the church at Antioch of Syria were Barnabas, Simeon (called "the black man"), Lucius (from Cyrene), Manaen (the childhood companion of King Herod Antipas), and Saul. One day as these men were worshiping the Lord and fasting, the Holy Spirit said, "Dedicate Barnabas and Saul for the special work to which I have called them." So after more fasting and prayer, the men laid their hands on them and sent them on their way. (Acts 13:1–3)

On Paul's first journey he was accompanied by men named Barnabas and Mark. The journey began in Seleucia, the seaport of Antioch in what is now Syria (Acts 13:1–4). From there, Paul, who was still called Saul, sailed to the island nation of Cyprus. They landed in the city of Salamis, where they preached in the Jewish synagogues (13:5). They then traveled the entire southern coast of Cyprus until they reached a place called Paphos

(13:6), where the Roman proconsul Sergius Paulus was converted after Paul rebuked a sorcerer there (13:6–12). It was at this time that Paul became the leader in the missionary journey, and also when his name was changed from Saul to Paul (13:9, 13).

From there, Paul and Barnabas visited the following places:

- Perga, where John Mark left them (Acts 13:13)
- Pisidian, Antioch, where many were converted (13:14–41)
- Iconium, where many Jews and Gentiles alike were converted (13:51)
- Lystra, where Paul was stoned (14:8–19)
- Derbe (14:20)

The Bible says that after visiting Derbe, Paul and Barnabas returned by ship to their home base of Antioch (Syria) and that, "Upon arriving in Antioch, they called the church together and reported everything God had done through them and how he had opened the door of faith to the Gentiles, too" (Acts 14:27). Paul and Barnabas stayed in Antioch for a period of time (probably around a year) after that first missionary journey, dealing with various issues and questions in the church there. But it was only a matter of time before Paul had the urge to go and do what God had called and prepared him to do.

Study Questions

- ○ How was Barnabas referred to when he is first introduced in the book of Acts (Acts 13:1)?
- ○ While in Salamis, where did Paul and Barnabas preach?

Paul's Second Missionary Journey (Acts 15:36–18:21)

Paul's second missionary journey started like this: "After some time Paul said to Barnabas, 'Let's go back and visit each city where we previously preached the word of the Lord, to see how the new believers are doing'" (Acts 15:36).

Of course, Barnabas was all for a follow-up visit to the cities where he and Paul had preached the gospel message, but that was followed by an unfortunate disagreement. Acts tells us that Barnabas wanted to take John Mark, who had left them on their first missionary journey and returned home, but Paul didn't think it was wise. That led to something of a split between Paul and Barnabas. Although there was no animosity between the two—in fact, Paul later spoke very highly of Barnabas and also made up with John Mark (Colossians 4:10, 2 Timothy 4:11)—the two never traveled together again.

point of interest

It was during Paul's second missionary journey that Luke, the writer of the book of Acts, personally joined the missionary party. From Acts 16:10 on, the narrative changes and uses the pronoun *we*. ("So we decided to leave for Macedonia at once, having concluded that God was calling us to preach the Good News there.")

The apostle's second missionary trip was far longer than the first. It started around A.D. 49 and lasted for about three years. This time, instead of traveling with Barnabas, Paul was accompanied by a man named Silas. The second trip was over land, through Syria and Cilicia, so that Paul could visit the Asian churches he had established in his first journey.

Among those churches were the ones at Derbe and then the one at Lystra, where a young preacher-to-be named Timothy joined him (Acts 16:1–5). From there they went north through places called Phrygia and Galatia (16:6), the home of the church to which Paul wrote the book of Galatians, which is in the New Testament.

The Biblical account of Paul's second missionary journey is filled with incredible adventures and spiritual visions on the part of Paul, including the following:

- After leaving Galatia, Paul wanted to travel to Bithynia, which is located on the shore of the Black Sea, but he and his companions were stopped when, "the Spirit of Jesus did not allow them to go there"

(Acts 16:7). Instead, they traveled to a seaport called Troas, which was on the shore of the Aegean Sea, and preached and taught there (16:8).

- After staying in Troas for a while, Paul had a vision of a man in Macedonia begging him to come and help the people there (Acts 16:9). Realizing that this was a message from God, Paul and his companions set sail for Macedonia, where he worked to establish churches in Philippi (16:11–39), Thessalonica (17:1–9), and Berea (17:10–15).

- Facing threats of death, Paul was sent away from Berea while Silas and Timothy stayed behind. Paul, leaving instructions for Silas and Timothy to rejoin him as soon as possible, was taken to Athens, Greece, a city filled with pagan idolatry. While there, Paul observed a huge altar to "an Unknown God" (Acts 17:23). Paul pointed out to the high council of Athens that they had been worshipping a deity they didn't even know, but he could tell them who God really was and that this God was the one who had power over death (17:24–32). Some who heard Paul's message laughed at him, but some—including a council member named Dionysius and a woman named Damaris—joined him in believing in Jesus Christ.

- From Athens, Paul traveled to Corinth, which was the seat of the Roman government of Achaia. Paul stayed there for a year and a half successfully preaching the message of Jesus Christ to Jews and Greeks alike. While in Corinth, Paul wrote two letters to the church at Thessalonica, which are in the Bible today as First and Second Thessalonians.

Following several other visits in the region, many of them quite fruitful, Paul began working his way home to Jerusalem because he, being a devout Jew, wanted to celebrate Pentecost in Jerusalem. Later, he returned home to Antioch (Acts 18:18–23).

Study Questions

○ Read again what Paul said to Barnabas as he prepared him to set out on another missionary journey (Acts 15:36). What was Paul's motivation in visiting those churches again?

○ Read Acts 16:7. What does Paul's change in course tell you about his relationship with God?

Paul's Third Missionary Journey (Acts 18:22–21:16)

Paul's third and final missionary expedition was launched from the same place as the other two: Antioch, Syria (Acts 18:23). The first leg of his third missionary trip was over land in Asia Minor (modern-day Turkey). He visited cities in the regions of Galatia and Phrygia before settling for nearly three years in the city of Ephesus (19:1–41), where he founded a church that would receive one of the letters that later would be included in the Bible.

Like many ancient cities of that time, Ephesus was rife with pagan religious worship and practices. But as Paul preached, taught, and performed miracles for all the people to see—including the healing of sick people and the casting out of demons—many people turned to Christ, including sorcerers who burned very expensive sorcery books (Acts 19:17–20).

factum

Acts 20:7–12 gives the account of Paul doing what Jesus himself had done: raising a person from the dead. A young man named Eutychus fell three stories from a windowsill to his death. But Paul bent down and took the man in his arms: " 'Don't worry,' he said, 'he's alive!' " (20:10). As Paul had said, the young man lived.

While in Ephesus, Paul found himself in trouble from the local idol worshipers. This time, Paul had exposed the fraud of the pagan god Artemis and the craftsmen and artisans who were in the business of supplying the public with the idols. After Paul spoke out, a near riot broke out and he was nearly killed in the melee (Acts 19:28–41).

Paul left Ephesus for Macedonia and eventually arrived in Greece, where he stayed for three months before learning of a plot against his life (Acts 20:1–3). At that time he was preparing to sail back to Syria—most likely Antioch—but decided to return through Macedonia. After arriving in the city of Philippi, he sailed to Troas (20:6). From there, Paul traveled through Assos, Mitylene, Kios, Samos, and Miletus (20:13–16).

While in Miletus, Paul sent for the elders of the church at Ephesus and asked them to come meet him. They did, and Paul told them:

> You know that from the day I set foot in the province of Asia until now I have done the Lord's work humbly and with many tears. I have endured the trials that came to me from the plots of the Jews. I never shrank back from telling you what you needed to hear, either publicly or in your homes. I have had one message for Jews and Greeks alike—the necessity of repenting from sin and turning to God, and of having faith in our Lord Jesus. (Acts 20:18–21)

Paul then told them that he would be returning to Jerusalem and encouraged them in their work in their church. In the end, when Paul had finished speaking to the elders, "he knelt and prayed with them. They wept aloud as they embraced him in farewell, sad most of all because he had said that they would never see him again. Then they accompanied him down to the ship" (Acts 20:36–39).

Paul then finished the final leg of his voyage, stopping in the island of Cos, Rhodes, Patara, Cyprus, and then to Tyre, Syria. He then traveled through Ptolemais, Caesarea, and then finally to Jerusalem.

Study Questions

○ What was the tone of Paul's farewell to the elders of the Ephesian church?

○ Read Acts 20:25–35. What specific encouragements did Paul give the elders of the Ephesian church and how do they apply to your life of faith today?

Paul in Jerusalem (Acts 21:17–23:22)

As Paul began his journey back to Jerusalem, he was faced with an ominous prophecy from a man named Agabus. When this prophet visited Paul and his companions, he took Paul's belt and tied his own hands and feet with it, then told Paul that the owner of the belt would be bound likewise by the Jewish leaders in Jerusalem and handed over to the Romans (Acts 21:10–11).

Those words certainly came to pass. Paul was welcomed by the Christian church leaders in Jerusalem (Acts 21:17), who listened as he told them of the things God had done during his travels and who later asked him to deal with some misunderstandings about his teachings among Jewish believers. It wasn't long, however, before he was beaten and nearly murdered in a mob scene near the Temple that arose over the perception that Paul had broken Jewish law. It was only because he was taken into custody by a Roman authority that Paul survived (Acts 21:27–36).

point of interest

It has been pointed out that this part of Paul's life is very similar to the final few days of Jesus's own life. What was to happen to both was foretold. Both were taken into custody in Jerusalem. Both were falsely accused, and both had to stand trial for crimes they didn't commit.

Some of those opposed to Paul's teachings wanted him dead on the spot, but it was only because of his knowledge of the law of that time that he survived. What followed was an arrest by the Roman authorities and a series of defenses on Paul's own part.

The book of Acts records many instances where Paul defended himself: in front of the crowd who wanted him dead (Acts 22:1–21), before the body of Jewish religious authorities (23:1–10), before Governor Felix, the Roman procurator of Judea at that time (24:10–21), and before King Agrippa (26:1–29).

Study Questions

○ How do you think believers God has called to service should respond in the face of fear and opposition to the work they are doing?

○ How would you respond if you were falsely accused or even punished as Paul was even though he'd committed no crime?

Paul in Caesarea and Rome (Acts 24:10–28:10)

There were plots afoot to have Paul killed, so he was sent away by the Roman authorities to Caesarea, where he stood before Felix, who, in an effort to win favor with the Jewish people, had Paul put in custody. Paul did have some limited freedoms and privileges, but he was left there for two years (Acts 24:22–27).

Two years after Paul's imprisonment there was a change in Roman leadership, and Paul, himself a Roman citizen, appealed his case to Caesar. He did that because there was a plan afoot to have him taken to Jerusalem so that he could be intercepted and killed on the way. For that reason, Paul was sent to Rome to be tried in a Roman court. It was because Paul was a Roman citizen that his appeal was heard.

factum

It was during Paul's time as a prisoner in Rome that he wrote his epistles to the Colossians, the Ephesians, the Philippians, and to Philemon. Also, if he is the writer of the epistle to the Hebrews (as many believe he is), it was most likely that he wrote that while in Rome as well.

Paul's voyage by sea to Rome was a long and perilous one. At one point, they fought through a long and terrible storm, and no one on the ship had eaten in a long time. Paul, however, received assurance from God in a dream that he would eventually arrive safely in Rome and stand trial before Caesar and bear witness to the gospel (Acts 27:19–25). But that would happen only after the ship was torn apart by a storm off the shore of the Mediterranean island of Malta. Miraculously, everyone on the ship was able to make it to shore, where they stayed for three months and where Paul was able to perform some miracles for some of the locals.

Paul finally made it to Rome, where he was put under what could be considered house arrest. He was allowed to have his own private lodging, but he was under constant guard by a Roman soldier (Acts 28:16). Three days after his arrival, Paul met with the local Jewish leaders and pleaded his case with them, telling them, "Brothers, I was arrested in Jerusalem and handed over to the Roman government, even though I had done nothing against our people or the customs of our ancestors" (Acts 28:17). He went on to explain how the Romans had tried him and acquitted him of any wrong-doing but that when the Jewish leaders protested the decision, he felt it necessary to appeal to Caesar for his own safety. He finished by telling them that he called them together to tell them that the Messiah had come in the person of Jesus Christ (28:18–20).

From that time on, Paul preached the gospel message, telling everyone who would listen that salvation had come to the Jews and to the Gentiles alike. For the next two years he lived in his own rented home, where he welcomed everyone who came to visit him and told them about Jesus Christ. And no one, the final verse of Acts tells us, did anything to stop him.

Study Questions

○ Despite a terrible shipwreck, Paul believed God when he was told that he would one day be in Rome. How do you respond when it appears that the promises God has given you might not come to pass because of some circumstance?

○ Do you believe you would have the courage to preach the gospel of Christ if you were in Paul's situation?

CHAPTER 15

Romans: The Basics of the Christian Faith

Paul's letter—or epistle—to the Roman Christians is the first of the thirteen letters known to have been authored by Paul to appear in the Bible. (Some ascribe Hebrews to Paul, but that is far from certain.) Romans has been praised as Paul's greatest printed work—mostly because its simplicity and direct approach to the message of the gospel of Jesus Christ makes it accessible and understandable to even the most novice Bible readers.

The Upshot of Romans

The writers of the four Gospels tell us about the words and works of Jesus Christ, but Paul tells us what they mean to those who would put their faith in him after his death, resurrection, and ascension back to heaven. It is through reading Romans that we come to an understanding of the meaning of Jesus's sacrificial death on the cross as well as how that event should change the way we think and live.

factum

It isn't certain who founded the Roman church, but it is believed that visitors from Rome to Jerusalem for the Passover and Pentecost may have been converted then took the message of Christ back to Rome. Paul's epistle to the Romans is believed to have been written around A.D. 54 or 55.

This chapter provides a study or overview of the first eight chapters of Romans. As you begin reading and studying this epistle for the first time, large portions of the first two or three chapters might seem a little dark—even hopeless. But don't allow yourself to stop just because the early reading might seem like bad news. Make sure you read on so that you can more fully understand the Good News of the salvation God has provided freely through the work of Jesus Christ on the cross.

What Happens to All Sinners (Romans 1:18–2:10)

One of the most common misconceptions about God is that since He is a God of love, there is no way He would allow anyone to miss out on heaven and end up in the other place. But it is hard—even impossible—to read the Bible and make a case for that kind of thinking.

The apostle Paul—following some greetings to the Roman church, including stating his desire to visit them—points out that there is a price to be paid for all sin, even what we might consider the little ones. He begins this section by stating very clearly that "God shows his anger from heaven against all sinful, wicked people who suppress the truth by their wickedness" (Romans 1:18). Paul goes on to say that sin starts in the heart of humans who won't acknowledge God for who He is or even recognize Him for what He has done.

Because of these things, Paul tells us, God allowed all of humankind to go into every kind of sinful behavior:

Their lives became full of every kind of wickedness, sin, greed, hate, envy, murder, quarreling, deception, malicious behavior, and gossip. They are backstabbers, haters of God, insolent, proud, and boastful. They invent new ways of sinning, and they disobey their parents. They refuse to understand, break their promises, are heartless, and have no mercy. (Romans 1:29–31)

Still, many people might look at the things that Paul has written in Romans 1 and say, "I haven't done any of those things, so I must be doing all right!" But Paul writes, "You may think you can condemn such people, but you are just as bad, and you have no excuse! When you say they are wicked and should be punished, you are condemning yourself, for you who judge others do these very same things" (Romans 2:1).

Then comes the unavoidable truth about the sin for which each and every human being is guilty: "And we know that God, in his justice, will punish anyone who does such things. Since you judge others for doing these things, why do you think you can avoid God's judgment when you do the same things?" (Romans 2:2–3).

Paul gives his readers a hint of the Good News, pointing out that God is kind, tolerant, and patient with each and every one of them and that this kindness, tolerance, and patience is designed to bring them to repentance and away from punishment (Romans 2:4–6) if they will just turn from their stubborn ways. Paul writes, "But he will pour out his anger and wrath on those who live for themselves, who refuse to obey the truth and instead live lives of wickedness" (Romans 2:8).

Paul is coming to the Good News for all of us—Jew and Gentile alike (Romans 2:10), but before he gets to that, he has another point to make when it comes to the sinful condition of all humankind.

Study Questions

○ What does this passage say God has in store for sinners?
○ What kinds of behaviors does the apostle Paul condemn as sinful in this passage?

The Lowdown, Dirty Truth: We're All Sinners (Romans 2:11–3:20)

No one likes to be thought of as a sinner, as someone who has nothing to offer God. We all like to think of ourselves as fundamentally good people who have a good grasp on right and wrong and whose lives are by and large pleasing to God. While most of us know we're not perfect, at least we aren't out doing the really bad stuff.

But Paul is very clear in his letter to the Romans that each and every one of us—Jew and Gentile alike—are all sinners who deserve eternal separation from God. Quoting from the Old Testament, he states, "No one is righteous—not even one. No one is truly wise; no one is seeking God. All have turned away; all have become useless. No one does good, not a single one" (Romans 3:10–12).

point of interest

When Paul wrote of the universal sinfulness of humankind in Romans 3:10–18, he quoted from several Old Testament sources: Psalms 14:1–3, 53:1–3, 5:9, 140:3, 10:7; Isaiah 53:7–8; Psalm 36:1. Having been a former Pharisee, Paul knew the Old Testament Scriptures very well.

Paul, a Jewish religious leader prior to his conversion and therefore one who knew well the Law of Moses, pointed out in Romans 2:11–16 that all people would be judged the same. Those who sinned without the law would be judged the same as those who sinned under it, he said.

Paul pointed out in Romans 3:19 that the purpose of the law was to show all of humankind that it was sinful, that it had missed the mark when it came to the righteousness of God. He wrote, "For no one can ever be made right with God by doing what the law commands. The law simply shows us how sinful we are" (Romans 3:20).

symbolism

In citing the writings of Moses (found in the first five books of the Old Testament, also known as the Pentateuch) and the prophets, Paul is pointing out that God's ultimate plan of redemption for humankind through Jesus Christ ran throughout the Bible, starting with the book of Genesis and running through the final book of prophecy.

This is bottom-line preaching, and it tells us that no matter how good we are, no matter how well we keep the letter of the law, no matter how many acts of kindness we take part in, we are still sinners in the eyes and by the standards of a holy God.

So what is the good news in all this? Paul goes on to tell us that it is the fact that God justifies us or makes us righteous through our faith in Christ, not in following the letter of the law.

Study Questions

○ Read Romans 3:10–18. What does this tell us we as humans lack when it comes to being righteous?

○ What is the true purpose of the law of God, according to Paul?

Now for the Good News! (Romans 3:21–31)

If you take them alone, most of the first three chapters of Romans can seem kind of bleak. Paul is essentially telling his readers that keeping the law of God even to the very letter isn't going to do them any good when it comes to being truly righteous—not to mention truly saved.

But the apostle isn't going to leave his readers hanging over a pit of despair. He has set them up to see the beauty and wonder of God's plan of salvation for Jew and Gentile alike, a plan that has nothing to do with keeping the law or with our own acts of goodness: "But now God has shown us a way to be made right with him without keeping the requirements of the law, as was promised in the writings of Moses and the prophets long ago. We are made right with God by placing our faith in Jesus Christ. And this is true for everyone who believes, no matter who we are" (Romans 3:21–22).

Paul has gone to great pains to establish the fact that all men and women—no matter what their background, ethnic heritage, or religious pedigrees—are sinners on their way to eternity in hell. "For all have sinned; all fall short of God's glorious standard," he summarizes (Romans 3:23), then concludes, "Yet now God in his gracious kindness declares us not guilty. He has done this through Christ Jesus, who has freed us by taking away our sins. For God sent Jesus to take the punishment for our sins and to satisfy God's anger against us. We are made right with God when we believe that Jesus shed his blood, sacrificing his life for us" (Romans 3:24–25).

factum

One of the key themes in Paul's letter to the Romans is the Good News of salvation in Jesus Christ. That phrase appears in Romans sixteen times in all, compared with twenty-six times in the four Gospels. That is one of the reasons this book has been referred to as the Gospel according to Paul.

This passage brings to mind a courtroom scene in which each of us as individuals stand absolutely 100 percent guilty before God. We not only don't have adequate defense, we have no defense at all. God is well within His rights to pronounce judgment on us, but His Son, Jesus, steps between the Father and us and pronounces us not guilty. Yes, we've sinned, but because Jesus willingly took the punishment for our sins on the cross, God sees us as pure and sinless.

Some people may believe that God judges people on a scale that weights the good things we've done against the bad things we've done. If the good outweighs the bad, then we've punched our own ticket into heaven.

However, Paul points out that this kind of thinking is completely wrong and backward: "Can we boast, then, that we have done anything to be accepted by God? No, because our acquittal is not based on our good deeds. It is based on our faith. So we are made right with God through faith and not by obeying the law" (Romans 3:27–28).

That's the Good News in a nutshell: Each of us is guilty—guilty as sin, as it were. But because of God's incredible graciousness and mercy, we are made right with Him. And that's not because of anything we are or anything we do. It's all because of who God is and what He is like.

Study Questions

○ According to Romans 3:24, on what basis does God save sinners?
○ According to Romans 3:25, what exactly did Jesus do in order to bring salvation to those who believe in him?

Justified Through Faith (Romans 3:29–5:1)

A beloved humanitarian and the lowliest nobody who never lifted a finger in his life to help his fellow man have one thing in common: Without faith, neither of them will see the kingdom of God.

Forgiveness means that God has removed from us the stain of our sin so that He can't see it anymore. Justification means that He's made us right before Himself through the work of Jesus Christ on the cross. Those two things—which are absolutely essential to the one who wants to inherit God's heavenly, eternal kingdom—are accessed through faith and faith alone.

Faith can be defined simply as taking God at His word. It means that you believe Him when He tells you that He's taken care of everything it takes for you to be made right with Him. Again, for Jew and Gentile alike, faith is what it takes to be made right before God. As Paul points out, God is the God of all people—Jew and non-Jew alike—and He has made faith the common denominator for everyone to approach Him.

"There is only one God, and there is only one way of being accepted by him. He makes people right with himself only be faith, whether they are Jews or Gentiles" (Romans 3:30). And that faith, Paul points out, doesn't replace the law but in fact fulfills it (Romans 3:31).

point of interest

The theme of justification through faith is hardly unique to the New Testament. In the book of Genesis, Abraham is said to have believed God and been justified through his faith. Paul cites that passage of Genesis in several other of his epistles to the various churches.

Paul pointed out that Abraham, who was the earthly father of the Jewish people, wasn't declared righteous through anything he did but because of who he believed: "Abraham believed God, so God declared him to be righteous" (Romans 4:3). Paul tells us that Abraham, while he wasn't a perfect man, never wavered in his faith. He continued through his life to believe God in all things, and because of that the life of Abraham was a benefit to all of humankind (Romans 4:16–17). It was through Abraham's people that God brought into the world the Messiah, Jesus Christ, who died for the sins of all humanity.

That is why Paul wrote, "Therefore, since we have been made right in God's sight by faith, we have peace with God because of what Jesus Christ our Lord has done for us" (Romans 5:1). Being made right in God's sight is a wonderful place to be. It's a place of forgiveness and justification, and a place of many other benefits.

Study Questions

○ What part does faith play in personal salvation through Jesus Christ?
○ What "works" make us worthy in God's eyes of salvation?

The Benefits of Being Made Right with God Through Faith (Romans 5:1–5)

Paul echoed what the book of Genesis said about Abraham, the father of the Jewish people, namely that he believed God and was declared righteous because of that faith. That is the number one benefit each and every one of us who place our faith in Jesus Christ receive: being right with God.

symbolism

It has been said that the word *justified* as Paul uses it in his letter to the Romans means that when God looks at those who have put their faith in Jesus Christ, He sees perfection because He sees only His own righteousness, which was lived out perfectly in the life of His only begotten Son.

But there are many other side benefits that flow out of that one, and they are all important for us to enjoy as we grow and mature in our faith in Christ. According to Paul in his letter to the Romans, when we are "made right in God's sight" by placing our faith in Jesus Christ, we have the benefit of:

- being at peace with God (Romans 5:1);
- being in a position to receive undeserved blessing and freedom (5:2);
- confidently and joyfully looking forward to sharing in God's eternal glory (5:2);
- knowing that everything we go through, including trials and problems, helps us to mature (5:3);
- knowing that all we endure develops character, which strengthens our confidence in our salvation (5:4);
- knowing how dearly God loves us, simply because He's given us His own spirit (5:5);
- being called "friends of God" (5:10–11).

All of these things flow out of God's unmerited favor, which has been seen as the very definition of His grace. It is also reflected in these words Paul wrote about the sacrificial death of Jesus Christ: "When we were utterly helpless, Christ came at just the right time and died for us sinners. Now, most people would not be willing to die for an upright person, though someone might perhaps be willing to die for a person who is especially good. But God showed his great love for us by sending Christ to die for us while we were still sinners" (Romans 5:6–8).

Romans tells us that when Christ did those things for us, he made us right with God, and that he will certainly save us from the condemnation that has come upon all humankind because of the sin of Adam.

Study Questions

○ What does it mean to you to be at peace with God?
○ What benefits have you personally received through your faith in Jesus Christ?

A New Life in Christ (Romans 6–7)

The sacrifice of Jesus Christ on the cross ensures that each and every person who puts their faith in him is forgiven, justified, and guaranteed a place in God's eternal kingdom. But a change in eternal destination isn't the only way our lives are altered. In addition, Paul tells us that we are given the freedom over the effects and bondage of sin.

point of interest

Romans 5:12–19 outlines what is known as the doctrine of original sin, which states that sin entered the human race through one man, Adam, and that all of his descendants (which are all of us) are born with that sin. This doctrine further states that through one man, Jesus, that sin is removed.

In Romans 1–5, Paul outlines how we can be saved, but in Romans 6–8 he tells us what that means to our lives in the here and now. This passage is, in other words, instructions on how to live the Christian life.

In these three chapters, Paul tells us that we have the potential to live holy lives because we know Christ (Romans 6) but that we find living those kinds of lives impossible through our own efforts because we still live in sinful bodies (Romans 7). The answer to this problem is spelled out in chapter 8, which tells us that we are empowered to live godly lives because God gives each of those who put their faith in Jesus Christ His Holy Spirit to aide and guide them.

Chapter 6 begins, "Well then, should we keep on sinning so that God can show us more and more of his wonderful grace? Of course not! Since we have died to sin, how can we continue to live in it? Or have you forgotten that when we were joined with Christ Jesus in baptism, we joined him in his death?" (Romans 6:1–3).

Paul then goes on to explain that those who have received Christ have, through baptism, symbolically and spiritually died with him, been buried with him, and been raised from the dead with him (Romans 6:4–11). When we died with him, our sinful natures died and were buried. What was raised was a new person, one who has had the power of sin broken in his or her life.

Because of that, we are no longer slaves to sin, as we once were. Instead, we are slaves to God, and that means we are free to live lives that lead to holiness and eternal life (Romans 6:20–23).

Study Questions

○ How does God's grace affect how you view sin in your personal life?
○ How has your faith in Christ changed how you view sin?

Power for Godly Living (Romans 8)

The eighth chapter of Romans begins with this powerful message: "So now there is no condemnation for those who belong to Christ Jesus. And because you belong to him, the power of the life-giving Spirit has freed you from the power of sin that leads to death" (verses 1–2).

This tells us that although we will never be completely free of sin while we live in these mortal bodies (see Romans 7), we are freed from the power of sin over our bodies and free from the control of indwelling sin—meaning sin within us. Paul tells his readers that the law—meaning the Law of Moses—could do nothing to release us from the power of sin, that it could only show us how sinful we really are. The power of the life-giving Spirit of God, on the other hand, has freed all who believe "from the power of sin that leads to death." Yes, even those who have put their faith in Jesus Christ are prone to sin at times, but they are never to be controlled by or dominated by the sin that once so cruelly ruled over them.

Romans 8 opens by telling us that there is no condemnation for those who belong to Christ Jesus, and it ends by telling us that there is nothing that can separate us from his love:

> And I am convinced that nothing can ever separate us from God's love. Neither death nor life, neither angels nor demons, neither our fears for today nor our worries about tomorrow—not even the powers of hell can separate us from God's love. No power in the sky above or in the earth below—indeed, nothing in all creation will ever be able to separate us from the love of God that is revealed in Christ Jesus our Lord. (Romans 8:38–39)

This is what the life in Christ is all about. We aren't condemned, but we are loved and freed to live a godly life. And no matter what happens—no matter what kind of opposition comes our way—nothing can remove us from God's love, which was demonstrated through Jesus Christ.

Study Questions

○ How does knowing that there is no condemnation for you affect your life for and in Jesus Christ?

○ What part do you think God's Holy Spirit plays in your personal daily walk with Jesus Christ?

CHAPTER 16

Ephesians: Engaging in Spiritual Warfare

Jesus came to earth as the Prince of Peace, but what he left behind after going back to his Father in heaven was a people he had called to go to war on his behalf—spiritual war that is. This chapter is a study of a section of the apostle Paul's letter to the Ephesian church in which he encourages them to go to spiritual war but to make sure they are fully equipped to fight before they go.

The Look of the Church (Ephesians 1–5)

The apostle Paul, writing to a group of Christians (also called "the church") in a city called Ephesus, wrote about the blessings they had received in Jesus Christ, how they were to be united in Christ, and the mission Christ had performed when he was on earth. He followed that by writing about the diversity of the church and what holiness within the church looked like.

One of the main themes of the book of Ephesians is that all Christians have been given "every spiritual blessing in the heavenly realms, because we belong to Christ" (Ephesians 1:6). One of those blessings is listed in Ephesians 6, and it's probably the best known in this particular epistle. It is in this section that Paul writes about what has come to be known as spiritual warfare.

Paul wanted the believers in Ephesus to understand that they have tremendous power in Christ—power they had hardly even begun to harness and use to their advantage—and that their victory in the spiritual realm was absolutely guaranteed, simply because Jesus had delivered them the victory. This section on spiritual warfare was Paul's final message of encouragement to the Ephesians, and it started like this:

A final word: Be strong in the Lord and in his mighty power. Put on all of God's armor so that you will be able to stand firm against all strategies of the devil. For we are not fighting against flesh-and-blood enemies, but against evil rulers and authorities of the unseen world, against mighty powers in this dark world, and against evil spirits in the heavenly places. (Ephesians 6:10–12)

Before telling the Ephesians what the weapons for spiritual warfare are, Paul tells them to put on the "full armor of God" so that they will be able to withstand evil and stand their ground (Ephesians 6:13).

Belt and Body Armor (Ephesians 6:10–14)

After telling the believers in Ephesus to put on every piece of their spiritual armor, and after telling them who the battle is really against, he goes on to tell them what those pieces are. He starts that section by saying, "Stand your ground, putting on the belt of truth and the body armor of God's righteousness" (Ephesians 6:14).

You don't have to be an expert on all things military to know that the belt and body armor are used to protect a warrior from a frontal assault—not to protect him from behind. That is why Paul starts this section by telling the Ephesians to stand their ground.

symbolism

> There are only a few things God cannot do, simply because they would violate His perfect nature. Among them is telling an untruth: "So God has given both his promise and his oath. These two things are unchangeable because it is impossible for God to lie" (Hebrews 6:18).

The belt of truth means God's truth. God speaks only truth. It is not in His nature to lie in any way. If He has said it in the pages of the Bible, you can bank on it!

On the other hand, the enemy and his cohorts are liars and deceivers. Of course, we would expect them to lie and deceive in order to win a war by keeping us from seeing the truth about ourselves, about the power we have in Christ, about the authority of God's written Word, and about God Himself. But Paul tells us that the truth of God will keep us from being blinded, deceived, or confused by the devil or by the worldly influences he attempts to use in spiritual war.

The breastplate of righteousness refers to God's righteousness. That's because God has declared all believers righteous—meaning right or justified before him—because of what Christ has done for us on the cross. (See Romans 5:18–19 to read about that wonderful truth.) That declaration makes our souls and spirits untouchable as far as Satan's attacks are concerned. Yes, he may harass us and try to keep us from doing the things God calls all believers to do, but as long as we are protected by God's body armor, he can never strike anything coming close to a mortal blow. Paul wanted to remind the Ephesian Christians that they possessed an impenetrable piece of armor that would protect them as they went on the offensive against the devil and against the ungodly world around them.

Study Questions
○ What are believers to do as they put on the belt of truth and the body armor of God's righteousness?
○ What is the purpose of the belt of truth and the body armor of God's righteousness?

Wearing the Shoes of Peace (Ephesians 6:15)

Paul's "full armor of God" includes weapons of defense and weapons of offense. And it also includes shoes. Paul wrote, "For shoes, put on the peace that comes from the Good News so that you will be fully prepared" (Ephesians 6:15).

point of interest

The word *peace* is one that has many meanings in the Bible. It's used in a spiritual, emotional, and sometimes even physical sense. All of these meanings are important to God, but it is still important you use a concordance and a Bible dictionary and that you pay close attention to how the word is used when you study it.

At a glance, shoes might seem a little out of place when you're talking about dressing for war. But think about it for a minute. What a soldier wears on his feet may be just as important as what he uses to cover his torso or head. If you don't believe that, try hiking ten miles in one day in a really uncomfortable pair of boots. Furthermore, if the Bible tells us to put on shoes or other footwear, that means God intends for us to be on the move.

And that would tell us that we are to be moving forward in an offensive against the devil, not sitting back just playing defense. It would also tell us that we are to walk on and in the peace we have as Christians because we have received the Good News of salvation through faith in Jesus Christ.

One application of that idea of peace is found in Paul's epistle to the Romans: "Therefore, since we have been made right in God's sight by faith, we have peace with God because of what Jesus Christ our Lord has done for us" (Romans 5:1). There are many other references to the word peace in the Bible, some of which refer to our peace with God, others that talk about the inner peace Christians are to have, and still others that talk about peace with one another.

Thinking of peace as one of the pieces of armor for spiritual war may seem a little backward, but it implies that being at peace with God means being in a war of offense against the ungodly elements of our world and, of course, against the devil.

Study Questions

○ What part do the shoes play in the full armor of God?
○ According to Ephesians 6:15, where does peace come from?

A Shield of Faith (Ephesians 6:16)

No first-century soldier in his right mind would have headed out for battle without his shield. Without that all-important piece of equipment, he would be easy prey for his well-armed counterpart, who was probably carrying spears, swords, and other projectile weapons.

factum

The apostle Peter also warned people to be on the alert for the devil, but he used a different metaphor: "Stay alert! Watch out for your great enemy, the devil. He prowls around like a roaring lion, looking for someone to devour" (1 Peter 5:8). While the wording was different, the idea was the same: Be alert and ready!

Likewise, no Christian would dare head out and attempt to do spiritual war without taking along the shield of faith. That is why Paul wrote, "In addition to all of these, hold up the shield of faith to stop the fiery arrows of the devil" (Ephesians 6:16).

Paul knew that while the devil was defeated by what Jesus did on the cross, he wasn't about to lie down and acknowledge his defeat without trying to take down as many people with him as possible. He is an angry adversary who still had some fight left in him, even if the outcome of the battle was settled.

The devil has an array of weapons he likes to use against believers: fear, doubt, lust, anxiety...the list goes on and on. But Paul says that God has given us a means to repel the devil's use of those weapons: faith. Having faith—meaning taking God at his word and believing He keeps His promises, and knowing that God Himself is bigger and more powerful than anything the devil can throw at us—renders the devil's weapons of offense against the believer absolutely worthless.

Study Questions

○ What specific spiritual weapons has the devil been trying to use against you?
○ In what areas of your spiritual life is God challenging you to have more faith today?

The Helmet of Salvation (Ephesians 6:17)

Very few soldiers can survive a direct shot to the head. Paul wanted his readers to understand that a great deal of the war they were engaged in would be taking place between their ears—in their minds. And he wanted them to understand that the devil wanted nothing more than to take their thinking away from the kind of thinking God wanted them engaged in.

Furthermore, Paul wanted the Ephesians to understand that they had a means of protection for their heads and their minds: "Put on salvation as your helmet" (Ephesians 6:17). That meant making sure that their minds were fixed on what God had done for them through Jesus Christ and on what it meant to them in their present lives.

But a helmet—be it one used in war, one used in sports, or one used on a construction site—won't do its owner a bit of good unless it is worn. So how do we put on the helmet of salvation?

It's by keeping in mind who you are in Christ—that you have been saved and are on your way to heaven, that you have been given the ability to serve God, and that you are given the authority over the devil and the ability to battle him and win. It's knowing that no matter what you have to endure in this life, God has your very best in mind and that He won't allow you to be tempted beyond your ability to withstand it and that He'll cause everything to work for your best. (See Romans 8:28.)

It is knowing with absolute certainty that in Christ, you are:

- a child of God (John 1:12)
- chosen and enabled to do good things on this earth for God (John 15:16)
- a prized possession of God (1 Corinthians 6:19–20)
- forgiven of all your sins (Colossians 1:13–14)
- able to do all things through the strength of Christ (Philippians 4:13)
- on your way to heaven (Philippians 3:20)

During times of spiritual attack, the devil loves to try to get inside our minds and tell us that we aren't some or any of the things listed above, but when we put on our helmet of salvation, he is unable to sway our minds away from who and what God says we are.

Study Questions

○ Look up the word *salvation* (and its variations) in the New Testament. What do these messages say to Christians about their salvation?

○ Use your concordance and find instances in the New Testament where it says, "You are." What does the New Testament say about who and what Christians really are in Christ?

God's Word: The Sword of the Spirit (Ephesians 6:17)

Earlier in this book, you read that one of the uses of the Word of God, the Bible, was as a weapon of spiritual warfare. That is why Paul referred to it as "the sword of the spirit."

God wants us to understand that the truths and promises contained in the Bible, when they are illuminated by the Holy Spirit—and when we are empowered to receive and apply them—are tremendous weapons in the spiritual battle that is going on this very day. Remember, it was Jesus himself who repelled the devil and his temptations by using the Scriptures correctly (the devil had twisted them in an attempt to tempt Jesus into something God hadn't sent him to do), answering each temptation with the words, "It is written...."

symbolism

The book of Psalms starts out saying this of those who hold to the Word of God: "Oh, the joys of those who do not follow the advice of the wicked, or stand around with sinners, or join in with mockers. But they delight in the law of the Lord, meditating on it day and night" (Psalm 1:1–2).

The power of God's Word to repel the attacks of the devil didn't end when Jesus went back to heaven. In fact, because God later sent His Holy Spirit to help remind us of the things Jesus did and taught and to shed some light on the Scriptures themselves, we have all the power we need to use the Bible the same way Jesus did. Here are some of the things the Bible says about the Scripture:

- that it will not return to God unfulfilled (Isaiah 55:10–11)
- that it is like a consuming fire and a hammer (Jeremiah 23:29)
- that it will never pass away (Matthew 24:35)
- that it is quick, powerful, and sharp (Hebrews 4:12)
- that it is "inspired by God" (2 Timothy 3:16)

Knowing all these things about the Bible, it's hard to imagine living the Christian life—including fighting spiritual battles against the devil—without reading, studying, and meditating on the Bible. In fact, it can't be done!

Paul is encouraging us to take up our swords by making the Bible a regular and consistent part of our daily lives. When we do that, we will be able to wield a weapon of offense against the devil.

Study Questions

○ In what ways have you personalized the Word of God and used it as a weapon against the devil?

○ Is there anything in your life today toward which you can use the Word of God in order to take victory? What is it and what step will you take next to claim that victory?

Don't Forget to Pray! (Ephesians 6:18–19)

One of the themes we find throughout the Bible is that nothing we attempt to do on God's behalf or to further His kingdom is going to go anywhere unless we have His blessing. And how do we get his blessing? Through prayer!

Paul finishes his spiritual call to arms for the Ephesian Christians by telling them, "And pray in the Spirit at all times and on every occasion. Stay alert and be persistent in your prayers for all believers everywhere" (Ephesians 6:18).

factum

Paul told us who to pray for when he wrote to the young pastor named Timothy: "I urge you, first of all, to pray for all people. Ask God to help them; intercede on their behalf, and give thanks for them" (1 Timothy 2:1). When you do spiritual warfare and pray for people, pray for everyone God brings to your mind.

Over the centuries, there has been much debate about what exactly it means to "pray in the Spirit," but there can be little question that Paul is reminding believers that if the weapon of choice against the devil is the

Word of God, then prayer should be the fasteners that hold the armor of God in place.

We are encouraged throughout the Bible to pray in all situations and for all things. We are encouraged to pray privately and publicly, in groups or alone. There are many models for prayer in the Bible, but the apostle Paul himself wrote this about prayer: "Don't worry about anything; instead, pray about everything. Tell God what you need, and thank him for all he has done" (Philippians 4:6).

Paul is telling us to pray according to the teaching of the Word of God and through the power of the Holy Spirit. When we are in the midst of spiritual warfare, we must pray for ourselves and for other believers who are in the midst of the very same battles we are fighting.

Paul wants believers to understand that the devil is our spiritual enemy and that we will only be successful in defeating him through using all the weapons at our disposal, including prayer.

So if you forget anything today—your lunch, your car keys, your driver's license—make sure you remember to pray.

Study Questions

○ What kinds of spiritual battles are you fighting now, and how are you praying about them?
○ What groups of people and which individuals do you believe God through his Holy Spirit is asking you to pray for today?

CHAPTER 17

Philippians: Real Joy in the Midst of Suffering and Adversity

One of the recurring themes you will find in the Bible—particularly in the New Testament letters from Paul, John, and the others—is that of the believer having joy in the midst of suffering and trials. This chapter is a study of Paul's letter to the Philippian church, focusing on his encouragements to live and think in terms of joy—even when times are tough, which they certainly were for the first-century church.

What the Bible Really Says about Suffering

Right now you may be scratching your head and asking yourself, "Does the Bible really say that I'm supposed to be happy because I'm suffering?" Well, that's not exactly what the Bible teaches.

God doesn't expect us to look at difficulties in our lives, such as the loss of jobs, broken relationships, sicknesses, injuries, and the like, and be happy that they are happening to us. In fact, he knows that there is absolutely no way we can be happy about those kinds of things. What God does want, however, is for us to be able to acknowledge that we are hurting and suffering but at the same time know that He is doing something good in us and for us through those times of suffering.

The apostle Paul knew a little bit about suffering. He went through arrests, beatings, imprisonments, shipwrecks, threats, and just about every other difficulty you can imagine. Even as he wrote his letter to the Philippian church, Paul sat in chains in a Roman prison, not knowing whether he would ever see freedom again or if he was going to live or die. Yet in the midst of all that, he was able to say from the heart, "always be full of joy in the Lord" (Philippians 4:4).

point of interest

In the short letter of Philippians, the apostle Paul uses the word *joy*—or variations—no fewer than eight times and the word *rejoice* no fewer than five. Obviously, Paul wants to convey the idea that our relationships with God through Jesus Christ give us many reasons to feel joy in our hearts.

It was the fact that Paul wrote these things while in stocks and chains in a Roman prison that makes his letter to the Philippians not just a beautiful letter to a church he loved but also a study in rejoicing in even the worst of times and situations.

Always be full of joy in the Lord. That is exactly what Paul himself was. In spite of his present circumstances, he writes a joy-filled love letter to his friends, his brothers, and his sisters in Philippi. For that reason, this book of the Bible is in itself an encouragement to all believers to live in the joy of the Lord no matter what circumstances they face. In his letter to the Philippians, Paul has many things to teach us about joy in the midst of adversity and suffering.

There Is Joy in Jesus Christ, Even When We Suffer

If you were to read a letter someone had written while being confined to a jail cell with only the bare essentials for survival, it's very likely that the tone of the letter would be very dark and dismal. That is exactly the situation Paul was in when he wrote the letter to the Philippians, but his tone is filled with joy and without even a hint of darkness, complaining, or suffering. That is because Paul had learned to have joy in Christ, no matter what his present circumstances.

In fact, as Paul sits in his prison cell, all he can think to say about his situation is that it is benefiting others by bringing them the message of salvation and by emboldening those who are already Christians: "And I want you to know, my dear brothers and sisters, that everything that has happened to me here has helped to spread the Good News. For everyone here, including the whole palace guard, knows that I am in chains because of Christ. And because of my imprisonment, most of the believers here have gained confidence and boldly speak God's message without fear" (Philippians 1:12–14).

factum

The apostle Paul, along with his co-missionary Silas, founded the Philippian church during his second missionary journey (Acts 16:12–40). Their first convert was a woman named Lydia and her family, followed by a jailer in Philippi (who heard the message of Christ while guarding Paul and Silas) and his family.

This is far more than optimistic thinking. It's a man who seems to take no thought of his suffering other than in what it can do for the good of the kingdom of God. It is a man who, humanly speaking, had every reason to complain and feel sorry for himself but who could do nothing but thank God that his imprisonment had helped further his own missionary work.

As you read through the first chapter of Philippians, ask yourself if you could be as positive and filled with joy as Paul obviously was if you were going through the kind of suffering he was going through.

Study Questions

O How specifically does Paul describe his feelings for the believers in Philippi?

O Who did Paul say heard the message of Christ through his imprisonment?

Joy in Our Relationship with Christ (Philippians 2)

A common misconception is that being a Christian means being protected from any physical harm, any kind of sickness or injury, or from persecution at the hands of those who don't like what Christianity stands for. Paul wants his readers—his friends in Philippi—to know that this just isn't the case. He's in what any right thinking person would consider a negative situation, and yet he constantly and repeatedly speaks positive words, words that convey his joy.

In the first chapter of Paul's letter to the Philippians, we read that there is joy not just in knowing Christ but also in suffering for Christ. True Christian joy, which emanates from within the person who knows Jesus Christ as his or her Lord and Savior, will always triumph over even the worst suffering.

In the second chapter of this letter, Paul tells us that it is also the fact of our salvation in Christ that gives us joy, even in the worst of times. This means that no matter what happens to us, we can rest assured that we have been welcomed in as one of God's own children and that we have been marked among those who will spend eternity with Him in heaven.

The second chapter of this letter starts with Paul asking three rhetorical questions: "Is there any encouragement from belonging to Christ? Any comfort from his love? Any fellowship together in the Spirit? Are your hearts tender and compassionate?" (Philippians 2:1)

Paul wants his readers to see that the obvious answers to all three are a resounding "Yes!" But he goes on in verses 2–5 to show the Philippians how that inner joy should show itself both within the church and to the outside world.

Study Questions

○ According to Philippians 2:1, what do we as believers receive from Christ, in good times and bad alike?

○ Read Philippians 2:2–5. What should be the outward, visible effects of a believer's joy in his or her salvation?

Joy in Being Made Truly Righteous Before God (Philippians 3:1–11)

When you're sitting in a prison in chains, not sure if you'll ever again see the light of day, you do a lot of reflecting about your life—where you've been, the things you've done, and what those things mean to you now. Paul writes to the Philippian church about those things:

> Yes, everything else is worthless when compared with the infinite value of knowing Christ Jesus my Lord. For his sake I have discarded everything else, counting it all as garbage, so that I could gain Christ and become one with him. I no longer count on my own righteousness through obeying the law; rather, I become righteous through faith in Christ. For God's way of making us right with himself depends on faith. (Philippians 3:8–9)

Paul lists the "everything else" in verses 4–7, in which the apostle writes of his earthly pedigree and lists his credentials as a religious leader. Paul explains that he had followed all the Jewish laws to the letter, that he was from the "right" family, and that he had even been educated as a Pharisee, the Jewish religious leaders who were known for their zealous and strict obedience to the Law of Moses and other legal traditions.

point of interest

In the short letter of Philippians, the apostle Paul uses the word *joy*—or variations—no fewer than eight times and the word *rejoice* no fewer than five. Obviously, Paul wants to convey the idea that our relationships with God through Jesus Christ give us many reasons to feel joy in our hearts.

Those things, he said, could have given him reason to boast in his own accomplishments and credentials. But he also wanted the Philippian Christians to understand that as far as he was concerned, those things meant nothing to him now. He had renounced his own pedigree and credentials—as far as their having anything to do with his righteousness before God—and had placed his trust completely in the work of Jesus Christ.

Paul took great joy in knowing that he belonged to Jesus Christ and that no matter what happened to him, his ultimate destination in heaven was sealed forever. But not only that, he took deep joy and great encouragement in the fact that his own suffering helped him identify with the sufferings of Jesus Christ, who had died on a cross of wood for him and who was raised from the dead (Philippians 3:10–11).

Study Questions

○ According to Philippians 3:8–9, what are the results of Paul's laying aside his own credentials as a Jewish religious leader and committing himself in every way to Jesus Christ?
○ Reread Philippians 3:10–11. In what event should all believers draw encouragement and joy, especially in times of adversity and suffering?

Joy at Looking to Future Perfection in Christ (Philippians 3:12–16)

When a man is imprisoned and not sure if he'll ever be released alive, he's not prone to think or talk a lot about the future—unless it's to wonder if he has one. But Paul, in the midst of the suffering and persecution he's going through in that Roman prison, takes a forward-looking approach to his faith:

> *I don't mean to say that I have already achieved these things or that I have already reached perfection. But I press on to possess that perfection for which Christ Jesus first possessed me. No, dear brothers and sisters, I have not achieved it, but I focus on this one thing: Forgetting the past and looking forward to what lies ahead, I press on to reach the end of the race and receive the heavenly prize for which God, through Christ Jesus, is calling us. (Philippians 3:12)*

Essentially, Paul is saying that he knows that God has a plan for him to reach spiritual maturity, which was what He had called Paul to in the first place. And Paul speaks as if finishing that race is a certainty. Paul wants his readers to understand that what lay behind them is nothing compared with what is ahead, and that is the heavenly prize God has called each believer to receive at the end of the race He has for each of us to run.

symbolism

Focusing on the future God has for us is a recurring theme in the Bible, and it's the subject of one of the best-known and most beloved Old Testament verses: "'For I know the plans I have for you,' says the Lord. '"They are plans for good and not for disaster, to give you a future and a hope'" (Jeremiah 29:11).

For that reason, the apostle stands as an example to us modern-day Bible readers of looking forward to what is ahead, not looking back longingly at better days or regretfully at what used to be. This passage shows us that Christianity is very much a religion of looking forward and not backward. God calls each of us to keep our eyes focused ahead and not behind as we press on.

- ○ What kinds of things in the past do you believe God wants believers to put behind them as they "press on to reach the end of the race and receive the heavenly prize"?
- ○ Why do you think Paul strongly implies that it's not a good idea to focus on the past but a great idea to focus on the future?

Joy in God's Provision (Philippians 4:1–7)

"Always be full of joy in the Lord," Paul tells the Philippians. He then punctuates that command by writing, " I say it again—rejoice!" (Philippians 4:4).

In times of suffering, adversity, or need, it's difficult for us humans to allow ourselves to feel much of anything good, let alone feel joyful. But Paul isn't just telling his readers to feel joy in the midst of suffering, adversity, and need, he's doing it in writing for them!

Paul wrote: "Don't worry about anything; instead, pray about everything. Tell God what you need, and thank him for all he has done. Then you will experience God's peace, which exceeds anything we can understand. His peace will guard your hearts and minds as you live in Christ Jesus" (Philippians 4:6–7).

factum

Jesus was teaching something very similar to what Paul is saying in this passage, "When you pray, don't babble on and on as people of other religions do. They think their prayers are answered merely by repeating their words again and again. Don't be like them, for your Father knows exactly what you need even before you ask him" (Matthew 6:7–8).

This sounds like a simple formula, and in some ways it is. Paul is telling his readers that when they are in a tough spot or in a time of need, just do the following:

1. Stop worrying.
2. Pray and tell God what you need.
3. Thank God for what He's already done and for what He's going to do.
4. Rest in the peace of God, which is itself beyond human understanding.

That sounds like a tall order for a lot of believers, especially those who are going through difficult times. It's hard not to worry when you or a loved one is sick and you don't know what's going to happen next. It's hard sometimes to tell God what you need, especially when you may not know specifically what kind of difficulty you are looking at. It's hard to be thankful when things aren't going well. And it's hardest of all to rest in the peace of God when life is anything but peaceful.

But Paul tells us it can be done, and he tells us that there is something of a supernatural intervention on the part of God himself when we simply take the steps laid out for us in Philippians 4:6–7. Again, this is all coming from a man who knew all too well the need for inner peace in the face of trials and tribulations. So if you're looking for someone with some credibility when it comes to such things, look at the apostle Paul, who in all things, no matter how difficult or insurmountable they may have seemed, knew to look to his heavenly Father who always provided what Paul needed when he needed it.

Study Questions

○ Can you think of times when God provided—maybe even miraculously—for something you needed but didn't see any way of getting? How did you respond?

○ What seemingly impossible trial or test are you facing right now? How are you responding to it?

Joy in Focusing on the Right Things (Philippians 4:8–9)

Paul finished his encouragements to the Philippian church by telling them: "And now, dear brothers and sisters, one final thing. Fix your thoughts on what is true, and honorable, and right, and pure, and lovely, and admirable.

Think about things that are excellent and worthy of praise. Keep putting into practice all you learned and received from me—everything you heard from me and saw me doing. Then the God of peace will be with you" (Philippians 4:8–9).

point of interest

Paul had plenty of opportunity in Philippi to put what he taught into practice. It was shortly after he led a woman named Lydia to Christ that he and his companion, Silas, were arrested, severely beaten, bound in stocks and chains, and thrown in prison. Despite everything, Paul and Silas sang songs of praise in prison (Acts 16:16–40).

This was many centuries before anyone talked about anything like the power of positive thinking, but Paul pointed out the importance of right thinking. He encouraged the Philippians to put their focus on what is:

- true and not on what is false
- honorable and not on what is dishonorable
- right and not on what is clearly wrong
- pure and not on what is polluted
- lovely and not on what is horrible
- admirable and not on what is unworthy

Today, the question remains: How do we know what are good things to think on? Simply put, those are the things that God Himself thinks on, and we can find that out by reading, studying, and memorizing the Bible. It is there that we find out what God thinks about every subject important to our faith—where we learn truth, where we learn right from wrong, where we see what is honorable, where God shows us what is pure, lovely, and admirable.

Paul learned that in the midst of suffering, it's important to make sure that you fix your thoughts on the things that will fill your mind and heart with joy—even when your present situation might make joyful thinking humanly difficult or even impossible. That is his final word to the Philippians, and it's his message of hope and joy in Jesus Christ that has withstood 2,000 years of time.

Study Questions

O What do you tend to think of when life seems difficult or even unfair? What do you think God wants you to think of?

O Reread Philippians 4:8–9. What specific things should you think on at all times, particularly difficult times?

CHAPTER 18

Hebrews: The "Betterness" of Jesus

The writer of the epistle to the Hebrews (it isn't certain who wrote it and exactly when) was writing to Jewish people who had become Christians but who later wanted to reverse course in order to escape persecution by their Jewish brothers and sisters. The theme of the book of Hebrews is the superiority of Jesus Christ over the Jewish system of priesthood, laws, and sacrifices. Jesus, the writer tells them, is better than angels, better than Moses, better than the established Jewish priesthood, better than the Law of Moses.

Encouragement Toward Maturity

Hebrews paints a word picture of Jesus that is specially designed for the Jewish people, and it gives all readers an overview of who Jesus really is—to them and to other believers who would come behind them. The writer's goal is to keep these Jewish Christians on course toward spiritual maturity. As he wrote, "So let us stop going over the basic teachings about Christ again and again. Let us go on instead and become mature in our understanding. Surely we don't need to start again with the fundamental importance of repenting from evil deeds and placing our faith in God" (Hebrews 6:1). That he does by explaining to them—in unmistakably Jewish terms—who Jesus was, is, and will always be and how he was better than anything or anyone who had come before him or would come after him.

Jesus: Better Than the Angels and Other Created Beings (Hebrews 1:5–14)

Jesus lived and ministered in a time when the people of Palestine had what can only be seen as an unhealthy and unbalanced view of angels. The believers of that time had some understanding of the role that angels played in bringing about the plans of God, and that was a good thing. But there were many people—especially in the Jewish community—whose ideas about angels had become superstitious or even idolatrous. They had come to believe that angels were mediators between God and man, the position Jesus held himself.

This gave the writer of Hebrews the opportunity to set the people straight about what angels really were. In doing that, he set Jesus apart as being far above any created thing—including the angels and the humans to whom angels would be subject.

The writer spells out that the relationship between God the Father and His Son was infinitely superior than the relationship between God and the angels simply because it was a father-son relationship and not a creator-created relationship: "For God never said to any angel what he said to Jesus: 'You are my Son. Today I have become your Father.' God also said, 'I will be his Father, and he will be my Son.' And when he brought his firstborn Son into the world, God said, 'Let all of God's angels worship him'" (Hebrews 1:5–6)

Indeed, there were several examples in the Gospels of angels doing what they had been created to do: minister to Jesus and to those he loved. In fact, it was an angel who first announced the coming birth of Christ (Luke 1:26–38) and an angel who announced his resurrection from the dead (Luke 24:1–7).

discussion question

Who was the writer of the epistle to the Hebrews?
It is believed that the apostle Paul wrote the book of Hebrews, but that is not certain. Other candidates are Barnabas (a leader in the early church), Luke (the writer of the Gospel of Luke and Acts of the Apostles), Apollos (a believer mentioned in Acts and in the epistles of Paul), and several others.

Angels are wonderful creations of God, the writer of Hebrews tells us, but they are just that—creations. And God doesn't call us to worship what He has created, He has called us to and allowed us the privilege of worshipping Him by worshipping His Son.

Study Questions
- What does Hebrews 1:5–14 tell us is the true place of angels in God's kingdom?
- According to Hebrews 2:9, what place did Jesus hold in comparison with the angels at his death on the cross?

Jesus: Better Than Moses (Hebrews 3:1–6)

In first-century Jewish culture, there were a few men of the past who qualified as heroes of the culture and of the faith. One of those men was Moses, who answered—although somewhat reluctantly at first—God's call to lead the people of Israel out of captivity in Egypt. The first-century Jews had a very high opinion of Moses, and rightly so. And while the writer of Hebrews doesn't downplay the faithfulness or faith of Moses or the importance of what he did, he wrote that "Jesus deserves far more glory than Moses, just as a person who builds a house deserves more praise than the house itself. For every house has a builder, but the one who built everything is God" (Hebrews 3:3–4).

factum

Jesus himself didn't downplay the importance of Moses's part in God's plan of redemption. In his famed Sermon on the Mount, Jesus said, "Don't misunderstand why I have come. I did not come to abolish the law of Moses or the writings of the prophets. No, I came to accomplish their purpose" (Matthew 5:17).

In other words, Moses, just like every other human being, was created by God, the same God Jesus represented perfectly in everything he did. But still, Moses played his part in the plan to bring salvation to the world: "Moses was certainly faithful in God's house as a servant. His work was an illustration of the truths God would reveal later. But Christ, as the Son, is in charge of God's entire house. And we are God's house, if we keep our courage and remain confident in our hope in Christ" (Hebrews 3:5–7).

Moses was called to fulfill his part in God's plan of redemption for all of humankind, and he played that part. While he wasn't perfect in everything he did and said—as Jesus was—he faithfully and obediently did as God had called him to do.

Jesus, on the other hand, was perfect in everything he said and did—perfect in his obedience to God and in his service to humankind. He was everything that Moses and other servants of God had been before him as they prepared the world for his arrival. But he was far, far more.

While Moses was a great leader of the Jewish people and a man who is to be revered, he was only a foreshadowing of what Jesus Christ would be. Jesus is our Savior, the One sent of God to seek out and save the lost (Luke 19:10). He is God in the flesh, and as such he is worthy of infinitely higher praise and reverence than Moses.

○ How did the writer of Hebrews describe Moses?

○ How did the writer of Hebrews compare and contrast Moses and Jesus?

A Better Rest in Jesus Christ (Hebrews 3:7–4:11)

The first eleven verses of Hebrews 4 are about a new and better kind of rest that God gives those who believe Him, who take Him at his word, and who have the kind of faith it takes to enjoy God's salvation. This passage is a continuation of the latter parts of Hebrews 3, which recount the tragedy of the deaths of untold thousands of Israelites in the desert outside the Promised Land of Canaan. They died there, the writer tells us, because they "rebelled against God, even though they heard his voice" (Hebrews 3:16). In this passage, the Hebrew believers are warned and encouraged to continue on in their faith so that they could enter into a much better rest even than the one the people of Israel missed out on because of their unbelief and rebellion. (See Chapter 6.)

point of interest

When the writer of Hebrews wrote, "So in my anger I took an oath: 'They will never enter my place of rest,'" he was quoting Psalm 95:11, which refers to the generation of Israelites who, because of their unbelief and rebellion, died in the wilderness without seeing the Promised Land.

Hebrews 4:1–2 says, "God's promise of entering his rest still stands, so we ought to tremble with fear that some of you might fail to experience it. For this good news—that God has prepared this rest—has been announced to us just as it was to them. But it did them no good because they didn't share the faith of those who listened to God." But there is one condition for entering into this rest, the better rest in Jesus Christ: We have to believe! (Hebrews 4:3).

The writer of Hebrews tells us, "So there is a special rest still waiting for the people of God. For all who have entered into God's rest have rested from their labors, just as God did after creating the world" (Hebrews 4:9–10). This is a different rest, a better rest, because it is an everlasting rest. It is the rest Jesus gives us that allows us to cease from all work when it comes to earning our salvation, and it is the rest we have in knowing that we don't need to rely on our own strength to live the lives God wants us to live.

Study Questions

○ What does the writer of Hebrews tell us is God's reaction to unbelief?
○ What is the condition we must meet before we can enter into and enjoy God's perfect rest?

Jesus: A Better High Priest (Hebrews 4:14–5:11)

Jesus is referred to in the Bible by dozens of names, one of which appears late in the fourteenth chapter of Hebrews: "So then, since we have a great High Priest who has entered heaven, Jesus the Son of God, let us hold firmly to what we believe" (Hebrews 4:14). In speaking of Jesus as a newer, better high priest, the writer of Hebrews is speaking the language of the Jews. The Jewish people understood that they just couldn't walk into the tabernacle or temple and approach God. They needed to approach through the high priest, who was in their system of worship the only one through whom they could approach God and offer their prayers and offerings.

That all changed with this new high priesthood of Jesus Christ, the one Hebrews tells us is vastly superior to the old one, first, because he was like us in all ways except that he never sinned, and also because he gives us direct access to God: "This High Priest of ours understands our weaknesses, for he faced all of the same testings we do, yet he did not sin. So let us come boldly to the throne of our gracious God. There we will receive his mercy, and we will find grace to help us when we need it most" (Hebrews 4:15–16).

symbolism

The apostle Peter pointed out that believers are to join Jesus as priests in this life and to this world: "You are royal priests, a holy nation, God's very own possession. As a result, you can show others the goodness of God, for he called you out of the darkness into his wonderful light" (1 Peter 2:9).

Hebrews 5 starts where chapter 4 left off, explaining to the reader the duties and qualifications of the high priesthood. It tells us that the office of high priest wasn't one someone could have simply because he wanted it. Rather, it was an office to which God Himself had to call someone—just as He called and appointed Jesus to it (Hebrews 5:1–5).

But there is more to the superiority of Jesus' priesthood. Hebrews tells us: "And in another passage God said to him, 'You are a priest forever in the order of Melchizedek'" (Hebrews 5:6).

By that, God meant that Jesus wasn't just priesthood but royal priesthood. Melchizedek was the king-priest mentioned in Genesis 14:18–20, and he came long before the Jewish priesthood had been established. His priesthood was considered timeless—without beginning and without end. Hebrews ends this section this way:

While Jesus was here on earth, he offered prayers and pleadings, with a loud cry and tears, to the one who could rescue him from death. And God heard his prayers because of his deep reverence for God. Even though Jesus was God's Son, he learned obedience from the things he suffered. In this way, God qualified him as a perfect High Priest, and he became the source of eternal salvation for all those who obey him. (Hebrews 5:7–9)

In other words, this passage is saying that Jesus was a perfect example in all he did, including how to pray and how to live a life of perfect obedience to God. That is why he is a high priest who is not only better than any who came before him, but he is a perfect high priest.

○ What, according to Hebrews 5:1–3, were the duties of the high priest and how do they compare with what Jesus does for us today?

○ How should knowing Jesus as our high priest change how we approach God?

Jesus: The Bringer of a New—and Better—Covenant (Hebrews 8:1–9:10)

We've already seen that Jesus brought with him a priesthood that was better than the one established centuries before him. But he also brought with him—and purchased through his sacrificial death on the cross—what the epistle to the Hebrews referred to as a "new covenant" (Hebrews 8:8), meaning a new promise or agreement with his people.

point of interest

Jesus spoke of the "new" aspect of worship that the writer of Hebrews seems to refer to when he said, "But the time is coming—indeed it's here now—when true worshipers will worship the Father in spirit and in truth. The Father is looking for those who will worship him that way" (John 4:23).

The writer of Hebrews wrote of those who worshipped under the old covenant:

They serve in a system of worship that is only a copy, a shadow of the real one in heaven. For when Moses was getting ready to build the Tabernacle, God gave him this warning: "Be sure that you make everything according to the pattern I have shown you here on the mountain." But now Jesus, our High Priest, has been given a ministry that is far superior to the old priesthood, for he is the one who mediates for us a far better covenant with God, based on better promises. (Hebrews 8:5–6)

This tells us that Jesus brought us something new when it comes to worshipping God, something the writer stated very directly when he wrote: "When God speaks of a 'new' covenant, it means he has made the first one obsolete. It is now out of date and will soon disappear" (Hebrews 8:13).

And what was it that God made obsolete? What is now out of date and will soon disappear? The writer of Hebrews goes on to explain that it was the complex system of worship—the places and ways people could worship God—that was a part of the Law of Moses.

This new covenant means that no longer would God pay attention to where people worshipped Him or whether they followed rigid rules of worship. Now He would focus on the hearts of those who came to Him and would write His laws and His ways in their hearts and not on tablets. This would be a covenant based not on laws and regulations but on a personal one-on-one relationship with a God who extended His grace to the people of Israel—the Hebrews—and the rest of the world.

Study Questions

○ What do you think studying and understanding this new covenant will do to your relationship with Jesus Christ?

○ How would you describe your Christian faith when it comes to the personal relationship with God through Jesus Christ?

Jesus, a Better—Perfect—Sin Sacrifice (Hebrews 9:11–10:18)

The target audience of this epistle—Jewish converts to Christianity—were no doubt aware of the system of animal and grain sacrifices set up during the time of Moses in order to deal, temporarily anyway, with sin. But the writer of Hebrews pointed out that the sacrificial system was temporary and nothing more than a precursor to what Jesus would do on the cross: "The old system under the law of Moses was only a shadow, a dim preview of the good things to come, not the good things themselves" (Hebrews 10:1).

The tenth chapter of Hebrews points out that the sacrifice of Jesus Christ was superior to the old system of animal and grain sacrifices in the following ways:

- Under the old system, the sacrifices were done yearly, but Christ's was done once and for all (verse 1–3).
- Under the old system, the sacrifices made someone "clean" enough to be able to worship, but the sacrifice of Christ completely cleanses us from all sin and guilt (verse 2–3).
- The blood of animals can't completely take away sins, but the sacrifice of Christ has done just that (verse 3–6).
- Under the old system, there were several different sacrifices for different occasions, but Christ willingly offered himself so that we could be made holy and pure (verses 11–12).
- Christ's sacrifice negates any need for further sacrifices (verse 18).

The sacrifice of Jesus Christ is infinitely superior to those spelled out under the Law of Moses. That is because what Jesus did on the cross provided not just forgiveness of sin but also power against it. Jesus destroyed once and for all the works of the devil, and he has made those who would put their faith in him right before God.

Study Questions

- How do you personally approach the Law of Moses as it is written in the Old Testament?
- What is your response to knowing that the work of Jesus on the cross completed what was started in the Law of Moses?

CHAPTER 19

First Peter: The Look of the Christian Life

The apostle Peter, the man who spent three-plus years traveling with Jesus during his earthly ministry and the man Jesus charged with taking the gospel message of salvation to the Jewish world, wrote his first epistle to the Christians in the Black Sea coastal area. These believers were facing intense suffering and persecution over their faith, and Peter wants them to know that they should not be surprised or alarmed because of the opposition that was coming their way.

The Importance of Gladness

Peter's first epistle—one of two bearing his name—is amazingly practical in how it sets forth guidelines and offers wisdom for living the Christian life in the midst of a corrupt, evil, and sometimes violent world. Peter tells these believers:

> *So be truly glad. There is wonderful joy ahead, even though you have to endure many trials for a little while. These trials will show that your faith is genuine. It is being tested as fire tests and purifies gold—though your faith is far more precious than mere gold. So when your faith remains strong through many trials, it will bring you much praise and glory and honor on the day when Jesus Christ is revealed to the whole world. (1 Peter 1:6–7)*

As these Christians go through the faith-testing trials, Peter wants them to know about the joy that is ahead and the life Jesus Christ has for them right now. That is the focus of this chapter, which is a study of the principles found in the book of 1 Peter.

Growing in the Faith (1 Peter 2:1–11)

One of the most daunting questions a new Christian faces is how to properly live now that he or she has left behind a life in the world and in the flesh and joined God's eternal family through faith in Jesus Christ. In his first epistle, Peter explains how Christians are to live: "So get rid of all evil behavior. Be done with all deceit, hypocrisy, jealousy, and all unkind speech. Like new-born babies, you must crave pure spiritual milk so that you will grow into a full experience of salvation. Cry out for this nourishment, now that you have had a taste of the Lord's kindness" (1 Peter 2:1–3).

Another way of looking at this passage is that believers are to abandon all those things we know are sinful—dishonesty, jealousy, unkindness, and the like—and replace them with the things that help us to grow to maturity. That is what Peter meant when he wrote, "crave spiritual milk so that you will grow into a full experience of salvation."

Peter starts with the assumption that when we are first saved through our faith in Jesus Christ, we are immature believers—newborn babies who have nothing to offer God or anyone else. If you've ever been around an infant, you know that it is completely incapable of doing anything for itself. A little girl or boy is completely dependant on others to be fed, clothed, and changed. You also know that there is nothing that infant craves more than its own mother's milk.

If you were to try to feed a newborn infant steak and potatoes, then the poor little thing would likely starve within a few days. That's because that sort of food isn't appropriate for a baby; babies aren't meant to eat those kinds of foods.

As Christians, especially new Christians, God doesn't intend for us to be feeding on our old ways of life, on behavior and thought patterns we know to be unhealthy for our spiritual lives. Instead, we are to abandon all those things and make sure that we nourish ourselves with the milk of God's Word, which can be found in the pages of the Bible.

Study Questions

○ What kinds of behaviors does Peter tell believers to rid their lives of?
○ What does Peter tell us is necessary to grow into the "full experience of salvation?"

A Life Worthy of a Priest (1 Peter 2:4–11)

If someone were to ask you how a priest lives, how would you answer? Most of us think of priests as people who hang around the local parish, who can't marry, who listen to people confessing their sins all day long, and who wear funny-looking collars.

But there is more to being a priest than doing all those things. Being a priest—or any other kind of minister for that matter—means living under a higher standard of conduct, making sure that everything said and done properly reflects the position entrusted to the person. The very same thing applies to those who have been welcomed into God's eternal family through their faith in Jesus Christ.

Peter points out in this passage that there will be people who "stumble" because they don't obey God's Word, and the consequences are that they meet a fate other than the one reserved for those who have put their faith in Jesus Christ (1 Peter 2:8). True believers, on the other hand, are different because: "you are a chosen people. You are royal priests, a holy nation, God's very own possession. As a result, you can show others the goodness of God, for he called you out of the darkness into his wonderful light. Once you had no identity as a people; now you are God's people. Once you received no mercy; now you have received God's mercy." (1 Peter 2: 9–10).

symbolism

Peter's teaching on the priesthood of the individual believer was one of the assertions made by Martin Luther and other reformers during a sixteenth-century event in the history of Christianity known as the Protestant Reformation. Luther believed that the Catholic Church at the time was going against this teaching by asserting so much control over individuals.

As God's chosen people—as those who are royal priests and members of a holy nation—God has called us all to live in this world as "temporary residents and foreigners" (1 Peter 2:11). That means we are to "keep away from worldly desires that wage war against your very souls. Be careful to live properly among your unbelieving neighbors. Then even if they accuse you of doing wrong, they will see your honorable behavior, and they will give honor to God when he judges the world" (1 Peter 2:11–12).

In other words, since God has taken us as His own possession and called us "royal priests," we are to live lives befitting those God has called to such a high spiritual position. We are to live lives that people around us will see as different, as above reproach. And when we do that, others will see Jesus Christ in us.

Study Questions

O Who does Peter tell us we are in relation to God because of the work of Jesus Christ?

O What does Peter say God has called believers into?

Properly Responding to Authority (1 Peter 2:13–17, 3:1–7)

Peter wrote that good Christian behavior included submission to and respect for those in authority over us, including those in civil positions. Peter used the example of kings and his officials, but the modern-day application of this principle would include local, state, and federal authorities as well as those we've put ourselves under in the spiritual sense.

The reason for doing that is simple: "It is God's will that your honorable lives should silence those ignorant people who make foolish accusations against you. For you are free, yet you are God's slaves, so don't use your freedom as an excuse to do evil. Respect everyone, and love your Christian brothers and sisters. Fear God, and respect the king" (1 Peter 2:15–17).

factum

> The apostle Paul also had something to say about how husbands and wives were to relate to one another. In Ephesians 5:21, Paul indicates that wives and husbands are to submit to one another "out of reverence for Christ." He later instructs wives to submit to their husbands and husbands to love their wives (Ephesians 5:22–28).

Peter also directed wives to submit to the authority of their husbands because in doing so they may through their examples win over an unbelieving spouse to the faith (1 Peter 3:1). He also encouraged them not to be concerned about their outward appearance—fancy hairstyles, expensive jewelry, beautiful clothes, and the like—but to "clothe yourselves instead with the beauty that comes from within, the unfading beauty of a gentle and quiet spirit, which is so precious to God" (1 Peter 3:4).

Peter also commanded husbands to honor their wives and to treat them with understanding and respect. He told them, "She may be weaker than you are, but she is your equal partner in God's gift of new life. Treat her as you should so your prayers will not be hindered" (1 Peter 3:7).

While this might sound older than old school by today's standards, it was quite radical for that time and in that culture. Back then, wives were considered just barely above personal property and servants.

Study Questions

○ How does the preceding passage apply to how believers are to respond to authority today?

○ How can this passage be applied in marriage today?

Patiently Endure Wrong Treatment (1 Peter 2:18–25)

One of the most amazing aspects of Jesus Christ going to the cross in order to pay for our sins is that he did it willingly and without complaint. As the prophet Isaiah said about the Messiah Jesus, "He was oppressed and treated harshly, yet he never said a word. He was led like a lamb to the slaughter. And as a sheep is silent before the shearers, he did not open his mouth" (Isaiah 53:7).

There are few things that demonstrate to the world the transformation Jesus Christ has done in believers more than their following his example of patiently enduring being wronged and treated unjustly. When Christians do that, people clearly see that there is something different about them.

point of interest

Peter's teaching in this passage is consistent with that of Jesus: "You have heard the law that says the punishment must match the injury: 'An eye for an eye, and a tooth for a tooth.' But I say, do not resist an evil person! If someone slaps you on the right cheek, offer the other cheek also" (Matthew 5:38–39).

That is the more modern application of Peter's encouragement to slaves of that time: "You who are slaves must accept the authority of your masters with all respect. Do what they tell you—not only if they are kind and reasonable, but even if they are cruel. For God is pleased with you when you do what you know is right and patiently endure unfair treatment" (1 Peter 2:18–19).

Today, slavery is seen as a dark part of the Western world's past, but we know that there was a time when humans were allowed to own other humans and that those precious human souls who were held as slaves were sometimes subjected to abominable treatment. Apparently, the same thing was true in Peter's day.

While none of us in our culture today are held as slaves, it is still possible that we may have to sometimes endure cruel mistreatment at the hands of people God has put in our lives. Sometimes that mistreatment is in the form of cruel words or actual wrongs committed. Either way, Peter tells us that as believers we are to "patiently endure unfair treatment."

God doesn't credit us for being punished for doing wrong, but if we patiently endure mistreatment when we are innocent of any wrong, then God is pleased with us. Why? Because in doing so, we follow Jesus's example and reflect him to the world around us (2:20–21).

Study Questions

○ How do you respond when people speak wrongly about you or treat you in a way you think is unfair?

○ How do you think you are to respond when people don't treat you fairly or justly?

Living for God So That Others Will See (1 Peter 4:1–6)

Jesus told his followers, "Let your good deeds shine out for all to see, so that everyone will praise your heavenly Father" (Matthew 5:16). And so began the New Testament theme of believers living lives that brought glory to God and caused nonbelievers to see the differences Jesus has made in our lives.

One of the subthemes in Peter's first epistle was that of allowing people in the world to hear in our words and see in our attitudes and actions the transformation Jesus Christ has done within us. And one of those differences is fairly obvious for all to see: "You won't spend the rest of your lives chasing your own desires, but you will be anxious to do the will of God. You have had enough in the past of the evil things that godless people enjoy—their immorality and lust, their feasting and drunkenness and wild parties, and their terrible worship of idols" (1 Peter 4:2–3).

point of interest

The apostle Paul provided the church at Corinth a list of the sins and behaviors that people are to leave behind when they become Christians. He also warns that those who practice those things have "no share in the kingdom of God" (1 Corinthians 6:9–11).

Of course, Peter points out, some of our former friends will be surprised at the changes in our lives, and some may even insult or slander us. But he wants us to remember that each of us will have to face a God who will righteously judge everyone and call to account the things they have done.

God doesn't save people so that they can go on living as they once did. Being a part of God's eternal family means allowing Him to make changes in your thoughts as well as your deeds in this life. Some will notice and laugh, but others will see the changes in your life and be drawn to what God can also do in their own lives (1 Peter 4:4).

Study Questions

❍ What effect do you think your behavior and attitudes have on those who know you are a Christian?

❍ What attitudes or behaviors do you believe God wants you to give up so that you can glorify him in front of others?

Serving the Body of Christ (1 Peter 4:7–11)

Peter told his readers that the end of the world was coming soon, and for that reason they needed to be both "earnest and disciplined" in their prayer lives. But more important than that, he said they needed to show love for one another. Peter himself heard Jesus tell the disciples, "Your love for one another will prove to the world that you are my disciples" (John 13:35), and he wanted his readers to understand the importance of believers having deep love for one another, "for love covers a multitude of sins" (1 Peter 4:8). He even gave believers a practical way to demonstrate that love when he told them to cheerfully share their homes with those who needed a meal or a place to stay (1 Peter 4:9).

Peter also said that believers are to use the spiritual gifts God has given them in service of one another. Be it speaking, helping others, or whatever gifts we have, we are to use them with all the strength God gives us so that everything we do will bring glory to God through Jesus Christ (1 Peter 4:10–11).

Study Questions

○ Read 1 Corinthians 12. What are some of the abilities the Holy Spirit gives us so that we can serve the body of Christ more effectively?
○ What gifts do you believe God has given you to serve his kingdom and the body of Christ?

Glorifying God in Our Suffering (1 Peter 4:12–19)

Peter lived and served in a time when just being a Christian could subject you to unspeakably harsh treatment. Believers were routinely rounded up, imprisoned, tortured, and killed—all because they practiced a religion different from that of the Roman world.

Peter teaches the importance of glorifying God in our suffering—or to put it another way, suffering the right way. And what is the right way? The way Jesus himself suffered as those who persecuted and murdered him looked on. Peter wrote in 1 Peter 4:1: "So then, since Christ suffered physical pain, you must arm yourselves with the same attitude he had, and be ready to suffer, too."

Just hours before he was about to endure some of the most brutal physical punishment ever inflicted, Jesus told his disciples, "If the world hates you, remember that it hated me first....Do you remember what I told you? 'A slave is not greater than the master.' Since they persecuted me, naturally they will persecute you. And if they had listened to me, they would listen to you" (John 15:18, 20).

symbolism

Thriving and growing in our faith in the midst of suffering is one of the main themes, if not the main theme, of 1 Peter. The word *suffer*, or variations of it, is used no fewer than seventeen times in this epistle, while the word *trial* is used five times.

One thing those who have suffered for their faith can tell you is that persecution, opposition, and other kinds of suffering have a way of either killing you or making you stronger. That is partly why Peter, who was with Jesus when he gave the above warning, wrote, "Dear friends, don't be surprised at the fiery trials you are going through, as if something strange were happening to you. Instead, be very glad—for these trials make you partners with Christ in his suffering, so that you will have the wonderful joy of seeing his glory when it is revealed to all the world" (1 Peter 4:12–13).

We live in a world where most people can avoid any kind of suffering or discomfort. It's also a world in which even the most outspoken Christians have to endure little more than verbal abuse. But Peter, who lived in a place and time of incredible danger for Christians, encouraged his brothers and sisters in the faith of that time to:

- not be surprised at the "fiery trials" they were going through
- be glad about the suffering, because they make them partners with Jesus Christ in his suffering.
- know that suffering in a way that glorifies God gives them the privilege of seeing God's glory revealed to the world

In other words, when we suffer for Christ in any way, enduring it without complaining but with a sense of joy, peace, and faith, it is sure to get the world's attention and reflect positively on the faith you have and on the One in whom you have that faith.

factum

The first chapter of James gives an excellent overview of the purpose God has in our spiritual lives for trials and suffering. In that passage, James points out that suffering produces endurance and endurance produces strength of character (James 1:2–4).

In this passage, Peter does give his readers a small addendum to let them know that while there is no shame but only joy and reward for suffering for Christ, it is important to make sure we are suffering for the right reasons. He wrote, "If you suffer, however, it must not be for murder, stealing, making trouble, or prying into other people's affairs" (1 Peter 4:15).

This is in keeping with making sure that our lives continue to be a reflection of the Christ we serve. And Peter seems to indicate that if we suffer because of our own ungodly, unacceptable actions, then there is no reward in that—only the consequences of our own shameful behavior.

However, Peter tells us that there is no shame in suffering for being a Christian, so we can praise God for the privilege of being called by His name. And if we suffer in a way that pleases God, if we keep doing the right things, if we keep trusting in our Creator, He will never fail us—no matter what we have to endure (1 Peter 4:16–19).

Study Questions

○ How do you typically respond when you are criticized or chided for being a Christian? In light of Peter's teaching, how do you think you should respond?

○ What behaviors and thought patterns do you think cause you to suffer needlessly?

CHAPTER 20

First John: A Life of Love

Central to the message of the gospel of Jesus Christ is love. Jesus explained his presence on earth beginning with, "God so loved the world" and later left his disciples with the command that they "love one another." The message of the Bible is that God loved us so we are to love Him in return. Not only that, we are to love one another just as He has loved us—in a sacrificial, selfless way. That is the message of this chapter, which is a study of 1 John.

John's Central Message: Love

The apostle John, who spent three-plus years of his life following Jesus—watching him perform miracles, preach powerful sermons, and demonstrate love—was the writer of the gospel that bears his name and the three letters that appear late in the New Testament (First John, Second John, and Third John), as well as the book of Revelation. In his first letter—or epistle—John writes very caringly and lovingly about what the Christian life should look like, giving emphasis to the kind of love Jesus repeatedly taught about when he was on earth.

It was John who recorded these words of Jesus just prior to his arrest, trial, and crucifixion: "So now I am giving you a new commandment: Love each other. Just as I have loved you, you should love each other" (John 13:34). And it is in the apostle's first letter that we read of what that love looks like.

Jesus wanted his disciples to know that what they were about to embark on—taking the message he had preached to the world around them once he was gone—could only be done if they were bound together in the kind of love Jesus showed them every day. That is why John so strongly echoed in his first letter the teachings of Jesus when it came to love.

In 1 John, we read of our love for God and what that means, and we read how our love for him motivates, encourages, and empowers us to love one another. The book of John, then, is a love letter to believers throughout the centuries.

Why We Obey God's Commandments (1 John 2:4–6)

You can't have marriage—not a good one, anyway—without love. The very same thing is true when it comes to our love for God. If we love God, we will prove it because we obey His commandments. That is what John meant when he wrote, "If someone claims, 'I know God,' but doesn't obey God's commandments, that person is a liar and is not living in the truth. But those who obey God's word truly show how completely they love him. That is how we know we are living in him" (1 John 2:4–5). Love and obedience: You can't have one without the other!

symbolism

Jesus himself spoke of the keeping of God's commandments as proof of our love for him when he told his disciples, "If you love me, obey my commandments" (John 14:15). This tells us that our love for God and our obedience to God are inseparable. You truly can't have one without the other.

John goes on to tell his readers that they are to live out their lives of love for God in the very same way Jesus did (1 John 2:6). Jesus was perfectly obedient to God, and that was because he loved God and communed with God intimately. Everything Jesus said and did were perfect reflections of a deep and abiding love for his Father in heaven.

And while we can't in this life and on this earth be perfect in our love for and obedience to Jesus, we can follow Jesus's example and continue growing in our love for God. As our love for Him grows, so does our ability to obey Him better and better.

Study Questions

○ What kind of person, according to 1 John, claims to love God but lives a life of disobedience?

○ What does this passage tell us is the proof of our love for God?

Why We Are Called Children of God

The third chapter of John 1 begins, "See how very much our Father loves us, for he calls us his children, and that is what we are! But the people who belong to this world don't recognize that we are God's children because they don't know him" (1 John 3:1).

The theme of believers being children of God is repeated throughout the Bible and is especially prevalent in 1 John. In that epistle, John repeatedly refers to his readers using the obvious term of love and affection: "dear children."

John wanted his readers to know that as Christians we weren't just saved from going to hell, but we were also given the privilege of being called God's children, a point he also made early in his gospel (John 1:12–13).

factum

The apostle Paul echoed this theme of the loving Fatherhood of God when he wrote, "And because we are his children, God has sent the Spirit of his Son into our hearts, prompting us to call out, "Abba, Father" (Galatians 4:6). The word *Abba* implies a familiar, loving father/child relationship similar to the English word *Daddy*. (See also Romans 8:15.)

God did that out of a love that fallen, sinful humanity can't fully grasp. It is in many ways a complex love, but it is also simple in many ways, too. It is a love that:

- moved God to reach out to a lost and sinful world (John 3:16)
- was given to us directly through Jesus Christ (John 15:9)
- is radiated out of us through the Holy Spirit (Romans 5:5)
- is a source of comfort to the afflicted (2 Corinthians 1:3–6)
- existed before we even knew God through Christ (Romans 5:8)
- causes God to discipline His children (Hebrews 12:1–13)

These are just a few examples of what God's love for His people really looks like. There are dozens and dozens of other examples and descriptions of God's love of those He refers to as His children in the Old and New Testaments.

As you study the love of God in the Bible, you'll find that it is a love that comes with a variety of rights and privileges. And it is also a love that comes with some responsibilities, all of which God empowers us to carry out as we demonstrate His love to the world around us—just like Jesus did so perfectly.

Study Questions

○ What does God call those who belong to Him?

○ Why don't people in the world understand that believers are actually God's own children?

The Proof That We Are Really Born Again (1 John 3:10–15)

John taught that the love that Jesus showed would be an outgrowth of someone who had made him his or her Savior. "So now we can tell who are children of God and who are children of the devil. Anyone who does not live righteously and does not love other believers does not belong to God" (1 John 3:10).

John goes on to say that loving one another is the message his readers had heard from the very beginning (1 John 3:11). But then he tells them that brotherly Christian love is the proof that someone has really been saved: "If we love our Christian brothers and sisters, it proves that we have passed from death to life. But a person who has no love is still dead. Anyone who hates another brother or sister is really a murderer at heart. And you know that murderers don't have eternal life within them" (1 John 3:14–15).

discussion question

How exactly do we demonstrate Christian love?
The apostle Paul gives some of the best examples and instruction when it comes to loving one another in the thirteenth chapter of his first letter to the Corinthian church—also known as the Love Chapter. In that passage, he tells us that love is, among other things, patient and kind and that it is not jealous, vain, proud, rude, or selfish.

John's teaching about love being the proof of one's Christianity fits in with what Jesus told his disciples late in his earthly ministry: "Your love for one another will prove to the world that you are my disciples" (John 13:35).

In other words, love is proof to the world, to ourselves, and to other believers that we really are children of God.

Study Questions

○ What, according to John, are the two proofs that someone is a child of God?

○ What does John say about those who don't love other Christians?

Jesus: A Perfect Example of Love (1 John 3:16–17)

One of the great things about love is that the Bible shows us a perfect example of how to do it every day and in every way. This perfect example is what John was referring to when he wrote, "We know what real love is because Jesus gave up his life for us" (1 John 3:16).

Jesus himself said, "There is no greater love than to lay down one's life for one's friends" (John 15:13). And that is exactly the kind of love Jesus demonstrated to his "friends"—those who had made a lifetime commitment to follow him.

But how, according to John, do we imperfect humans reflect God's perfect love? Most of the time, it's just a matter of being practical. John goes on to write, "So we also ought to give up our lives for our brothers and sisters. If someone has enough money to live well and sees a brother or sister in need but shows no compassion—how can God's love be in that person? (1 John 3:16–17).

symbolism

Sacrificial love is central to the Christian faith and was demonstrated perfectly by Jesus, who "gave up his divine privileges; he took the humble position of a slave and was born as a human being. When he appeared in human form, he humbled himself in obedience to God and died a criminal's death on a cross" (Philippians 2:7–8).

In other words, love, in order to be love, must be demonstrated through actions, not just through feelings and words. And while there are numerous references in the New Testament letters to feelings of affection and friendship from one believer to another, real love—the kind of love Jesus had for his followers—has to be demonstrated and not just felt.

Jesus demonstrated his love for others by speaking soothing words of comfort as well as difficult words of truth, by meeting people's physical needs through some of his miracles, and by healing those who were sick or injured. But his greatest act of love—the greatest act of love in all of history—was when he willingly gave himself up to die a horrible death on a cross of wood.

From the very beginning of his life, Jesus, John tells us, is our perfect example of love. While it is highly unlikely that any individual believer is going to have to die for another, it is a certainty that we all will have opportunities to "give up our lives for our brothers and sisters" by demonstrating the kind of compassion Jesus demonstrated every day.

Study Questions

O What should it mean, practically speaking, to the believer today to love as Jesus loved when he was on earth?

O Why do you think Jesus spent so much time meeting the physical needs of people through his many miracles when his ultimate mission was to save people's souls?

God the Father: Another Perfect Example of Love (1 John 4:8–12)

John tells us that it is God's nature to love. But he goes a step further in telling us that God Himself is love (1 John 4:8). That means that God in His very essence is love, and it's a love that needs to be displayed and given away: "God showed how much he loved us by sending his one and only Son into the world so that we might have eternal life through him. This is real love—not that we loved God, but that he loved us and sent his Son as a sacrifice to take away our sins" (1 John 4:9–10).

factum

In what may be the best-known verse in all of the Bible, Jesus told Nicodemus, a Pharisee with whom he had engaged in a deep spiritual conversation, "For God loved the world so much that he gave his one and only Son, so that everyone who believes in him will not perish but have eternal life" (John 3:16).

The one who knows God knows that it is in His nature to love, to give of Himself, and to extend kindness to even the most lost and hurting sinner. That is what moved Him to send Jesus Christ to earth to die on the cross so that we could be freely forgiven for our sins and adopted into the family of God. It is beyond human ability to fully and adequately explain this love of God, but it is simple to point others to the ultimate display of that love: Jesus Christ on the cross, dying a sacrificial death for unworthy sinners.

When we respond to God the Father's love—and to the expression of that love through Christ—we become His children and inherit eternal life with Him. But there is a here-and-now aspect to this love. Since God has so loved us and given His Son for us, John says, we should be willing to love one another. After all, he states, if we in whom God lives love one another, God is alive in us and has expressed our love in and through us (1 John 4:11–12).

It has been said that love isn't love until it is given away. And our heavenly Father has given us a perfect example of what giving away love looks like.

Study Questions

○ In light of 1 John 4:11–12, what specifically should be your response to the love of God?

○ How do you think your loving others can more perfectly express the love of God for humankind?

Living and Growing in God's Love (1 John 4:17)

Christianity isn't just a system of beliefs or something we carry with us like an identification card. It's a life of faith in God, a life that changes as we grow stronger and more mature in our faith. And it's a life of love that brings us to maturity in all areas of our lives, including how we love God and others.

The apostle John points out that the love that is within us—and that radiates out of us—will grow toward perfection as we grow more perfect in our relationship with God: "And as we live in God, our love grows more perfect. So we will not be afraid on the day of judgment, but we can face him with confidence because we live like Jesus here in this world" (1 John 4:17).

The point John makes here is that there will be a day when each of us will appear before God, a day when we will give an accounting of what we did and didn't do. And this verse tells us that when we grow in our love, when our loves becomes "perfect"—meaning more like the love of Jesus— then we'll have every reason to face God Himself with confidence because we know and love His Son—our Savior—Jesus Christ, and because we allowed him to love others through us.

point of interest

The apostle Paul wrote of the centrality of love to the Christian life: "Three things will last forever—faith, hope, and love—and the greatest of these is love" (1 Corinthians 13:13). Love, then, is the beginning and the end and everything in between when it comes to our relationships with God. That's because we get to love God and love others because God loved us first.

When Jesus was asked which commandments were most important, he replied that the two most important were to love God with all of our being and to love our neighbors as we do ourselves (see Matthew 22:35–39). Jesus finished his point by saying, "The entire law and all the demands of the prophets are based on these two commandments" (Matthew 22:40). That means that there is nothing we can do in the Christian life—no kind word, no act of charity, no religious performance—that can please God if it isn't done with a pure heart of love, both for Him and for others.

When we love God, our obedience to Him comes not out of a dread of God or out of fear that He will punish us—although we are told in the Bible that it is a good thing to fear God—but out of a heart of love for Him and for our brothers and sisters in Christ. When we do those things willingly and joyfully, it is a sign that we are maturing spiritually, that we are becoming, in John's words, "more perfect" in our love.

We aren't to love God because we're afraid not to, and we aren't to love the people He has put in our lives because we know there is eternal reward in doing so. While outside the love of God is certainly a scary place to be, and while there is reward in performing those acts of love for our brothers and sisters, we are to love from our hearts without worrying about the costs of not loving and without concern for the rewards of loving.

The Christian life is a life of faith in and obedience to God, but more than anything it is a life of love. And when we respond to God's love by loving Him in return, we will find that our lives become fountains of love to God Himself and to the people He puts around us.

Study Questions

○ What does it mean to you to be "more perfect" in God's love?

○ What steps are you taking now to grow "more perfect" in God's love? What other steps can you take?

CHAPTER 21

Revelation: How It All Ends Up

Back in Chapter 5 you studied Genesis, the book of beginnings. Now you will study the book that closes out the Bible, the book of Revelation, the book on how it all ends up—how God's divine plan of redemption is finally brought to completion. The meaning of much of Revelation may be difficult to decipher, but it is still filled with messages that are as relevant today as they were when they were written two thousand years ago.

John's Prophetic Message

Written by the apostle John (the writer of the gospel and the epistles that bear his name) during a time of exile on the island of Patmos, the book of Revelation is the only New Testament book whose focus is primarily on prophetic events. John wrote Revelation near the end of the first century, a time of terrible suffering and persecution for a lot of Christians. It was a time when Roman emperors demanded deitylike worship, and Christians and Jews who refused to worship these emperors were routinely pressured economically, tortured, and even put to death. John himself was banished to Patmos.

Before you delve into reading and studying the book of Revelation, a warning or caution is in order. This book is filled with oftentimes strange and mystifying imagery whose meanings have been a source of debate for centuries. As you study this book, it is especially helpful to purchase a study guide—or several for that matter—to give you a leg up in deciphering this book. Even at that, it is likely that you will find contradictory interpretations on what this book really means and what context it should be read under. When you read and study the book of Revelation, do it with an open heart and mind that takes what it sees at face value.

Christ and the Seven Churches (Revelation 1–3)

The book of Revelation begins with a stunning description of someone that John identifies as the glorified Jesus Christ. John was one of the men who spent three years with Jesus during his earthly ministry, but his description of his Lord is nothing like what we think of when we read John's gospel account. In John's vision, he saw seven gold lampstands:

And standing in the middle of the lampstands was someone like the Son of Man. He was wearing a long robe with a gold sash across his chest. His head and his hair were white like wool, as white as snow. And his eyes were like flames of fire. His feet were like polished bronze refined in a furnace, and his voice thundered like mighty ocean waves. He held seven stars in his right hand, and a sharp two-edged sword came from his mouth. And his face was like the sun in all its brilliance. (Revelation 1:13–16)

When John saw this vision, he goes on to say: "I fell at his feet as if I were dead. But he laid his right hand on me and said, 'Don't be afraid. I am the First and the Last. I am the living one. I died, but look—I am alive forever and ever. And I hold the keys of death and the grave'" (Revelation 1:17–18).

Then John received the meaning of the mystery of the seven gold lampstands, namely that they were the seven churches who would be addressed in Revelation 2–3.

symbolism

While the meaning of some of John's imagery in the book of Revelation is open to debate, what isn't open to debate is the main theme of the book: remain true to Jesus Christ, even in the face of persecution, even in the face of suffering, even in the face of losing all you have, even in the face of death.

The next two chapters of the book of Revelation are a collection of letters to seven churches in Asia Minor (modern Turkey)—the churches of Ephesus, Smyrna, Pergamum, Thyatira, Sardis, Philadelphia, and Laodicea. Here is what Jesus had to say to those churches:

- **Ephesus:** This church received praise for doing good things but was also criticized for not loving Christ or one another as much as it did at first (Revelation 2:4). Christ called this church to turn back to doing the things it did at first.
- **Smyrna:** Though this church was in poverty and being slandered by the outside world, it was a church of great spiritual riches (Revelation 2:9).
- **Pergamum:** This church is praised for remaining true to Christ, even in the face of intense persecution, but it is also chided for compromising when it came to the kind of teaching it received (Revelation 2:12–27).
- **Thyatira:** Jesus spoke highly of this church's love, faith, service, and endurance. The problem, however, was that idolatry and sexual immorality had crept its way into the church (Revelation 2:18–29).

- **Sardis:** Jesus's message to this church indicated that it was spiritually dead and in need of a reawakening (Revelation 3:1–6).
- **Philadelphia:** This church also received high praise for its faithfulness and perseverance—even in the face of persecution by "Satan's synagogue," or false Jews who were making life rough for these believers (Revelation 3:7–13).
- **Laodicea:** This church was a spiritual mess. That is because they were "neither hot nor cold" but lukewarm. Jesus wanted them to decide which they wanted to be. "But since you are like lukewarm water, neither hot nor cold, I will spit you out of my mouth!" (Revelation 3:14–22). The word *spit* in this context means "vomit," meaning that Jesus was saying, in effect, "You make me sick!"

Jesus's final words in this message for the churches were these:

Look! I stand at the door and knock. If you hear my voice and open the door, I will come in, and we will share a meal together as friends. Those who are victorious will sit with me on my throne, just as I was victorious and sat with my Father on his throne. Anyone with ears to hear must listen to the Spirit and understand what he is saying to the churches. (Revelation 3:20–22)

This was quite a promise to those believers who lived during such a dangerous time. It assured those who put their faith in Jesus Christ that, no matter how bad things got for them, their endurance would mean incredible blessings to come.

Study Questions

○ What are some of the things Jesus praises his church for in Revelation 2:4-3:22?

○ What are some of the things Jesus chides his church for?

Christ's Throne and the Seven Seals (Revelation 4–5)

Chapter 4 of Revelation opens with an invitation to view the throne of God and the scene surrounding it: "Then as I looked, I saw a door standing open in heaven, and the same voice I had heard before spoke to me like a trumpet blast. The voice said, 'Come up here, and I will show you what must happen after this' (Revelation 4:1).

John, now in the Spirit, saw a throne with a figure on it who was as brilliant as gemstones. The glow of an emerald circled the throne like a rainbow, and twenty-four thrones surrounded it. On the thrones were "twenty-four elders"—all of whom were clothed in white and wearing gold crowns. From the main throne came lightning flashes and thunderclaps. In front of the throne were seven torches with burning flames, which represented the sevenfold Spirit of God. Also in front of the throne was a shiny, sparkling sea of glass.

There were four living creatures—each of them covered with eyes front to back—in the center and around the throne. One of them looked like a lion, another like an ox, the third like a human, and the fourth like an eagle in flight. Each of them had six wings, which were also covered with eyes. Day in and day out, night in and night out, these creatures spoke these words: "Holy, holy, holy is the Lord God, the Almighty—the one who always was, who is, and who is still to come" (Revelation 4:8).

John saw that whenever one of these beings gave glory and honor to the one sitting on the throne, the twenty-four elders fell and worshipped him also and laid their crowns before the throne.

John also saw in his vision a scroll in the right hand of the one sitting on the throne—Christ, the Lamb of God. There was writing on both sides of the scroll and it was sealed with seven seals that no one on heaven or earth was able to open and read.

John was bitterly distraught that no one was worthy to open the scroll, but one of the elders told him, "Stop weeping! Look, the Lion of the tribe of Judah, the heir to David's throne, has won the victory. He is worthy to open the scroll and its seven seals" (Revelation 5:5). John saw a vision of a lamb looking as if it had been slaughtered but which was standing. It had seven horns and seven eyes (which represented the sevenfold spirit of God). As the lamb stepped forward and took the scroll, the four living beings and the twenty-four elders fell down before him. They sang a "new song."

Study Questions

○ What did the one sitting on the throne look like?
○ What are the words of the "new song" being sung in this scene (Revelation 5:9–13)?

The Breaking of the Seals (Revelation 6–7)

Revelation 6 begins with John's vision of the lamb breaking the first of the seven seals on the scroll. When he broke the first seal, John saw a white horse with a rider wearing a crown and holding a bow. He rode out to win many battles and "gain the victory" (Revelation 6:2).

When the lamb broke the second seal, a red horse appeared who brought horrible war and death on the earth (Revelation 6:4). He was followed by the black horse of famine and scarcity (Revelation 6:5–6). Finally, the pale green horse of pestilence and death is brought forth as the fourth seal was broken (Revelation 6:7–8).

At the opening of the fifth seal, John saw a vision of the souls of those who had died on account of their faith and heard their voices asking how much longer it would be before God avenged their deaths and set things on earth right (6:9–11). The sixth seal brings earthquakes, environmental catastrophes, celestial occurrences, and such chaos that everyone on earth would hide themselves in the caves and such places, wishing for the mountains to fall on them so that they could avoid the wrath of God (Revelation 6:12–15).

Before the seventh seal was broken, John saw four angels who held "back the four winds so that they did not blow on the earth or the sea, or even on any tree" (Revelation 7:1). He also saw another angel coming from the east carrying the seal of the living God and telling the four not to harm the land or sea or the trees until they had placed the seal of God on His servants' foreheads (Revelation 7:2–3). John saw a throng of 144,000 people—12,000 from each of the tribes of Israel—who had been marked with that seal (Revelation 7:4–8).

symbolism

The time of tribulation described in Revelation is commonly accepted to be the same event described by Jesus, who referred to it as a time of "greater anguish than at any time since the world began" and said that "unless that time of calamity is shortened, not a single person will survive." (Matthew 24:21–22).

John also saw a crowd so huge that it was impossible to count—from every nation, tribe, and language—standing in front of the throne and in front of the lamb, all shouting, "Salvation comes from our God who sits on the throne and from the lamb!" (Revelation 7:10).

Finally, the lamb broke the seventh seal, and there was silence in heaven for about half an hour. After that, John saw seven angels standing before God, and each of them were given seven trumpets. This was the calm before the storm!

Study Questions

○ What did the first seal reveal when it was broken?
○ How were the other seals different from the first?

The Trumpets (Revelation 8–11)

The seven angels with the seven trumpets were ready to blast away, and when they did all hell breaks loose upon the earth. After the first angel blew his trumpet, a mixture of hail and fire and blood showered the earth, setting a third of its surface on fire (Revelation 8:7).

The second trumpet blast brought with it a mountain of fire, which was thrown into the sea, turning a third of the water the color of blood and killing a third of all things in the sea and destroying a third of the ships.

The third trumpet blast brought a huge star, which burned "like a torch," falling from the sky, turning a third of the water on earth so "bitter" that it killed people who drank it (Revelation 8:10–11). When the fourth angel blew his trumpet, a third of the sun's light and a third of the moon's light was struck, and a third of the stars became dark. "Then I looked," John writes in Revelation 8:13, "and I heard a single eagle crying loudly as it flew through the air, 'Terror, terror, terror to all who belong to this world because of what will happen when the last three angels blow their trumpets.'"

That is exactly what happens, too. Hell is loosed on earth as the fifth and sixth angels blow their trumpets. There are visions of horrible locust-like creatures up from hell, creatures with stings like scorpions who were told to injure only people who did not have God's seal on their foreheads. Those they stung wouldn't die—as much as they wanted to—but would be tortured for five months.

The sixth trumpet blast brought four angels who would kill one-third of the people on earth through three plagues—fire, smoke, and burning sulfur coming out of the mouths of horrible horselike creatures (Revelation 9:13–19). Still, those who didn't die from these horrible plagues refused to repent and turn to God.

Between describing the seventh trumpet, John describes two witnesses for God—men who will have powers much like Moses and Elijah—but who would be killed after they were done testifying by "the beast that comes up out of the bottomless pit" (Revelation 11:7). The wicked people of the world will celebrate their deaths, but three and a half days later, they would rise from the dead.

factum

The name or word *Antichrist* doesn't appear in the book of Revelation, but it does appear in one of the apostle John's own epistles where he writes, "Dear children, the last hour is here. You have heard that the Antichrist is coming..." (1 John 2:18).

After that, the seventh trumpet would be blown, and there would be loud voices from heaven praising God: "The world has now become the

Kingdom of our Lord and of his Christ, and he will reign forever and ever" (Revelation 11:15). Also, the twenty-four elders would fall on their faces and worship God and acknowledge that the time of judgment and wrath had come (Revelation 11:16–19).

Study Questions

O What sorts of natural events do you think will bring to pass all the things written of in the book of Revelation?

O How do you reconcile the fact of a loving God with what is happening in the world described in Revelation?

The Arrival of the Antichrist (Revelation 12–14)

As Revelation 12 begins, John has a vision of a woman "clothed with the sun, with the moon beneath her feet, and a crown of twelve stars on her head" (Revelation 12:1). The woman was pregnant and in labor.

John also saw a large red dragon with seven heads and ten horns, with crowns on each head. He saw a war in heaven, as Michael and his angels defeated the dragon—identified as Satan, the deceiver of the whole world—and his angels and threw him out of heaven (Revelation 12:9). When the dragon realized he'd been kicked out of heaven, he pursued the woman and her male child, but she was protected from the dragon (Revelation 12:13–14).

Then John saw a beast rising up out of the sea—a beast with seven heads and ten horns and ten crowns on its horns, and on each head were blasphemous names. The beast looked like a leopard but had the feet of a bear and the mouth of a lion. The dragon, who had waited on the shore, gave the beast his own power and throne (Revelation 13:1–3).

The beast was allowed to blaspheme God and to do whatever it wanted for forty-two months, including wage war against God's people and even to conquer them. The people who were of the world—not those whose names were written in the Lamb of God's Book of Life—worshipped the beast (Revelation 13:5–8).

Then John saw a second beast, one who came up out of the earth. This beast had two horns like those of a lamb but spoke with the voice of a dragon.

He had the same authority as the first beast and required all people to worship the first beast, with anyone refusing to worship being put to death.

This beast "required everyone—small and great, rich and poor, free and slave—to be given a mark on the right hand or on the forehead. And no one could buy or sell anything without that mark, which was either the name of the beast or the number representing his name. Wisdom is needed here. Let the one with understanding solve the meaning of the number of the beast, for it is the number of a man. His number is 666" (Revelation 13:16–18).

point of interest

The apostle Paul also makes mention of the beast—or the Antichrist—referring to him as "the man of lawlessness—the one who brings destruction" in his second epistle to the Thessalonians. This was because Paul wanted to deal with some confusion on the part of the Thessalonians about the second coming of Jesus Christ.

Things don't look at all good for believers in the world at that time, but John gives them some hope, telling them about 144,000 people who refused to take the mark of the beast but instead took God's seal (Revelation 14:1–5). Three angels arrived—the first announcing the need to fear God and give glory to Him, the second proclaiming the fall of the city of Babylon because of her immorality, the third warning all who could hear that those who worship the beast or accept his mark would face God's wrath (Revelation 14:6–12).

Then came a voice from heaven saying, "Write this down: Blessed are those who die in the Lord from now on. Yes, says the Spirit, they are blessed indeed, for they will rest from their hard work; for their good deeds follow them!" (Revelation 14:13). What followed was the deaths of the wicked people of the earth as God's judgment came down (Revelation 14:14–20) as well as the rewarding of those who refused to worship the beast or take his mark (Revelation 15:2–4).

⭕ How are the destinies of those who "die in the Lord" different from those who are wicked?
⭕ Why do you think those who "die in the Lord" from this time on are blessed?

The "Bowl" Judgments (Revelation 15–18)

John's vision of God's wrath and judgment continues in chapter 15, which begins, "Then I saw in heaven another marvelous event of great significance. Seven angels were holding the seven last plagues, which would bring God's wrath to completion" (Revelation 15:1). Those last plagues were "bowls of the wrath of God" (Revelation 16:1), and He commanded them to go and pour them out on the earth. These bowls of wrath are:

- terrible sores on those who received the "mark of the beast" (Revelation 16:2)
- the sea turns to blood (16:3)
- the waters turn to blood (16:4–7)
- people are scorched by the sun (16:8–9)
- darkness and pain for humanity (16:10–11)
- the Euphrates River dries up and the battle of Armageddon takes shape (16:12–16)
- the earth is terribly shaken with the worst earthquake in human history (16:17–21)

This obviously is a horrible time of suffering on earth, but it wouldn't last forever. There would be a new heaven and a new earth, but only after the final conflict between good and evil, between God and Satan.

When the seventh bowl is poured out, a loud shout came saying "It is finished!" The city of Babylon was split into three sections, and the cities of many nations were reduced to piles of rubble. This was the wrath of God falling on Babylon for its sins, and it included the disappearance of every island, the leveling of every mountain, and falling hailstones weighing seventy-five pounds each. Still, people continued to curse God (Revelation 16:17–21).

symbolism

> While there are other verses and passages of the Bible that imply a final conflict between good and evil, it is in Revelation 16:16 that we find the only mention in the Bible of Armageddon. Many other of Israel's biggest military battles have taken place at that location, which is on the plain at the foot of Mount Megiddo.

Another angel appeared, announcing the fall of Babylon and that all the world leaders who had "committed adultery" with her would cry and mourn when they saw her burning. Merchants would mourn because they would no longer have Babylon as a business partner. There would be absolutely no hope for the future of the city.

Study Questions

○ What would be your response if you were in the midst of everything described in Revelation 15–18?

○ How much of what you read in Revelation do you take absolutely literally and how much do you believe is meaningful symbolism?

The Rider to the Rescue (Revelation 19–20)

Right after reporting the announcement of the destruction of Babylon, John hears what sounded like "a vast crowd in heaven shouting, 'Praise the Lord! Salvation and glory and power belong to our God. His judgments are true and just. He has punished the great prostitute who corrupted the earth with her immorality. He has avenged the murder of his servants'" (Revelation 19:1–2).

As words of praise like these continued, John saw heaven opened and a white horse whose rider was named "Faithful and True, for he judges fairly and wages a righteous war" (Revelation 19:11). His eyes were like blazing fire and he had many crowns on his head. He wore a robe dipped in blood, and he was called "the Word of God" and on his robe and thigh were written the name "King of all Kings and Lord of all Lords" (Revelation 19:11–16).

Then John saw the "beast and the kings of the world and their armies gathered together to fight against the one sitting on the horse and his army" (Revelation 19:19). In other words, they were preparing to fight against Jesus Christ himself! The beast and the false prophet were captured and thrown alive into a lake of fire. An angel then descends from heaven, binds the devil, and throws him into the "bottomless pit," where he stays with the beast and the false prophet for a period of a thousand years (Revelation 20:1–5).

At the end of the thousand years, the devil is released from the pit and allowed to deceive people once again. He even attempts to gather an army and surrounds God's people, but fire falls from heaven and destroys the army. Then the devil is thrown into a "fiery lake of burning sulfur," where he, the beast, and the false prophet would be tormented for all of eternity.

With the devil put in his eternal place, the end of this age comes as all those who had died were judged before a "great white throne," which was God's throne (Revelation 20:11–12). The dead would then be judged according to the things they had done, and those whose names were not found in the Book of Life were thrown into the lake of fire, along with death and the grave itself.

Study Questions

○ How does knowing the devil's ultimate end affect your life of faith?

○ Do you find the prophecies in the book of Revelation more frightening or more comforting? Why?

A New Heaven and New Earth (Revelation 21–22)

As horrible, disturbing, and frightening as some of John's images in the book of Revelation may seem, his description of what was ahead for those who had placed their faith in Christ will make enduring those things worth it. The prophecies in Revelation are difficult to decipher, but the description of how faithful believers will be rewarded once all those things have come to pass is fairly clear and straightforward. This, John said, is "a new heaven and a new earth, for the old heaven and the old earth had disappeared" (Revelation 21:1). Also gone was the sea, and John also saw the "new Jerusalem," coming down out of heaven like a bride beautifully adorned for her groom (Revelation 21:2). Then John heard a voice from the throne, saying, "Look, God's home is now among his people! He will live with them, and they will be his people. God himself will be with them. He will wipe every tear from their eyes, and there will be no more death or sorrow or crying or pain. All these things are gone forever" (Revelation 21:3–4).

John heard that same voice saying, "Look, I am making everything new!... Write this down, for what I tell you is trustworthy and true... It is finished! I am the Alpha and the Omega—the Beginning and the End. To all who are thirsty I will give freely from the springs of the water of life. All who are victorious will inherit all these blessings, and I will be their God, and they will be my children" (Revelation 21:5–7). Indeed, everything will be new—a new heaven and earth (Revelation 21:1), a new people (21:2–8), a new bride of Christ (21:9), a new home (21:10–21), and a new Temple (21:22).

factum

The Bible more or less begins and ends with the Tree of Life. Back in the Garden of Eden, a fallen Adam and Eve were not permitted to eat from it or even go near it (Genesis 3:22–24), but in the New Jerusalem, everyone is allowed to eat from it (Revelation 22:13, 19).

The book of Revelation presents a pretty disturbing picture of what the end times will look like. But it also gives us the ultimate happily ever after ending, one where the devil will be handed his defeat—a defeat he's had coming for thousands and thousands of years—for all of eternity and one where those who have put their faith in Jesus Christ will find that all things truly have become new.

Study Questions

O Which of the "new" things Jesus Christ has promised do you look forward to most?

O Reread Revelation 21:5–8. How does the contrast in that passage change your approach to sharing your faith with others?

Help for Studying the Bible

Study and Devotional Bibles

The Disciple's Study Bible. Eugene, OR: Harvest House Publishers, 1984.

Life Application Study Bible. Wheaton, IL: Tyndale House Publishers, 1988.

The New Jerusalem Bible, Reader's Edition. New York: Doubleday, 1990.

The New Oxford Annotated Bible with the Apocrypha: Revised and Expanded. New York: Oxford University Press, 1994.

The NIV Quiet Time Bible. Downer's Grove, IL: Intervarsity Press, 1994.

The NIV Serendipity Bible: For Personal and Small Group Study, Revised and Expanded. Grand Rapids, MI, and Littleton, CQ: Zondervan Publishing House and Serendipity House, 1988.

The One-Minute Bible: The Heart of the Bible Arranged into 366 One-Minute Readings. Kohlenberger, John R., III, ed. Bloomington, MN: Garborg's, 1992.

Ryrie Study Bible, Expanded Edition. Chicago: Moody Press, 1994.

The Thompson Chain Reference Study Bible. Nashville: Thomas Nelson Publishers, 1983.

Bible Study Series

Faithwalk Bible Studies. Wheaton, IL: Crossway Books, 2000.

Fisherman Bible Study Guides. New York: Random House, Inc., 1992.

God's Word for Today's Bible Studies. St. Louis, MO: Concordia Publishing House, 1995.

Bible Reference Books

HarperCollins Bible Dictionary. Achtemeier, Paul J., Gen. ed. San Francisco: HarperCollins Publishers, 1985.

Where to Find It in the Bible: The Ultimate A to Z Resource. Anderson, Ken. Nashville: Thomas Nelson Publishers, 1996.

The Moody Atlas of Bible Lands. Beitzel, Barry J. Chicago: Moody Press, 1985.

Roget's Thesaurus of the Bible. Day, A. Colin. New York: Harper Collins, 1992.

The New Bible Commentary. Guthrie, D., and J.A. Motyer, eds. Grand Rapids, MI: William B. Eerdmans Publishing Company, 1970.

Living by the Book. Hendricks, Howard G., and William D. Chicago: Moody Press, 1991. [inductive Bible study method]

What the Bible Is All About, Revised Edition. Mears, Henrietta C. Ventura, CA: Regal Books, 1983.

Manners and Customs of the Bible. Packer, J.I., and M.C. Tenney, eds. Nashville, TN: Thomas Nelson Publishers, 1980.

The New Strong's Exhaustive Concordance of the Bible. Strong, James. Nashville, TN: Thomas Nelson Publishers, 1995.

Unger's Bible Handbook. Unger, Merrill F. Chicago: Moody Press, 1967.

Description of the Books of the Bible

There are a grand total of sixty-six books in the Bible—thirty-nine in the Old Testament and twenty-seven in the New Testament. Here is a quick overview of each of those books.

The Old Testament

Genesis

The word *genesis* means "beginnings," and that makes it a fitting title for the first book of the Bible. The book of Genesis, which is commonly believed to have been written by Moses, contains the stories of the beginning of the universe, the beginning of the planet Earth, the beginning of humankind, the beginning of human civilization, the beginning of sin, the beginning of the Jewish race, and the beginning of God's plan for the salvation of all humankind.

Exodus

Also commonly accepted to have been recorded by Moses, the book of Exodus tells us the story of how Moses, despite his own misgivings about his ability to lead, obeyed God's call to lead the Hebrew people out of Egyptian slavery. It also tells the story of how God gave His people the Law of Moses, including the Ten Commandments.

Leviticus

The third book of the Bible, Leviticus, was also recorded by Moses, and it deals with the laws, regulations, and commandments concerning sacrifices to God, the priesthood, ceremonial purity, and dietary and other laws the people of Israel were to observe.

Numbers

The book of Numbers is important historically because it gives the details of the route the Israelites took out of Egypt and also their important encampments on their way to the Promised Land. Numbers includes the numbering of the Israelites, an account of the journey from Sinai to Moab, and the Jewish people's rebellion because of their fear.

Deuteronomy

This book, which was also recorded by Moses, consists of four addresses to the Israelites by Moses shortly before his death. The first address (chapters 1–4) covers the historic events during the Israelites' forty years in the wilderness. This book also contains the laws and guidelines for the Israelites' conduct in Canaan, the Promised Land. As Deuteronomy closes, Moses prepares himself for death and appoints Joshua to take his place.

Joshua

Moses, who led the people of Israel out of Egyptian captivity, has died, and in his place God has raised up Joshua as the leader who will now—forty years too late because of their own rebellion—guide the people of Israel into the Promised Land. This book covers the conquest of Canaan (chapters 1–12), the allotment of the land to the twelve tribes (13–22), and the farewell speeches from Joshua (23–24).

Judges

This book, which contains some of the greatest stories in the Bible, tells us the history of Israel from the death of Joshua to the beginning of the monarchy under Saul, Israel's first king. The book gets its name from the fact that it records the history of Israel's government under fourteen judges who ruled over the nation prior to the monarchy.

Ruth

The story of Ruth is set during the time of the judges—a time when the nation of Israel had plunged into a time of unfaithfulness to God. Ruth, on the other hand, was faithful, and she was rewarded with a new husband, Boaz, and with a place in the lineage of King David (she was his great-grandmother) and, eventually, Jesus Christ.

1 Samuel

First Samuel records the leadership transition in Israel from judges to kings. It is named for Samuel, the last judge and first prophet of Israel, and it includes the account of the monarchy of Saul and the preparation of David, who has been anointed but wasn't yet recognized as Saul's successor.

2 Samuel

The book of Second Samuel records the highlights of the reign of King David—first over the territory of Judah and later over the entire nation of Israel. It records David's ascension to the throne, his sin of adultery and murder, and the consequences of those sins for himself, his family, and his nation.

1 Kings

This book tells the story of Solomon, the son and successor of King David. It was under Solomon's leadership that Israel rose to the peak of its power and influence worldwide and the holy Temple was constructed. This book also tells the sad story of how Solomon's zeal for God faded in his later years.

2 Kings

Second Kings picks up where 1 Kings leaves off, and it tells the terrible story of a kingdom divided into two nations—Israel and Judah—and of those two nations' rebellion and their path toward captivity. Second Kings also records the ministry of the prophet Elisha, who ministered during terrible times.

1 and 2 Chronicles

These books cover the same period in the history of Israel as 1 and 2 Kings but with a different emphasis. The books of Chronicles are not just repetition of what has already been recorded. They give the reader a more spiritual look at the terrible events that led to the fall and captivity of a once great and blessed nation.

Ezra

The book of Ezra, named for an important priest by that name, tells the story of the two returns of the people of Judah from captivity in Babylon. The first of those returns was led by Zerubbabel, and it was to rebuild the temple (chapters 1–6). The second was led by Ezra, and it was to begin a spiritual awakening or revival of the people (7–10).

Nehemiah

This book, which is thought to be an autobiography of Nehemiah, can be seen as a continuation of the book of Ezra. It tells the story of the rebuilding of Jerusalem (chapters 1–7), the spiritual state of the Jewish people at that time (8–10), and other events, including the dedication of the wall around Jerusalem and the spiritual reforms carried out by Nehemiah (12–13).

Esther

The inclusion of the book of Esther in the Scriptures has been a source of debate for centuries. For one thing, God is not mentioned at all in the book, and there are only passing references to any kind of spiritual disciplines. However, if you read closely, you'll see that the hand of God in the affairs of His people is evident throughout the book.

Job

This is believed to be the earliest written book of the Bible. The story is set during the time of the patriarchs (Abraham, Isaac, Jacob, and Joseph) and tells the story of a man whose faith and devotion to God is challenged when he loses everything he has—his wealth, his family, even his health—and is left asking why.

Psalms

Written over a period of several centuries, the book of Psalms is a collection of individual writings—by several authors—that cover the full range of humanity's interactions with its Creator. There are many themes in the Psalms, the most prominent ones being prayer, praise, and worship of God. Outside of Isaiah, the Psalms are the most quoted Old Testament writings in the New Testament.

Proverbs

The Bible tells us that King Solomon prayed for one thing, wisdom (2 Chronicles 1:10), which can be defined as the ability and knowledge it takes to live a Godly life. The book of Proverbs gives the reader some of Solomon's wisdom, covering such topics as work, pride, greed, friendship, anger, words, sex, procrastination, and many others.

Ecclesiastes

King Solomon is traditionally believed to be the author of the book of Ecclesiastes, which has as its main theme the vanity or futility of a life—even what appears to be a successful, comfortable, happy life—outside of a real relationship with God. Nothing, we learn from reading this book, can take the place of living with and for God.

Song of Solomon

Written by King Solomon, this book—also called the Song of Songs—is a love song filled with erotic imagery and metaphors. It depicts Solomon's joyful courtship of and wedding with a shepherdess named Shulamite, but metaphorically it has been seen as a picture of God's love for Israel and for Christ's church.

Isaiah

The prophet Isaiah ministered over a span of at least forty years and under the reigns of four kings of Judah. His book of prophecies records the dire warnings of coming judgment for a wayward people, but it also contains wonderful promises of coming redemption and salvation—salvation through the coming Messiah and Savior—for all humankind.

Jeremiah

This book contains the prophecies of the man who has been called "the weeping prophet," and it carries a heartbreaking message of doom and judgment on a people Jeremiah repeatedly points out have "forgotten God." Throughout his sermons and warnings, Jeremiah staunchly declares that the only hope for the people of Judah is to return to their God.

Lamentations

This book, written by Jeremiah, is a continuation of the messages of the book of Jeremiah, and it describes the horrible aftermath of the invasion of Jerusalem by the Babylonians. There is death and destruction all around, and Jeremiah is heartbroken over what has happened to this great city and to the people who lived there.

Ezekiel

The prophet Ezekiel ministered during the worst time in the history of Judah: the seventy-year period of Babylonian captivity. His prophecies can be seen as companions for those of Jeremiah, but while Jeremiah focused on death and destruction, Ezekiel focused on God's eventual restoration and salvation for his people.

Daniel

Like the book of Ezekiel, Daniel is set during the Babylonian captivity. Daniel was one of the many Jewish people who had been taken from his home to Babylon, and he was picked for government service, a position he used to speak God's prophetic message to Jews and Gentiles alike.

Hosea

The prophet Hosea, whose name means "salvation," ministered to the northern kingdom of Israel, which is enjoying a time of national prosperity but which is also in a state of spiritual decay. In order to dramatize the unfaithfulness of his people, God calls Hosea to marry an immoral and unfaithful woman named Gomer.

Joel

Sudden disaster has struck the land of Judah in the form of a black cloud of locusts, which devour every living green thing in their path. While it's not clear in this book whether the locusts were literal or a vision of things to come, the prophet Joel uses the occasion to call his countrymen to repentance.

Amos

Like Hosea, the prophet Amos ministered to Israel in a time of national prosperity and expansion. But also like Hosea, he ministered in a time of religious and spiritual decay. Amos, a farmer turned prophet, speaks out fearlessly against the sin of the people, warning them of coming judgment if they don't turn back to God.

Obadiah

The shortest book of the Old Testament, Obadiah centers on a centuries-old feud between the Israelites, the descendants of Jacob, and the Edomites, the descendants of Esau. In this book, God has pronounced judgment against Edom for its continued hostility toward Israel.

Jonah

Called by God to go and preach to the wicked people in Nineveh, the prophet Jonah refuses and instead boards a boat and heads in the opposite direction. But God never lets Jonah out of His sight and eventually brings him back to a place where he can minister as God had called him to in the first place.

Micah

The prophet Micah was a contemporary of Isaiah, and he spoke a message of reproof for the rich and influential people of Jerusalem who had been mistreating or neglecting the poorest and neediest among them. He rebukes those who would use their power for personal gain. His message was for the people to "do what is right, to love mercy, and to walk humbly with your God" (Micah 6:8).

Nahum

The Assyrian capital of Nineveh, where Jonah had preached, resulting in repentance and a stay of God's judgment, has a hundred years later turned back to evil ways and is about to feel the wrath of God. Nahum prophesies the utter destruction of the city, which will come at the hands of the Babylonians.

Habakkuk

The prophet Habakkuk ministers to the kingdom of Judah during her final moments prior to the Babylonian invasion, which God will use to mete out His wrath on His rebellious people. Although they have repeatedly been called to repentance, the people stubbornly refuse to change their ways. Habakkuk, knowing the sinfulness of his countrymen, asks God how long it can continue.

Zephaniah

Judah's political and religious history included occasional reform, the kind of reform preached by the prophet Zephaniah. His book contains the twin themes of the severity and lovingness of God, and it also speaks of God's judgment on sin and of God's restoration and salvation of the nation He loves.

Haggai

The terrible period in Jewish history known as the Babylonian captivity is past, and they have returned to their homeland and started rebuilding the temple. But sixteen years after the project is started, it has yet to be finished—all because the people have allowed their personal affairs to keep them from God's work. The book of Haggai contains fiery calls to finish the work so that God can bless His people.

Zechariah

The prophet Zechariah was a contemporary of Haggai, and he addressed the same issue: the unfinished temple. However, Zechariah is more positive in his tone, focusing on the presence of God to give the people strength to finish the task before them. He gives great encouragement to the governor Zerubbabel.

Malachi

Years after God had lovingly and graciously returned His people from Babylon to the Promised Land, they again began backsliding and falling into the same kinds of sins that led to the Babylonian captivity in the first place. Malachi directs his message of judgment to a people who had a false sense of security when it came to their relationship with God.

The New Testament

Matthew

While the message of Matthew's gospel is for everyone today, it was written especially for the Jewish people of his time, a people who had waited for centuries for the promised Messiah. Matthew, one of the twelve apostles, continually points out that Jesus was the One they had waited for simply because he fulfilled the Old Testament prophecies—more than forty of which Matthew lists in his gospel account.

Mark

The shortest of the four Gospels, Mark portrays Jesus as a servant of his Father in heaven, as a preacher, teacher, and healer who took care of the needs of others all the way to his death on a cross. Mark himself is identified as "the son of Mary of Jerusalem" (Acts 12:12) and as "John Mark" (Acts 12:25).

Luke

The Gospel of Luke—which, along with the Acts of the Apostles, was written by the physician Luke—focuses on the perfect humanity of Jesus Christ. Luke tells his readers upfront that he wasn't one of Jesus' apostles or even an eyewitness to the earthly ministry of Christ. Luke's gospel was the only one of the four written by a Gentile, and it includes many details left out of the other accounts.

John

While Luke presents Jesus as the perfect human, or "the Son of Man," the apostle John presents him as the perfect, sinless Son of God. One of the recurring phrases in the Gospel of John is "I am," which was spoken by Jesus several times as he identified himself as the Son of God, the Messiah, and the Savior.

Acts of the Apostles

Dr. Luke, apparently an avid historian and researcher, compiled and wrote the account of how the church got its start. In this book we read of how the believers received the Holy Spirit (chapter 2), and many of them—including Peter, John, and the apostle Paul—went out into the world and preached what Jesus Christ had taught.

Romans

Paul's epistle to the Romans is considered his greatest work. The Gospels recount the life of Jesus and present his words and deeds, but the book of Romans explains the significance of his life and of his death and resurrection, namely that these events were accomplished so that all humanity—Jew and Gentile alike—could have fellowship with God.

1 Corinthians

The city of Corinth was one of the most important in Greece during Paul's day. As a port city, it was the hub of commerce and trade. But it was also a center of immorality and idolatrous religious practices. It was the influences of these things that Paul addressed as he wrote his letter to a church he had founded earlier.

2 Corinthians

Since Paul had written his first letter to the Corinthian church, it had been infiltrated by false teachers who had stirred the people against his teachings. Upon hearing about that, Paul sent an associate, Titus, to deal with the problems. Upon the return of Titus, Paul was overjoyed to hear of the Corinthians' change of heart. This letter is Paul's expression of thanksgiving to the church for its about-face.

Galatians

The Galatian church has been influenced to leave the life of faith and follow after teachings based on works of the law and the flesh. Paul was disturbed at this development and wrote this epistle in an attempt to get them to follow a gospel based on faith.

Ephesians

Paul's epistle to the Ephesians is addressed to a church that doesn't quite seem to understand what riches they have in Jesus Christ. They are called to higher living, yet they live like paupers only because they don't understand what they have in him. Chapters 1–3 of this epistle spell out for these Ephesians what they have, which is every spiritual blessing they could ever need.

Philippians

Paul's letter to the Philippians is different from his others simply because he isn't correcting any major problems within the church. Instead, he writes with great warmth and affection to these believers in Philippi, who had helped him out in his hour of need. In writing this letter, Paul spells out the central truth that it is only in Christ that believers can have real unity and joy.

Colossians

This letter has as its emphasis the works, the person, and the character of Jesus Christ. Paul wanted his readers to understand that Christ should be first and foremost in people's lives and that their lives should reflect that fact. The first two chapters of this letter give the readers the doctrine of who Jesus is, while the second two spell out what that means in how we live.

1 Thessalonians

Paul's first letter to the newly founded Thessalonian church expresses his words of praise for their faith, hope, love, and perseverance—all in the face of the severe persecution that churches faced in those days. He also encourages them to grow in their faith and in their love for one another and to continue praying, rejoicing, and giving thanks in all things.

2 Thessalonians

Since Paul's first letter to the Thessalonian church, some false teaching had made its way into the church causing these believers to falter in their faith. In writing 2 Thessalonians, Paul was attempting to rid the church of this false teaching and put them back on the right path of faith.

1 Timothy

This is a letter Paul wrote to his young protégé Timothy, a pastor at the church in Ephesus who was faced with the challenging tasks of ridding the church of false teaching, making sure public worship was conducted properly, and developing mature leadership. Paul wanted Timothy to understand that his youthfulness could be used as an asset in his ministry and that he had to be on his guard against false teaching and pursue the things a godly man should.

2 Timothy

This epistle is one of several Paul wrote from prison, and like the others it is a letter of encouragement. Again, Paul is encouraging Timothy to be on the alert for false or faulty teaching and to cling to the truth—even though there would be those who wanted to hear something other than the truth of Jesus Christ.

Titus

Titus, like Timothy, was a young pastor who faced some daunting challenges. In this case, it was setting in order the church in Crete. Paul wants him to understand the importance of making sure that the leadership in the church were the kind of men who would lead by example in the area of spiritual maturity.

Philemon

Paul's letter to Philemon, a fellow Christian, is the shortest of his epistles that appear in the Bible. In it, he is pleading the case of Onesimus, a runaway slave who had become a Christian. Paul is pleading with Philemon to take Onesimus back in the spirit of brotherly love and forgiveness.

Hebrews

The first Christians recorded in the Bible were Jewish people who had converted. Many of them struggled with the persecution by their countrymen and from the Roman authorities and were considering leaving Christianity and going back to Judaism. The writer of Hebrews (it's not certain who that was) wanted to encourage them to continue on, and he did so by showing them the superiority of Christ over any of the religious systems they knew.

James

While no one can be saved on the basis of their deeds, true faith in Christ will manifest itself in the deeds we do. That is the point the apostle James—it isn't certain who this is, but it has been generally accepted as the one referred to as "the Lord's brother" (Galatians 1:19)—was making when he wrote, "faith is dead without good deeds" (Galatians 2:26). Faith takes us through trials, repels temptation, and motivates us to obey the Word of God.

1 Peter

Jesus never told anyone that following him would be easy or that they wouldn't face opposition. In fact, he promised exactly the opposite. The apostle Peter, who followed Jesus for nearly the entirety of his earthly ministry, wanted the readers of this epistle to understand that following Jesus meant facing trials but that those who persevered through those things would receive the reward.

2 Peter

In his second epistle, Peter warns believers about false teachers who were sure to come into their midst trying to sell false and damaging teaching. He wanted them to understand that they would need to be diligent in examining their personal lives and in pursuing the kind of personal conduct God had called them to.

1 John

The apostle John, who had enjoyed close fellowship with Jesus while he was on earth and who still enjoyed close fellowship with him as he was in heaven, wanted his readers to see that God is three things: light, love, and life. And because of those things, those of us who know Jesus Christ are allowed to walk and live in those three things.

2 John

The apostle John had already said that loving one another is the equivalent of walking according to God's commandments. However, John wrote that love must also be discerning. It can't be naïve, ignorant, or open to anything and anyone. That is because there are a lot of false teachers who do not acknowledge Christ as having come in the flesh.

3 John

In this letter, the apostle John encourages Christians to have brotherly fellowship with one another. John expresses his love for a person named Gaius, then assures him of his prayers for his health and proclaims his joy over Gaius's steady walk with the Lord.

Jude

This epistle—which was likely written by Jude, the brother of James—encourages believers to fight and contend for the faith, particularly when people fall away, when false teachers appear, and when the truth of God comes under attack. In the face of such things, Christians should not be caught off guard but should be ready to contend for their faith.

Revelation

Revelation, written by the apostle John, is the book of finalities—or how things turn out for us. In this book, we see God's final plan for the redemption of humankind and the judgment of all evil unfold. This is the book of unveiling or disclosure of all things eternal.

How the Bible Came to Be

Have you ever looked at the copy of that leather-backed book on your bookshelf or nightstand and wonder how we got it? How the individual books came to be or how these particular books ended up in the Bible we have today? Was it the result of someone just randomly choosing a bunch of interesting stories for bedtime reading? Or did it happen when some committee of religious people got together and decided what to leave in and what to leave out?

In truth, very few people open their Bibles and give thought to how it came to be or how or why the sixty-six books in it are there. Most of us just open the Bible and start reading, feeling comfortable in our belief that what's in the Bible is what God wanted to be included. The way it all came about is actually a very interesting story—far more interesting than the scenarios listed above.

Becoming a Part of the Canon

The recording of the written Word of God began in around 1400 B.C. when Moses received the Ten Commandments on the stone tablets. By around 400 B.C., all of the original Hebrew manuscripts that make up the thirty-nine books of the Old Testament had been completed.

In the third century B.C. these books—as well as fourteen books of what is called the Apocrypha—were translated into Greek, the dominant language of the time. This translation was called the Septuagint. Legend held that it took seventy-two scholars seventy-two days to get the job done, but it in fact took much longer than that. This version was very popular in the Greek-speaking early church as well as with Jews in and around Palestine who no longer spoke Hebrew.

All of the original copies of the Hebrew Scriptures are long gone, but the copying was done with meticulous care and precision, ensuring that the copies were completely accurate. Traditionally, the Jews held the text of the Scriptures in such high esteem that they buried copies that had aged to the point where they had become difficult to read.

By the end of the first century A.D.—or around seven decades after the death of Jesus Christ—all of the books included in the New Testament today—from Matthew to Acts to the epistles to Revelation—had been written. In the second century all these books as a group comprised the collection of writings that would become the New Testament. But it would not be until a few centuries later that the books in the list were canonized, meaning that they were accepted as having been divinely inspired and, therefore, included in the Bible we have today.

Why the Canon?

There were numerous reasons why the church needed to come up with a final, official list of readings for its members. First of all, the apostles and other eyewitnesses to the life, work, and words of Christ had long since died, and the members of the church wanted something in writing that would spell out for them the messages of Jesus and the apostles.

Another reason the church needed the list was that it was customary at the time for church leaders to read to the people in the congregation. At first, all of the readings done in the church were taken from the Old Testament—after all, there was nothing else to read at that time—but later the leaders also began reading to the congregation what were called the Memoirs of the Apostles. These leaders wanted to make sure they had readings that reflected the message of God as it came through Jesus Christ himself and the apostles who continued his work on earth.

Obviously, there was a need for a list of readings to be compiled. But how was it going to be accomplished?

The Standard for Canonization

The early church fathers—those second- and third-century writers and teachers who took the place of the apostles as leaders in the church—knew they needed to figure out which of the many books and letters available from various sources belonged in their collection of accepted readings—also known as the canon.

The church fathers believed that the only requirement for inclusion in the canon was that the books and letters be inspired—specifically inspired by God—meaning that they were the words God would speak to them if He were to allow His voice to be heard in the congregations.

The obvious problem with that kind of test was figuring out how a book or letter—and there were many of them to choose from—was truly inspired by God. It didn't take too long before the early church fathers realized that they would need other tests in order to decide on the canon of Scripture.

One of those tests for canonizing a book or letter was whether it was written by an apostle or someone who was close to an apostle. So the books by the apostles Matthew, John, Peter, and Paul were included. Luke the physician, who wrote the gospel that bears his name as well as the Acts of the Apostles, was not an apostle. However, he had a very close relationship with the apostle Paul and even traveled with him during his missionary journeys. For that reason, two of his writings ended up as part of the New Testament we have today.

Gradually, over the course of centuries, the canon developed. It is believed that by about A.D.175, the canon included essentially the same books as our present day New Testament. By the year 200 the church widely accepted this list as canonical, and it was used widely in church services. Clement, the Bishop of Alexandria, recognized the books, as did many other church leaders of his time.

Still, it would be nearly 200 years before the canon of Scripture was officially recognized. In the year 397 a meeting of church leaders, called the Third Council of Carthage (modern-day Tunis)—it wasn't actually a general council but a regional council of African bishops, heavily influenced by Augustine, the Bishop of Hippo—acknowledged the twenty-seven books of the New Testament as we know them today. Most of the books had already been treated as Scripture for years, but around a half dozen books needed further discussion for final acceptance.

While the Third Council of Carthage acknowledged the twenty-seven books of the New Testament as we now have them, it wasn't until the Council of Chalcedon that the canon was officially accepted and approved by the church. Interestingly enough, there were several books included in the canon at the Third Council of Carthage that can no longer be found in modern-day Bibles—with the exception of some Catholic Bibles. These other books—known as the Apocrypha—were included in the original King James Bible but were removed in 1885, leaving the sixty-six books we have today.

Not long after the canon was officially recognized at the third Council of Carthage and adopted at the Council of Chalcedon, another historic milestone concerning the Bible took place. On or around the year 400, the entire Bible was translated, primarily by a Christian leader named Jerome (340–420), into Latin. This version was known as the "Vulgate" which means "written in the language of the people." Since that time, the Bible has been translated into more than 500 languages and dozens of versions or translations, some of which got the translators in major hot water with the ruling religious authorities of the time.

Putting the Bible in the Hands of the People

There was a time when the government/religious authorities (they were one in the same back then) kept the general public from reading the Bible for themselves. But many of the reformers—including the ones prior to the sixteenth-century Protestant Reformation—believed that the general public needed the right and privilege of reading the Bible and even owning one.

That led to several translations of the Bible, including a hand-copied one by John Wycliffe, who in the late 1300s was the first person to produce a copy of the complete Bible in English. Many other translations followed over the next several centuries, and in around 1455, a German named Johann Gutenberg developed a printing press that revolutionized printing and allowed for easier dispersal of all printed materials, including the Bible.

In a time when we can often obtain a Bible for free, or at least buy one for a small amount of money, it's hard to imagine a time when people couldn't even afford one. But that was the situation during the Middle Ages, when a Bible cost the equivalent of one year's wages. It was Gutenberg's development of the printing press that began to change that situation.

The first book off Gutenberg's press was a Bible, and it didn't take long for the Scriptures to become available throughout Europe and in all European languages.

The All-Time Number One Bestseller

The best-known of all Bible translations is the King James Version, which was commissioned by King James I of England in 1611 and completed by a team of fifty-four of the world's finest linguists. These were incredibly well-qualified men who had an excellent grasp on the Hebrew, Aramaic, and Greek languages of the Bible. On top of that, they were all devout Christians who held the Bible in the highest esteem. Their work is still praised for its accuracy in holding to the original manuscripts, and it has become by far the world's best-selling book of all time. Since that time, there have been many translations and paraphrases of the Bible.

Here is a timeline of some of the key dates in the writing and translation of the Bible, courtesy of *www.greatsite.com* and adapted for this book. Please note that some of the dates may be approximate:

- **1400 B.C.**—the first written Word of God: the Ten Commandments delivered to Moses

- **400 B.C.**—completion of all original Hebrew manuscripts that make up the thirty-nine books of the Old Testament

- **200 B.C.**—completion of the Septuagint Greek manuscripts that contain the thirty-nine Old Testament books and fourteen Apocrypha books

- **First century A.D.**—completion of all original Greek manuscripts that make up the twenty-seven books of the New Testament

- **315**—Athanasius, the Bishop of Alexandria, identifies the twenty-seven books of the New Testament that are today recognized as the canon of Scripture

- **382**—Jerome's Latin Vulgate manuscript produced, which contains all eighty books (thirty-nine Old Testament, fourteen Apocrypha, and twenty-seven New Testament)

- **500**—Scriptures have been translated into over 500 languages

- **600**—Latin was the only language allowed for Scripture

- **995**—Anglo-Saxon translations of the New Testament produced

- **1384**—Wycliffe is the first person to produce a (hand-written) manuscript copy of the complete Bible (all eighty books)

- **1455**—Johann Gutenberg invents the printing press; books may now be mass produced instead of individually hand-written; the first book ever printed is Gutenberg's Bible in Latin

- **1516**—Erasmus produces a Greek/Latin parallel New Testament

- **1522**—Martin Luther's German New Testament

- **1526**—William Tyndale's New Testament, the first New Testament printed in the English language

- **1535**—Myles Coverdale's Bible, the first complete Bible printed in the English language (all eighty books)

- **1537**—Tyndale-Matthews Bible, the second complete Bible printed in English; done by John "Thomas Matthew" Rogers (all eighty books)

- **1539**—the Great Bible printed, the first English language Bible authorized for public use (eighty books)

- **1560**—the Geneva Bible printed, the first English language Bible to add numbered verses to each chapter (eighty books)

- **1568**—the Bishops Bible printed; the Bible which the King James revised (eighty books)

- **1609**—the Douay Old Testament is added to the Rheims New Testament (of 1582) making the first complete English Catholic Bible; translated from the Latin Vulgate (eighty books)

- **1611**—the King James Bible printed, originally with all eighty books; the Apocrypha was officially removed in 1885 leaving only sixty-six books

- **1782**—Robert Aitken's Bible, the First English language Bible (KJV) printed in America

- **1791**—Isaac Collins and Isaiah Thomas respectively produce the first family Bible and first illustrated Bible printed in America; both were King James Versions with all eighty books

- **1808**—Jane Aitken's Bible (daughter of Robert Aitken); the first Bible to be printed by a woman

- **1833**—Noah Webster's Bible; after producing his famous dictionary, Webster printed his own revision of the King James Bible

- **1841**—English Hexapla New Testament, an early textual comparison showing the Greek and six famous English translations in parallel columns

- **1846**—The Illuminated Bible; the most lavishly illustrated Bible printed in America. A King James Version, with all 80 books

- **1885**—the English Revised Version Bible, the first major English revision of the KJV

- **1901**—the American Standard Version, the first major American revision of the KJV

- **1971**—the New American Standard Bible (NASB) is published as a modern and accurate word for word English translation of the Bible

- **1973**—the New International Version (NIV) is published as a modern and accurate phrase for phrase English translation of the Bible

- **1982**—the New King James Version (NKJV) is published as a modern English version maintaining the original style of the King James Version

- **2002**—the English Standard Version (ESV) is published as a translation to bridge the gap between the accuracy of the NASB and the readability of the NIV

Prayer

Top Ten Things You Need to Know
about Prayer

1. Without prayer, we never fully understand what it means to be human, nor do we gain a full understanding of life's big issues—the big picture.

2. We can be good people without prayer. We can be strong and courageous and compassionate. But with prayer, we're even better—we know where our source of strength is.

3. Prayer helps us better understand and yield to God's commands.

4. Going to God in prayer can help us see beyond our immediate situation and start sorting out the details.

5. Prayer can reveal things that play a bigger role in our lives than we'd like them to.

6. It can be hard to know which direction we should take in life when we only rely on our own thoughts and feelings. Asking God for His opinion can help us get a better idea of the road we should travel.

7. It is important to seek God's wisdom through prayer so that we can better align our decisions with what He has in mind for us.

8. We don't know what the future holds for us from God's point of view unless we seek Him through prayer.

9. Prayer makes sense. If it didn't, we wouldn't feel called to do it. Nor would the billions of other people who make a conscious effort to connect with God on a regular—if not daily—basis.

10. Praying is the only way to learn how to pray.

Introduction

HUMAN BEINGS HAVE SEARCHED for understanding since the earliest of times. We were born with inquiring minds and an innate need to understand the "big picture"—how the world around us came to be, and where we fit into the scheme of things. From those earliest of times, we have sensed that the answers lie not in what we can see, but in that which we cannot see. Prayer has been our means of communicating with the greater being or spirit that lies beyond human understanding.

Although we were born with the desire to pray—some call it "being wired for prayer"—prayer frustrates many people. They find it difficult to make time for it. They wonder if they are doing it right, and if they could do it better. Is it better to pray alone or with others? Silently or out loud? Should they kneel, sit, or stand? Should they call that which they pray to "God," "Goddess," "Father," or "Mother"? Does any one prayer style or any specific posture ensure that they'll be heard? Does prayer really get them anywhere?

The truth is, there is no one perfect prayer, no perfect way to pray, and no perfect pray-er. In this particular arena, there are no yes or no answers, no scales of comparison. There is simply the practice of prayer, in whatever form it takes. And that is what this book is all about.

Prayer is often written about in a fairly lofty manner, which can make it seem like we need to be experts at it before we can do it, and that we have to be on our best behavior when we do it. In the pages ahead, you'll find a great deal of evidence to the contrary. Everyone has to begin somewhere in prayer. In this particular practice, not only are we all beginners, we remain beginners. Prayer is meant to be a lifelong experience. There is always something new to learn, another path to explore, another door to open. This is what makes prayer both challenging and exciting . . . even fun.

There is no need to be perfect angels when we pray. We can be angry, happy, sad, or elated. Throughout time, the people who pray have been all these things, and more. You'll see many examples in this book of people praying just as they were, without any pretense or artifice. They prayed, as is often said, with their warts on. They simply had a chat with God.

The "G" word—God—may be how you experience your creator. Then again, it might not. He goes by many names—Allah, Father, Jehovah, and of course God—which makes it difficult to choose one name when writing about Him. To keep things simple here, we refer to our creator as God, and sometimes the Almighty. This choice reflects the name that many people are familiar and comfortable with. But, it may not work well for some. If you are one of them, feel free to substitute the word or words that resonate with you whenever you see the word God.

Referring to God as "He" or "Him" may also be a problem for some. It's definitely a problem for anyone who writes about God. Truthfully, there's no pronoun that accurately reflects what God is. God isn't male, female, or "it." He transcends all genders. Here again, the pronoun Him used throughout this book to refer to God was chosen as it works well for many people. Feel free to substitute any word that you find more acceptable.

If you are new to prayer, you may be wondering what it takes to pray. Not much, really. The desire to pray, of course, is a big part of it. The fact that you're curious about prayer shows that you've got this one covered. Prayer also requires having some sort of a relationship with the Divine, which being curious about prayer also speaks to. The rest of prayer is all about details.

You may also be wondering what you'll get from prayer. Maybe the better question is, what don't you get? Without prayer, we never fully understand what it means to be human, nor do we gain a full understanding of life's big issues— the big picture. We can be good people without prayer. We can be strong and courageous and compassionate. With prayer, we're even better. With prayer, we know where our source of strength is. With prayer, we know God.

CHAPTER 1

The World of Prayer

Mother Teresa often said that everything starts from prayer. This was her take on the importance of prayer, and, frankly, she hit the nail on the head. History shows us that prayer has played a central role in the human experience from the very beginning of recorded time. And it continues to do so to this day.

Prayer All Around

The word *prayer* comes from the Latin word *precari*, which means to entreat. Interestingly, the word *precarious*, which means "dependent upon the will or favor of another person," is based on the same Latin word.

Even if you're not much of a pray-er, it's hard to find an aspect of life where prayer—either the act itself or some sort of reference to it—doesn't play a part. It appears in song lyrics and movie titles. Walk into any bookstore, or browse any online bookseller, and you'll find hundreds of books on every conceivable aspect of prayer—walking prayer, listening prayer, prayers for babies, prayers for parents, prayers for celebrating life, prayers for the dying.

We have prayer breakfasts and national days of prayer. There are prayer circles, prayer warriors, and prayer partners. Sometimes we ask people to pray for us. Sometimes we are called upon to pray for others. Sometimes we think certain people haven't got a prayer. And, sometimes, it seems like we're the ones who are lacking in this particular arena.

factum

In a 1997 *Newsweek* poll, 52 percent of American adults said they prayed on a daily basis; 29 percent reported praying more than once a day. An overwhelming majority of those—87 percent—said they believe that God answers their prayers atleast some of the time.

Yet, we live—well, at least most of us do—in a secular society, one that isn't governed by a religious body or bodies or controlled by religious or spiritual matters. In general, the world around us is defined more by ideas and concepts that can be scientifically proven than things that lie beyond the realm of human knowledge, which prayer, being the key thing that connects us to God, definitely is.

As the lines of scientific discovery continue to extend, more and more of the world's mysteries are being uncloaked. Thanks to such endeavors as space and deep-sea exploration, we now have a better understanding of the various physical forces that created our universe. We now know the secrets behind how we're genetically programmed, which has allowed researchers to start knocking at the doors of cures for cancer and other chronic diseases. But such knowledge can only take us so far. As human beings, we also need to know how and where we fit into the bigger picture. We still seek the presence of God to help us find the answers to such questions, and, as we have done since the earliest of times, we do so through prayer.

quote

Your brain is hardwired to find God. Until you do, you will not know who you are.
—Deepak Chopra, in *How to Know God: The Soul's Journey into the Mystery of Mysteries*

Why We Pray

Scientific inquiry has even extended into prayer, resulting in our being given lots of reasons why we shouldn't pray, and, on the other hand, why we should. Some of the strongest affirmations of what prayer can do, interestingly enough, have come from the medical and scientific communities, which had previously discounted its effectiveness in matters of health and healing.

The first scientific study of healing prayer, conducted in the early 1980s, showed that hospital patients who were being prayed for fared considerably better than those who weren't. Prayer was also put to the test in the field—literally—by researchers probing its effect on corn seeds. The kernels that were prayed for did better than the seeds that received no spiritual boost.

What science can't tell us, however, is why we pray. While prayer is considered by many to be an essential component of a rich and full religious life, and it plays a key role in formal religious ceremonies, the call to prayer clearly goes beyond any sense of obligation. Many people who claim no adherence to any one faith, or who don't even define themselves as particularly religious, do identify themselves as pray-ers. There is no need to be in a house of worship to pray.

Regardless of who you are, how you were raised, or what your spiritual

discussion question

Do you have to be a "religious" person to derive the full benefits of prayer?
While having a relationship of one sort or another with the Almighty is an essential component of prayer, an allegiance to a specific religion or church is not a prerequisite for experiencing a rich and fulfilling life of prayer.

Some people believe that the urge or desire to pray is an indelible part of the human psyche. In other words, we're programmed to pray. Herbert Benson, the physician who founded the Mind/Body Medical Institute at Harvard Medical School, believes that people are, in his words, "wired for God," and that our desire to worship and believe in the Almighty is a deep and intrinsic part of our genetic programming. As the psychologist and philosopher William James wrote, ". . . we cannot help praying. It seems probable that, in spite of all that 'science' may do to the contrary, men will continue to pray to the end of time, unless their mental nature changes in a manner which nothing we know should lead us to expect."

Beyond any desire or programming, however, lies our simple need to be fed. We can handle the physical aspects of nourishment (many would argue all too well), but when it comes to providing for the mind and spirit, our attention must turn to God. As the following Psalm illustrates, the benefits of doing so are great indeed.

God is our refuge and our strength,

A very present help in trouble.

Therefore we will not fear,

Even though the earth be removed,

And though the mountains be carried into the midst of the sea;

Though its waters roar and be troubled,

Though the mountains shake with its swelling.

There is a river whose streams shall make glad the city of God,

The holy place of the tabernacle of the Most High.

God is in the midst of her, she shall not be moved;

God shall help her, just at the break of dawn.

The nations raged, the kingdoms were moved;

He uttered His voice, the earth melted.

The Lord of hosts is with us;

The God of Jacob is our refuge.

Come, behold the works of the Lord,

Who has made desolations in the earth.

He makes wars cease to the end of the earth;

He breaks the bow and cuts the spear in two;

He burns the chariot in the fire.

Be still, and know that I am God;

I will be exalted among the nations,

I will be exalted in the earth!

The Lord of hosts is with us;

The Lord of Jacob is our refuge.

The Changing Face of Prayer

What has changed somewhat over time is how we choose to come before the Almighty. Like our perceptions of God, prayer doesn't stand still. It is instead an evolutionary process, and it changes when and as necessary. The English theologian Karen Armstrong notes that humans have always created gods, and that when one worship form or religion has ceased to work or has lost its relevance, it's simply been replaced with another.

The same appears to be true about prayer. It has taken various forms and styles throughout history and continues to do so. At times, communal or corporate prayer has been emphasized over other forms. It was believed that it was best to come to God in a set place of worship, and through a set liturgy.

At other times, people went to God through an intermediary, someone who could act as a "go-between" and petition the Almighty on behalf of people because it wasn't believed appropriate to approach God directly.

factum

> Another term for liturgy is order of service. The word *liturgy* stems from a Latin term meaning "public servant." It refers to both the sacrament of the Eucharist as well as the overall set form for public worship.

God Is Dead

In the 1960s, "God is dead" was a popular proclamation of the hippie subculture. Their words echoed the beliefs of many intellectual pioneers of the last century or so. The work of such brilliant thinkers as Karl Marx, Charles Darwin, Friedrich Nietzsche, and Sigmund Freud had presented new ways of looking at the human condition, and God didn't factor much at all into the brave new world that they envisioned. The world had become more based in the secular and, in turn, increasingly less devoted to the sacred, or convinced that the sacred even existed.

Perhaps some people had indeed lost their belief in God. As history has shown us, however, it wasn't that people believed that God had gone away as much as they had once again changed the way in which they perceived Him. The increasingly dominant focus on the physical and material aspects of life lessened the emphasis on matters of a more spiritual nature. This made God seem extremely far away, and perhaps nonexistent.

What was definitely clear was that many people had lost their commitment to worshipping in the same ways that their parents did. Traditional religious practices—regular attendance at church, heads bowed in supplication at prescribed times during set-in-stone liturgies—didn't cut it for the "Me" generation, which was more interested in personal enlightenment than formal worship services. Institutional religion and religious doctrine became irrelevant for many people.

In Search of Spirit

For some, the answers seemed to lie beyond many of the better-known traditions of Western religion. Eastern spirituality, including Zen practice, became one of many alternative paths to a deeper spiritual experience. Others moved beyond the religion of their childhood and explored different pathways to spirituality, including yoga, transcendental meditation, and the more contemplative and mystical forms of prayer that had played a significant role in ancient worship dating back to the early days of Christianity. In so doing, they blurred the lines between the prayer forms that had come to define traditional religion and those that were perhaps less familiar but in no way any less valid or effective.

symbolism

While many use the terms religion and spirituality interchangeably, they do mean different things. In his book *The Best Alternative Medicine*, Kenneth R. Pelletier, director of the Complementary and Alternative Medicine Program at Stanford University School of Medicine, defines spirituality as "an inner sense of something greater than oneself, a recognition of a meaning to existence," and religion as "the outward expression of spiritual impulses, in the form of a specific religion or practice."

As more people embarked on their journeys to self-enlightenment, those trips often took them far beyond their previous spiritual experiences. Some integrated what they learned into their own religious traditions, whereas others found it difficult to do so. They left behind the religious traditions they had been raised with, and created their own personal brand of spirituality.

The "Define-It-Yourself" Age

Today, the manner in which we approach the Almighty can best be described as eclectic. In general, there is less emphasis on institutional religion or doctrine, although they continue to play an important role. More and more, however, spirituality—or the quality or condition of being spiritual—is the focus. In fact, a 2000 poll by the magazine *Spirituality & Health* reported that one in five Americans considers himself spiritual rather than religious.

As Robert Owens Scott noted in the Spring 2001 issue, ". . . our spiritual journeys are now taking us down paths that were not available to previous generations. Not only are we exposed to a wider variety of religious practices, but the word spirituality has stepped out on its own. It now signifies a multitude of indispensable indefinables that give our lives meaning."

Many people seeking spiritual enlightenment are exploring a variety of points of view from many different faiths. Instead of asking their ministers to advise them, they're increasingly going it alone or employing the help of spiritual directors or guides. Prayer is often one of a number of practices—including such things as meditation, visualization, drumming, and so forth—that are done to keep body, mind, and spirit in touch with God. As such, it also takes various forms, with a decided shift being seen in more meditative or contemplative methods that emphasize being able to experience God in a very personal manner. Some people decry this "define-it-yourself" spirituality, but there's no question that it is the approach that works for many today.

factum

Spirituality & Health's poll reported on many aspects of the "new American spirituality." Among its other findings: 59 percent of Americans think of themselves as both religious and spiritual; 23 percent view spirituality as the broader concept that embraces religion. An overwhelming majority—91 percent—see praying as a spiritual activity; 81 percent described attending worship services as spiritual.

Types of Prayer

Prayer has traditionally been defined as "asking, pleading, or petitioning." You'll find versions of this definition in virtually any dictionary, and examples of these prayer forms in all of the world's religions, as well as in the Bible.

Pleading or petitioning prayers could also be the kinds of prayers that you are most familiar with, and, perhaps, were raised to believe are most acceptable. That's fine, but to think of prayer in this manner barely scratches the surface. Ask anyone who has made prayer a part of his spiritual journey, and he'll tell you that his understanding—and experience—of prayer goes far beyond this.

Prayer can—and does—take innumerable forms. There are short prayers of less than a sentence, and prayers that go on for pages. Prayers can follow a specific form, or they can be simply prayers of the heart, offered directly and simply in no specific form at all. They can be vocal or silent, spoken or sung. Prayers can make requests of God—the Bible, in fact, is full of examples of petitionary prayer, with the ones attributed to the authors of the Psalms leading the list as being some of the most passionate and heartfelt. They can glorify and praise Him, they can simply thank Him, and they can ask Him for His forgiveness.

quote

I like to speak of prayer as listening. We live in a culture that is terribly afraid to listen. We'd prefer to remain deaf. The Latin root word of the word *deaf* is "absurd". Prayer means moving from absurdity to obedience. Let the words descend from your head to your heart so you can begin to know God. In prayer, you become who you are meant to be.

—Henri Nouwen, Jesuit priest

We can pray indoors and out, in places of worship or in our cars in the middle of rush hour. We can pray collectively or individually, with our loved ones, with congregations, or with total strangers.

Communicating with God

Central to all types of prayer, however, is a sense of communicating with God. Sometimes you'll see this communication described as talking or listening to God. These two-way dialogues are meant to take place at any time, day or night, just like you would chat with a friend. Through them, God comes to us and works with us, no matter where we are or the manner in which we've addressed Him. As we continue our conversations, we grow in our relationship with the Almighty. We draw closer to Him, and we allow Him to draw closer to us.

Saint Ignatius called the prayer conversations that people have with God colloquies, and believed they should be no different in tone or content than two friends talking to each other, or a parent talking to a child. Many of the world's great spiritual leaders, both past and present, have described or defined prayer in similar fashion.

However, not everyone is comfortable with the concept of talking to God "one on one," such as it were. Some even find the notion of treating the Almighty with such familiarity somehow irreverent. If you do, it might take you some time to break through your current beliefs. But, as you'll see in the chapters that follow, developing an intimate relationship with God is a cornerstone of a fulfilling prayer life. As many people believe, it's what He wants us to do.

Getting Down and Dirty

God literally asks us to get "down and dirty" with Him. While there is nothing wrong in coming before the Almighty in a formal way, such as through liturgical services and proscribed prayers, the truth is that there is no need for formality in this particular relationship. We don't have to be washed clean and dressed in our Sunday best. It is perfectly all right to let our guard down and be ourselves in God's presence throughout the course of everyday life.

Going Formal

There are certainly times when it is appropriate to pray in a more formal fashion. Worshipping during a formal liturgical service in a church, synagogue, or mosque calls for following the order of service as it's set down in the prayer book. If you were at a wedding or a funeral, a casual colloquy with God would most likely not be in order.

At these times, following the prayers that others have written and allowing their words to substitute for ours is necessary, and it's the right thing to do, even if we feel like we're talking more at God than with God. But on an everyday basis, there is less need for such formality. We can just let the words flow.

Coming Clean

It is also not necessary to be squeaky clean and free of problems before going to God in prayer. Many people are reluctant or even afraid to pray because they feel they're not worthy of having a relationship with God for some reason. Some people feel they've "been too bad" and would in some way offend the Almighty. They're ashamed to turn to God because they're afraid of what He might say. Or they'd like to believe that such a relationship is possible, but they have a hard time getting one started because they've been disappointed in prayer in the past. Others are simply afraid to go where they haven't gone before, and fear that opening themselves to God will force them into examining behaviors and beliefs that they'd rather leave untouched.

It's easy to understand these fears, and even easier to put them to rest. Here's why: God knows us better than we know ourselves, and He understands better than we ever could. Nothing is going to come as a surprise to Him, nor is it necessary to try to explain it all to Him. All that is necessary is to come to Him and tell Him what's going on.

quote

Where can I go from Your Spirit? Or where can I flee from your presence? If I ascend into heaven, You are there; If I make my bed in hell, behold, You are there. If I take the wings of the morning, And dwell in the uttermost parts of the sea, Even there Your hand shall lead me, And Your right hand shall hold me.

—Psalm 139:7–10

As hard as it might be, the times when we're feeling "less than," for any reason, are exactly when it is most important to talk to the Almighty. We might not always get the answers we want, or answers that we understand, but it is essential to keep the conversation going. Doing so not only deepens our relationship with God, it helps us remain open to the changes in ourselves that come about through that relationship.

Getting the Conversation Going

If prayer is as simple as talking to God, it should be easy to do, right? Perhaps so, but many people find that it isn't easy, at least not at first. They are concerned over doing it "right," although there isn't one right way to pray, or one way that's any better than any other. The way that works best for you is simply the "right" way. And, as you'll see in this book, there are many ways to go about it.

As human beings, we tend to make things more difficult than they need to be, and our tendency to complicate things can stand in the way. When it comes to prayer, we sometimes get tied up in knots worrying about how we're doing it. When we don't immediately see the benefits of our prayers, we think we're doing it wrong.

The answer to these concerns should be pretty obvious by now. Just pray. Put aside any fears or concerns that you have, and start talking to God. And don't forget to listen.

CHAPTER 2

The Power of Prayer

Prayer, purely and simply, is about being in union with God. When we make the commitment to experience that union on a regular basis, all sorts of things can happen, and do happen, both to us and to the people we pray for.

Changing Things Through Prayer

It's often been said—you've probably heard it more than once—that prayer changes things. In fact, you might have experienced firsthand some of the changes that prayer can bring about. You might have prayed for something and had your prayer answered. Maybe someone you know joined a prayer group and seems to be happier and more at peace because of it. Or you know someone who made a pretty miraculous recovery from a serious illness and gives prayer the credit for being able to return to wellness.

What you may not know, however, is exactly how these changes come about. But here's the inside story on that: No one really knows. Not for sure, anyway. Even the world's greatest theologians—men and women who have

discussion question

What is it about our relationship with God that can change life's circumstances?
There's not an easy answer to this question, but it begins with the changes in ourselves that come about through that relationship. When we say that God changes things, the most important things He changes are the people who walk with Him in prayer.

What we do know for sure is that God promises to answer our prayers. In the Book of Matthew, Jesus tells his disciples that, "Everyone who asks receives," which is about the best testimony to the power of prayer that anyone could ask for. On the other hand, the Bible also tells us that if we don't ask, we don't get, which is pretty good justification for getting close to God in prayer. He might be all-knowing and all-seeing, but He's not going to answer our prayers unless we offer them to Him.

But what does "answering our prayers" really mean? If we ask God to help us become prosperous, will He help? If we pray for healing, will He heal? If we ask for His guidance, will He guide us? Yes, in all these things God will answer us. But the changes in circumstances that we're seeking will often manifest themselves differently than how we think they will. Sometimes, in fact, they won't happen at all because His answer to our prayer was "No."

Personal Transformations

Another word for the changes that take place through prayer is *transformation*. Every relationship you enter into alters you in some way. So, too, does the relationship you have with God. In fact, the changes that God makes in the people who love Him are some of the most compelling examples of the power of prayer.

Through prayer, as we get to know God better, we also get to know ourselves better. We gain a greater understanding of what makes us tick, and what motivates us to do the things we do. We get smarter about how we handle the challenges of life. As we get to know ourselves better, we also are better able to understand others, and we become more compassionate and caring. In short, we learn how to be better people. It's a relationship, in biblical terms, that bears a lot of fruit, as the apostle Paul puts it in his letter to the Galatians: "But the fruit of the Spirit is love, joy, peace, longsuffering, kindness, goodness, faithfulness, gentleness, self control" (Galatians 5:22–23).

What God refrains from doing is telling us exactly how we should live our lives—He leaves the freedom of will up to each one of us. Instead, by talking to Him—that is, praying to Him—we gain a greater understanding of our actions and the motivations behind them, and, for that matter, the actions and motivations of others.

As we grow in our relationship with God, we also get better at knowing how to keep our dialogue with Him flowing smoothly. In other words, we understand what it takes to pray. In a nutshell, it boils down to five basic principles:

1. **Having faith.** As mentioned in Chapter 1, belief in God is a prerequisite for prayer. But having faith in prayer goes beyond this; it takes our believing that God is capable of doing anything and everything—including answering our prayers. It also means that we have to believe that God works for good in all things, even during times when it doesn't seem like He is doing so at all.

2. **Being humble.** Humility before God means understanding where we are in relation to Him. Simply put, He is God, and we're not. It means accepting the fact that we're pretty puny when compared to Him, and that we very much need His help. And, it means being willing to allow Him to work within or through us, and to accept His will. His will, not ours.

3. **Being honest.** God has a great sense of humor, but He doesn't like being fooled with. While it's not even possible to do it, you'd be surprised at how many people do try. Being honest with God means coming before Him as we are, with all our earthly foibles. It also means asking God for His forgiveness if we've not been obedient to His word in some way.

4. **Being patient.** We are, by nature, a pretty impatient people. We don't like waiting any longer than we think we need to, whether it's when we're stopped at a red light or when we're trying to access a Web site that's loading more slowly than we'd like it to. We want what we want, and we want it now. Well, there isn't much "now" when it comes to God. If there's one lesson that God teaches us more than any other, it's learning how to wait on Him. We have to wait, as the prophet Elijah had to do, for God's "still, small voice."

5. **Being thankful.** Giving thanks to God is also part of coming before Him with a humble heart. When we thank God, we're acknowledging the importance of our relationship with Him.

If there were such a thing as a magic formula for effective prayer, it would consist of something like these five principles. Come before God with these precepts firmly in place and you'll be able to offer up the kinds of prayers that He can do something about. Not only that, you'll better understand the reasons why you don't always get what you pray for.

When Prayer Fails

One of the things that keeps people from experiencing the power of prayer is that they've been disappointed in it. They've asked God for certain things, and they haven't received what they asked for. In other words, prayer failed them. Or did it?

factum

Even the prayers that we think have failed are powerful prayers. While they may not deliver the results we had hoped for, their power can be seen, and felt, in other ways.

Sometimes, yes, prayer can feel like failure. If we've prayed for healing, and it doesn't happen, it can be hard to believe that prayer can be effective. If we ask God for a new house, a new job, or a new car, and we don't get them, it's pretty hard not to be disappointed.

What is behind failed prayers? Some will tell you that prayers fail because the people who pray them are lacking in faith. In other words, they didn't believe strongly enough in what they were praying about, and they didn't truly believe that God could answer their prayers. There's some truth to this, but it's only part of the answer.

The Flip Side of Failed Prayers

As hard as it can be to deal with the disappointment and frustration that failed prayers can create, it is important to realize that they don't work against us. Instead, they work for us. To understand how this can be, you have to look at things from a different perspective. Instead of pointing a finger at God and accusing Him of not helping out, we have to take a closer look at why our prayers are ineffective. Maybe we're not asking for things in the right way. Or we're asking for things that may not be in our best interest. Maybe, in fact, we're the problem, not God.

In *Be Careful What You Pray For . . . You Just Might Get It: What We Can Do About the Unintentional Effects of Our Thoughts, Prayers, and Wishes*, author Larry Dossey notes that one of the key issues behind failed prayers is our inappropriate involvement in what he calls a "tightly coupled system." For the most part, that system performs pretty well, but when it doesn't, we try to fix things through prayer. But, instead of making things better, our involvement often makes them worse.

As Dossey puts it, "The issue is not that we pray, but how we pray. When something goes wrong in our life, we tend to invoke prayers involving highly specific, designated outcomes. We're certain that we have the knowledge to set things right, and we waste no time telling the Absolute what to do. We do not realize that we are interfering in a highly complex, tightly coupled system that, when tweaked, often responds in unpredictable ways."

The Problem of Playing God

What Dossey is getting at is that we tend to play God a bit when we pray for certain things. We let our egos get in the way of prayer. Instead of praying, "Thy will be done," we're saying to God, "My will be done." This isn't prayer, but rather it's our thinking that we can manipulate God into giving us what we want. But we can't manipulate God. Things just don't work this way in prayer.

To justify this sort of "naming and claiming" prayer, many people single out the biblical verses that seem to support it. In Jesus' "Sermon on the Mount," he tells his listeners to "Ask and it will be given to you; seek, and you will find; knock, and it will be opened for you. For everyone who asks receives, and he who seeks finds, and to him who knocks it will be opened" (Matthew 7:7–8).

quote

If God had granted all the silly prayers I've made in my life, where should I be now? The best antidote for our folly may be, as we've seen, not in praying for anything at all, but in adopting an approach in prayer such as "Thy will be done" or "May the best outcome prevail." This approach might offer fabulous protection from the most serious threat we face: ourselves.

—C. S. Lewis, in *Letters to Malcolm*

These are pretty powerful words. Taken literally, they tell us that God will answer our prayers, no matter what, and give us whatever we want. But Jesus, who was a master at allegory and metaphor, and used them extensively in his teachings, was, in fact, speaking metaphorically here. The lesson he's teaching is on the importance of having faith in God, and the results of our putting our faith in Him. Everyone who asks does receive, but the gift we get is God's perfect love for us, not a shiny new BMW.

The Real Meaning of Unanswered Prayers

The bottom line is this: We're not God. His words in the Book of Isaiah make this very clear:

"For My thoughts are not your thoughts, nor are your ways My ways," says the Lord. "For as the heavens are higher than the earth, So are My ways higher than your ways, And My thoughts than your thoughts" (Isaiah 55:8–9).

Because we don't have God's insight and wisdom, we have no way of knowing about factors that might be working against our immediately having our prayers answered. Or having them answered at all. Maybe it's not the right time. Maybe God has something better in store for us. Maybe we need to learn how to be more faithful or more patient. Maybe, simply, the answer is "no" because what we're asking for may actually make things worse.

In not answering our prayers, God teaches us one of the most powerful lessons of all: to trust Him, and trust in Him, no matter what. When we get that lesson down, well, miracles can happen, and often do.

Healing by Faith

Some of the greatest miracles brought about by prayer, interestingly enough, have taken place in the realm of health and healing. In biblical times, people routinely asked God to heal them. The Second Book of Kings, in the Old Testament, describes how King Hezekiah prayed for healing from a terminal disease:

> Then he turned his face toward the wall, and prayed to the Lord, saying, "Remember now, O Lord, I pray, how I have walked before you in truth and with a loyal heart, and have done what was good in your sight . . . Then it happened, before Isaiah had gone out into the middle court, that the word of the Lord came to him, saying, "Return and tell Hezekiah the leader of My people, Thus says the Lord, the God of David your father: I have heard your prayer, I have seen your tears; surely I will heal you. On the third day you shall go up to the house of the Lord. And I will add to your days fifteen years. I will deliver you and this city from the hand of the

*King of Assyria; and I will defend this city for My own sake, and for
the sake of My servant David."*

—2 Kings 21:2–6

The New Testament contains a number of examples of how Jesus healed
various ailments of the faithful. In fact, he even told his disciples the secret to
it: ". . . if you have faith as a mustard seed, you will say to this mountain, 'Move
from here to there,' and it will move; and nothing will be impossible for you"
(Matthew 18:20).

In this era of modern medicine, we've tended to put our faith more in the
healing power of physicians and less in the healing power of God. Recent
studies, however, suggest that each has a place in the continuum of healing.
Not only that, most of us prefer to have God be an active part of the equation.

factum

A survey conducted in 1995 to assess the relevancy of religion and
spirituality in medicine found overwhelming support for the inter-
mingling of the practical with the spiritual. Fifty percent of hospital-
ized patients told surveyers they believed that their physicians
should not just pray with them, but for them as well.

One of the most intriguing areas in which the power of prayer has been
put to the test is in remote healing. In several experiments, people from many
different spiritual backgrounds have been asked to pray on behalf of certain
individuals in need of healing. Their long-distance prayers were shown to be
pretty effective. In one study, about 1,000 heart patients who were admitted to
a hospital's critical care unit were divided into two groups. For a year, a group
of volunteers and the hospital's chaplain prayed for one half of the group. The
result: The patients in the prayer group had 11 percent fewer heart attacks,

strokes, and life-threatening complications. One of the cardiologists who participated in the study commented that it offered some interesting insights into the possibility that God influenced lives on earth. As a scientist, he added, he had no way of explaining how He did so.

The question of prayer's effectiveness when patients prayed for themselves was also put to test. Here, the focus was on how prayer could affect the mental status of critically ill heart patients. Again, prayer proved helpful—almost 100 percent of the individuals who prayed for themselves before undergoing major surgery reported that praying had been extremely helpful in helping them manage the stress and anxiety that so often arise when serious illness strikes.

Another study tested the power of remote prayer on critically ill AIDS patients. The twenty patients in the study received basically the same medical treatment. Half were prayed for by spiritual healers representing a number of religious traditions—Christianity, Buddhism, and the traditional practices of Native Americans among them. The others received no prayer support. All ten of the prayed-for patients remained alive throughout the course of the six-month study. Four of the others died, reflecting a standard mortality rate for AIDS patients as critically ill as these individuals were. A follow-up study conducted by the same researcher found that people who received prayer and remote healing spent far less time in the hospital, both in terms of frequency of admission and length of stay.

Clearly, the final verdict on prayer isn't in. But it sure looks like it couldn't hurt. Or could it?

The Negative Power of Prayer

It's clear that prayer can definitely be good medicine. But it can be bad medicine as well. As it turns out, prayer has a dark side, too.

For many, this is an unspeakable subject. The fact that it is has a lot to do with our having whitewashed God's personage over the years. Most people won't even admit that prayer can be anything else but good. There is some pretty strong evidence, however, to the contrary.

If you know your Old Testament at all, you know that the Almighty could be pretty vengeful when He needed to be. The Israelites felt the hand of God on a fairly regular basis. Remember the story of Sodom and Gomorrah? God destroyed these two cities because the people who lived in them were so wicked and depraved. David, the beloved Jewish king, often called upon God to wreak vengeance on his enemies. David wouldn't have done so if he didn't get some results.

O Lord God, to whom vengeance belongs—O God, to whom vengeance belongs, shine forth.

Rise up, O Judge of the earth; Render punishment to the proud.

—Psalm 94:1–3

The New Testament also contains examples of negative prayer. In the Book of Acts, Paul calls upon God to blind a false prophet who was trying to turn a righteous man away from God (Acts 13:6–12). Say what you will about the righteousness of his intentions, the outcome was a negative one.

Even Jesus prayed a negative prayer when he called on God to wither away a barren fig tree (Matthew 21:19). Admittedly, his actions were part of a lesson in faith to his disciples, but let's not whitewash what really happened here. The fig tree was alive, it just wasn't bearing fruit for some reason. Jesus said "Let no fruit grow on you ever again," and it died.

It isn't important to dwell on this topic to excess. However, to fully understand the power of prayer, you also need to accept the fact that there are negative prayers, and negative pray-ers. As much as we might like to think that these individuals are not aware of what they're doing, we know otherwise. In 1994, *Life* magazine reported the results of a Gallup poll that contained some pretty startling data: Five percent of the Americans polled admitted to having prayed for something bad to happen to others. Five percent may not sound all that bad, but keep in mind that this figure represents only the people who were honest enough to admit praying in this manner. The actual numbers are probably quite a bit higher.

The Nature of Negative Prayer

When we think about negative prayers we often put them in the context of intentional hexes and curses such as those cast by witches in children's fairy tales. More often, however, they're much more casual than this, and we're often not aware of them when we launch them. We can be praying negatively simply by thinking negatively about another person. All those little "damn you's" and "God damn its"—they're negative prayers, too.

Negative prayers can be as innocent as asking God to put us ahead of someone else as equally deserving of His favor. In *Be Careful What You Pray For . . . You Just Might Get It*, Larry Dossey calls these random and seemingly innocent prayers "prayer muggings," and issues a strong caution about making them, as they're usually made without any consideration for the effect they might have on the other party.

discussion question

Should I pray for someone who hasn't asked for it?
Some people believe that it can be risky to pray for someone who hasn't specifically requested it, as doing so may not be aligned with that person's desires or religious beliefs. If you know a person who has asked someone else to pray for him or her, it's probably okay for you to join in. But it's a good idea to ask before you do so.

Even praying for someone without his or her consent may be seen as a negative prayer. Mary Baker Eddy, the founder of Christian Science, made this point clear when she wrote, "Who of us would have our houses broken open or our locks picked? And much less would have our minds tampered with? . . . Our Master said, 'when we enter a house, salute it.' . . . I say, When you enter mentally the personal precincts of human thought, you should know the person with whom you hold communion desires it."

If you take anything away from this discussion of negative prayer, it should be this: Know that prayer can be very powerful, and be careful how you use it.

Avoiding Negative Prayer

One of the simplest ways we can keep from uttering negative prayers is to always remember that our prayers never exist in a vacuum. In some way or another, they will have an effect on something or somebody. What might seem like a positive prayer in your eyes may be very much the opposite to someone else. When you're praying to God, be mindful of your prayers. Ask Him for His guidance on them as well. He'll direct you to the positive side if you ask Him to.

What can you do if you feel like you're the target of negative prayers? Well, you can pray for yourself. Doing so may very well be your best defense. There are a number of different prayers that you can use if you feel like you want to harness the power of someone's words. "The Lord's Prayer"—the prayer that Jesus taught his disciples when they asked him how they should pray—is one of the best prayer covers you could ask for. In fact, it even asks God to protect us from those who wish to harm us.

Our Father, who art in heaven, hallowed be thy name.

Thy kingdom come, thy will be done

on earth as it is in heaven.

Give us this day our daily bread,

And forgive us our trespasses

as we forgive those who trespass against us.

And lead us not into temptation,

but deliver us from evil.

For thine is the kingdom,

and the power, and the glory,

forever and ever.

Amen.

CHAPTER 3

How the Faiths Pray

One of the basic things to know about prayer is that it doesn't belong to any one religion or spiritual tradition. Prayer is universal, and it plays a key role in all of the world's leading religions. To understand how your prayer practice fits into the grand scheme of things, it can help to know something about the prayer traditions of the different faiths. We'll look at some of them in this chapter.

The History of Prayer

While there isn't an exact history of prayer in and of itself, we do know quite a bit about how people have sought to understand the world around them, both seen and unseen, and the religions that developed as a result of their efforts. It is in the history of these religions where we find the rituals and traditions that shape how people communicate with God.

quote

> What a strange fellowship this is, the God-seekers in every land, lifting their voices in the most disparate ways imaginable to the God of all life.
>
> —Huston Smith, in *The World's Religions*

From the earliest of times, we have realized that there is something greater than we are out there. We have sought ways to understand what it is as well as ways to develop some sort of a connection with it. What's interesting about our efforts is that they're very similar to those around us. No matter how we come at it, we all end up in the same place. There is one spirit—a Divine spirit—that unites us all, regardless of how we perceive it or how we choose to experience it.

When you pray, you're both honoring that shared history and extending it to the generations that will come after you. As you pray, whether you choose to honor the traditions of a specific religion, prefer to pull from many in an eclectic mix, or you wing it on your own, you're tapping into a rich spiritual pool that goes all the way back to prehistory.

Of the world's religious traditions, the three that share a common theology—Judaism, Christianity, and Islam—also claim the largest number of followers. These faiths are linked by a belief in one God, known as monotheism, as well as their shared history. In all of them, prayer takes the form of a personal relationship with God.

But prayer is not the only way in which people connect to that which is greater than themselves. There are a number of religions and beliefs throughout the world, primarily outside of the Western hemisphere, that acknowledge a greater being or spirit, but not God as we understand Him to be. They also experience the Holy in ways that are similar to, yet different from, the prayer forms that we are most familiar with. Buddhists, for example, don't pray to a God-like figure as most of us would understand one. However, Buddhists do pray. In Buddhist practice, prayers often take the form of meditation, and are directed toward acquiring spiritual enlightenment or illumination. Similar meditative practices are also performed by members of other religious faiths. What this illustrates is that there are many ways in which we can connect with the Absolute. Our spiritual beliefs will influence how we perceive this entity. It can be God or Allah. It can also be Brahma, the Universal Mind, the Tao, or the Void. It can even be the Great Goddess.

factum

Buddhists sometimes pay their respects to images of Buddha, but not as a form of religious veneration. Buddha is not a deity, but the title of the being who achieved supreme enlightenment in accordance with the teachings of Buddhism.

Other religions pray to or commune with the energy, spirit, or power within and its connections to the universe. We know less about some of these religions—such as the ones practiced by indigenous peoples in Africa and Australia—because their histories are oral instead of written. Yet, they too are part of the mix.

The Search for Meaning

As previously mentioned, people have sought a connection to that which is greater than they are from the beginning of civilization. They have sought this link for a variety of reasons—for guidance, direction, or simply to ask "why?" In the earliest times, our ancestors experienced the world in a far more intuitive and organic manner than we do today. Their lives revolved around food and the pursuit of food (although some would argue that today ours do as well). They were astute observers of nature—and especially the weather—as they understood that the forces of nature governed their food supply.

For this reason, the gods they worshipped were also a part of nature. They worshipped the god of the storm and the god of the sun. There were gods in mountains, and in animals.

symbolism

To ancient peoples, gods didn't create the flora and the fauna; their gods were the flora and the fauna. When a lightning bolt split the sky during a storm, it wasn't a god who sent that bolt—the bolt itself was a god making his presence known. Rain wasn't controlled by a water god; rather, it was part of a water god.

During this period, the family structure as we know it today had not yet developed. Instead, people gathered together in tribes, and the tribes worked together as a unit. Each tribe had its own gods.

The Sumerians and Their Gods

The beliefs of the earliest people carried forward to the first great civilization—the Sumerians. They too worshipped gods that were tied closely to nature and natural phenomena. The Sumerians, however, made their gods in the image of themselves—in other words, their gods had human form. They couldn't be seen, however, because they lived in the heavens.

The Sumerians believed that they had been created to work for their gods, and that everything belonged to them. Originally, each Sumerian city had its own god. Over time, the many gods were consolidated and organized into a hierarchy where some gods were more important than others. There were four main deities, each with a specific activity or role:

1. Anu, the father of the gods
2. Enlil, the god of the sky (the most important, because without him nothing was possible)
3. Ninmakh, or Ninkhursag, the great mother (who personified the fertility of the earth)
4. Enki, the god of the underground waters (who personified the masculine powers of creativity and life in the earth)

In addition to these deities, there was also a collection of minor gods, including Nanna, the moon god; Utu, the sun god; and Inanna, the god of the morning star.

The gods demanded a lot of the Sumerians. Elaborate rituals assured prosperity and a long life, but little more. But the Sumerians also felt a sense of protection from their gods. They understood that their gods controlled the environment and sustained life.

The Gods of Other Civilizations

The tradition of worshipping many gods also continued with the Egyptian civilization, which had gods in many forms, both human and animal, and also in the abstract and the inanimate. Like the early Sumerians, each Egyptian town had its patron deity or deities and its own religious community. The Egyptian pantheon, or collection of gods, was huge, numbering at least 2,000. Worship was in the form of cults led by pharaohs and priests. The gods they worshipped controlled the heavens and the earth as well as the world of the dead. Some of the basic myths of creation, divine kingship, and cosmic order can be found in the earliest Egyptian civilization.

Polytheism, or a belief in many gods, was the norm in most of the ancient world. In India, the Aryans worshipped nature gods, including Indra, the god of the air and of the storm; and Agni, the sacrificial fire. The intoxicant they drank during worship was the god Soma. Varuna was worshipped as the guardian of cosmic regularity. Hinduism had its gods, too. Siva personified the cosmic forces of destruction and reproduction; Vishnu was the god of sacrifice who took two forms—Krishna and Rama. There was also Brahma, the great Creator.

symbolism

The tradition of worshipping many gods is called polytheism, as opposed to monotheism, which is the belief or worship of a single god. Deism is the belief that a single god created the universe and then left it to its own devices without any influence at all.

The Romans had a simpler hierarchy, mostly based on the worship of Mars, who was an agricultural deity first, a god of war later. Religious ceremonies were simple but had to be orchestrated in a specific way in order to please the gods. Only then would they act. Failure to get the desired results was blamed on faulty ceremonies, not on the gods.

The Babylonians held close to the Sumerian tradition and had a system of gods. Each controlled a specific cosmic force—the heavens, air, ocean, sun, moon, and so on—and had a main temple in a particular city. Over time, however, one god—Marduk—elbowed out the others and took the lead as the primary Babylonian god.

From Many Gods, One

The Babylonians weren't the only ones who were beginning to place their faith in one deity instead of many. A small nomadic tribe that had wandered the Fertile Crescent of the Middle East for some time had entered into a covenant with the god Yahweh. Yahweh, the god of the Hebrews, was a mighty leader, creator, and judge. He was just as powerful as other ancient gods, but He stood apart from the others because He had no pantheon of lesser gods to accompany Him.

"I Am the Lord Your God"

Like the other civilizations of the ancient world, the Hebrews had a polytheistic heritage. The tribes who were their forerunners believed that there were many gods. However, they worshipped only their own god. When they strengthened that agreement by entering into a covenant with Him, whereby Yahweh agreed to return them to their promised land, they also agreed to dispense with their beliefs that there were other gods. In other words, there were no other gods before God. Nor was there ever to be, as long as the covenant between the two parties remained in place. God made this abundantly clear when He laid down the law to Moses, and Moses made it very clear to the Hebrews in turn:

> I stood between the Lord and you at that time, to declare to you the word of the Lord; for you were afraid because of the fire, and you did not go up the mountain. He said: I am the Lord your God who brought you out of the land of Egypt, out of the house of bondage. You shall have no other gods before me . . . For I, the Lord your God, am a jealous God . . .
>
> —Deuteronomy 5:5–9

The religious belief in one god set the Hebrews apart from all other ancient civilizations. The way in which they perceived their god did as well. Unlike the others, the god of the Hebrews took no human form. He was a transcendent deity, the creator of everything, who existed independently of His own creation. As Huston Smith describes it in *The World's Religions*:

> Where the Jews differed from their neighbors was not in envisioning the Other as personal but in focusing its personalism in a single, supreme, nature-transcending will. For the Egyptians, Babylonians, Syrians, and lesser Mediterranean peoples of the day, each major power of nature was a distinct deity . . . When we turn to the Hebrew Bible we find ourselves in a completely different atmosphere. Nature here is an expression of a single Lord of all being.

factum

> The Hebrew word for prayer is *tefilah*, which, loosely translated, means "to judge oneself." This meaning sheds light on the introspective nature of prayer and its importance to people of the Jewish faith.

The Lord God All Around

The belief that the entire world belongs to God and reflects God's glory continues to shape how Jews pray to God to this day. No matter where they are, no matter how they're praying—in formal worship services or on their own—Jews find a way to praise God and His work in virtually everything. In doing so, they constantly remind themselves of God's presence and their relationship to Him.

Jews pray both formally and informally, publicly and privately, as has been done since the earliest times of the faith. Some observant Jews (especially the Orthodox, the most stringent adherents to the traditional aspects of the faith) pray three times daily—in the morning, the afternoon, and the evening—and follow a specific pattern of prayer. Praying in the morning and the evening is a directive from the Shema, the oldest daily prayer in Judaism, which commands the faithful to pray "when you retire and when you arise." Saying the Shema, which consists of verses from the Old Testament books of Deuteronomy and Numbers, fulfills the prayer commitment at morning and night. The afternoon prayer was added later.

In addition to the three formal prayer services, Jews also say blessings over just about every daily activity. These prayers fall into three general categories:

1. Blessings recited before eating, drinking, or smelling something pleasant
2. Blessings recited before fulfilling a commandment of the Lord or performing a good deed
3. Blessings that praise and thank God for His wonderful works, or that ask God for His help

In the Shema can also be found the basis for two of the key visual symbols of the Jewish faith: the tefillin, or phylacteries; and the mezuzah. Tefillin, the symbols of faith that Jewish men wear on the head (above the eyes) and on the arm during prayer are symbolic of God's urging the Jews to bind His word "as a sign upon your hand, and . . . a reminder before your eyes." God's instructions to write His word "on the doorposts of your house and upon your gates" is symbolized by the mezuzah, which observant Jews (and even many Jews who aren't as observant) place inside the frame of the front doors of their homes to serve as a constant reminder of God's presence in their lives.

factum

The tradition of praying three times a day dates back to the sixth century B.C.E. At that time, the Jews were in exile in Babylon, and weren't able to offer their sacrifices in the temple, which was the central place of worship in ancient Jerusalem. Prayer was substituted for that practice. Since sacrifices had been held three times daily, a third prayer time was added to the two called for by the Shema.

God Made Man

Christianity is a historical religion that is based on concrete events and historic facts that center on the life of Jesus Christ—or, to be more exact, on his brief ministry of teaching and healing. During his short career, Jesus went from being the son of a poor carpenter to being a prophet and a healer. He preached the need for repentance in the face of the end of time and Judgment Day, and both told and showed people what they needed to do to reach the kingdom of heaven.

Jesus had a firm education in Jewish scripture, and he was devoutly Jewish. During his life, he both upheld his Jewish heritage and was deeply critical of it. He was a strong opponent of many of its precepts as they had come to be practiced, and believed that they erected barriers between people instead of bringing them together. This, in Jesus' eyes, was not what God was all about. He saw God as compassion and love, and his visions of God formed the basis for his teachings.

To this day, prayers made in the Christian tradition follow the prayer pattern that Jesus taught to his followers when they asked him how to pray—to adore God, confess to Him, offer thanksgiving, and to petition Him. "The Lord's Prayer" is considered by Christians to be the perfect prayer, and is valued for its simplicity, its beautiful imagery, and its timeless instruction.

factum

The first four books of the New Testament—the gospels of Matthew, Mark, Luke, and John—tell the story of Jesus' ministry from different yet similar points of view. The remaining New Testament books document the early formation of a new religion—Christianity—based on Jesus' teachings and works.

The prayer's opening words, "Our Father, who art in heaven, hallowed be thy name," describe how to approach God—with reverence and adoration. "Thy kingdom come, thy will be done, on earth as it is in heaven," reflects the desire to experience God's perfect kingdom and speaks to the necessity of living under His authority. "Give us this day our daily bread" again illustrates the need to rely on Him for all things.

The next line, "And forgive us our trespasses as we forgive those who trespass against us," asks God to pardon us as well as to give us the wisdom to pardon others. "Lead us not into temptation, but deliver us from evil," again asks for God's protection. The final lines of "The Lord's Prayer," "for thine is the kingdom, and the power, and the glory, forever and ever. Amen," takes us back to where we began as they adore Him and speak to His dominion over all.

In the Beginning . . . Allah

Islam, like Christianity, is a history-based religion. Chronologically, it came about after Judaism and Christianity, and it shares many theological concepts with its forerunners: There is just one God, and He is incorporeal and invisible. It also has a shared history with the other great monotheistic religions. As you may remember from the Old Testament, Abraham had a wife named Sarah. She couldn't bear children, so Abraham took another wife in order to fulfill God's commandments to "be fruitful and multiply." Hagar, Abraham's second wife, bore him a son whose name was Ishmael. Miraculously, Sarah also conceived and had a son, named Isaac. But Sarah was jealous of Hagar and Ishmael, and she demanded that Abraham banish them both from the tribe. According to the Quran, they traveled to Arabia. Muhammad, the founder of Islam, was a descendant of Ishmael.

"God Is Great"

Islamic worship is based on the five Pillars of Islam as they were set down by Muhammad. They include:

1. Declaration of Faith, or shahada (witness, testimony)
2. Prayer (salat)
3. Purification (zakat)
4. The Fast of Ramadan
5. Pilgrimmage, or Hajj

Muslims demonstrate their faith in God through prayer. The prayer rituals they follow are exact, and exacting. There are five daily prayer periods—daybreak, noon, midafternoon, sunset, and evening. The prayers offered during these periods are considered "contact prayers"—a means for remembering God and for staying on the right path. The prayers must be recited in Arabic. They can be performed individually or in a congregation.

symbolism

The rough translation of *Islam* is "submission." A Muslim, or adherent to Islam, translates to "submitters" in English. This refers to the Islamic belief that a true follower fully submits his or her self to God.

In many Muslim countries, followers of the faith are called to prayer by a mosque official called a muezzin who sits in a mosque's minaret, or tower. As they prepare to pray, Muslims face Mecca, the holy city. Before approaching God, Muslims must cleanse both the mind and body to ensure they are spiritually and physically pure. While Muslims can pray in any clean environment—alone or together, in a mosque or at home, at work or on the road, indoors or out—it is preferable to pray with others, if possible, as one body united in the worship of God. Doing so demonstrates discipline, brotherhood, equality, and solidarity among the people of Islam.

The Sequence of Movements

The prayers Muslims recite consist of readings from the Quran interspersed with phrases that glorify God. Each time of prayer begins with the declaration, "God is most great" ("Allahu Akbar"), and is followed by fixed prayers that include the opening verse of the Quran. They're accompanied by a sequence of movements, followed in exact order:

- standing
- bowing
- kneeling
- touching the ground with one's forehead (prostration)
- sitting

factum

Muslims aren't the only people who prostrate themselves during prayer. In fact, prostration is a common posture in many world religions, and is assumed both by clergy and laypersons at various times as part of their prayer life.

Both the words that are spoken and the movements that accompany them reflect humility, submission, and adoration of God. After all the required prayers are said, there is a brief period for personal prayer, during which time private petitions can be offered to God. Pray-ers can pray in Arabic, assisted by recommended texts. If they prefer, they can address God in words and language of their own. At the end of the prayer period, a declaration of faith is again recited, and the peace greeting—"Peace be upon all of you and the mercy and blessings of God"—is repeated twice.

The Path to Enlightenment

Buddhism was founded by a Hindu named Siddhartha who lived 2,500 years ago in what is now Nepal. His father was a king, and he was a prince. However, Siddhartha gave up his princely role in his early twenties and went out to seek understanding. The result of his search became the basis for Buddhism.

What Siddhartha saw on his journeys was a great deal of pain and suffering, disease and death. It made him despair of finding fulfillment on earth. This meant that fulfillment had to lie elsewhere. His quest for knowledge led him to the leading Hindu masters of the day. He also studied with a band of ascetics, with whom he tried to gain the knowledge he sought by going on what amounted to a fast. In so doing, he believed he would break the hold his body had on him, which would allow him to then be enlightened. He ended up sick and weak, and no more enlightened than he had been when he started out.

symbolism

The title "Buddha" means the "Enlightened One" or the "Awakened One." It is based on the Sanskrit word *budh*, which means both "to wake up" and "to know." In Buddhism, enlightenment also refers to a person attaining nirvana, or a state of no care or concern.

In the final stage of his quest, Siddhartha took up a form of yoga that taught mystic concentration. One evening, he sat down under what has come to be known as the bodhi tree, or tree of enlightenment. There, he sensed that he was on the verge of an enlightenment breakthrough, and he pledged to himself that he wouldn't move until he had grasped the golden ring. He remained in that spot—which Buddhists call the Immovable Spot—for forty-nine straight days. And he got what he was after.

After the Buddha received his enlightenment, he began to preach it to others. He taught them the Four Noble Truths, which remain the basis for Buddhism:

1. Life, as typically lived, is suffering, unfulfilling, and filled with insecurity
2. Human beings suffer because we live in an almost constant state of desiring private fulfillment
3. We know how to train our minds to cure our selfish cravings and reach new levels of satisfaction and cravings
4. We can end our suffering by following a specific course of treatment

Buddha believed that the way to end suffering was to live fully in the moment, in the here and now. He taught his followers not to project into the future, nor to carry the past forward. Instead, one should face all thoughts that flow through the mind and then just simply let them go. Doing so would allow a return to one's "true nature," or "Buddha nature." It also allows entering into a blissful state called nirvana. This state is what the spiritual practices of Buddhism are directed toward and is the ultimate goal of Buddhist worship.

CHAPTER 4

From the Good Book

Some of the greatest testimonies to the power of prayer can be found in the Bible. It's also one of the best resources you could ask for when it comes to the things that can help you live a prayerful life. People often turn to the Bible in times of trouble because it makes them feel good. But you don't have to be in a bad spot to benefit from what the Bible has to offer.

Getting to Know God's Word

References to prayer and examples of prayer can be found throughout the Bible, which is why many people consider it an essential component in their prayer life. If you're like most people, you probably own at least one copy of the Bible.

And, if you're like a lot of people, your Bible probably spends more time on the bookshelf than it does in your hands. If you're not very familiar with the Bible, you might feel somewhat uncomfortable about reading it, especially if you don't know your way around it very well.

But the best way to learn about the Bible, and mine the riches that it holds, is to simply start reading it. You can use this chapter to get you started. We'll sketch the journey for you by telling you how the Bible came about and how it is put together. We'll also point you to some of the pithiest prayer spots within its pages.

Bible Background

The book that we call the Bible is a compilation of many texts that reflects the creative work of a whole host of people—most of whom are anonymous except for their writings—dating back some 4,000 years. It is a stunning literary work, truly unlike any other with its potpourri of historical narrative, teachings, poetry, philosophy, exhortations, and prophetic visions of the future.

symbolism

The English word *Bible* comes from the Greek *biblia*, a variation of Byblos, the ancient Phoenician coastal city where the Phoenicians exported the papyrus, or paper, used to copy early books. *Biblia* originally meant papyrus; however, since all early books were written on papyrus, *biblia* eventually came to mean "book."

The Bible tells the story of the people of the ancient world with their warts on, as they really were, with all their strengths and faults. In it, people cry out to God in joy and in sorrow. They both worship the Almighty and question whether He exists at all. The Old Testament books that chronicle the life of David contain stirring narratives that detail his military and political genius. You'll also see passages of an intensely personal nature where a king over-wrought with emotion asks God to rescue him from his persecutors, pleads for God's forgiveness after he steals another man's wife (and then sends her husband to certain death in the frontlines of battle).

Be merciful to me, O God, for man would swallow me up;

Fighting all day he oppresses me.

My enemies would hound me all day,

For there are many who fight against me, O Most High.

Whenever I am afraid,

I will trust in You.

In God (I will praise His word),

In God I have put my trust;

I will not fear.

What can flesh do to me?

All day they twist my words;

All their thoughts are against me for evil.

They gather together,

They hide, they mark my steps,

When they lie in wait for my life.

Shall they escape by iniquity?

In anger cast down the peoples, O God!

You number my wanderings;

Put my tears into Your bottle;

Are they not in Your book?

When I cry out to You,

Then my enemies will turn back;

This I know, because God is for me.

In God (I will praise His word),

In the Lord (I will praise His word),

In God I have put my trust;

I will not be afraid.

What can man do to me?

Vows made to You are binding upon me, O God;

I will render praises to You,

For You have delivered my soul from death.

Have you not delivered my feet from falling,

That I may walk before God

In the light of the living?

—Psalm 56

Some of the world's greatest storytelling takes place in the Bible. If you're looking for meaty morality tales and passionate love stories, you'll find them on the pages of this great book. Some of what the Bible contains rivals the best television miniseries. You'll also find a spirited blend of historic fact, myth, and legend that reflect how the ancients perceived the wonders and mysteries of the world around them.

Both the Christian and Jewish faiths accept the Bible as having been inspired by God and of Divine authority, which is what places the Good Book at the center of both religions.

factum

The Quran, the sacred text of the Islamic faith, contains many verses that mirror those in the Bible. What is interesting about this is that it is very unlikely that Muhammad was ever exposed to the Bible.

It really doesn't matter what you choose to believe about how the Bible became what it is today. Whether you think it's the word of God dictated verbatim, divinely inspired, or merely a fanciful grouping of fairy tales devised to educate the ancient masses, it still serves as one of the best resources on prayer ever written.

The Bible consists of two parts: The Old Testament contains the Jewish scriptures, which are also called the Hebrew Bible. The New Testament contains the Christian scriptures, and tells the story of Jesus Christ's life and ministry, and how the Christian church was formed.

The Books of the Old Testament

The actual process of writing down the Bible dates back to approximately 1500 B.C.E., which was when the earliest Hebrew scriptures—the first five books of the Bible—were written. In total, the Hebrew Bible contains twenty-four books in three groupings: Torah, or Law; Nevi'im, or the Prophets; and Kethuvim, or the Writings.

Books of the Torah

Consisting of five books—Genesis, Exodus, Leviticus, Numbers, and Deuteronomy—the Torah is the oldest part of the Bible, dating back to approximately 1000 B.C.E.

These five books are often called the Mosaic books in honor of the belief, now disproven, that held that Moses was their author. They are also known as the Pentateuch. The Torah tells the rich story of the earliest days of Judaism and reflects a time when God was experienced on a highly personal level. You'll see various facets of Him in scripture detailing:

- The Creation
- Adam and Eve
- Moses and the Ten Commandments
- The parting of the Red Sea

factum

The scripture of the Jewish Bible, also known as the Old Testament, was originally written in Hebrew and Aramaic. The books of the New Testament, which detail the life of Jesus Christ and the establishment of the Christian church, were written in Greek.

The Prophets

The next section of the Bible, the prophets, consist of two subdivisions: the Former Prophets (Joshua, Judges, 1 and 2 Samuel and 1 and 2 Kings) and the Latter Prophets (Isaiah, Jeremiah, Ezekial, and The Twelve, which includes Hosea, Joel, Amos, Obadiah, Jonah, Micah, Nahum, Habakkuk, Zephaniah, Haggai, Zechariah, and Malachi).

These books reflect the experiences of men and women who had received Divine messages and who passed them on to others, either verbally or symbolically. They delivered their messages to individuals, groups, the entire nation of Israel, and to foreign nations.

symbolism

While the prophets often had important messages to convey, the messengers themselves weren't always held in the highest regard. Kenneth Davis, author of *Don't Know Much About the Bible*, notes that they were "itinerants who roamed the countryside, sometimes in bands." Some of them were fairly powerful; many were considered troublemakers.

The Writings

The writings consist of three subdivisions: the Poetical Books (Psalms, Proverbs, Job), the Five Rolls (Song of Songs, Ruth, Lamentations, Ecclesiastes, Esther), and the Historical Books (Daniel, Ezra, Nehemiah, Chronicles).

Of the books contained in the writings, the Book of Psalms is the one that people are often the most familiar with. Psalms, the largest book in the Bible, is a compilation of 150 hymns, or poems, with almost every one containing some words of praise to God. They cover a wide time span and were written to different audiences under many different conditions. For this reason, they run the gamut on emotion and themes, ranging from jubilation to lamentation.

The Psalms served as the hymnbook and devotional guide for the Jewish people, and continue to play a role in both Jewish and Christian worship services to this day. Because virtually every psalm contains words of praise to God, it is a rich resource for prayer. Everyone has his favorite psalm. Psalm 23 is one of the more famous:

The Lord is my shepherd;

I shall not want.

He makes me to lie down in green pastures;

He leads me beside the still waters.

He restores my soul;

He leads me in the paths of righteousness

For His name's sake.

Yea, though I walk through the valley of the shadow of death,

I will fear no evil;

For You are with me;

Your rod and Your staff, they comfort me.

You prepare a table before me in the presence of my enemies;

You anoint my head with oil;

My cup runs over.

Surely goodness and mercy shall follow me

All the days of my life;

And I will dwell in the house of the Lord

Forever.

—Psalm 23

While the Psalms make for great reading, there are other books in the writings that are worth spending some with. Proverbs is a wonderful book of wisdom, with pithy sayings like, "When pride comes, then comes shame; But with the humble is wisdom" (Proverbs 11:2). The Book of Job is a morality story that tells the tale of a man whose faith in God couldn't be shaken, no matter what. Song of Solomon is a love song written by King Solomon that depicts his courtship and marriage to a Shulamite sheperdess. No one is quite sure whether it's a piece of fiction, an allegory, or an historical account. Read it, and see what you think. Be prepared for some erotic metaphors when you do. Here's an example:

Awake, O north wind,

And come, O south!

Blow upon my garden,

That its spices may flow out.

Let my beloved come to his garden

And eat its pleasant fruits.

—Song of Songs 4:16

The Books of the Apocrypha

One of the things you'll notice if you compare different Bibles is that some versions contain more books than others. This doesn't mean that these Bibles are any better than others, or that some versions are incomplete because they don't have as many books as others. The differences exist because some religious traditions recognize certain books as holy or authoritative, and include them in their canon, while others do not.

symbolism

The word *canon* is Greek, meaning "rule." The canon can refer to the religious laws themselves, the book that contains the laws, or even the members of the council that creates the laws.

Going by "The Rules"

The various biblical canons comprise scriptures that have been deemed authoritative according to certain rules. When compiling its canon, the Protestant church rejected some books, as well as parts of books, that had long been part of the Greek translation of the Old Testament. Church leaders did so because they didn't feel these works belonged to what they believed to be the authentic canon of scripture. In doing so, they sided with Jewish religious leaders, who had come to the same conclusion sometime before when they excluded all works from the canon of the Jewish Bible that they believed to be written after the age of Ezra, the great sage of the fifth century B.C.E., at which time it was believed that inspiration or prophecy had ceased.

The collection of fifteen religious writings rejected by the Protestant church were part of the Septuagint, the ancient Greek translation of the Hebrew scriptures, and were preserved in the Vulgate, the first Latin translation of the Bible. They are commonly referred to as the Apocrypha, which means "things hidden away," although they were never really hidden, just removed from the Jewish and Protestant canons. In the Roman Catholic church, they are referred to as deuterocanonical, which translates to "secondary rule," meaning that they belong to a second layer of the canon but aren't of lesser value than the other books of the Bible.

discussion question

Why is the Old Testament included in the Bible that Christians use?
Jesus often quoted Jewish scripture when he taught. After his death, his followers turned to these scriptures to better understand his life and his teachings. To this day, the Christian church honors the role that the Old Testament played in the formation of Christianity, and considers the Jewish scriptures a cornerstone of Christian life, thought, and worship.

Pick up anything other than a Protestant or Hebrew Bible, and you'll see that some or all of these books have been included, usually inserted between the Old and New Testaments. The Bible used by the Roman Catholic church, for example, includes Tobit, Judith, the Wisdom of Solomon, Sirach, Baruch, the Letter of Jeremiah, and 1 and 2 Maccabees, as well as Greek additions to the books of Esther and Daniel, including the Prayer of Azariah and the Song of the Three Jews, Susanna, and Bel and the Dragon. The Orthodox churches, which primarily stick to the books that were included in the Greek Septuagint, include a few more, such as 1 Esdras, 3 and 4 Maccabees, and Psalm 151.

The Value of the Apocrypha

There has never been much agreement among the various religious traditions on the value of the Apocryphal books. The Calvinists discouraged their use and felt they were no better than anything written by any other human. The Church of England requires their inclusion in Bibles distributed for public use, and includes them in its lectionary, but also directs its followers to disregard them as doctrine. Lutherans have decided that these books aren't as important as the other books of the Hebrew Bible, but they may also study them along with other scripture.

For a long time the majority of Bibles didn't include the books of the Apocrypha. Modern discoveries of ancient texts gave new insights on how the Jewish canon was established, however, and it became clear that the writings, which comprise the third part of the Hebrew Bible, weren't as engraved in stone as they were previously thought to be. This put into question the argument against including the books of the Apocrypha as they are also considered to be part of the writings.

As interest in biblical research and interpretation grew, the Apocryphal books began to appear more frequently. Various stand-alone editions of the Apocrypha have also been published. They provide interesting historical narrative not found in other parts of the Bible, much of it covering the period between the Old and New Testaments. They also contain a number of morality tales, ethical teachings, and apocalyptic revelations.

The Books of the New Testament

In contrast to the thousands of years that are detailed in the books of the Old Testament, the New Testament contains writings that cover a very short period of time—just about 100 years. It tells the story of Jesus' life—his birth, works, teachings, execution, and resurrection. It also details the beginnings of Christianity and documents its early growth.

The New Testament falls into two main divisions. The first five books tell the story of Jesus' life and how his followers established Christianity. The twenty-one books that follow contain letters written by various leaders of the early Christian church that expand upon or interpret Jesus' teachings.

factum

The Book of Revelation, the last of the twenty-seven books of the New Testament, contains a fantastical account of the days leading to Jesus' revelation. It is written in apocalyptic language, warning of the destruction and devastation accompanying the end of the world, and the resulting triumph of good over evil.

The Gospels

The writings of Matthew, Mark, Luke, and John describe the career of Jesus Christ from four similar but different viewpoints. Also contained in these books are details on Jesus' teachings and the healings he performed.

factum

At the time that the New Testament was compiled, there were some thirty variations of the Gospel in circulation. Of the four that were included in the New Testament canon, three are believed to have similar roots—the authors of Matthew and Luke used the gospel of Mark along with a second outside source. John was believed to have drawn on other contemporary sources.

Acts

Also known as Acts of the Apostles, this book records the earliest history of the Christian church, covering a period of about thirty years after Jesus' death and resurrection. Written by the same author as Luke, it was originally written as a sequel to the gospel of Luke.

Letters

Paul, one of the Christian church's earliest missionaries, was also quite a letter writer. Many of the twenty-one letters contained in the New Testament are believed to be his missives to the early churches and other missionaries. They are full of encouragement to the new churches and instruction for Christian living.

The Book of Revelation

The last book in the Bible is rich with symbolism and imagery depicting the second coming of Christ. It is apocalyptic literature, meaning that it warns about and predicts the future. In it are a series of divine revelations made by a prophet named John that detail the events leading to the establishment of God's kingdom on earth.

New Testament Apocrypha

Other works related to the New Testament are also considered apocryphal. They were written by various authors and for various reasons. In some cases they were meant to shed additional light on writings already in circulation; other works were penned merely as entertainment. Still others were written to spread practices and beliefs that were contradictory to church doctrine. None of these works are included in any official versions of the Bible, although they have been published in various forms.

One Bible, Many Translations

Over the years, the Bible has been translated into many different versions and into many different languages. In the English-speaking world, the King James Version, first published in 1611, was for many years the translation used in most Protestant churches. To this day, it remains the most widely circulated Bible in existence.

As the Elizabethan-style Old English contained in the King James Version became increasingly out of date, many people found it difficult to read. To make the Bible more accessible, new translations were produced. Today, the following are in wide use:

- **King James Version/New King James Version**—Still "the Bible" to many, especially those who love the poetry of its words. The New King James Version, published in 1982, retains much of the phraseology of the original, but in a modern and updated format.
- **New Revised Standard Version**—Published in 1990, this Bible is a revision of the earlier Revised Standard Version. It is similar to the King James Version in tone and feeling. Unlike the King James, it includes the Apocrypha. It is a gender neutral Bible, with words like people and humankind substituted for man and men.

- **New International Version/New International Reader's Version/Today's New International Version**—This Bible, in all its versions, is the best selling Bible today. Easier to read than the previous versions, it uses contemporary English and is gender accurate, meaning that it doesn't eliminate distinctions between genders as some modern translations do. There is also a gender-neutral edition available.
- **Living Bible**—This version of the Bible is actually a paraphrase that was written to help children understand the scriptures. Its simple, everyday English makes the Living Bible very easy to read, which makes it popular among people who are new to reading the Bible or whose first language isn't English.
- **New Living Translation**—One of the newer translations of the Bible, published in 1996, it too uses vocabulary and language structures that are familiar to today's readers. Although considered a new translation, it's also a revision of the Living Bible. A team of biblical scholars went back to Hebrew, Aramaic, and Greek texts to revise the previous version. In so doing, they also made some accuracy and style changes that sets the NLT apart from its predecessor. This translation is also gender neutral.
- **New American Standard Bible**—This Bible's formal tone is off-putting to some, but it's said to be the most exact English translation available.
- **Amplified Bible**—This popular translation uses a system of brackets and parentheses to convey the original meanings of Greek and Hebrew words.
- **New American Bible**—This is the Catholic version of the Bible, published under the direction of Pope Pius XII. All editions include the deuterocanonical books.

Choosing Among the Translations

With so many different Bible translations available, it can be difficult to know how to choose the one that best suits your needs. If you're new to reading the Bible, you may want to stick with a paraphrase as they're often easier to understand. However, if you want a Bible that more closely reflects the original language in which it was written, you'll want to avoid paraphrases.

Beyond this, find a Bible that speaks to you when you read it. If you're serious about studying it, definitely consider a literal translation such as the New King James, the New International Version, or the New Revised Standard Version. If you're a rookie, you might prefer a study Bible, which combines text and study materials in one volume. Other options would be a text and reference Bible, which cross-references passages for easy comparison, or a parallel Bible, which contains different Bible translations placed side-by-side for easy comparison between versions.

discussion question

Is any one translation of the Bible better than others?
Not necessarily, although Bible scholars will tell you that they're not all of the same quality or theological level. The translations are written to different reading levels, and some were created at different points in time, which can also alter the reading level of the text.

Studying the Bible

There are many ways to mine the Bible's resources. Some people crack it open randomly and look for inspiration on the pages that happened to open up. Others take a more structured approach and use study aids like an index or concordance to search for passages that deal with specific issues or that are attributed to certain authors. There is really no right or wrong way; only the one that works the best for you.

Martin Luther compared Bible study to gathering apples. First, he said, study the Bible as a whole and shake the whole tree. Then shake every limb and study book after book. Then shake every branch, paying attention to the chapters. Then shake each twig by carefully studying the paragraphs and the sentences. Finally, ". . . you will be rewarded if you look under each leaf by searching the meaning of the words."

If you're serious about studying the Bible, however, it is best to have a direction or plan of attack so you know where you're going and how to get there. Along these lines, there are various tried-and-true approaches, each with its own particular merits. Study guides are available for you to follow if you need direction, and many houses of worship offer Bible study groups you can join.

quote

> The very best way to study the Bible is simply to read it daily with close attention and with prayer to see the light that shines from its pages, to meditate upon it, and to continue to read it until somehow it works itself . . . into the very warp and woof of one's being.
> —Howard A. Kelly, a scientist and medical doctor

Regardless of the approach you take, read prayerfully. Let God speak to you through His words. And don't rush things. You'll gain a better understanding if you read slowly and reverently.

By the Book

One of the most popular ways of studying the Bible involves reading each book, in order, from cover to cover. Members of the Christian faith sometimes prefer to start with the New Testament first. Either way, this is a good method for getting a feel for the majesty and scope of the Bible if you're unfamiliar with it.

If you're reading the Bible for the first time, focus more on your general impressions of the purpose of the book and its ideas rather than on its details. You can get more specific on subsequent readings.

Studying for Knowledge

Another popular approach involves identifying a specific idea, subject, or doctrine and studying it throughout the Bible. Also called doctrinal Bible study, you'll need a study Bible or concordance (if your Bible doesn't have a good one) to help you find the relevant passages.

discussion question

Is it okay to write in or underline passages in my Bible?
If you're new to Bible study you might feel uncomfortable doing it, but there's nothing wrong with marking your Bible. As you grow in your prayer practice, you'll come to cherish the notes and underlining as marks of your spiritual journey.

These are just a few of the many ways you can study the Bible. For information on other methods, check any of the many books available on the subject. Online Bible study resources exist as well. Some study Bibles even contain their own study outlines. Regardless of the method you choose, it's a good idea to take a different approach on occasion. It will keep your study fresh and lead to new insights and discoveries.

CHAPTER 5

Books of Prayer from Around the Globe

The Bible is a great prayer resource, but it's by no means the only one. There are many other written works, ranging from holy scripture to prayer books to devotionals, that can also help you learn more about prayer as well as help you develop your relationship with God. We'll give you a taste of the various types in the following pages.

Tapping into Wisdom from Other Faiths

You might be wondering why you should read other books about spirituality and prayer, especially those that don't relate to your own spiritual background. You may also wonder if it's all right if you do. Is it all right to read the Quran if you're not Muslim, or the siddur (prayer book) if you're not Jewish? Yes, it is.

There is a great piece of wisdom from the Bible that says, "All Scripture is given by inspiration of God, and is profitable for doctrine, for reproof, for correction, for instruction in righteousness, that the man of God may be complete, thoroughly equipped for every good work" (2 Timothy 4:16–17). To put this piece of wisdom into secular terms, it tells us that there is something of value in the spiritual writings of other faiths, and that reading these works may give us a fuller understanding of our relationship with God.

One of the benefits of exploring the history and culture of other religions through their writings is that it allows us to be more informed and tolerant in our global society. This isn't to say that you are going to agree with everything you read, or that you'll find everything you read enjoyable. On the other hand, you might find some surprises. The Quran, for example, contains many references to people and events central to both Judaism and Christianity. Interesting parallels are to be found between the teachings of Buddha and Jesus.

symbolism

When reading holy books that are outside of your spiritual background, it can be helpful to put the words into context by reading texts that explain some of the concepts within the religion itself.

One of the great things about the world today is that many of us have a great deal of control over just about every area of our lives. There is no one standing over us telling us what we can and cannot do. We can choose to believe what we want to believe, pray how we want to pray, read what we want to read. In this context, it's good to step out of your own belief system and see what someone else has to say once in a while. You might find something really beautiful there.

With this said, you'll find the suggestions that follow to be somewhat eclectic. Don't take our selections, or lack thereof, as a reflection of any bias. Some of what is here is included because we have personally enjoyed these books and have found them helpful in our own prayer lives. Others reflect works that form the basis for a well-rounded spiritual education. They all lead to a better understanding of how God is experienced in the world religions.

The Book of Common Prayer

Often referred to as "the BCP" by those who use it on a regular basis, The Book of Common Prayer (its full title is The Book of Common Prayer and the Administration of the Sacraments and other Rites and Ceremonies of the Church) is the official prayer book of the Anglican and Episcopal churches.

If you belong to one of these churches, you get to know this book pretty well as it's what you pray with whenever you attend a church service. But The Book of Common Prayer is also a great guide for individual prayer.

factum

The term common prayer refers to the shared cycle of services of the Anglican and Episcopal churches, which include the Daily Office, the Litany, and the Eucharist. You don't have to be an Anglican or an Episcopalian to use it. In fact, the BCP is a cherished guide to prayer for many Christians of many denominations.

How the BCP Came About

The BCP was the work of Archbishop Thomas Cranmer, who produced it in 1549 as a service book for the new Church of England—a church that he played a hand in bringing about. Remember King Henry VIII and his six wives? Cranmer had gained the king's favor by suggesting ways to implement Henry's much desired divorce from his first wife, Catherine of Aragon. In fact, Cranmer ended up granting the annulment himself on the grounds that the king and his wife were relatives—her first husband, who had died, was Henry's brother—and therefore could not be legally married.

Grateful for Cranmer's assistance, King Henry VIII made Cranmer the Archbishop of Canterbury in 1533. He couldn't write his service book while Henry was alive, however, as the two didn't see eye to eye on many theological matters. After Henry died, Cranmer penned the first version of the BCP as a part of the reforms that were being introduced by the church during the reign of the new king, Edward VI.

symbolism

If you are interested in seeing how the BCP has changed over the years, do an Internet search on it. You'll find many editions of the BCP, including the full text of the 1559 edition as well as one written in Hawaiian by King Kamehameha.

That first attempt at the BCP was revised many times, first by Cranmer, and then later by others. The book Cranmer first came up with was based on medieval Catholic prayer books and on the liturgies written by the early fathers of the Orthodox Church. Cranmer revised much of the other liturgies, and in doing so emphasized the reading of scripture over elaborate ceremonies as the basis for the new church's worship services. He removed other elements of Catholic ceremonies as well, and wrote the service in English instead of Latin to make it easier for more people to follow. But there were problems with this first effort, and many felt it didn't reflect the reformed nature of this new church. In 1552, Cranmer produced a rewritten version of the first book.

It's been said that no other prayer book or missal includes as complete a collection of worship services and devotional materials as The Book of Common Prayer. If you're looking for a way to put some order into your prayers, and you want to do so by following formal, written prayers, the BCP is a top pick.

What You'll Find in the BCP

Thomas Cranmer set out to write a book of prayer that would serve all the needs of the church and its members. For this reason, much of the book is devoted to corporate prayer and worship. You'll see references to "the officiant" and "the people" throughout the BCP, even in the prayers that can be said individually. If you're praying alone, consider yourself to be both parties—you read (or think) both the officiant's and the people's parts.

The Daily Office is the order of service followed by the church. It also contains prayers that can be said privately:

- The Morning Prayer, which, as its name suggests, is to be prayed in the morning.
- The Evening Prayer, which is said in the early evening.
- Compline, which is said in the final hours of the evening, usually before going to bed.

factum

The Daily Office has its roots in Judaism, with its ancient traditions of gathering for corporate prayer (and sacrifice) in the morning. Members of the early Christian church followed the traditions of their ancestors and continued to worship together regularly.

You'll find two versions of many of the prayers in the BCP. Rite I is written in Elizabethan English. Rite II uses more contemporary wording. You can use either one. If you're new to the BCP, you may prefer the more contemporary styling of Rite II.

In addition to the prayers from the Daily Office, the BCP also contains daily devotion services. These follow the same pattern as the Daily Office prayers, but are shorter and have the psalms and readings included right in the service, which makes for much less flipping around. There is also a section called Prayers and Thanksgivings, which can be said during the Morning or Evening Prayer as well as separately. They cover just about every subject you can think of, ranging from prayers for the world to general thanksgivings.

Praying with the BCP can be somewhat confusing at first. While the prayer service itself follows a specific order, the readings vary from day to day. You'll have to get used to flipping back and forth from the service to the parts of the BCP where those readings appear. After you've done it a few times, however, it begins to make sense. The Daily Office also calls for readings from scripture, which aren't included in the book, so you'll need a Bible to pray the full office.

The Siddur

Another example of a prayer book that orders one's prayers, the siddur is the prayer book used by followers of the Jewish faith. The word *siddur*, which means "order" in Hebrew, is a good reflection of what this prayer book is all about: it specifies the order of the set prayers for the various Jewish services.

factum

Jews treat their siddurim with great reverence as they contain the name of God. If one is dropped, it is kissed when it is picked up. Some people kiss the siddur when they're done praying with it. When a siddur is no longer usable, it is buried, not casually thrown away.

As previously mentioned, Jews say set prayers at home and in the synagogue. The siddur contains both the basic form of Jewish prayer—the blessings, when they give thanks to God at various times during the day, always prefaced with "Blessed art Thou, O Lord our God, King of the Universe"—and the three set services that are prayed in the morning, afternoon, and evening. Like the BCP, there are many versions of the siddur. Many siddurim (the plural of siddur) are printed in both English and Hebrew. Some contain transliterated text, which consists of Hebrew sounds spelled out using the English alphabet, to assist people who can't read Hebrew.

Prayers in the siddur fall into four categories: prayers of petition, prayers of thanksgiving, prayers that praise God, and prayers of soul-searching and confession.

The Quran

Revered by Muslims as the eternal and literal word of God, the Quran is Islam's key book of faith. It contains God's revelations as they were delivered to the prophet Muhammad through the angel Gabriel.

The Quran's 114 chapters, called surahs, were revealed to Muhammad over a twenty-three-year period, from the time he was forty until his death in 632 C.E. About fifteen to twenty years after Muhammad died, the entire text of the Quran was gathered into a format and order that Muslims believe was commanded by divine revelation.

People outside of the Muslim faith often avoid reading the Quran for a variety of reasons. Many feel its contents aren't relevant to their own faith. Others think they shouldn't read it because they're not Muslims. And there are those who don't want to read it and never will because they mistakenly believe that it advocates violence.

Inside the Quran

The Quran isn't a very long work, only about four-fifths the size of the New Testament. Chapters are organized by length instead of chronologically or thematically, with the longest chapter first. Each paragraph within each chapter is considered an individual lesson to be learned and reflected on.

Similarities to the New Testament

One of the things you'll notice if you read the Quran is that parts of it parallel biblical scripture. There are references to names from the Old Testament, including Adam, Noah, Abraham, Ishmael, Isaac, and Moses, as well as references to the Garden of Eden, the parting of the Red Sea, the David and Goliath story, and the story of Joseph. Even Jesus' mother Mary appears, the only woman to do so in the Quran. These similarities are interesting because Muhammad never met Jesus Christ, and certainly never read the Bible. Nor did he have the Bible read to him. You'll also see a different interpretation of how Jesus began his life than what you'll see in New Testament.

factum

Ramadan, the holy month in the Islam faith, is important for Muslims because it is believed to be the month during which the Quran was revealed to Muhammad (all the revelations would later be recorded by scribes, a process that took twenty-three years). Ramadan is the ninth month of the year in the Islamic calendar.

The Quran contains language that is meant to instruct Jews and Christians as well as Muslims, such as this passage:

Surely Those who believe, Those who are Jewish, The Christians, the converts; anyone who

1) believes in God, and

2) believes in the Hereafter, and

3) leads a righteous life,

will receive their recompense from their Lord, they have nothing To fear nor will they grieve.

—Quran 2:62

Such writing reflects the shared heritage of the three monotheistic religions as well as Muhammad's belief that the revelations he received were an extension of Jewish and Christian scripture.

The Imitation of Christ

Revered as one of the greatest Christian devotional works of all times, The Imitation of Christ was written in the fifteenth century by the German monk Thomas à Kempis as a means of teaching monastery novices about spirituality.

symbolism

Although Thomas à Kempis is given the credit for writing The Imitation of Christ in its entirety, the works were more likely written by several monks who belonged to the same order, and compiled by à Kempis.

The Imitation of Christ remains a spiritual classic for anyone, not just monastics. It is full of good advice that rings just as true today as it has throughout the centuries. It encourages readers to become more like Jesus Christ in all aspects of their lives. But it also gives great advice on how to live a spiritual life in general. Although it's not organized in question and answer format (Book Three, however, takes the form of a dialogue between Jesus and "the disciple"), it often reads like it was written to answer specific questions posed by the novice monks. There weren't advice columnists in the fifteenth century (that we know about, anyway!), but à Kempis and his cohorts came pretty close to being the Dear Abby and Ann Landers of the Enlightenment.

Do not yield to every impulse and suggestion but consider things carefully and patiently in the light of God's will. For very often, sad to say, we are so weak that we believe and speak evil of others rather than good . . . Not to act rashly or to cling obstinately to one's opinion, not to believe everything people say or to spread abroad the gossip one has heard, is good wisdom.

—Thomas à Kempis, in The Imitation of Christ

The Imitation of Christ has been translated into more than fifty languages and thousands of editions. Several versions of this devotional classic also reside on the Internet. If you do a search for them, you'll notice that the language in some is more formal than in others. Translations do vary widely; it's a good idea to take a look at a couple of them before jumping in.

The *Bhagavad Gita*

Bhagavad Gita means "the Song of the Lord." The *Bhagavad Gita* is a Hindu religious poem that details a civil war in India. The participants are the sons of two families—the Kauruvas and the Pandavas—who are fighting over a kingdom that the Pandavas believe was stolen from them by the Kauruvas. This may not seem like the best setting for religious teachings, but it quickly turns into exactly that. During a break in the war, Arjuna, the third Pandava brother, has a chat with Krishna, his charioteer. During the conversation, Krishna gives Arjuna teachings on yoga practice—both physical and spiritual—to lead him to union with God.

quote

The person whose mind is always free from attachment, who has subdued the mind and senses, and who is free from desires, attains the supreme perfection of freedom from (the bondage of) Karma through renunciation.

—from the *Bhagavad Gita*

The *Bhagavad Gita* is actually part of the Mahabharata, one of two ancient historical texts that relate the events that took place in India from 1400 B.C.E. to 1000 B.C.E. The *Bhagavad Gita* contains teachings on the nature of duty and devotion; the Mahabharata details dharma, which in Hinduism relates to the moral code governing the actions of warriors, kings, and anyone else who is seeking immortality. Along with the Upanishads, the *Bhagavad Gita* represents the basic religious scriptures for Hinduism.

The Tao-te Ching

Tao-te Ching means "the Way and Its Power." This sacred text, which is the basis for Taoism, is attributed to a man named Lao Tzu. We know very little about him beyond the fact that he lived in China during the sixth century B.C.E., and that he was a keeper of the archives and sacred books.

According to legend, the Tao-te Ching is the result of a border crossing gone awry. As an old man, Lao Tzu was attempting to enter a different province in China when he was stopped by the guardian of that province and asked to write down his wisdom. In a period of three days, he produced a work of about 5,000 characters.

All the word says,

"I am important;

I am separate from all the world.

I am important because I am separate.

Were I the same, I could never be important."

Yet here are three treasures

That I cherish and commend to you:

The first is compassion,

By which one finds courage.

The second is restraint,

By which one finds strength.

And the third is unimportance,

By which one finds influence.

Those who are fearless, but without compassion,

Powerful, but without constraint,

Or influential, yet important,

Cannot endure.

—Tao-te Ching

The Upanishads

The word Upanishad means "sitting down near" and implies studying with a spiritual teacher. Written by sages of India between the eighth and fourth centuries B.C.E., The Upanishads are a blend of devotions, hymns, opinions, and reflections of holy men regarding the inner meaning of traditional religious truths. They also include some of the earliest ascetic teachings that would become a part of Indian religion.

By whom directed does the mind project to its objects?

By whom commanded does the first life breath move?

By whom impelled are these words spoken?

What god is behind the eye and ear?

That which is the hearing of the ear,

the thought of the mind, the voice of the speech,

the life of the breath, and the sight of the eye.

Passing beyond, the wise leaving this world become immortal.

There the eye does not go, nor speech, nor the mind.

We do not know, we do not understand how one can teach this.

Different, indeed, is it from the known,

and also it is above the unknown.

Thus we have heard from the ancients who explained it to us.

That which is not expressed by speech,

but that by which speech is expressed:

know that to be God, not what people here adore.

—The Upanishads

CHAPTER 6

First Steps Toward Prayer

Prayer is difficult for many people. Some say it doesn't satisfy them, or they don't see the value in it. Often, what this really means is that they don't know how to pray. While there isn't an instruction manual to follow, there are some things to know that can help you learn how to become an effective pray-er.

Learning How to Pray

Praying—not just going through the motions or mouthing the words, but really getting to know God on a very personal, intimate level—takes some work. It also requires some sacrifices. Hard work? Sacrifice? This may not be what you want to hear about prayer. Ask anyone who prays on a regular basis, however, and he'll tell you that all of his efforts in this particular arena are more than worth it.

The payoff of all that hard work and effort is being able to experience the nearness of God. And that, frankly, is an experience like no other. Those who commit to hearing the word of God do indeed hear His voice, often in some amazing ways.

quote

How to pray? This is a simple matter. I would say: Pray any way you like, so long as you do pray. You can pray the way your mother taught you; you can use a prayer book. Sometimes it takes courage to pray; but it is possible to pray, and necessary to pray. Whether from memory or a book or just in thought, it is all the same.

—Pope John Paul II, in *The Way of Prayer*

The idea that people have to learn how to pray, and that we have to keep on working at it, may seem odd to you. After all, if we're "wired for prayer," as some researchers believe, then we should instinctively know how to do it, right? To a certain extent, yes. One of the wonderful things about prayer is that it's really very simple. However, because we're human and we're concerned about doing things "right," we tend to make a bigger deal out of it than we need to. We read about it, we agonize over it, and we analyze it to death. We spend far more time thinking that we should pray, and wishing that we prayed, instead of just doing it. We forget what we already know, or we simply choose to ignore it.

Mother Teresa, who definitely knew a thing or two about prayer, said the best way to learn how to pray is by praying. There is a certain amount of paradox in her words. But like all paradoxes, there is also truth. Quite simply, while you can read all you want to about praying and how to pray, doing it is the only way you'll really learn how. And keeping at it is the only way you'll become effective at it. While it is possible to gain something from any effort at prayer, even the smallest and briefest dip into it, maintaining a regular prayer practice will move you forward faster and make you better at it. It's like an athlete training for a big event. Working out every once in a while does not make an Olympic champion. But doing a little bit on a consistent basis and building on those efforts can put you into medal contention.

symbolism

Even Jesus' disciples had to be taught how to pray. His answer to them was "The Lord's Prayer," which is revered by Christians as the greatest prayer of all.

It can be difficult to move from thinking about praying to actually doing it. However, there's not much to be gained from prayer if it remains an intellectual pursuit. How can you move from thinking to doing? First, by making the commitment to becoming a person who prays. Second, by using that commitment to anchor a plan—call it a prayer plan—to give you a framework for your prayer practice.

Making a Commitment to Prayer

Getting the greatest benefits of prayer does involve making a commitment to it. If you think of prayer as a relationship with God, this makes sense. We make commitments in the relationships we have with people, even the ones we have with pets. The relationship you have with God requires doing so as well.

Making the commitment to pray, however, means more than just saying you'll do it. It means taking some active steps toward it. It also means developing the discipline that will help you honor that commitment. Discipline is a negative word for a lot of people, and it might have negative connotations for you. But, in this context, discipline doesn't mean punishment or regimentation. Instead, it refers to establishing some ground rules for your conduct in your relationship with the Almighty. Or, in other words, a structure for your prayer practice.

Here's the lowdown on why this is important: Without a certain set pattern—a discipline—to govern how and when we pray, our desire to get to know God more fully remains just that. Without being committed to this particular goal, and having a game plan to govern our efforts, we won't get to where we want to go.

factum

The words *discipline* and *disciple* are both derived from the same Latin word, which means "pupil." In both cases, it refers to a teacher bestowing knowledge upon a student, or pupil.

Prayer itself is considered a discipline in Christianity. As such, it is one of a number of spiritual disciplines, such as meditation, fasting, and spiritual direction, some of which you'll be introduced to in other chapters of this book. When followed, these disciplines allow us to be transformed from within by God's spirit.

Discipline versus Legalism

As important as discipline is, it is also important to keep it in perspective. Discipline is not regimentation. It is not engraving things in stone. It isn't about making laws. Making it so, will only set you up for failure.

quote

> The Disciplines are God's way of getting us into the ground; they
> put us where He can work within us and transform us.
> —Richard Foster, in *Celebration of Discipline*

Feeling like you've completely blown it if you miss a scheduled prayer session isn't discipline, it's living by fear and shame. You're committing yourself to a lifetime of the same if you take discipline to the extreme. On the other hand, rescheduling a missed prayer session for later in the day, and doing it then, honors both your commitment to God and the discipline you've chosen to govern your time with Him.

Regimentation is not the goal here, but developing a routine and a rhythm to your prayer life can play a significant part in making prayer an ongoing part of your life.

Commitment as Covenant

Commitment and discipline can also be thought of as making a covenant with God. You'll find many examples of these special agreements in the Bible. There are two types: secular covenants made between leaders and people, and spiritual covenants made between God and man.

factum

In the Old Testament, covenants were promises made between God and the Israelites, who agreed to worship no other gods. Throughout the Bible, all serious promises are referred to as covenants.

As described in the *Oxford Companion to the Bible*, the covenants between God and the people are "all covenants of divine favor or grace. They express God's gracious commitment and faithfulness and thus establish a continuing relationship."

Some of the best examples of the covenants between God and His people can be found in the Old Testament Book of Deuteronomy. In fact, the entire book revolves around the concept of commitment and obedience. You might find it helpful to take some time to read through it as you are entering into your own covenant with the Almighty. Let the commandment to "fear the Lord your God, to walk in all His ways and to love Him, to serve the Lord your God with all your heart and with all your soul," (Deuteronomy 10:12) guide you in forming your own covenant with Him.

Scheduling Your Prayer Time

If it seems silly to talk about learning how to pray, it may seem even more ridiculous to talk about scheduling the time for doing it. However, honoring your commitment to God means putting aside a certain period of time every day during which you do nothing else but talk to Him. Determining when you're going to pray and how long you're going to do it is part of your plan for success.

quote

I strongly believe that one should have a personal spiritual discipline—whatever it might be—and regularly practice it. I start the day by reading a few verses from the Bible, since that is my tradition. I pray a morning prayer as soon as I get up. I keep a little icon near my bed right at the window so I can look out and see the world. My prayer has a whole series of things I say and it varies a bit from week to week in its pattern. This is a must for me.

—Harvard theologian Harvey Cox, in the journal *Sacred Journey*

It's somewhat of a sad statement about our world today that it's necessary to schedule prayer time, but this is indeed the case. A good majority of the people who pray say that their prayer lives would be sorely lacking if they merely tried to fit prayer into their schedules instead of setting aside a specific time for it.

factum

According to researchers at the Center for Media Studies at Rutgers, the State University of New Jersey, television has a hypnotic effect. It also acts as a sedative by increasing the brain's alpha waves and slowing its beta waves.

There is no one best time for prayer, but it's a good idea to choose a time when you won't feel rushed. If your schedule is so jam-packed that you don't see how you can avoid hurrying through your prayers, take another look at how you spend your time. There are lots of wasted moments in a day, time that could be better spent doing something else. If, like most Americans, you watch four or more hours of television a day, it's pretty obvious where your time is being wasted. Tuning into the "boob tube" has often been called an addiction, but there is new research that actually supports this claim. One of the best things you can do for your brain and your psyche is to kick this particular habit. What better to replace it with than some good conversation with your best friend?

The second consideration in choosing a prayer time is determining a time at which you can be at your most attentive. Many people prefer to pray early in the morning before they get caught up in the pressures and demands of their everyday lives. Spending time alone with God before the rest of your household is awake, or perhaps as everyone else is beginning to stir, can make a crazy world seem a little saner. However, if you're really not a morning person, don't set yourself up for failure by deciding that the wee hours of the day are for you. Praying at night can have the same benefits as it allows us to look back on the events of the day and reflect on how we experienced God in them.

quote

> The work of religion has been compared to the doing of exercises, wherein we desire to have our hearts engaged in God. Metaphors like "running the race," "wrestling with God," "striving for the great prize," and "fighting with strong enemies" are often used to describe the exercises we engage in.
>
> —Jonathan Edwards, in *Religious Affections*

Many beginning pray-ers feel most comfortable with the traditional times for prayer—upon arising in the morning and before going to bed at night. But they're by no means the only times of day during which praying can be done. If you're working in an office away from home, you might like to break up your day by praying during your lunch hour, or maybe during the ride to or from work. The idea is to find a time that works for you, and that will work for you regularly. If it's in your car during the afternoon rush hour, so be it.

Prayer Duration

The third part of your prayer plan calls for determining how long your daily prayer periods will be. There is nothing that dictates how much time you should spend praying, but there is lots of evidence to support the theory of more being better. The apostle Paul felt that prayer should be unceasing. In the Book of Thessalonians, he exhorted the followers of Christ to "Pray constantly, and for all things give thanks to God, because this is what God expects you to do . . ." (1 Thessalonians 5:17–18). John Wesley, the founder of the Methodist church, devoted two hours of his day to prayer. Martin Luther did him one better and prayed for three hours a day.

More, however, isn't necessarily better. In fact, focusing on God for short periods of time is definitely superior to praying for hours while your mind is elsewhere. Given the choice, it's better to work with less rather than more, and do it right. Emphasize quality over quantity.

If you're new to prayer, keep it short and simple. Start with a few minutes a day. If you feel like extending your prayer time, by all means do so. But don't feel like you have to spend hours in prayer, or that you're letting God down if you can only manage five minutes a day. You won't earn any gold stars if you go longer, or get demerits for brevity. On the other hand, the more time you spend talking to God, the more you'll get out of it. Let God's spirit lead you both into and out of your prayer time, and the amount of time you spend in prayer will be right and perfect.

Determining a Place for Prayer

The next step in your prayer plan is deciding where you're going to pray. Ideally, it should be a place that you can use every day of the year, come rain or come shine. While there's nothing that beats the experience of talking to God in the midst of nature, having to deal with the "come rain or come shine" factor often means praying indoors at home.

There's a basic practicality to home-based prayer, which is why it's the dominant choice for those who pray daily. You can't beat the convenience, and the doors are always open. If you want to visit a Web site as part of your prayer routine, you can do so without your boss or coworkers wondering what the heck you're doing. No one cares if you're in your pajamas and your hair isn't combed. God certainly doesn't, anyway.

On the downside, praying at home can pose real problems if you have young children who don't understand why Mommy or Daddy can't come out and play right now, or you have a particularly pesky pet who insists on being fed at this exact moment and won't leave you alone until you do something about it.

If you're going to pray at home, do yourself and everyone else a favor and set aside a specific place in which to do it. Preferably, the spot you choose should be far enough away from your house's main traffic pattern so you don't have to deal with noise, clutter, and interruptions. Your space doesn't have to be spacious. In fact, it can be as small as a corner in your bedroom. Even a pantry or a linen closet will do as long as there is enough ventilation.

Room permitting, you might want to spiff up your prayer space by turning it into a sacred space. This can be a real boon to your prayer practice, especially if you live in an area where it's difficult to get away and connect to nature. You can make your space as simple or lavish as you wish. Possible elements include plants, a fountain, a meditation cushion, a table-top Zen-style sand garden, a finger labyrinth—really, just about anything goes. Other options (you'll read more about them in Chapter 8 as well) include candles, icons, a cross, or a crucifix.

quote

We can pray perfectly when we are out in the mountains or on a lake and we feel at one with nature. Nature speaks for us or rather speaks to us. We pray perfectly.

—Pope John Paul II, in *The Way of Prayer*

What you're after is a contemplative environment that supports all aspects of your prayer practice and helps you stay focused. Make it special, and make it yours. After all, this relationship you're working on—the one between you and God—is a pretty special thing. Spending the time with Him in a space dedicated to mindfulness can make what is already a pretty wonderful experience into a joyous celebration of spirit.

CHAPTER 7

Finding Your Prayer Style

Each of us experiences God in a different way, and we stand before Him as unique beings. No two people pray exactly alike, but the results are the same. We enter into fellowship with God. We learn more about Him, and in the process, learn more about ourselves as well.

Lots of Ways to Pray

There is no right or wrong way to pray, only different ways—in fact, many different ways—in which to do it. What's more, you can decide the approach you want to take. There are no exact rules to follow, nor any boundaries to mind.

People who are new to prayer tend to think that one method of praying is better than the others, or that there is one specific way of praying that will guarantee that their prayers will be heard. In fact, they may even have been told these things at some point or another. But they are wrong on both counts.

There are no objective or subjective scales when it comes to prayer. In other words, there is no one prayer style that is any better or any worse than the others. This isn't to say that you won't find some methods of praying more to your liking than others. These will be the ones that will be more effective for you. Prayers said while kneeling have no greater chance of reaching God's ears than those said when sitting upright. What's important is that we pray, not that we pray in a way that we think we have to.

A full and balanced prayer life consists of many different kinds and styles of prayer. What's more, the best pray-ers tailor their approach to meet their needs. Since those needs change, so too do their prayer styles. Casual prayers, ones that are offered up to God at all times of the day and night, are the foundation of living a life of prayer. But this doesn't mean that praying casually is the only way in which we should pray. There will also be times when we'll need to talk to God in a more formal manner, both on our own and when we're praying with others.

Private Prayer

Private prayer—spending time alone with God—is the dominant prayer style for most people. It's the easiest style to fit into busy schedules as you can do it anywhere and at any time. You're not constrained by anything other than your own limits. There is no waiting for church doors to open or other people to arrive.

If you're going to follow the biblical precept to "pray without ceasing," it stands to reason that you'll spend most of your life praying to God on your own. But there are other reasons beyond unceasing prayer to spend lots of personal time with God.

factum

> You can think of private prayers as "instant prayers," as you can do them at any time without constraint. You can pray a private prayer any time you have a spare minute or two. When you do so, you share an intimate moment with God.

Private prayer is, more than anything else, intimate. These are the times in which you'll feel most closely connected to the Almighty. When it's only you and God together, wherever and whenever it may be, you can communicate with Him in any way you choose. You can talk out loud or speak your words silently. You can pray whatever is on your mind or follow a set order of prayer. You can sing to Him, laugh with Him, cry with Him, even yell at Him. You can dance with Him or simply sit still and be at rest with Him. Because there are no constraints in place, you can run the gamut of emotions if you need to and not worry one bit about what anyone else might think or say.

Praying privately is also a reflection of where you are in your relationship with God. It means you're not afraid to come before Him alone. Since there is no one else to see or hear you pray, it also means that you're praying for the right reasons. You're not praying to please anyone else or to show the world how devout and dedicated you are to prayer. In other words, you're not, as Jesus put it in the Book of Matthew, "practicing your piety before others."

Take heed that you do not do your charitable deeds before men, to be seen by them. Otherwise you have no reward from your Father in heaven. Therefore, when you do a charitable deed, do not sound a trumpet before you as the hypocrites do in the synagogues and in the streets, that they may have glory from men. Assuredly, I say to you, they have their reward. But when you do a charitable deed, do not let your left hand know what your right hand is doing, that your charitable deed may be in secret; and your Father who sees in secret will Himself reward you openly. And when you pray, you shall not be like the hypocrites. For they love to pray standing in the synagogues and on the corners of the streets, that they may be seen by men. Assuredly, I say to you, they have their reward. But you, when you pray, go into your room, and when you have shut your door, pray to the Father who is in the secret place; and your Father who sees in secret will reward you openly.

—Matthew 6:2–6

Private prayer generally takes one of two forms. The first is rational prayer, or prayers of the mind, in which we express our thoughts to God in words and sentences, either out loud or silently. This is the type of prayer that is familiar to most people, and the style of prayer followed by most. When we refer to talking with God, this is the prayer style we're talking about.

symbolism

Praying without ceasing may be a difficult concept to grasp if you're new to prayer. It doesn't mean that you're going to spend your entire life praying at the exclusion of everything else. What it does mean is carrying out your daily activities with God at your side, and talking to Him on a regular basis.

The other form of private prayer relies more on connecting to God in a deeper, more holistic or intrinsic way. Instead of using words to communicate with God, we use our hearts. We stay quiet. We listen to Him instead of talking at Him. We open our minds, hearts, bodies, and emotions to God, and allow Him to enter in.

Corporate Prayer

Corporate prayer means coming together with other people to pray. It can be done informally, such as in prayer groups, or formally in houses of worship such as churches, monasteries, synagogues, and mosques. Corporate prayer is also called communal prayer.

The gathering together of pray-ers goes back to biblical times and even before. There are numerous references to it in the Old Testament. While Jesus encouraged his disciples to pray alone, he also recommended that they experience the fellowship of praying together, saying, "For where two or three are gathered together in My name, I am there in the midst of them" (Matthew 18:20). The early Christians clearly took Jesus' words to heart as they prayed together often.

When we come together with others in prayer, we're linking to them by having similar intentions and purposes. We become a community of faith, and we can draw on the resources of that community to help us in many ways. If we need strength, the members of the community can strengthen us. If we need caring, they can care for us. If we need prayer, they can pray for us.

If you are praying in a small group, such as a prayer or Bible study group, your prayers can still be fairly intimate, especially if you are with people you know, or feel you can come to know, and you feel comfortable in their presence.

quote

Doing spiritual practice in the midst of busy activity is like lifting the heavy weights. Just because you can do it only once, for a moment, does not mean that it has no effect. On the contrary, it exercises your spiritual "muscles" as much as doing many repetitions with the light weights, just in a different way.

—Lewis Richmond, in *Work as a Spiritual Practice*

Praying with larger groups, such as those in churches and other houses of worship, however, is often a very different ballgame. You may be with a group of people that you know well, you like, and you feel comfortable with. Then again, you may be surrounded by complete strangers. Because of this, prayer in large groups is oftentimes much less personal in nature. Instead of praying for your own needs, you're praying for the corporate body—the church, the synagogue, and its people. This kind of prayer is important as it takes you out of yourself—it shifts your focus to the interests and needs of your prayer community, and it makes you a part of the community's concerns.

discussion question

How can I find a church with a worship service that will fit my own prayer style?
There isn't any one type of church that will. Nor will the church that your best friend really connects with necessarily be one that speaks to your heart. Your best bet is to visit a few different churches and experience their worship services for yourself.

The hallmark of public or corporate prayer are worship services, or liturgies. They range from informal to very formal. You'll find the greatest range of style in Christian churches, which fall into two basic categories:

1. Churches that follow a traditional liturgy, consisting of written prayers from a prayer book, a short sermon, and the sacraments. This is the worship style followed by Roman Catholic, Episcopal, Orthodox, and Lutheran churches, as well as some Methodist and Presbyterian churches.
2. Churches that follow a free form, or free-worship form. Here, the emphasis is less on following a formal liturgy and more on extemporaneous prayers. The sermon, rather than the sacraments, is a big part of the service. Many churches that follow this style don't use prayer books. This is

the worship style that you'll find in many Protestant churches, including Baptist, Assembly of God, Church of God, Nazarene, Evangelical Free, and Wesleyan, as well as independent churches that are not affiliated with any particular denomination.

Jewish liturgies also vary in format and style. You'll find the most formal services in Orthodox synagogues. Reform congregations generally have the least formal liturgy, while Conservative congregations are somewhere in between.

Some people find great beauty in the formality of traditional liturgical worship services. To others, they're complete yawners.

quote

> One of the advantages of having a written and printed service is that it enables you to see when people's feelings and thoughts have changed. When people begin to find the words of our service difficult to join in, that is of course a sign that we do not feel about those things exactly as our ancestors.
>
> —C. S. Lewis, in *God in the Dock*

What is definitely true is that it can be hard to find a personal connection to God through the words of others, no matter how beautifully crafted and patterned they might be. At the same time, more extemporaneous or free services that allow worshippers greater rein in how they pray during the service can also miss the mark.

On first blush, it may seem like private prayer has a distinct edge over corporate prayer. In many respects, it does. When you're talking to God on a one-on-one basis, you have substantially more control over the situation. You can choose how you want to talk to Him, where you want to talk to Him, and how long you're going to do it. When you pray with a group, you have to follow along with the pack for the most part. However, it's best not to have either form of prayer take precedence over the other in your prayer life. This isn't to say that you should, or need to spend as much time praying with others as you do on your own. However, spending too much time on your own in prayer is also not desirable. There's a certain synergy that develops when you combine corporate prayer with personal prayer. Do one to the exclusion of the other, and you miss out on what the other style has to offer.

Patterning Your Prayer

When you pray as part of a group in a house of worship, your prayers will follow a certain pattern as set by the order of service followed by the group. When you pray by yourself, on the other hand, you don't have to follow a set pattern unless you want to. You can speak extemporaneously, simply saying what's on your mind if you so choose. Or you can be more formal. You can structure your prayers in a certain order or pattern. This can be especially helpful if you're new to prayer and you're not sure what you should pray about.

Acting Up

When we pray, our prayers generally fall into four basic categories. We're either praising God, humbling ourselves before Him by admitting we're not perfect people, thanking Him, or asking Him for His help. ACTS, which stands for Adoration, Confession (or Contrition), Thanksgiving, and Supplication, is a prayer pattern based on these four categories, bringing them together in a neat little bundle.

Adoration

Prayers of adoration are prayers that simply bless God. When we say them, we're both praising Him and telling Him how much we appreciate our relationship with Him. As we bless Him, we in turn are blessed.

Some people have a hard time praising God. They get awestruck and tongue-tied when trying to express their appreciation to God. If you're one of them, know that a simple "Bless you, God," will suffice. You can also rely on the adoration prayers of others, and there are plenty of these to choose from in the Bible. Once again, your greatest resource is the Book of Psalms, as the majority of the psalms praise God in some way. Choose the ones that speak to you.

Confession

Confession, which calls for declaring your sins before God, is a part of prayer that some people have trouble with. Why is this important? Unconfessed sin can stand in the way of your prayer life, and keep you from both wanting to pray and from receiving all that God can bestow upon you. Yes, it is important to come before God in whatever place you're in. But that doesn't mean trying to cover things up that you should be telling Him about. He knows about them anyway, and it's important for you to come before Him and take ownership and responsibility for your actions.

What kinds of things should you confess? Any action or thought that you're not particularly proud of. If you feel bad about yelling at the dog, tell God. If you think you could have been a little more compassionate when a coworker came to you seeking some advice, out with it, too.

Some people change ACTS into CATS so they can begin their prayer sessions by "coming clean" to God.

Thanksgiving

It is always important to give thanks to God, even at times when we don't much feel like doing it. Thanking Him for what we have serves as a reminder of where we are in relationship to Him. It acknowledges God's love for us and our love for Him, and it reminds us of what He has done in our lives. Perhaps most important, taking the time to reflect on the things we have and thanking God for them helps us put into better perspective the things that we do not have.

quote

Praising [God] is not something we do because we feel good; rather it is an act of obedience. Often the prayer of praise is done in sheer teeth-gritting willpower; yet when we persist in it, somehow the power of God is released into us and into the situation.

—Merlin R. Carothers, in *Prison to Praise*

Supplication

Supplication, the last part of ACTS, is when we make requests of God and ask Him for His help on various matters. These prayers are offered for ourselves and for others. Supplication means addressing humble requests and prayers to somebody with the power to grant them—in this case, God.

There are many things that you can pray to God for in this final stage. Here are just a few:

- Yourself, for your physical daily needs and to help you grow in devotion to God.
- Your family, including children, parents, siblings, and so forth.
- Your community, and especially those in power and authority, that they will seek God's counsel in making wise decisions.
- The sick, both for their restoration to health and for spiritual peace and strength.
- The poor and oppressed throughout the world.
- Those who do not know God.

Following the Hours

Another way to order your prayer is to follow the Liturgy of the Hours. Also known as the Divine Office, this is a liturgy with very deep and ancient roots. The Liturgy of the Hours consists of prayers, psalms, and meditations for every hour of every day. If you're looking for a way to pray without ceasing, you'll find it in the Hours. Furthermore, the readings change every day.

While the Liturgy of the Hours is often associated with the Catholic Church, it can be prayed by anyone. Online resources are available to keep you going through the liturgy, as well as a version that can be downloaded to PDAs (personal digital assistants). The basic structure looks like this:

- Lauds, or the Morning Prayer, to be said the first thing in the morning.
- The Little Hours, also known as Prayer through the Day. (These are short prayers said at certain times during the day.)
- Vespers, also known as Evening Prayer or Evensong.
- Compline, also called Night Prayer, which is the last prayer of the day.

The Liturgy of the Hours also includes the Office of Readings, which can be said at any time of the day.

Finding Your Prayer Posture

People pray in all sorts of positions—standing up, sitting down, kneeling, even lying prostrate. They stretch out their hands to God or fold their hands neatly in supplication. They look up to the heavens, or cast their eyes downward.

Where did all of these prayer postures come from? They're ancient as the hills. The custom of praying with the arms outstretched and raised dates back to antiquity and was common to both Jews and Gentiles.

The posture you choose to pray in is of no great importance in and of itself, but it is important in that it shows respect and reverence to God. In the past, some churches specified that people should stand during public prayer and kneel when praying privately, but most don't get quite so specific anymore. Certain positions are more helpful for some people than for others. Some simply work better at certain times than at others. Kneeling and prostration, for example, are appropriate when we are saying prayers of petition, confession, or repentance. Raising our hands to God just comes naturally when we're praising Him or giving Him thanks. Sitting in a lotus position (or as near as you can get to one) is the classic position for more meditative forms of prayer.

How to choose which prayer position is right for you? Try the ones that appeal to you, and maybe add one that doesn't. Pick one that allows you to be relaxed, yet attentive. And don't be afraid to mix them up. There is nothing that says that one prayer position is more effective than any other.

Here are a few to consider, along with passages from the Bible that talk about them:

- **Kneeling**—"Now when Daniel knew that the writing was signed, he went home. And in his upper room, with his windows open toward Jerusalem, he knelt down on his knees three times that day, and prayed and gave thanks before his God, as was his custom since early days" (Daniel 6:10).

- **Sitting**—"Then King David went in and sat before the Lord; and he said: Who am I, O Lord God? and what is my house, that You have brought me this far." (2 Samuel 7:18)
- **Bowing**—"Then the man bowed down his head and worshiped the Lord." (Genesis 24:26)
- **Standing**—"Then Solomon stood before the altar of the Lord in the presence of all the congregation of Israel, and spread out his hands toward heaven." (1 Kings 8:22)
- **Hands raised**—"Therefore I desire that the men pray everywhere, lifting up holy hands, without wrath or doubting." (1 Timothy 2:8)
- **Face down**—"So Moses and Aaron went from the presence of the assembly to the door of the tabernacle of meeting, and they fell on their faces. And the glory of the Lord appeared to them." (Numbers 20:6)
- **Walking**—"And what does the Lord require of you But to do justly, To love mercy, And to walk humbly with your God?" (Micah 6:8)

discussion question

Is it okay to pray in bed?
Absolutely. Many people spend a few minutes in prayer before they go to sleep at night and in the mornings when they wake up. If you find yourself falling asleep while you're praying, simply resume your prayers when you wake up.

Some people feel that you should stay in one position during your prayer time, as moving around may be disruptive to your prayers. Others will tell you that there is nothing wrong with moving around at will when you're praying. Contemplative prayers, however, do call for staying very still and in one position throughout the prayer period. The best approach to take is to match your prayer position with the kind of prayer that you're doing.

CHAPTER 8

Prayer Tools

Getting into a prayerful state often entails removing ourselves from the distractions that sight and sound can create. This is just one way in which we can more closely focus our efforts on prayer, but it's by no means the only one. Sometimes that focus can be found by keeping our eyes and ears open and treating them to prayer aids that delight the senses. In this chapter, we'll discuss various aspects of the more sensual side of prayer, and how these tools can be used to enhance your prayer experience.

Visual Prayer Tools

The world's religions are rich in visual imagery, symbols, and icons, with many of them dating back to the earliest recorded history. The Christian church used paintings and mosaics to teach and enlighten followers from its earliest times. Images from the Old and New Testaments have adorned most aspects of church architecture, including ceilings, walls, altars, and windows. They are also used to decorate furniture, liturgical vessels, and books. Other commonly used images were inspired by the lives and legends of the saints and from mythology.

symbolism

The various tools of prayer—crosses, icons, candles, prayer beads, and such—are meant to enhance the prayer experience, not supplant it. Thinking about how much you love God while you're lighting some incense doesn't substitute for spending some time in prayer with Him.

Visual symbols were also not foreign to ancient followers of Judaism. God had forbidden the creation of graven images in the Second Commandment—"You shall not make for yourself any carved image, or any likeness of anything that is in heaven above, or that is in the earth beneath, or that is in the water under the earth; you shall not bow down to them nor serve them" (Deuteronomy 5:8–9). However, God's directive only prohibited making images of anything in heaven or earth for the purposes of worship. In other words, there was a distinction made between graven images that would be worshipped, and graven images in general.

Images of bull calves, cherubim, palm trees, and flowers covered the walls and the doors of the temple. Two cherubs decorated the top of the Ark of the Covenant. Biblical figures dating back to 235 C.E. were also found on the walls of a synagogue in Syria that was discovered in the 1920s. Such Old Testament scenes as Moses descending from Mount Sinai, the parting of the

Red Sea, and David in scenes of battle, often rendered in stained glass, grace some modern synagogues. However, in keeping with Jewish tradition, there are never any physical representations of God.

But remember to be careful when adding visual elements to your prayer space. Adding so many visual aids to your prayer space that they distract you rather than help you focus on God makes them, rather than God, the object of your attention. When adding prayer aids to your prayer practice, remember their proper place, and keep their use in perspective.

factum

In biblical times, cherubim were supernatural creatures associated with the presence of God. Today we think of them as angels. They are often depicted in artwork as beautiful young children with wings.

Crosses and Crucifixes

One of the key symbols of faith, the cross is today associated almost wholly with the Christian faith. In reality, however, this particular symbol predates Christianity. Primitive cruciform signs can be traced back to early Oriental and Indian religious practices, where, it is believed, they represented the sun or the sacred fire of the ancestors. In ancient Egypt, a form of the cross called a tau, which looks like a capital "T," was the symbol of life. The Greeks were also familiar with the form of the cross, and associated its four points with the four elements—earth, water, fire, and air. Cruciform signs have also been found in pre-Columbian ruins in North America, and in ancient Western European megaliths.

Unlike other ancient civilizations, the Romans never viewed the cross as a symbol of faith or spirituality. Instead, they used it as an instrument of torture. It was, of course, used to crucify Jesus, and it was also used to punish many others, in particular individuals who could not prove their Roman citizenship or who stole or committed other crimes. In many respects, it's ironic that an object with such a history would become such an important symbol of faith. Soon after Christ's death, however, it became symbolic for all that Jesus stood for. Early followers of Christianity placed crosses in their homes to symbolize their dedication to their beliefs, and the cross soon became a key element in Christian worship.

symbolism

According to church legend, the St. Andrew's cross leans on its side because St. Andrew didn't feel worthy of being crucified in the same manner as Jesus was and asked that his cross be made differently. However, more modern sources identify this cross form with the saint only from the fourteenth century onward.

As the leading symbol of Christian faith, crosses and crucifixes abound. They come in a variety of forms. The Latin cross, with its single longer vertical element, is the most commonly seen. The Greek cross, which has four arms of equal length and looks like a "+" sign, is also a familiar version.

Other cross forms include:

- **The St. Andrew's cross**—One of the most ancient, and often seen in ancient sculpture; it resembles the letter "X".
- **The Celtic cross**—First used in sixth-century Ireland by Celtic Christians, it is essentially a Latin cross with a circle in its center overlying the axis of the horizontal and vertical elements. The circle signifies eternity.
- **The Eastern Orthodox cross** (also called Byzantine Cross, the Eastern Cross, and the Russian Orthodox Cross)—This cross of early Christianity has three horizontal bars of different lengths crossing one vertical bar. A short bar at the top represents the inscription that Pontius Pilate posted above Christ's head. Close to the bottom is a tilted lower bar that is a bit longer than the top bar, which represents a footrest.

- **The Maltese Cross**—The arms on this cross are all equal in length. Each arm looks similar to an isosceles triangle, with the single points meeting in the middle of the cross. The eight points formed by the arms represent the eight Beatitudes of Matthew.

When a cross is affixed with a representation of the body of Christ it is called a crucifix. The carved figure of Christ's body is called the corpus.

Icons

An integral part of the traditions of the Orthodox church, icons are depictions of holy figures—often the Holy Trinity, the Holy Family, or Jesus and Mary—and religious events. They can be and often are beautiful works of art, but they are meant to do much more than merely delight the eyes. To followers of the Orthodox faith, they are the means through which the kingdom of God can be experienced on earth. For this reason, icons are often referred to as "windows into heaven."

Jesus himself is believed to be the first iconographer, having created an image of his face on a linen cloth as a healing gift for a king. This icon, known as "Not Made by Human Hands" or the "Holy Face," no longer exists in its original form, but copies of it are still being produced to this day. A similar story credits the first icon as having appeared on a cloth given to Jesus by Veronica, one of the women who comforted him as he was carrying the cross. According to church history, the apostle Luke was the first to actually paint an icon. He painted a living subject—the Virgin Mary—whose face he had seen for himself. When he presented the images he had created to her, she gave them her blessing and said that Christ's grace would be imparted to them.

factum

At least three of the icons that Luke created of the Virgin Mary are still in existence, including a portrait of the Virgin Mary holding Jesus as an infant (the first such depiction). Luke is also credited with painting icons of Peter and Paul.

Many early church leaders kept icons front and center to inspire them during their studies and devotions. Over time, the practice was embraced by laypeople as well. Throughout the centuries, people have contemplated icons and have prayed before, with, and to that which the icons represent. In so doing, they have accessed the spirit of the saints they portray in order to deepen their connection to God.

Icons were traditionally created by monks who lived in seclusion. Instead of canvas, which was deemed too fragile to withstand the hard use that icons are often subjected to, the monks painted on solid blocks of wood, using as many as thirty layers of paint and lacquer to create the holy images. As opposed to other forms of sacred art, in which subjects are often depicted in more natural or representational styles, the rules of iconography dictate that the saints not be portrayed as they appeared in real life. Instead, their images are meant to reflect their spirit, and especially that spirit as experienced and interpreted by the iconographer.

To this day, iconographers create their images using specific artistic devices that are unique to iconography. To a casual observer, these techniques may seem rather odd and rudimentary. Faces and bodies are highly stylized and flat, bearing no shadowing or shading to make them look three-dimensional, and therefore lifelike. Details are minimal, with scenery and other settings, and are rendered as simply as possible. Perspectives are placed in such a way that the viewer's eye is drawn into and toward the subject of the icon. Clothing takes the shape of geometric forms—triangles, rectangles, and ovals—that demonstrate a heavenly order.

symbolism

Orthodox icons were originally meant to be used only for religious veneration. In the twentieth century, however, they became highly sought after as collectible works of art, especially after the fall of communism and the resurgence of the Orthodox faith in many Eastern European countries where its practice had been prohibited.

Even the colors used in icons are dictated by tradition to a large extent, although there will be some differences based on local traditions, the materials available, and the iconographer himself. Blue, the color associated with heaven, mystery, and the mystical life, is primarily used for Christ's outer garment or mantle as well as the clothing of Mary. Red, associated with life and vitality, is used for Christ's tunic or inner garment. A deeper red or wine color is used to depict the Virgin Mary's outer garment.

Candles

With their warm flames leaping and dancing with life, candles have long been used to enhance religious ceremonies, worship, and prayer, far beyond their basic function of bringing light into darkness. It's hard to think of a religion where candles, flame, or fire don't play a role in one way or another.

In Judaism, the flame symbolizes the soul. A special candle called a yartzeit candle (meaning "year" and "time" in Yiddish) is customarily lit on the anniversary of a family member's death to commemorate the travel of the individual's soul from its earthly plane. Candles are lit both at the beginning of the Sabbath observance and at its end. Some families light a candle for each member of the family, or for each person who is present at the beginning of the Sabbath. The candle that closes the Sabbath—the Havdallah candle—is braided and has more than one wick, which symbolizes harmony, love, and the coming together of the souls during the Sabbath remembrance. During Hanukkah—the Festival of Light—the rededication of the Temple in Jerusalem in 165 b.c.e. is symbolized by eight days of candle lighting.

Blessed are You, Lord, our God, King of the Universe, who sanctifies us with his commandments, and commands us to light the candles of Shabbat.

—The blessing said over the Sabbath candles

Flame, or fire, is a common symbol for God's presence in scripture. In 1 Kings, Elijah tells the children of Israel that the God "who answers by fire" is the true God (I Kings 18:24). In Hebrews, God is described as a "consuming fire" (Hebrews 12:29). In Deuteronomy, God's voice is described as "speaking out of the midst of the fire" (Deuteronomy 4:33).

For Christians, the flame also symbolizes Christ's divine presence. Candles are used to symbolize him as the "true light," and to remind those who follow him of their commitment to their faith. Candles are also lit in memory of the dead and in other special devotions. Catholics light candles as part of the veneration of saints. When praying privately, many Christians light a candle when they pray to signify Christ's presence in their lives.

The Sweet Smell of Incense

Fragrancing is as old as history itself, and the use of fragrance—primarily as incense—in worship dates back to the earliest times as well. The people of the ancient Near East used it both cosmetically and in religious ceremonies, and its application spread widely from there. Both Ovid and Virgil document the use of incense in early Roman worship.

Frankincense and myrrh, the two main types of incense used in ancient times, come from two types of resinous trees that grow in parts of the Middle East, Africa, and India. Both are obtained by cutting or peeling the bark of the tree and harvesting the resins and gum that flow out.

The ancient Egyptians were particularly fond of incense and used it widely for fragrancing, in religious rituals, and in preparing bodies for entombment. Images of kings burning incense in censers similar to those that are still used today in Roman Catholic, Orthodox, and Anglican churches can be seen in the carvings on Egyptian tombs and temples.

factum

A censer is a fireproof vessel, usually suspended from chains, used for burning incense. Also called a thurible, a censer consists of a cup or bowl, which rests on a firm base, and a hollow movable pan for holding ignited charcoal, plus a lid.

Over time, incense was used to both enhance prayer practice and to symbolize prayers as they traveled upward to God. Incense also factored heavily in ancient Jewish rituals, and there are numerous references to its use in the Old Testament. In the Book of Exodus, Moses was commanded by God to "take sweet spices, stacte and oncycha and galbanum, and pure frankincense with these sweet spices . . . You shall make of these an incense, a compound according to the art of the perfumer . . . And you shall beat some of it very fine, and put some of it before the Testimony in the tabernacle of meeting where I will meet with you. It shall be most holy to you" (Exodus 30:34–36). In Leviticus, Moses' brother Aaron was instructed to present a bull to God as a sin offering. To protect himself from the presence of God, he was also told to ". . . take a censer full of burning coals of fire from the altar before the Lord, with his hands full of sweet incense beaten fine, and bring it inside the veil. And he shall put the incense on the fire before the Lord, that the cloud of incense may cover the mercy seat . . . lest he die." (Leviticus 16:12–13). According to the gospels of the New Testament, frankincense and myrrh mixed with gold were given to the infant Jesus by the Magi, or the Three Kings.

The use of incense in Christian worship services also dates back to ancient times as many of the church's rites and ceremonial observances were based on Jewish worship forms. However, there aren't many references to burning incense in the New Testament, and its use fell out of favor when the practice of blood sacrifice was halted after the destruction of the Jewish temple in 70 c.e. It's not known exactly when or why incense was reintroduced to Christian worship, but its use is documented from the fifth century on and most believe that it played a role in Christian ceremonies earlier than this.

discussion question

Can the same kind of incense that's burned while praying be used at other times during the day?
While reserving the incense you use during prayer to these periods can add a special significance to the practice, there is nothing that says you can't use your prayer incense at other times of the day. Many people like to light some incense to create a sense of calm and peace when they get home from work or before they go to bed.

Incense continues to play a key role in the spiritual practices of many of the world's faiths. Buddhists burn it during festivals and initiations in addition to daily prayer. The Hindus use it for ritual and domestic offerings. In China incense is burned to honor ancestors and household gods. In Japan it is part of many Shinto rituals. Many American Indians burn fragrant herbs as part of their prayer rituals, either as an element of cleansing or as an offering to the Great Spirit.

Incense is also a wonderful adjunct to home worship. It engages a very ancient part of the brain called the limbic system, which is the brain's emotional and memory center and also houses the sense of smell. Depending on the type of incense burned, the practice can be healing, soothing, or uplifting.

factum

Resin incense, such as that used in ancient times, comes in small chunks or powdered form. If it's in chunk form, users typically grind it into a powder using a mortar and pestle. The powder is then sprinkled on a piece of long-burning charcoal that is held in a heat-resistant container. Stronger forms of resin incense, such as frankincense and myrrh, are often combined with milder forms like copal and benzoin, or with other additives.

Prayer Counters

Another prayer tradition shared by Eastern and Western faiths is the use of beads or other objects to count or focus prayer. This, too, is an ancient tradition, with evidence of it dating back to the Assyrian empire of the Old Testament. In early times, people would drop tiny pebbles into their laps to keep count of their prayers. About 500 years before Christ, it became customary to tie knots in strings. Christians, Buddhists, Hindus, and Muslims today use various kinds of prayer counters to assist them when they're praying repetitive prayers.

Ropes and Rosaries

One of the best-known forms of prayer counters are the rosaries used by Roman Catholics. They consist of a string of 150 beads, divided into groups of ten. Prayers, such as the "Hail Mary" and the "Our Father," are said while fingering each bead. The term rosary comes from the Latin word *rosarius*, which means "garland," "bouquet," or "garden of roses."

According to legend, the rosary was developed by St. Dominic in the thirteenth century, given to him by the Virgin Mary who appeared to him when he was praying for a weapon to use against those who opposed Christianity. In honor of this tradition, Dominican priests still wear a rosary on the left side of their belts in the same place that a knight would wear a sword.

symbolism

Primitive prayer beads were made of fruit pits, dried berries, pieces of bone, and hardened clay. The wealthy used precious stones, jewels, and even nuggets of gold to count their prayers.

There is, however, more myth than fact to this story. More likely, rosaries came into Christianity from Islam during the Middle Ages, and were used as a tool to help people learn and remember teachings from the Bible. At the time, most people couldn't read, and even those who did could rarely get their hands on a Bible. Instead, they learned their lessons by hearing them and committing them to memory as they fingered the beads on their rosaries.

In the Orthodox church, the rosary takes the form of a prayer rope, which consists of a series of small knots. Commonly referred to as komboskini by the Greek Orthodox and chotki by the Russian Orthodox, prayer ropes are used to say the "Jesus Prayer"—"Lord Jesus Christ, Son of God, have mercy on me, a sinner," or other short prayers. Usually made of black yarn, prayer ropes are marked off at intervals by wooden or glass beads, and come in various lengths, ranging from thirty-three knots (each knot represents a year in Jesus' life) to 100 knots. Prayer ropes are also used to count a silent "breath prayer," with "Lord Jesus Christ, Son of God," prayed on inhalation, and "have mercy on me, a sinner" prayed on exhalation.

Praying the Rosary

The Rosary prayer, which differs from the prayer counters, helps worshippers pay attention to mysteries in the history of their salvation, and to thank and praise God for them. There are twenty mysteries reflected upon in the Rosary, and these are divided into the five Joyful Mysteries, the five Luminous Mysteries, the five Sorrowful Mysteries, and the five Glorious Mysteries. When praying the Rosary, you pick one of the categories of mysteries to pray on. Each of the Mysteries is also referred to as a decade, as each involves the reading of five "Hail Mary's."

Generally, the Joyful Mysteries are said on Monday and Saturday, the Luminous on Thursday, the Sorrowful on Tuesday and Friday, and the Glorious on Wednesday and Sunday (with these exceptions: Sundays of Christmas season—the Joyful Mysteries; Sundays of Lent—the Sorrowful Mysteries).

The Five Joyful Mysteries

The Five Joyful Mysteries are as follows:

1. The Annunciation of Gabriel to Mary
2. The Visitation of Mary to Elizabeth
3. The Birth of Jesus
4. The Presentation of Jesus
5. Finding Jesus in the Temple

The Five Luminous Mysteries

The Five Luminous Mysteries are as follows:

1. The Baptism of Jesus
2. The Manifestation of Christ
3. The Proclamation of the Kingdom of God
4. The Transfiguration
5. The Last Supper

The Five Sorrowful Mysteries

The Five Sorrowful Mysteries can be found in the following verses:

1. The Agony of Jesus in the Garden
2. Jesus Scourged at the Pillar
3. Jesus Is Crowned with Thorns
4. Jesus Carries the Cross to Calvary
5. The Crucifixion of Jesus

The Five Glorious Mysteries

The Five Glorious Mysteries are reflected in the following:

1. The Resurrection of Jesus
2. The Ascension
3. The Descent of the Holy Spirit at Pentecost
4. The Assumption of Mary into Heaven
5. The Coronation of Mary as Queen of Heaven and Earth

Saying the Prayers

Every bead on the rosary corresponds to a prayer. To properly pray the Rosary, first you make the sign of the cross and recite the Apostles' Creed:

I believe in God, the Father almighty, creator of Heaven and earth.

I believe in Jesus Christ, his only Son, our Lord.

He was conceived by the power of the Holy Spirit and born of the Virgin Mary.

He suffered under Pontius Pilate, was crucified, died, and was buried.

He descended to the dead.

On the third day he rose again.

He ascended into heaven, and is seated at the right hand of the Father.

He will come again to judge the living and the dead.

I believe in the Holy Spirit, the holy catholic church, the communion of saints, the forgiveness of sins, the resurrection of the body, and the life everlasting.

Amen.

Following the "Apostles' Creed," say the "Lord's Prayer" (Our Father):

Our father, who art in heaven

hallowed be Thy name

Thy kingdom come

Thy will be done on earth as it is in heaven.

Give us this day our daily bread

and forgive us our trespasses as we forgive those who trespass against us,

and lead us not into temptation; but deliver us from evil.

Amen.

Following the "Lord's Prayer," pray three "Hail Mary's":

Hail Mary, full of grace,

the Lord is with thee

blessed art thou among women,

and blessed is the fruit of thy womb, Jesus.

Holy Mary, Mother of God, pray for us sinners,

now and at the hour of our death.

Amen.

Following the three "Hail Mary's," say the "Glory Be to the Father":

Glory be to the Father,

and to the Son,

and to the Holy Spirit.

As it was in the beginning,

is now, and ever shall be,

world without end.

Amen.

Next, announce the first Mystery followed by the "Lord's Prayer." Then say ten "Hail Mary's" while keeping the mystery in your mind. Following this, say the "Glory be to the Father," and then say:

O my Jesus,

forgive us our sins,

save us from the fires of hell,

lead all souls to Heaven,

especially those who have most need of your mercy.

Do the same for the second, third, fourth, and fifth mystery. When you have completed the entire rosary, pray the "Hail, Holy Queen":

Hail, Holy Queen,

Mother of Mercy, our life,

our sweetness and our hope!

To thee do we cry, poor banished children of Eve;

to thee do we send up our sighs, mourning and weeping in this valley of tears.

Turn then, most gracious advocate, thine eyes of mercy toward us,

and after this our exile, show unto us the blessed fruit of thy womb, Jesus.

O clement, O loving, O sweet Virgin Mary!

Other Prayer Counters

Buddhists and Hindus also use prayer counters called malas to count mantras, typically in 108-bead cycles. For Buddhists, the usual mantra is "om mani padme hum," meaning "Jewel in the heart of the lotus," which is one of the names of the Buddha. For each mantra that is uttered, the fingers advance one bead. Followers of Islam use prayer beads strung in thirty-three- or ninety-nine-bead strands to give glory to Allah in several prayer forms or simply to pray the ninety-nine names of Allah.

factum

Mantra is the practice of using specific "sacred sound" syllables for spiritual and material transformation. The power of the mantra is believed to come not from what the syllables specifically mean, but from their vibrational effect on the body's physiological and energy systems.

Although not a universal tradition in the Episcopalian church, prayer beads are also becoming a popular prayer tool for members of this denomination. Developed in the 1980s, Anglican prayer beads are ropes of thirty-three beads, divided into groups of seven. The thirty-three beads signify the number of years that Jesus lived on earth. The divisions of seven relate to the seven days of creation, the seven days of the week, or the seven seasons of the church year. A large bead called a cruciform bead separates each set. There is no official set of prayers for these beads as the practice is still too new. Popular choices include the "Jesus Prayer" and excerpts from The Book of Common Prayer.

Music to the Ears

Music is a powerful expression of human emotion, and it has long enhanced prayer and worship services. References to music abound in the Bible, and scripture from the Bible has formed the basis for some of the world's most beautiful songs. It is a cornerstone of all major religions, taking a variety of forms ranging from chanting to hymns to ringing bells and singing bowls. Researchers have found that soothing music induces states of deep relaxation. Simply chanting "om" can affect metabolic rate, heartbeat, and respiration rate.

Many people feel a special connection to God through music, and for some, prefacing their personal prayer time by listening to music helps them get into a prayerful state. What they listen to runs the gamut from Gregorian chant to contemporary instrumental music composed especially for prayer and meditation. Other choices include Sufi or Native American chanting, music from the Celtic tradition, modern sacred music, and classical music.

The resonant tones of Tibetan bells and singing bowls have long been used by Buddhists to help spiritual seekers enter into meditation. They can also be used at the beginning of a prayer session to cue the start of the session and as a focus for quieting the mind. The bowls are struck with a padded mallet or a soft piece of wood, or rubbed around the rim to produce a harmonic ringing. Each produces a different sound, with smaller ones usually pitched higher. Tibetan bells, also known as ghantas, are played by ringing or by rubbing a stick around the rim. Tingshaw, another type of Tibetan bell, come in matched pairs coupled together with a leather cord. They are played by striking them against each other.

You can buy recordings of singing bowls and bells, or you can buy the real thing and learn how to play them yourself. You'll find resources for both in Appendix B, along with some suggestions of music to use before or during prayer.

CHAPTER 9

Praying Simply

All relationships have to start at the beginning. So, too, does our relationship in prayer with God. Simple prayer, or beginner's prayer, honors our newcomer status by sticking to the basics. What could be easier?

Starting with Fits and Starts

Stepping out in prayer can be as nerve-wracking as going out on a first date. It shouldn't be, but there's something about starting a relationship with God that can be, well, tongue-tying. We might think we know what to say, or what we want to say, but when we start talking the words either don't come, or they don't come the way we'd like them to. We can't just sit down and have a heart-to-heart talk with the Almighty—which, by the way, is what simple prayer is all about. Then the self-doubt kicks in. "I'm not doing it right," we think. "Boy, God must think I'm one heck of a dodo. Why did I ever want to do this in the first place?"

Blush, blush, stammer, stammer, end of first date. Maybe there will be another one. Maybe not.

Negative Tapes

There are lots of reasons why there are fits and starts at the beginning of a life of prayer. The one that seems to be the biggest is that our rational minds are often too much in control. In other words, we spend too much time thinking about what we're doing instead of just doing it. Because of this, there's usually some pretty negative chitchat going on inside our heads. You might replay every old tape you've ever heard about prayer—it's dumb, it's silly, it's ineffective, it doesn't work, it's archaic, it has to be exactly right or God won't answer—you name it, while you're trying to pray. If prayer is all these things, your brain is saying, "Then why are you even remotely thinking about doing it, much less trying to do it? Give this up, go back to something that makes sense." The only problem is, we don't know what that "something that makes sense" would be.

Prayer does make sense. If it didn't, we wouldn't feel called to do it. Nor would the billions of other people who make a conscious effort to connect with God on a regular—if not daily—basis. This isn't to say that there won't be times when you'll have some of the same feelings. In fact, you can expect to.

Being in Control

When we first start out in prayer, we often try to control the outcomes. While we might go to God with the greatest of intentions and desires to get everything we can out of the time we spend with Him, we can't help trying to anticipate what the outcome should be. In other words, we won't hand over the controls to God. However, as the following words from the Book of Proverbs point out, this is exactly what needs to happen:

Trust in the Lord with all your heart,

And lean not on your own understanding;

In all your ways acknowledge Him,

And He shall direct your paths.

Do not be wise in your own eyes;

Fear the Lord and depart from evil.

It will be health to your flesh,

And strength to your bones.

—Proverbs, 3:5–8

As human beings, we often think we want things to be different. At the same time, we tend to resist change. Our status quo, the place we're in at the moment, is vastly more comfortable to us than the unknown is. Even if the place we're in isn't that great, if we've been there for a while we've grown comfortable with how it feels and we're reluctant to see if anything else could or would be better. Or, we tell ourselves that a little bit of change is okay. We don't want to be made anew. That would be too drastic. Instead, we just want to be a little different.

Prayer, however, is all about change. In fact, change is prayer's inevitable outcome. What's more, we can't control how things will change, when they'll change, or how even much they might change. Much as we might want to have our hands on the outcomes, we can't. We have to turn those controls over to God. If we don't, we'll be stalled out in the same awkward place for a very long time.

Starting from Scratch

Another big stumbling block to getting started in prayer is that we're self-conscious about doing it. Frankly, we're not very good at being beginners at anything. As adults, we're too out of touch with what it feels like to start to learn anything from scratch. We pride ourselves in being good, if not expert, at everything we do, and we tend to avoid the things that we are less than expert at. If we can't sail into a dialogue with God with as much grace and aplomb as anything we've ever heard or read, well, then, we'll just let that one sit for now. Or maybe we'll try again later, when we're better at it.

The problem is, the expertise we want to have in prayer doesn't come unless we start praying, and keep at it after we start. In other words, you don't get better at prayer unless you do it. This means that you have to start somewhere. It also means that you have to be a beginner.

Being a Good Beginner

Throughout the long history of humankind talking to God, some of the most effective prayers—if not all of them—have been offered up to the Almighty by people who considered themselves absolute beginners at the process. In fact, no matter how much they prayed, how long they prayed, or how fervently they prayed, they never thought of themselves as being experts at it. You might find this hard to believe, but it's absolutely true. Mother Teresa sure knew a thing or two about talking to God, but in her eyes she was always a beginner. To her dying day, she communicated with God very simply, like a child would talk to a parent. She always felt that there was something new to be learned from Him, and the best way to learn it was to keep things simple. In her words, everyone who prayed should, ". . . go to God like a little child. A child has no difficulty expressing his mind in simple words that say so much."

Other spiritual greats also valued the simple prayer of the beginner.

quote

> Prayer is strange in being an activity where no success is possible. There is no perfect prayer—except insofar as it corresponds to one's real situation and represents a total turning toward God.
>
> —Michael Casey, in *Toward God*

Jean-Nicholas Grou

An eighteenth-century Jesuit priest, Grou spent most of his time writing and speaking about spiritual growth and especially about how the practice of prayer furthered it. In *How to Pray*, he wrote, "Every Christian ought to say to the Savior as humbly as [the disciples]: "Lord, teach us to pray." He went on to say, "God must teach us everything concerning the nature of prayer: its object, its characteristics, the disposition it requires, and the personal application we must make of it according to our needs. In the matter of prayer we are as ignorant of the theory as of the practice."

Brother Lawrence

Brother Lawrence (given name Nicholas Herman) was a lay brother in a monastery in seventeenth-century Paris. He lived the simplest life, focusing his efforts on living every moment in the presence of God. As such, he also valued the importance of simplicity when praying, and wrote, "I have since given up all forms of devotions and set prayers except those which are suitable to this practice (conversing silently with God). I make it my business only to persevere in his holy presence wherein I keep myself by a simple attention and a general fond regard to God . . ."

Thomas Merton

Thomas Merton, a Trappist monk for twenty-seven years, wrote *The Seven Story Mountain*, an autobiography that dug deep into his own soul and ended up becoming a spiritual bestseller. As a Trappist, he spent his entire life in prayer, and understood the paradox of always being a beginner in prayer very well. As he put it, "We don't [enjoy] being beginners but let us be convinced of the fact that we will never be anything except beginners, all our life!"

Learning to Be Humble Before God

Allowing ourselves to be beginners activates one of the fundamentals of a successful prayer life. Admitting that we know very little, perhaps even nothing, about what we're about to do is a pretty humbling experience for most of us. However, being able to do so also signifies our intention, and our desire, to open ourselves to God and allow Him to work with us. And that's a good thing. As Benedict of Nursia put it: "The fifth step of humility is to keep no secrets from the one to whom we confess. We must humbly confess all of our evil thoughts and all of our evil actions."

Keeping no secrets means coming before God just as we are. It also means:

- Not trying to speak to God in the Queen's English. No one really does this.
- Not trying to make things pretty for God. In other words, you're going to blurt out exactly what's on your mind, no matter how ugly it is.
- Not trying to be anything that you aren't. Remember, God knows you better than you know yourself.

Pretty simple, right? If you can stick to these rules . . . well, you'll be praying. Now, how simple could that be?

But wait, you're thinking. Surely, it can't be this easy. I mean, after all the stuff I've read about ordering my prayer life, structuring my prayers, deciding where to pray, how to pray, and whether I should sit, stand, or kneel when I'm doing it, now you're going to tell me that praying is this simple? That all I have to do is follow these guidelines and I'll be okay with God? That I'll be praying?

Absolutely.

quote

> And you shall remember the Lord your God, for it is He who gives you power to get wealth, that He may establish His covenant which He swore to your fathers, as it is this day.
>
> —Deuteronomy 9:18

The Power of Praying Just as You Are

As previously mentioned, one of the things that tends to trip us up when we go to pray is that we think we have to come before God in our Sunday best. We think we have to look our best, act our best, and pray our best. But this isn't what God wants. Not by a long shot.

All God wants us to do is come before Him just as we are. This is what simple prayer is all about. As Richard Foster described it in *Prayer: Finding the Heart's True Home:*

> *In Simple Prayer, we bring ourselves before God just as we are, warts and all. Like children before a loving father, we open our hearts and make our requests. We do not try to sort things out, the good from the bad. We simply and unpretentiously share our concerns and make our petitions.*

As you can see, simple prayer is the easiest kind of prayer that you can do. All you have to do is open your mouth and say what's on your mind. Just talk about the ordinary events of your everyday life. If you're unhappy with things at work, you can talk about them. If someone in your life just threw you a curveball, out it comes. If you're beside yourself because you just got an unexpected raise, tell God how you feel. If you're disappointed beyond words because you didn't get that raise, tell Him too. Everything and any-thing that's on your heart is fodder for simple prayer. Simple prayer is what we can do when we think we can't pray. Another word for simple prayer is expository prayer, meaning that it sets forth facts.

You don't have to put a lot of thought into your words when you're praying simply. Instead, you just let the words tumble out, however they want. If you're a linear thinker, your words might align themselves in a fairly logical way. If you're not, they might be all over the place in a mad, free-association jumble, and they might not make sense at all. It simply doesn't matter.

Simple prayer is the kind of prayer that you see most often in the Bible. Some of the best examples of it can be found in the Psalms of the Old Testament. The following psalm, a psalm of David, reflects about every form that simple prayer can take. It also illustrates how praying simply allows us to air all our emotions, and all our dirty laundry, before God:

Be merciful to me, O God, be merciful to me!

For my soul trusts in You;

And in the shadow of Your wings I will make my refuge,

Until these calamities have passed by.

I will cry out to God Most High,

To God who performs all things for me.

He shall send from heaven and save me;

He reproaches the one who would swallow me up.

My soul is among lions;

I lie among the sons of men

Who are set on fire,

Whose teeth are spears and arrows,

And their tongue a sharp sword.

Be exalted, O God, above the heavens;

Let Your glory be above all the earth.

They have prepared a net for my steps;

My soul is bowed down;

They have dug a pit before me;

Into the midst of it they themselves have fallen.

My heart is steadfast, O God, my heart is steadfast;

I will sing and give praise.

Awake, my glory!

Awake, lute and harp!

I will awaken the dawn.

I will praise You, O Lord, among the peoples;

I will sing to You among the nations.

For your mercy reaches unto the heavens,

And your truth unto the clouds.

Be exalted, O God, above the heavens;

Let Your glory be above all the earth.

—Psalm 57

You can also get very angry with God during simple prayer, which is something that we are often afraid to do when praying in other ways. The following psalm is entitled "A contemplation of Heman the Ezarhite." Whoever he was, he had clearly experienced better days in his walk with the Almighty:

O Lord, God of my salvation,

I have cried out day and night before You.

Let my prayer come before You;

Incline Your ear to my cry.

For my soul is full of troubles,

And my life draws near to the grave.

I am counted with those who go down to the pit;

I am like a man who has no strength,

Adrift among the dead,

Like the slain who lie in the grave,

Whom You remember no more,

And who are cut off from Your hand.

You have laid me in the lowest pit,

In darkness, in the depths.

Your wrath lies heavy upon me,

And you have afflicted me with all Your waves.

You have put away my acquaintances far from me;

You have made me an abomination to them;

I am shut up, and I cannot get out;

My eye wastes away because of affliction.

Lord, I have called daily upon You;

I have stretched out my hands to You.

Will you work wonders for the dead?

Shall the dead arise and praise you?

Shall Your lovingkindness be declared in the grave?

Or Your faithfulness in the place of destruction?

Shall Your wonders be known in the dark?

And Your righteousness in the land of forgetfulness?

But to You I have cried out, O Lord,

And in the morning my prayer comes before You.

Lord, why do You cast off my soul?

Why do You hide Your face from me?

I have been afflicted and ready to die from my youth up;

I suffer your terrors;

I am distraught.

Your fierce wrath has gone over me;

Your terrors have cut me off.

They came around me all day long like water;

They engulfed me altogether

Loved one and friend You have put far from me.

And my acquaintances into darkness.

—Psalm 88

quote

Psychologically my relationship with God varies. There are better days, when we seem to get along well. Occasionally I get mad at him. I get bored with God often. Sometimes I wonder if I have any relationship with him at all and whether this whole business is not one big illusion.

—Jerry Ryan, in "Desiring Prayer," *America* magazine

Simple prayer is also the most dominant prayer form among modern-day pray-ers. It has so many fans because it's so simple to do. Because it follows no specific style, it appeals to people who don't like more formal prayer styles. It allows you to pray about what you want, when you want, and wherever you want to do it. You don't have to worry about carrying a prayer book or a devotional along with you. Other reasons why simple prayer is so popular:

- It allows us to experience God in a very personal way.
- The words you speak in personal prayer are yours and yours alone.
- You can speak to God about exactly what's going on in your life at any time.
- You can let your emotions run the gamut.

symbolism

It's a good idea to balance the freedom of simple prayer with some structured prayer time to keep your walk with God from getting too casual. Doing daily Bible readings, following the readings in a daily devotional, or using written prayers on occasion are all ways of keeping simple prayer from becoming too "me focused."

The Benefits of Simple Prayer

When we speak frankly and honestly with God through simple prayer, we're inviting Him into our hearts and allowing Him to walk with us in all aspects of our lives. As we do, something pretty wonderful happens. We get to know God better. We learn to trust Him with all of our thoughts, feelings, and emotions, even the ones we're not particularly proud of. We get a better feeling for what it's like to be in His presence, and it no longer intimidates us as it once did. We get over our feelings of inadequacy. Performance anxiety becomes a thing of the past. In other words, we learn how to pray.

Is simple prayer for everyone? While anyone can pray simply, this prayer form may be too undisciplined and spontaneous for some people. Taken to the extreme, it can perhaps lead to a fairly careless prayer life because it doesn't call for much effort. However, if you're moving forward in your spiritual walk, your desire to experience God in other ways will deepen, and you'll keep simple prayer in its proper perspective. It will always be a part of your prayer life, but it won't be all of it.

quote

> Each person brings himself along when he comes to pray; and if he is inexperienced in prayer, what he brings with him will mostly bear the stamp of his personal problems and daily life.
>
> —Attributed to Adrienne Von Speyr, a writer and convert to Catholicism

How to Do Simple Prayer

Simple prayer starts right where you are, with exactly how you're feeling at the moment you begin to talk with God. All you have to do is say something like this:

"God, it's really a great day today and I'm in a fantastic mood. Boy, the world you created is a wonderful spot. I'm having such a great time with it right now. I wish everyone could. It troubles me that everyone doesn't. There are hurting people in this world. I don't understand why. I wish I did. That Tom guy I work with—boy, he's a hurting person. He'd like to hurt me, no doubt about it. He sure shoots me the old evil eye whenever he can. Boy, I'd like to understand him better. Maybe I need to think about that one for a while. Things could be pretty crummy in his life. As a matter of fact, I think they are. I think his kid is having problems. He's taking them out on the family, and Tom's taking them out on the people around him. Hmmm . . . God, I don't know what to do about him. I'd like to be able to help him, but I don't like him very much, so I keep my distance. Oh well. Time to get back to work. Talk to you later, God. Oh, and thanks."

That's all there is to praying simply. Let your thoughts flow. Don't work at it. Let God do the work.

CHAPTER 10

Praying in Times of Trouble

Trouble in all its various forms is a pretty big part of the human condition. When we're kids we sometimes revel in being little troublemakers, but as adults we usually try to avoid it like the plague. Still, trouble can find us. Going to God in prayer can help us get through the times when a little—or a lot—of trouble comes our way.

Dealing with Difficulties

Times of crisis can turn life upside down. They're the times when the bottom falls out of our world. The things we may have believed to be true might no longer be. We may not know what to do, how to cope, or where to turn. We may be gripped with fear so great that we feel paralyzed and unable to do anything. We might even be afraid to ask anyone for help for fear of exposing our problems. Nothing seems right. Nothing feels right.

Crisis times can literally flip your world over and put it on its ear. The word *crisis* comes from the Greek *krisis*, meaning "decision." For many people, these are the times at which it's toughest to pray. But they are the times at which prayer can do the most good. In fact, some of the most powerful praying happens when it seems like prayer is the last resort. Not only can talking to God about our problems bring us peace and relief, it can also bring greater clarity and understanding to the situation at hand.

Let me not pray to be sheltered from dangers but to be fearless in facing them.

Let me not beg for the stilling of my pain but for the heart to conquer it.

Let me not look for allies in life's battlefield but to my own strength.

Let me not crave in anxious fear to be saved but hope for the patience to win my freedom.

Grant me that I may not be a coward, feeling your mercy in my success alone; but let me find the grasp of your hand in my failure.

—Rabindranath Tagore, Fruit Gathering

Being prayerful, staying with God, talking to Him, and telling Him what is going on, is what we should do at all times. When crisis strikes, however, it can sometimes be difficult to do so. For this reason, crisis also tends to redefine our prayer life and make us approach it in a very different way. For many people, times of trouble tear them away from prayer. Others draw closer to God and spend more time in prayer with Him than ever before.

Why Bad Things Happen

It is often said that times of trouble are tests of faith. This doesn't mean that the problems we face are God-sent, although some people do believe that they are, or can be. Why would God intentionally send trouble our way? Here are a few of the possible explanations for it:

- He is making us better people by repairing our character faults.
- He is trying to teach us a lesson.
- He is trying to punish us.

These may seem like plausible answers to the question; however, they are patently untrue. We may become better people, and learn some lessons as we travel through adversity, but God doesn't intentionally create problems for these reasons. He does not cause our suffering. Nor does He punish us.

quote

It is good for us to have trials and troubles at times, for they often remind us that we are on probation and ought not to hope in any worldly thing. It is good for us sometimes to suffer contradiction, to be misjudged by men even though we do well and mean well. These things help us to be humble and shield us from vainglory. When to all outward appearances men give us no credit, when they do not think well of us, then we are more inclined to seek God Who sees our hearts. Therefore, a man ought to root himself so firmly in God that he will not see the consolations of men.

—Thomas à Kempis, in *The Imitation of Christ*

If you're still looking for an explanation of why bad things happen, one of the best comes from Rabbi Harold S. Kushner's book *When Bad Things Happen to Good People*. In it, he offers a very simple answer: Sometimes they just do. However, because of our innate nature, we try to make sense of it by looking for reasons why they do.

Can you accept the idea that some things happen for no reason, that there is randomness in the universe? Some people cannot handle that idea. They look for connections, striving desperately to make sense of all that happens. They convince themselves that God is cruel, or that they are sinners, rather than accept randomness.

Understanding that problems can just happen for no particular reason may not bring you much comfort. You might still be wondering, "Why me?" What this understanding can do, however, is put adversity into better perspective.

Trouble's "Good" Side

No one in his right mind would ask for trouble to come his way, but when it does arise it can actually end up working for the good. It can sometimes take a while to realize the benefits, but they do manifest in time. They can include:

- Finding strength and courage that we never knew we had.
- Learning how to rise to the occasion in ways we never would have expected.
- Finding compassion and support from sources we never knew existed.
- Gaining a greater sense of how God works in our lives.

As odd as it may sometimes seem, the challenges that life presents are what make us better people. When we stand up to the bad times, we learn that we have the capacity to do so, and that we can continue to do so. We learn, as Eleanor Roosevelt said, to "do the thing you think you cannot do."

You gain strength, courage, and confidence by every experience in which you really stop to look fear in the face. You are able to say to yourself, "I lived through this horror. I can take the next thing that comes along. . . ." You must do the thing you think you cannot do.

It is never easy to face adversity. It's not meant to be. Psychiatrist and author M. Scott Peck notes that being on unfamiliar ground or doing things differently is always going to frighten us, but that it is necessary for all types of growth, including spiritual growth. Fear, he says, is "inescapable if they [people] are in fact to change."

Individuals who have gone through periods of immense difficulties will often say that their experiences during these times, and what they learned from them, are what made them who they are now. While they would never wish for dire things, in retrospect they're actually thankful that they happened. Through them, they learned their mettle, what they're really made of. Such times also made them more aware of their weaknesses, fears, and faults.

The Fear Factor

Fear often plays a key role in times of trouble. This is an emotion that can take many forms, but the one that pops up the most often is fear of the unknown. When the parameters of life have been shifted without our consent, we begin to sail uncharted waters. Like the seafaring explorers of centuries ago, we don't really know what is out there or what to expect. There could be monsters on the edges of the world. And they could be pretty awful indeed.

Dear Lord,

be good to me . . .

The sea is so wide

and my boat is so small.

—Irish fisherman's prayer

Some of the most legendary figures in the Bible knew firsthand what it was like to deal with fear of the unknown. The first time that Moses came into contact with God—in the form of a burning bush—he did so with a certain amount of trepidation. In fact, he turned away from what he did not know and chose not to "see this great sight." The children of Israel, whom Moses led to the Promised Land, were afraid to enter it because it was new territory—it was unknown and it frightened them. Even though the land offered the Hebrews all the abundance they could ever wish for, they found lots of reasons why they just didn't want to go there. After listening to a night's worth of crying and complaining, God had had enough.

> Then the Lord said to Moses: "How long will these people reject Me? And how long will they not believe Me, with all the signs which I have performed among them?
>
> —Numbers 12:11

Maybe the signs that God had sent weren't enough for the children of Israel, but they were enough for Moses. He trusted God, and he finally convinced his people that they needed to trust God as well if they wanted to get to where they needed to go.

We, too, need to remember to put our faith in God in all things. This means turning to Him when we fear the unknown. Simply telling God that we're afraid, even if we don't know what we're afraid of, can bring blessed relief, both physically and emotionally.

Suffering in Silence

People sometimes resist praying to God when they're troubled because they feel it's inappropriate to bother God with their problems. Instead of turning to a source of strength for comfort and guidance, they suffer in silence and bear the burden on their own.

As compassionate as we can be toward others, we often don't treat ourselves kindly at all. We are reluctant to expose our vulnerabilities. Instead, we often walk a pretty stoic walk. We maintain a stiff upper lip. We tough it out. Taking this approach, however, tends to make our problems worse. It isolates us from the people who could help us, and it isolates us from God, who will.

The belief that it is inappropriate to turn to God in times of trouble has no basis in any form of scripture. If you were to search the sacred writings, you wouldn't find anything to support this notion because there isn't one religion that considers God anything less than supremely compassionate. Instead, you would find some powerful words that attest to the fact that God will listen, no matter how large or small the problems we bring to Him.

Now that evening has fallen,

To God, the Creator, I will turn in prayer,

Knowing that he will help me.

Knowing that he will help me.

—A Dinka prayer, Sudan

The belief that it is inappropriate to pray our problems to God has its basis in some pious thinking that many believe is simply wrong. If you've been raised in religious traditions that espouse these beliefs, it might be difficult for you to take the first step. But there's an easy way to do it: talk to God. Keep talking to God. As you do, you'll realize that the benefits of doing so outweigh any concerns you might have about your prayers being "inappropriate."

Stopping the Spin Cycle

It can be difficult to think straight when our minds are spinning with problems. Prayer can stop the spin cycle long enough to let us begin to see what's really going on. We might not be able to determine what's at the root of the problem, but going to God in prayer can help us see beyond our immediate situation and start sorting out the details.

How to Pray in Times of Trouble

The prayers we pray when we're hurting, scared, or troubled for any reason can be some of the most fervent we'll ever voice. They can be emotional, beseeching, even pleading. This is as they should be. Simple prayer can be a good way to pray during these times as it allows you to get everything out in the open, all your thoughts and all your feelings. However, it is fine to pray in whatever manner works for you. If you're so overwrought that you can't even think straight, just find a quiet place where you can simply sit in God's presence for a while. Just listen, and let Him do the talking.

What should you pray for? Some people believe that it is best to be very specific about telling God what you want. However, this approach takes more of a "my will be done" than a "thy will be done" tone, and can lead to disappointment if the things you pray for don't come about. A better approach, often, is to simply turn to God, admit we can't manage things on our own, and ask for His help.

quote

> People who pray for miracles usually don't get miracles . . . But people who pray for courage, for strength to bear the unbearable, for the grace to remember what they have left instead of what they have lost, very often find their prayers answered . . . Their prayers helped them tap hidden reserves of faith and courage which were not available to them before.
>
> —Attributed to Rabbi Harold S. Kushner

When the Prayers Won't Come

There are times when the words won't come when we try to pray. It happens to everyone at some time or another. But it seems to happen especially often when we want to pray our way through a crisis.

What can you do when the words won't come? Praying scriptural prayers is always a great way of communicating with God. Finding some verses that speak to your heart when things aren't going well can be especially helpful. Psalm 23—"The Lord Is My Shepherd"—is one of the best known. Here is another from the Book of Psalms:

Hear my cry, O God;

Attend to my prayer.

From the end of the earth I will cry to You,

When my heart is overwhelmed;

Lead me to the rock that is higher than I.

For You have been a shelter for me,

A strong tower from the enemy.

I will abide in Your tabernacle forever;

I will trust in the shelter of Your wings.

For You, O god, have heard my vows;

You have given me the heritage of those who fear Your name.

You will prolong the king's life,

His years as many generations.

He shall abide before God forever.

Oh, prepare mercy and truth, which may preserve him!

So I will sing praise to Your name forever,

That I may daily perform my vows.

—Psalm 61

Leaning on the words of God and the experiences of those in the Bible can give you strength when you have exhausted your own supply of it. The stories of courage can help drive away your fears. If nothing else, focusing on someone else's problems for a while can give you a break from obsessing over your own.

The Story of Job

The story of Job, in the Old Testament, speaks volumes about human suffering. In the Book of Job, we learn about a man who was "blameless and upright, and one who feared God and shunned evil." In other words, he was so good and so perfect that there was no question that he walked in God's favor. But Job's goodness and perfection were put to the test.

One day, Satan appears before God to taunt Him about all the evil and sinful things that His people were doing. God holds up Job to Satan as an example of how wonderful His people could be. Satan then tells God that Job's piety and perfection were the result of God's having made it easy for him to be.

quote

Lord, hear my prayer, and listen when I ask for mercy. I call to you in times of trouble, because you will answer me.

—Psalm 86:6–7

To prove Satan wrong, God allows him to wreak havoc in Job's life without giving him so much as a clue that trouble was coming his way. In short order, Job's house is destroyed and his cattle, servants, and children are killed. But Job continued to bless God's name. Next, Job's health is attacked and he develops boils "from the sole of his foot to the crown of his head." Job's wife can't take it and urges him to curse God, even if doing so would cause God to strike him down. Job's friends come to comfort him, but then side with his wife. "Curse God," they tell him, "even if it means death." But Job won't budge. He remains devoted to God.

As long as my breath is in me,

And the breath of God in my nostrils,

My lips will not speak wickedness,

Nor my tongue utter deceit.

Far be it from me

That I should say you are right;

Till I die I will not put away my integrity from me.

My righteousness I hold fast, and will not let it go;

My heart shall not reproach me as long as I live.

—Job 27:3–6

Finally, God appears to Job and the two have a long talk. At the end, Job again proclaims his faithfulness to God, and the test is over. God rewards Job for remaining faithful, and restores his life to where it was before, giving him a new home, a new family, and a new fortune.

The story of Job is, of course, a morality tale, and it shouldn't be taken literally. In a literal sense, it is a "God giveth, and God taketh away" story, and the problems sent Job's way are of God's making, via Satan. Look beyond this, however, and the story of Job is a strong testimony to the power of faith. What it tells us is this: When disaster strikes, don't let it shake your faith in God.

CHAPTER 11

Praying in Times of Joy

We often pray big and heavy prayers when we pray to God. We pray these prayers so often, in fact, that we sometimes forget to talk to Him when all is well with the world. We forget to say thanks, to tell Him we're grateful, or praise Him for His works. While we often wait until times of joy to pray these prayers, the truth is that we should be doing so on a regular basis.

Giving Thanks and Praise

Joy can take many forms. We can have feelings of great happiness or pleasure tied to our life on earth. And, joy can also be more elevated and spiritual. Many religions speak to God being the source of joy. In the *Bhagavad Gita,* we are told that when one comes to know the Supreme Brahman one becomes fully joyful.

The Supreme Lord said: My dear friend, mighty-armed Arjuna, listen again to My supreme word, which I shall impart to you for your benefit and which will give you joy.

—Bhagavad Gita, 10:1

Many of the prayers in the Bible are of thanks and praise. David was almost a ceaseless thanker of God, and the Book of Psalms is full of his prayers.

Make a joyful shout to God, all the earth!

Sing out the honor of His name;

Make His praise glorious.

Say to God,

"How awesome are Your works!

Through the greatness of Your power

Your enemies shall submit themselves to You.

All the earth shall worship You

And sing praises to You;

They shall sing praises to Your name."

—Psalm 66:1–4

The Bible contains many other messages about joy. Among them:

- There is great strength in joy—". . . for the joy of the Lord is your strength" (Nehemiah 8:10).
- Being joyful helps those around us to be joyful as well—". . . having confidence in you all that my joy is the joy of you all" (2 Corinthians 2:30).
- God's mercy is a source of great joy—". . . I will be glad and rejoice in Your mercy" (Psalm 31:7).
- Being joyful is important to remaining strong—"A merry heart does good, like medicine, But a broken spirit dries the bones" (Proverbs 18:22).

Why Praying with Joy Is Difficult

There is so much that we can be joyous about in our everyday lives. However, it is a strange truth that many people find prayers of joy, thanks, or praise the most difficult of all to pray. This is somewhat understandable when we are feeling unhappy, or when things aren't going well in our lives, as it's hard to feel joyous during times of trouble. When you go through tough times, praying prayers of joy and thanksgiving can be extremely difficult, as they can seem almost irrational. It can seem extremely crazy to think of thanking God for something in the midst of tragedy. Doing so, however, can lift you out of the depths of despair and sorrow. But the reluctance to express joy to God, and praise Him for His role in creating that joy, even extends to the good times when it should be easy for us to do so.

symbolism

Try to find the time for giving thanks on a regular basis—daily, if possible. Learning how to pray joyously at all times can help you maintain feelings of gratitude when things aren't going as well as you would like them to.

The Myth of "Praying Correctly"

You might find prayers of joy or gratitude difficult to pray, too, especially if you were taught that "praying correctly" meant offering only prayers of petition or supplication. There isn't much room for expressing joy, or for thanking or praising God, when our prayers are focused on pleading to Him or petitioning Him.

As previously noted, believing that prayers should only take the form of petition or supplication is a formal, old-fashioned notion of prayer that should have been tossed out a long time ago. If it lurks in the back of your mind when you're praying, it's time to exorcise it, once and for all. Having some old, negative patterns is to be expected—after all, none of us comes into a life of prayer as empty slates just waiting to be written upon. We all have baggage. But thoughts like these can, and usually do, hinder your spiritual growth. It's important to recognize them so you can work on them, and it's important to work on them so you can put them aside.

factum

The word *thanks* is used more than thirty-five times in the Psalms. Hymns of thanksgiving and songs of appreciation are sung by followers of most, if not all, world religions, in recognition of God's greatness and the gifts He bestows.

Afraid of Feeling Joyous

Even for people who embrace prayer in all its forms, praying for joy can be difficult. We understand prayers of adoration and thanksgiving, but joyful praying—praise praying—does not come naturally for many. In *When in Doubt, Sing: Prayer in Daily Life*, author Jane Redmont noted that prayers of sorrow or anger seem to come more easily than joyous prayers, and wondered if "sometimes whether our fear of pain is matched only by our fear of joy."

Perhaps the problem is that we are not so much afraid of joy as we are afraid of admitting that we feel joyous. We live in a hurting world, a world in which there is a great deal of pain and suffering. Being outwardly joyous can seem a bit vain, egotistical, even cocky, especially when we are surrounded by so many other people who are suffering. Isn't keeping our mouths shut when we're happy the kind and compassionate thing to do? Perhaps you feel that expressing your feelings of joy would make people around you feel worse. But this doesn't mean that we should try to hide our feelings when we are talking to God. Doing so denies God the opportunity to know us in all ways. Not only that, not feeling comfortable in voicing feelings of joy during prayer is a poor reflection of what our relationship with God is all about, as so much of the joy we feel is a result of knowing Him.

symbolism

If you feel as though negative patterns or beliefs from your past are holding you back on your spiritual journey, consider talking with a spiritual adviser or director. Doing so can help you sort out your feelings and develop ways to replace negative patterns with more positive ones.

Another possible reason why many people find it so difficult to pray joyously is because they are afraid that doing so will somehow cause an end to their happiness. In other words, they are somehow afraid that being "too joyous" will put a hex on the source of their joy and derail their happiness. This concern might also be rooted in some old experiences or beliefs. "You shouldn't be too happy because it could end tomorrow" is unfortunately some negative programming that propagates this idea.

Being afraid of ending our happiness by paying attention to it has somewhat of a self-defeating aspect to it. If we don't pay some attention to the happy times in our lives, and recognize them by praising God for them, we end up not being able to appreciate them fully, or at all.

Being Unaware of Joy

In fact, one of the biggest reasons behind the lack of joyous praying may very well be that we are not very good at recognizing the joy that is present in our lives. In other words, we tend to be a bit ungrateful, whether we are aware of it or not.

Most people don't mean to block out or ignore all that is wonderful about life. Instead, they simply forget to pay as much attention to the grace notes, the good moments that come their way, as they should. Buddhist scripture tells us that "The worthy person is grateful and mindful of benefits done to him," yet we often take things far too much for granted.

quote

> The very act of praise releases the power of God into a set of circumstances and enables God to change them if this is his design . . . I have come to believe that the prayer of praise is the highest form of communication with God, and one that always releases a great deal of power into our lives.
>
> —Merlin R. Carothers, in *Prison to Praise*

In the whirlwind of activity that constitutes so much of what it's like to live in the twenty-first century, this can be easy to understand to a certain extent. It can be difficult to "stop and smell the roses" when life seems like one big to-do list. But being too busy is a poor excuse for not being grateful, or for not taking time to notice all the things that we should and can be grateful for. When we don't take the time to experience joy in life, and express that joy in prayer, we don't feed our souls.

Let joyous prayer lapse long enough, and hearts harden. Instead of being compassionate toward others, we feel miserable and sorry for ourselves. We allow ourselves to get too hung up on our feelings of joylessness. As we do, we become pretty miserable people to be around, and we wreck other people's joy. Rumi, the Sufi poet, put it well when he wrote, "Your depression is connected to your insolence and refusal to praise! Whoever feels himself walking on the path and refuses to praise—that man or woman steals from others every day—is a shoplifter!"

quote

> The basic response of the soul to the Light is internal adoration and joy, thanksgiving and worship, self-surrender and listening.
> —Thomas Kelly, in *A Testament of Devotion*

Being grateful calls for a shift in attitude, a shift in perspective. It calls for recognizing that life—in whatever shape it takes—is a gift. It means looking for silver linings in storm clouds, as pious as this might seem. It calls for being a little Orphan Annie-ish. You don't have to go about life skipping and singing "The sun will come out tomorrow," but the feeling that you could do so if you wanted to is pretty much what you are after.

If your take on the world is naturally a little dour or cynical, if the glass you see is half empty instead of half full, making the shifts in attitude necessary to see the bright side of life can take a great amount of effort. Herculean, in fact. However, if you can learn to do it—yes, it is a learning process, and it will take some time—you will see more positive things in your life. You will be able to find the good in the bad. As you do, you will find it easier to give thanks to God.

Developing an Attitude of Gratitude

Gratitude thinking, or having an attitude of gratitude, has received a lot of attention in recent years. We have been encouraged to work at gaining a better appreciation of what we have, and if we don't know how to do this, we have been encouraged to learn how. We have been told that we have "shut down or ignore[d] our authentic impulses" in order to conform to the world around us, and that happiness and joy lie in getting back in touch with our authenticity. According to author Sarah Ban Breathnach in *Simple Abundance Date Book of Comfort and Joy* (2003), this involves "appreciating everything that's right about you right now and giving thanks for it."

Gratitude is the most passionate transformative force in the Cosmos. When we offer thanks to God or to another human being, gratitude gifts us with renewal, reflection, reconnection. It is a choice of mind-set. When we put ourselves in a grateful frame of mind, we recognize all the bless-ings life has granted us.

If as a child you were told to "count your blessings" every time you seemed ungrateful about something, or wished you had something that you didn't have, gratitude thinking might have negative connotations for you. But there is good advice in this often pious-sounding directive. Sometimes we get so focused on the future, so intent on setting goals and pushing forward to meet them that we forget to be thankful for the things we already have. In other words, we forget to pay attention to the moment, and be mindful of where we are right now.

The Gifts of Gratitude Thinking

Gratitude thinking offers a great framework for praying joyously. It calls for making a habit of thanking God every day for the little things as well as the big things—our health, a beautiful sunrise, the love of family and friends, getting a college paper done on time, the small grace of a soft dog paw on your knee.

discussion question

Aren't we always supposed to give thanks when we pray to God? Yes, thanksgiving is a part of the ACTS prayer formula—adoration, confession, thanksgiving, and supplication. Prayers of joy, however, can also take the form of praise or adoration, where we acknowledge God's work in our lives in addition to thanking Him.

When you focus on giving thanks, and giving thanks for all that you have in life, an interesting thing happens. The more you exercise your "abundance muscles," the more you will get back. The results are often subtle or intangible. They may take the form of feeling more peaceful, happier, or just more content with life in general. But they can be tangible as well. There are numerous stories that describe the riches bestowed upon individuals who consistently go to God with prayers of thanks. Again, the Book of Job in the Old Testament is a good biblical example. No matter what life threw at him, his faith in God remained constant, and he continued to thank God for that which was good. Job lost everything he had at one point, but God restored it all to him, plus more.

The Benefits of Brakhat

In the Jewish faith, the spiritual practice of offering brakhat, or blessing prayers, is seen as a way to bring the sacred into every aspect of life. Praying brakhat serves both as a constant reminder of God's presence and increases the awareness of all the little blessings that are constantly being bestowed on us.

According to author Marcia Prager in *The Path of Blessing: Experiencing the Energy and Abundance of the Divine,* prayers of blessings and thanks made to God are part of a "sacred cycle of giving and receiving," and are necessary to keep this cycle in balance. Offering them completes our energy exchange with God. When we don't offer them, or forget to offer them, the energy exchange is thrown out of whack. "When we fail to praise," Prager says, "it is we who suffer. Without gratitude we become bored and depressed."

factum

Blessing prayers are central to Jewish prayer. These prayers always begin with "Blessed art Thou, Lord our God, King of the Universe." They may be prayers giving thanks to God, praising Him, or petitioning Him. They can also be offered in acknowledgment of His creation, such as blessings said over food, or in preparation for performing a mitzvah, or a good deed.

Journaling Joy

One of the ways in which we can become more aware of joy in our lives—and, in turn, find it easier to let God in on the things that make us joyful—is by jotting down the things that make us happy, or that we are grateful for, on a regular basis. What we write doesn't have to be much, maybe a line or two on a daily planner or in a prayer journal. Just little notes, like:

- I am grateful for my talent.
- I am grateful for my muscles.
- I am grateful for peace.
- I am grateful for new beginnings.

Other things you might wish to note are the little kindnesses that come your way ("Gee, didn't expect so-and-so to be so nice") and the times when you notice God's work ("Great sunrise!" "Beautiful day!" "Made the right decision," "Feeling like I'm walking in grace").

These simple notes can in themselves be prayers of joy and thanksgiving. Perhaps more important, writing things down that you are thankful for helps you to be more mindful of them. Doing so will also help foster a spirit of thanksgiving that makes it easier to pray joyously.

There are also special abundance journals available that can help you keep track of the things you are thankful for. One to take a look at is the *Simple Abundance Datebook of Comfort and Joy* by Sarah Ban Breathnach. Published annually, it includes thoughts on gratitude and abundance.

Reviewing the Details of the Day

Another way to increase awareness of the joyfulness of everyday life is to review the gifts of the day. Here are some steps you might take:

1. Pick a time—evenings are good, so you can go through the full events of the day. (In fact, this is a great exercise to practice right before you go to sleep as you'll fall asleep thinking of good things.)

2. Let your mind wander through the events of the past twenty-four hours. Don't judge them or sort them into good and bad. Review everything. Even if the day was really rotten, this will help you identify some good moments, even if they're along the lines of "I didn't get too wet in that downpour," or "That new door ding on my car could have been a lot worse."
3. As you remember the grace notes, the events of the day for which you can be grateful, thank God for them.

How to Pray Joyous Prayers

Prayers of joy can take many forms. They can be short quick prayers ("Thanks, God!") or lengthy colloquies. They can be simple or formal. They can be blessings to God offered before meals. They can take the form of songs, and of dance.

Praise the Lord!

Praise God in His sanctuary;

Praise Him in His mighty firmament!

Praise Him for His mighty acts;

Praise Him according to His excellent greatness!

Praise Him with the sound of the trumpet;

Praise Him with the lute and harp!

Praise Him with the timbrel and dance;

Praise Him with stringed instruments and flutes!

Praise Him with loud cymbals;

Praise Him with clashing cymbals!

Let everything that has breath praise the Lord.

Praise the Lord!

—Psalm 15

Some people write down everything they have to be thankful for on a daily basis and meditate on their lists as part of their regular prayer time. Others say prayers of joy and thanks on the fly, whenever and wherever they experience or see something that makes them happy and thankful.

If you're not in the habit of praying joyously, start simply. All it takes is a quick "thank you God" to let Him know when you're grateful. It's been said that if the only prayer you say in your entire life is "thank you," it would be enough.

CHAPTER 12

Praying for Special Needs

Throwing our hearts open before God and asking for His assistance can be some of the most difficult prayers to pray. These prayers, however, are also some of the most important. Our need to ask God for His help never goes away, no matter how well we think we can manage things on our own.

Going to God for Help

God likes to hear our calls for help. Not only this, He likes to answer them. Unfortunately, prayers that ask for help from the Almighty have received a bit of a bad rap over the years. Not from God—remember, He likes us to come to Him for assistance—but from humankind.

Some people believe that there is no need to ask God for help if they are living their lives as they should be. They believe that the people who do so are only interested in their own needs and wants. Because of this, the assumption goes, these selfish people focus on prayers that reflect their desires when they should be praying more exalted prayers.

Those opposed to asking for God's help often believe that the only kinds of prayers that should be spoken to God are prayers of adoration and thanksgiving. Asking Him for help is considered crass, crude, or the mark of an inexperienced or beginning pray-er.

factum

Prayers that ask God for help are called prayers of supplication—a humble appeal to someone who has the power to grant the request; petition—an appeal or request to a higher authority or being; and intercession—a prayer made on behalf of someone else.

While it is a bit of a stretch to characterize all pray-ers who ask for help as being unsophisticated or greedy, there are some people who are guilty as charged. Their prayers take the form of petition more than they should because they allow themselves to get too wrapped up in their own needs.

The Guilt Factor, Part 1

More often than not, however, the reverse is true. Many people who pray feel that it is only appropriate to ask God for help on behalf of others. When they do petition God on their own behalf, their prayers are accompanied with a good dose of guilt. There are a variety of reasons for why they feel this way. Among them are the following:

- A crisis in faith, resulting from not fully believing that God can help or is powerful enough to help in all situations.
- Feeling shameful about needing help.
- Not wanting to admit to needing help.
- Not wanting to believe that help is available.
- Feeling uncomfortable about bothering God with "little" problems when other people are in greater need of His help.
- Feeling that it is selfish to ask God for help.

What causes people to feel shame or guilt over petitioning prayer? There are no easy answers to this question, but we do know that part of the problem is cultural. We live in a society that values independence, self-reliance, and individualism, often at the expense of human emotion and need. These beliefs are reinforced by the messages we are sent through the media, either directly or indirectly. Magazines feature page after page of beautiful and happy celebrities who look like they haven't got a care in the world, or strong and forceful-looking business and political leaders who look like nothing would shake their confidence. Flip through the channels on your television and you'll see more of the same. The message? The "best people"—the most powerful and the most successful people—are beautiful, strong, and self-reliant, and they don't need anyone's help.

symbolism

Although God does encourage us to ask Him for help, it is important to remember that petitioning is just one form of prayer. To be most effective, prayers of petition should be balanced with prayers of adoration, confession, and thanksgiving.

This is an immensely powerful message, but it has both a positive and a negative side. On the positive side, we always need role models to look up to. Today, thanks to global communications networks, we not only are aware of more individuals that we can respect and admire, we know more about them than we ever did before. On the flip side, the negative message goes something like this: If you aren't like these individuals, or you can't be as strong or self-assured as they are, then you are weak, needy, and inferior. And, if indeed you are weak, needy, and inferior, you had better not let anyone else know it.

The Guilt Factor, Part 2

Another reason why many people feel guilty about asking God for help is because they've been raised in families that put a high value on self-reliance and independence. From an early age, the children in these families are encouraged to work things out on their own, to be strong, to "tough things out." When they grow up, these individuals are often some of the world's biggest success stories, but their success also often comes at a great personal price. Since they weren't allowed to admit that they needed help when they were growing up, they find it difficult or impossible to do so as adults. Many of them don't believe that anyone—including God—could help them even if they did ask for assistance. Because of this, they often experience problems at work and in relationships, and are often perceived as being aloof, cold, or as having a "mightier-than-thou" attitude. When they crash—and they almost all do at some time or another—the fall is often catastrophic.

One of the best things that parents can do for their children is to encourage them to seek help from others when they've reached the limits of what they can do on their own. If this lesson wasn't taught to you as you were growing up, you can learn it as an adult. In fact, you can ask God to help you do so.

Getting Beyond the Guilt

While feelings of guilt or shame about asking for help are understandable, living a full spiritual life necessitates overcoming them as they stand in the way of developing that life. These feelings don't allow us to be humble before God, which is one of the essentials of a successful prayer life. Not being willing to admit that we need help, and not feeling that we can ask God for it, is the antithesis of humility. It is false faith as it puts us in control instead of God.

If it is allowed to continue, it will lead to a shallow prayer life and a superficial relationship with the Almighty.

quote

What are the things that we should lay before the Almighty God in prayer? Answer: First, our personal troubles . . . The greatest trouble we can ever know is thinking that we have no trouble for we have become hard-hearted and insensible to what is inside of us.

—Attributed to Martin Luther

There are many passages in the world's sacred scriptures that warn against relying on one's own power, and that underscore the need for people to admit their weaknesses before God. And, there are many passages that talk to what the benefits are of doing so. *The Bhagavad Gita* says, "United with me, you shall overcome all difficulties by my grace." The Quran tells us, ". . . If you help God's cause, He will help you and will make your foothold firm."

Have you not known?

Have you not heard?

The everlasting God, the Lord,

The Creator of the ends of the earth,

Neither faints nor is weary.

His understanding is unsearchable.

He gives power to the weak,

And to those who have no might He increases strength.

Even the youths shall faint and be weary,

And the young men shall utterly fall,

But those who wait on the Lord

Shall renew their strength;

They shall mount up with wings like eagles,

They shall run and not be weary,

They shall walk and not faint.

—Isaiah 40:28–31

Not only can God not help us until we acknowledge our needs and ask for help, we deny ourselves the benefit of experiencing all that He can do for us until we turn to Him. As the Tao te Ching puts it: "To those who have conformed themselves to the Way, the Way readily lends its power. To those who have conformed themselves to the power, the power readily lends more power."

If you feel guilty about asking God for assistance, it might help to know a little more about the basic dynamic of these prayers. They are the classic embodiment of the parent-child model. God is our father; we are His children. In His eyes, we are always His children, and it is always appropriate to ask for His help. If going to a parent for help has negative connotations for you, try to remember that God is a parent like none other. There is no judgment, no blaming, no scolding, and no admonishments in our relationship with Him. There is only love.

Prayers of Petition

As mentioned, the prayers that we pray on our own behalf are prayers of petition. These are some of the most important prayers we can offer as only we know what is in our hearts. Only we know what we want to bring to God. We can't hope for God to hear our concerns unless we offer them to Him.

quote

> When we move from petition to intercession we are shifting our center of gravity from our own needs to the needs and concerns of others. Intercessory Prayer is selfless prayer, even self-giving prayer.
> —Richard Foster, in *Prayer: Finding the Heart's True Home*

What to Ask For

Prayers of petition acknowledge that we need God's help. For this reason, it is appropriate to pray them whenever we need God to help us do something we can't do for ourselves. People often say prayers of petition when they face obstacles or challenges that are new to them or larger than they have dealt with in the past. They pray for strength, courage, or simply the resolve to help them last through whatever it is that they are facing. As the late J. Robert Ashcroft, an Assemblies of God minister and educator put it, "Prayer is not just asking God to do things—it is helping him bring them to pass."

But asking God for His help can be as simple as saying "God, help me," when you are completely frustrated and almost out of strength after wrestling with something as simple as a tight lid on a jar. Silly? Maybe. But the next time you are in a similar situation, try it. Just taking a brief moment away from the object of your frustration can have surprising results.

factum

Many people pick and choose among their concerns, and only bring the ones they feel are the most meritorious to God. They forget that God wants to hear all prayers, not just the ones we think are most important.

Feelings You Might Get

If you haven't prayed for yourself before, you might feel somewhat self-conscious and maybe even a little smarmy about doing it at first. It can be hard to get over feeling uncomfortable about being the center of your own attention. Other negative thoughts that might arise include:

- Feeling that God has much better things to do.
- Feeling that God has people who are far worse off to listen to.
- Feeling that your needs are small and petty.

Again, remember that God wants to hear what is on your heart and mind, and that nothing is too small to bring to Him. Getting into the habit of petitioning Him will help you get over the negative feelings you might have about doing so. It will also help you better discern the results of your prayers. As is often the case in prayer, they may not be exactly what you think they would be, or would like them to be.

Whosoever keeps his duty to God, God will appoint a way out for him, and will provide for him in a way that he cannot foresee. And whosoever puts his trust in God, He will suffice him. Lo! God brings His command to pass. God has set a measure for all things.

—Quran 65:2–3

Keeping Track of Long-Term Petitions

If you are asking God's help regarding an ongoing concern, or an issue that has recently arisen in your life that you feel might turn into a larger one, it can be helpful to keep track of your concerns and your prayers—and their results—by writing them down. Keeping a prayer journal is one way to do this. For more information on prayer journals, and their role in an ongoing life of prayer, turn to Chapter 20.

Another way to keep track of long-term petitions—both yours and the ones you pray for others—is to make a list of them to refer to when you are praying. Following a list of prayer requests may sound like praying by rote, but it's better than wondering whether or not you remembered to include a specific request.

Intercessory Prayers

Intercessory prayers are very different than petitioning God on your own behalf. When you say these prayers, you are praying for someone else's needs. You are asking for God to step in and do something good for another person.

Kinds of Intercessory Prayers

There are many examples of intercessory prayers in the Bible. Moses interceded on behalf of the Israelites more than once, and was even willing to give up his own life so that his people could live. Abraham made an intercession when he pleaded to God on behalf of his son Ishmael. He also interceded on behalf of the people living in the wicked cities of Sodom and Gomorrah because they were his neighbors and he felt it was right to do so:

> And Abraham came near and said, "Would You also destroy the righteous with the wicked? Suppose there were fifty righteous within the city; would You also destroy the place and not spare it for the fifty righteous that were in it?"

> —Genesis 18:23–24

Many of the prayers that Jesus made were on the behalf of other people, including the one he prayed on the cross: "Forgive them, Father, for they know not what they do." Paul was another earnest intercessory pray-er, and offered up many prayers on behalf of the new church and its followers.

> Therefore I also, after I heard of your faith in the Lord Jesus and your love for all the saints, do not cease to give thanks for you, making mention of you in my prayers.

> —Ephesians 1:15–16

factum

People often refer to the act of intercessory prayer as "standing in the gap." This refers to their being willing to stand up for others before God, and to ask God for help on the behalf of others.

Matching Prayers to Needs

Many people believe that intercessory prayers should address specific concerns or requests in order to be most effective. Others feel that it is better to offer intercessory prayers of a more general nature, such as those that ask for strength, peace, or an overall resolution of whatever it is that is causing problems or concerns.

While it can be helpful to know exactly what you should pray for when you intercede for someone, it isn't always possible. Many people feel uncomfortable asking for prayer on their own behalf for the same reasons they find it difficult to pray their own petitioning prayers. When they finally muster whatever it takes for them to ask someone else to pray on their behalf, they might be uncomfortable discussing the specifics and will only ask for prayer of a general nature.

If you have been asked to pray for someone, but you don't know what you should pray for, it is perfectly all right to ask the person. Doing so shows that you are truly concerned about this person's needs, and that you want to provide the best help you can. If you don't feel comfortable asking, or you don't get an answer, it is also fine to bring the person's concerns before God in a more general manner. You can simply hold the person in your heart and pray that he or she finds relief through God's help.

Developing Your Intercessory Prayer Muscle

While intercessory prayer comes easily to some people, not everyone embraces it with zeal. If you fall into the latter group, don't feel guilty. It doesn't mean that you're a bad person, or a bad pray-er. It just means that praying for others isn't a prayer style that comes naturally to you. Some people get so many requests for prayers from others that they feel burdened by them. A heavy prayer load can diminish just about anyone's enthusiasm.

If you don't like to pray intercessory prayers, or you simply don't feel the desire to do so, it might help to ask for God's help on your own behalf first. *In Prayer: Finding the Heart's True Home*, Richard Foster suggests starting by praying for an increase in your ability to care and love others. "As God grows your capacity to care," Foster writes, "you will very naturally begin working for the good of your neighbors, your friends, even your enemies." In other words, you'll be praying for them.

When Intercession Goes Awry

As strange as it may seem, there are times when it may not be wise to pray for someone else. As mentioned in Chapter 2, we might have the very best of intentions in mind, but what we think is best may not be in line with the desires and beliefs of the individual we're praying for.

discussion question

What should I do if someone asks me to pray and I don't feel comfortable praying for him or her?
It can be difficult to pray for someone you don't know very well, or about whom you have mixed feelings for some reason. In these situations, just tell God what is on your mind. Tell Him that you know someone who needs His help and you're turning it over to Him. This is all you need to do.

There are times when we can pray for someone with assuredness, knowing that we are doing what is right for the person we're concerned about. If you get a request for prayer directly from the person who desires it, you can bet that this is exactly what he or she wants you to do. Even still, it is a good idea to ask exactly what you should pray for. Make sure that your prayers align with the individual's needs and desires.

Intercessory prayer is also appropriate in the following situations:

- When a friend asks you to pray on behalf of someone he or she knows who has asked for prayer.
- When you are part of a prayer group and you are praying as a body for individuals who have requested it.
- When you belong to a prayer chain and you are praying over requests submitted to the entire chain.
- When you are addressing the concerns of individuals as part of congregation.

Mary Baker Eddy, the founder of Christian Science, also believed that it was all right to pray for others without their knowledge if other means of intercession had failed. In these situations, she said, the end result could justify the intrusion into someone's privacy. She also believed that such prayer was warranted if the situation were so dire that there was "no time for ceremony and no other aide is near." As she put it, "It would be right to break into a burning building and rouse the slumbering inmates, but wrong to burst open doors and break through windows if no emergency demanded this."

quote

As for the faithful friends and acquaintances who pray so assiduously for my stained soul, I know it sounds churlish to say, "Please don't." But it's a somewhat queasy feeling, knowing that someone is praying for me to think differently or act differently or embrace a different God. Sort of like Mormons baptizing reluctant ancestors. If people are so convinced that prayer has magical powers of efficacy, how dare they use it to impose a change of their own devising?
—Jeannette Batz, "Be Leery of Anyone Who Wields Prayer as a Spiritual Weapon," in *National Catholic Reporter*

Asking for Specific Outcomes

Like healing prayers and discernment prayers, petition and intercessory prayers often revolve around our desire to receive specific answers to our prayers. The question then becomes: Should I ask for specific outcomes? Or should I keep my requests more general? There are several schools of thought on this. Some people believe that it is better not to be too specific with such prayers as it can be so disappointing if the outcomes don't match our requests. Others feel that God can't answer our prayers unless we tell Him what we want. Still others feel that it's important to believe that miracles can happen, and that specifically asking for them does not diminish the possibility of them taking place.

While the best prayer is always a variation of "Thy will be done," the ultimate decision regarding how specific to make your prayers is up to you.

For You O God know that which we need and want before we have thought of it and better than we can ever imagine.

—A prayer from the Armenian church

Perhaps the best way to approach the issue of specific outcomes is to remember that God already knows what is on our hearts and minds. If you desire specific outcomes, or you are praying on behalf of someone else who desires them, it isn't in the spirit of an honest prayer life to keep them from Him.

CHAPTER 13

Praying for Guidance and Wisdom

Living a full life calls for making decisions. We always want to make good ones, but it can be hard to know which direction we should take when we only rely on our own thoughts and feelings. Going to God and asking for His leading can help us get a better idea of the road we should travel.

Seeking God's Wisdom

One of the greatest joys of becoming an adult is the ability to make decisions on our own. The freedom of being able to decide where we want to live, what we want to do for a living, even what we want to eat for lunch—it can all be pretty wonderful. Even intoxicating at times.

quote

Ask God for what you want, but you cannot ask if you are not asking for a right thing. When you draw near to God, you cease from asking for things. "Your Father knows what things you have need of, before you ask him." Then, why ask? That you may get to know Him.
—Oswald Chambers

When we first step into the adult world of decision-making, we often do so knowing that we have a safety net to catch us if we should fall. We have the support and confidence of our parents or other older and wiser folks to fall back on should we need it. However, as we grow wiser and more mature during our spiritual walk with God, we gain an even greater safety net. In fact, it's the best fail-safe system we could ever hope for.

Getting a Grip on the Big Picture

If you are looking for the big picture, the macro view, on how to approach and handle life's turning points, you couldn't ask for a better guide than God. Here's why: When we ask the people around us—our friends and family members—for their opinions on what we should do, the responses they give us are going to be shaped and colored by their own experiences and their own belief systems. When we ask God for His advice, there are no such temporal filters. We don't get answers based on other people's experiences and beliefs. We instead are guided toward the proper course of action through the insights we gain as a result of asking His opinion.

This isn't to say that other peoples' opinions aren't worth anything, or that you should never ask anyone for an opinion or a piece of friendly advice. There is nothing wrong in doing so, and there is nothing about your relationship with God that would prevent you from doing so. What it does mean is that it can be a good idea to take the answers you get with a grain of salt.

quote

> Vain is the man who puts his trust in men, in created things . . . Do not be self-sufficient but place your trust in God. Do what lies in your power and God will aid your good will. Put no trust in your own learning nor in the cunning of any man, but rather in the grace of God Who helps the humble and humbles the proud . . . for God's judgments differ from those of men and what pleases them often displeases Him.
>
> —Thomas à Kempis, in *The Imitation of Christ*

The Folly of Following Your Own Advice

Taking matters into your own hands and following your own advice can be just as troublesome as leaning on the wisdom of others to help you make your decisions. The decisions you come up with on your own, without seeking God's wisdom and help, are just as biased as the ones you get from other people. They too are colored by your own experiences and feelings. The better answers, the ones that will serve you the best in the long run, will come when you have made them with the help of God's counsel.

Trust in the Lord with all your heart,

And lean not on your own understanding;

In all your ways acknowledge Him,

And He shall direct your paths.

Do not be wise in your own eyes;

Fear the Lord and depart from evil.

It will be health to your flesh,

And strength to your bones.

quote

Grant to me, O Lord, to know what I ought to know, to love what I ought to love, to praise what delights Thee most, to value what is precious in thy sight, to hate what is offensive to Thee. Do not suffer me to judge according to the sight of my eyes, nor to pass sentence according to the hearing of the ears of ignorant men; but to discern with true judgment between things visible and spiritual, and above all things to enquire what is the good pleasure of thy will.

—Thomas à Kempis, in *The Imitation of Christ*

Asking for Guidance and Wisdom

When we ask God for His guidance and wisdom, we pray prayers of discernment. These are prayers that help us see things that we can't see on our own, that help us gain a better understanding of the issues we face, or that help us make wise choices between the various courses of action that are open to us.

Discernment prayers are important because we can't predict the future, as much as we would often like to be able to do so. We also don't know what the future holds for us from God's point of view. Because of this, we need to ask for His help so we can better figure out what we should do and where we should go. It is important to seek His wisdom so that we can better align our decisions with what He has in mind for us, or what He wills for us. In other words, God's will.

factum

Discernment prayers help us better see things that are not very clear or obvious, to understand things better, or to be able to tell the difference between two or more courses of action or decisions. Another word for discernment is judgment, which describes the ability to form sound opinions and make sensible decisions or reliable guesses.

Bugging God

We can ask for God's help in making many different kinds of decisions. In fact, there really isn't an area in which we can't ask for His help. Some people believe that it's not a good idea to bug God all the time, however, to run to Him with every decision we need to make. Doing so, they say, activates something akin to a "chicken little" syndrome. In other words, God gets so tired hearing about all of our little questions that He doesn't pay attention to the big ones when they come His way.

Well, God is all-powerful, and He certainly knows a great deal more about things than we do. However, there is no evidence to suggest that He makes judgment calls when it comes to the issues in the lives of His people. He doesn't pick and choose, nor does He toss aside one question for another based on a scale of importance. In other words, He hears them all. If something is important enough to you that you want to ask God's opinion about it, it is important enough for Him to hear your request.

Knowing When to Ask for Advice

The best times to seek God's advice is when you are facing decisions that pertain to some aspect of how you live your life, or how you wish to live it.

Other times when it is wise to ask God's opinion is when your decision will affect the lives of the people you care about—family members, coworkers, friends—more than slightly. Examples of these decisions include:

- Caring for an elderly parent
- Job changes that may require relocation
- Relationship changes
- Starting a new business

These are broad brushstroke decisions, ones that can have a significant effect both on your own life and the lives of the people you care about. Making these decisions often calls for extending your field of inquiry beyond where it has been before. In other words, you are venturing into unknown territory, and these voyages almost always carry with them a certain amount of trepidation. Feelings of unease can too easily be translated into decisions if you try to make them in a vacuum. Pulling God into the process may not ease your butterflies, but it can help you recognize them for what they are.

Taking God's Point of View

If you still think that you need to filter your requests to God, and that you should only ask His advice on matters that you feel are important enough for Him to consider, think for a moment about what this says about your relationship with the Almighty. In effect, when you pick and choose the issues that you want God's advice on, you are taking matters into your own hands. In other words, you are playing God. You're assuming you know what He wants to hear. In so doing, you are also assuming that you know more than He does. This, of course, isn't the case, nor can it ever be.

quote

If any of you lacks wisdom, let him ask of God, who gives to all liberally and without reproach, and it will be given to him.

—James, 1:5

The greatest wisdom is not ours, it is that which we receive from God. If we ask Him for it, we will receive it.

Hearing God's Voice

When we say prayers of discernment, we are asking God for His advice. We want Him to give us His opinion. But how do we hear what He has to say? Will He speak to us? If so, what will He sound like? Will His words be those we can understand? How will we know that it is God speaking to us and not someone else? How can we tell that it is His voice, and not ours?

symbolism

When asking God for advice, it is important to step back and let Him do His work. Don't start trying to guide the outcome by searching for signs of God's direction. Be patient, and let it come to you.

The truth is, it can be extremely difficult to discern God's voice. Unlike biblical times, His words aren't accompanied by dramatic natural phenomena. The heavens don't open when He speaks. We don't hear His voice in a burning bush. The seas don't part. These days, God mostly speaks to us in ways that we can only learn to understand through talking—that is, praying—to Him.

A Bang or a Whisper?

Even in biblical times, however, God sometimes made His feelings known in much more subtle ways. In the Book of Elijah, God speaks in a "still, small voice" instead of in an eardrum-shattering revelation accompanied by earthquakes and thunderstorms. Other world scripture underscores the fact that God, as it is often said, is in the details.

Eye cannot see him, nor words reveal him;

by the senses, austerity, or works he is not known.

When the mind is cleansed by the grace of wisdom,

he is seen by contemplation—the One without parts.

—The Upanishads

Much is said about hearing the still small voice of God. It is the manner in which He usually speaks to us today. However, this isn't to say that you won't get a good old-fashioned revelation when you ask Him for His opinion. They do—and can—happen. Sometimes God's answer comes in a big "aha" moment. It might even be accompanied by something—a voice—that has no earthly presence. It may be a voice that you don't hear but you somehow sense deep inside of your being. On the other hand, you could possibly hear it loud and clear, just like you would when someone is talking to you.

To be honest, these types of revelatory experiences don't happen very often. Many people live their entire lives hoping to hear the voice of God, striving to hear Him, and yet they never do. You might not as well, but you can learn how to recognize the other ways in with He does answer you.

How to Recognize an Answer from God

As much as we might yearn and pray for definitive answers to the questions we throw up to God, He rarely issues concrete directives. He won't tell us to take one approach over another. He won't plant a road sign that says "Turn here," or put up a barrier that says, "Stop." Instead of words, we get nuances. And they can be very, very subtle.

While God's answers can take the form of external signs, His answers more often manifest themselves deep within our bodies and souls. In prayer, we turn our hearts and minds toward God. As we do, we become attuned to His presence. The more often we pray, the greater our sense of attunement becomes. It's as if we develop a special little antenna that picks up God's signals. What we sense or hear might be faint at first, but as we keep on praying, the signals get stronger. We become better able to sense how our actions do or don't line up with His will. In other words, we get our answers.

Answers from God are often described as feeling like being on the right path, even if it is a difficult one. Other indications of getting an answer from God include:

- An overall feeling of calm or peace
- Feeling like you've reached a resolution
- Feeling a sense of relief
- Feeling free of any need to second-guess your decision

Patience, Patience

It can take some time, and a great deal of prayer, to reach a resolution on important issues. God rarely works on the same schedule as we do, which can be a source of immense frustration at times. Although we know we need to be patient and wait for God, it is difficult to do so when we are seeking answers from Him. Because of this, we sometimes try to force God's hand. We search for specific signs or signals—often external—that we think could be an indication that He has answered us, and we use these signs to justify the actions we want to take. Or, we try to connect the lack of such signals to God's assent. If something doesn't happen, or we don't see a specific sign, it means that our plans meet with God's approval.

Seeking "Yes" or "No"

Searching for signs of God's answers can get a little silly at times. It can be amazingly easy to ascribe even the tiniest things to a yes or no answer from the Almighty. Here is one example of how it's possible to go a little overboard while seeking answers from God: Let's say you have been diligently asking God's advice regarding a relationship you'd like to pursue. You have been talking to Him for a while about it, and you don't feel like you've received much guidance either way. The person you're interested in hasn't changed in behavior toward you, or may not be aware that you even exist.

One day you happen to hear through the grapevine that this person has just ended a long-term relationship with someone else. "Aha," you think.

"There is my answer from God. It's a divine intervention, and it's been set up just for me. Green light, I'm good to go."

Or are you? Did God send a message? Did He intervene on your behalf and break up this person's relationship so you can step in? Or are you taking things into your own hands and reading something into the situation that has nothing to do with it?

There is no sure answer to this question beyond—you guessed it—continuing to seek your answers by turning to God in prayer. As you do so, you may sense a very different set of emotions than the ones previously described. Instead of feeling calm and peaceful, things might not seem right. You might feel confused and conflicted. Perhaps you are no longer sure that the events that have transpired have anything to do with God's will. That's good, because chances are pretty good that they don't. Instead, you made them fit what you wanted God's answer to be.

"My Will" Instead of "Thy Will"

When we look for God's answers instead of allowing them to come to us, we are again engaging in "my will" instead of "thy will" thinking. Even though it may not seem like we're taking things into our own hands, we are.

A better way of learning how to discern God's answers is to stick to the internal discernment approach described earlier. Pay close attention to how you feel when you are in His presence. As you do, you will gain a better sense of what God is doing in your life. You learn how to discern, or recognize, the messages He sends you. The more you go to Him, and the more attention you pay to how you feel, the better you will get at recognizing His answers when you get them. You won't have to go looking for them.

Getting to "Yes"

One of the biggest problems people have with discernment prayers is that they feel like God never gives them a clear answer. He is speaking, they sense something, but the message is garbled with static. Or, they get conflicting answers. God seems to be saying different things on different days. One day it's yes. The next day it's no.

In situations like these, the problem lies not with God but with us. As long as we continue to ask the same questions, His answers will be the same. Only our perceptions of what they are change. Problems with conflicting answers often arise when we are dealing with complex issues, and we are tossing up a lot of questions. It can also happen when the issues that we are dealing with are emotionally charged. It is always difficult to discern God's answer when your head is spinning.

quote

> The Master said, "Danger arises when a man feels secure in his position. Destruction threatens when a man seeks to preserve his worldly estate. Confusion develops when a man has put everything in order. Therefore the superior man does not forget danger in his security, nor ruin when he is well established, nor confusion when his affairs are in order. In this way he gains personal safety and is able to protect the empire. In the I Ching it is said: 'What if it should fail? What if it should fail?' In this way he ties it to a cluster of mulberry shoots [makes success certain]."
>
> —I Ching, Great Commentary

Sorting Out the Questions

When you can't get a firm handle on God's answers, it usually means that you need to sort out the questions that you are asking Him. The following six steps may help you to do so:

1. Write down the issues on which you are seeking God's leading.
2. Do a pro and con list for each. For example, if you are trying to figure out if you should accept a job offer, list all the reasons why you think you should accept the offer, and all the reasons why you think you shouldn't.
3. Next, list all the things you think might happen if you accept the job, and the things you think might happen if you don't.

4. Finally, list your concerns, your hopes, and your fears.
5. Find a quiet space, and spend a few moments just resting in God's presence. Then, ask for His help.
6. Read through your lists. As you do, pay attention to how you feel. Do some issues make you uneasy? Did you list some fears that now seem unfounded? Make note of your feelings.

After you are done with this process, you might find it helpful to simply let your thoughts stay in your head and heart for a while. As you do, you might get a sense that they are somehow moving around and shifting in importance. What may have seemed like a huge concern when you started your lists might now be at the bottom of the pile. Little things might have come forward. You might even have come up with some new feelings that you hadn't been aware of before. If they unsettle you, add them to your list.

You may have to repeat this process several times, if not more, before you feel like you've gained the clarity you're after. You'll know you've got it when you quit feeling unsettled and you start feeling at peace.

Seeking God's Voice in Sacred Literature

Another way to sort out the answers God is giving you is to read spiritual literature. Seek out both the words of others who have struggled with the same issues that you're facing, and words of wisdom from those they sought help from. Pay attention to how you feel as you read. As before, feelings of peace or calmness may be indications of God's answers for you.

Scripture from the Bible is an obvious choice for this, and you'll find some of the best words of wisdom you could ask for in the Book of Proverbs. Chapter One in Proverbs contains some especially good words of wisdom. But don't forget the sacred texts of other religions. There is wonderful guidance to be gained from these works as well.

CHAPTER 14

Praying for Healing

Healing prayer is controversial. Many people misconstrue what it is or reject it as nothing more than a placebo because they say it doesn't work. To a certain extent, such skepticism is understandable, especially in a world where science rather than spirit usually gets the credit for working miracles. But this doesn't mean that praying to God for healing doesn't also fit into the equation.

The Ancient Tradition of Healing Prayer

Prayer has played a significant role in healing since ancient times. In the earliest civilizations, people believed that gods, demons, and spirits both caused and cured diseases. Since they couldn't explain why disease happened, the only explanation for it had to lie in the unseen. So, too, did the cure. Because of this, priests and temples were the doctors and hospitals of the ancient world.

In ancient Greek and Egyptian civilizations, supernatural causes and cures for disease intermingled with more rational approaches. The Greeks believed that the god Apollo was the inventor of healing, and that he passed his sacred knowledge to Asclepius, a priest and medical practitioner who was eventually worshipped as a god. Temples and shrines to Asclepius were being built at about the same time that Hippocrates, the father of medicine, was practicing a more rational form of medicine, one that was based more on the powers of observation than on the supernatural powers of god and spirits. Hippocrates's refusal to blame the gods for causing illness and disease led to healing being thought of as a science instead of a religion.

factum

The Bible documents four major types of healing that can be experienced through prayer: forgiveness, physical healing, emotional healing, and deliverance from evil. Other things to pray for healing over include addictions and relationships.

Egypt, one of the ancient world's more advanced societies, was also the first to regard medicine as a specialty. Egyptian physicians treated people with plants, herbs, oils, magic charms, and surgery. However, they continued to both blame the gods and ask for their help when the treatments failed.

The belief that the supernatural was both responsible for and could cure disease is well documented in the Bible. There are numerous examples of

God inflicting illnesses and curing them in the Old Testament. There are fewer examples of God-sent diseases in the New Testament, and the ones that are here are vastly overshadowed by the healings that were such a significant part of Jesus' ministry. Healing of both the body and the spirit is a key theme in the New Testament. During his ministry, Jesus healed the lame, lepers, blind men, a hemorrhaging woman, and the demon-possessed. He even raised the dead. More than 20 percent of the Gospels are about the healings that Jesus did.

Healing, in fact, was so important to Jesus that he spent more time making people well than doing anything else. The early Christian church also emphasized physical healing, and considered it a component crucial to Christian life and faith. Some of the earliest monasteries built had hospitals where treatment relied on prayer and medical remedies. Later on, these monasteries housed some of the first medical schools.

quote

Ever since at least Moses was born . . . [divine medicine] has healed so many human beings; and not only has it not lost its proper power, but neither has any disease ever yet overcome it.
—St. John Chrysostom, in *Homily Against Publishing the Errors of the Brethren, or Uttering Against Enemies*

By the fourth century C.E., however, medical practice began to overtake prayer for treating disease. A number of Christians now believed that illness was sent by God as a way to punish or correct people. Since they couldn't go to the same entity who had caused the problem and ask for help, their only defense against it was to seek treatment from a physician. Faith became secondary to science. Still, there were some who believed that prayer could heal. Others, including St. Augustine, witnessed God's healing firsthand and became believers. Despite growing skepticism in the secular world about the power of prayer, the ministry of healing continued in the Christian church.

Many people continued to seek—and receive—God's grace in matters of health as the debate over body versus spirit continued.

To this day, many churches include requests for healing as part of their services. A growing number hold special healing services where prayers for healing are offered. Jewish healing services, held in synagogues and other settings, are also blossoming. Prayer is also regaining its place in medical practice as part of a growing emphasis on treating the mind, body, and spirit together. Not only are people praying to God for healing, they're doing so with the support of modern medicine.

factum

In 1992, only three medical schools in the United States were offering courses on spirituality and healing. Today, as many as two-thirds of all medical schools offer some kind of program that combines healing and spirituality. Even though there are some people who do not believe that prayer and spirituality have powers of healing, most everyone acknowledges that the peacefulness and serenity often achieved through prayer and spirituality can have tremendous benefits for the ill and injured.

The Nature of Healing Prayer

Like other types of prayer, we don't know exactly how praying for healing works. Skeptics, of course, will tell you that it doesn't, and that any healing that comes about through prayer is coincidental and more the result of good medicine than of good faith. That's fine, but what about healings that happen in the absence of medical intervention or treatment? Are they just a matter of coincidence, too? If a woman diagnosed with cancer recovers by doing nothing more than praying, and asking others to pray on her behalf, what is the basis for the recovery?

Healing prayer requires, more than anything else, the willingness to believe that anything—and everything—is possible. That requires a good amount of faith in God's abilities, including His ability to work miracles, which is something that an effective prayer life develops. It also means having an open heart. This isn't always easy when we're afraid or hurting, but not having one is one of the greatest obstacles to any kind of prayer.

The Faith Factor

Faith in God is clearly a big part of healing prayer. It is also the factor that gets blamed when prayers for healing don't deliver the hoped-for results. There is no scriptural basis for believing that healing was denied because a person was lacking in faith, or that the people praying for healing were lacking. But this type of causal thinking goes on. We're sometimes guilty of it ourselves.

The truth is that there is no cause-and-effect relationship between the amount of faith that one has and the healing that he or she either receives or doesn't. It is important, however, that our faith is aligned correctly. It's folly to say to God, "Hey Lord, I know you're going to heal so-and-so, so thanks in advance." That's telling God that we want a specific outcome that may or may not be aligned with what He has planned.

symbolism

Sometimes healing happens as a single miraculous event. More often, however, it manifests in things like finding the strength to stick to a long-term treatment program, or in developing a greater sense of peace about a lingering medical problem. However, if we fully put things in God's hands, we're focusing less on what we think should happen and more on believing that whatever happens is according to His divine plan.

Prayer Plus Medicine

What is also pretty clear about healing prayer is that it works best when coupled with medical practice. Research has shown that religious belief increases the effectiveness of medical treatment. There's no reason to believe that the reverse wouldn't also be true. While at times it may seem to be a good idea to emphasize one approach over the other, it's better to engage in both at the same time, and with the same level of commitment.

How to Pray for Healing

People who don't know much about healing prayer often believe that such prayers can only be offered by certain individuals—ministers and priests, for example—or other exalted beings who have somehow been chosen by God to utter these important prayers. Well, they're wrong. Anyone can pray for healing, both for themselves and for others.

factum

In biblical times, healing activities were often carried out by people who had a special relationship to God, or whom God had anointed for such service. In modern times, such precepts have often been interpreted as meaning that only people who felt specially called to healing, or who were "indwelt with spirit," could offer healing prayer.

Praying for healing does require certain attributes, such as:

- **The ability to listen**—Both to the needs of others, and to God.
- **The ability to discern**—You need to be able to tell if you're praying for the right thing.
- **Compassion**—Those with caring hearts offer the best prayers.
- **Belief**—Both in God and in His ability to heal.

- **Patience**—Healing doesn't usually happen overnight. If you're going to pray for it, you'll need to keep at it.
- **Humility**—Being able to accept what happens, good or bad.
- **Gratefulness**—The ability to give thanks to God, regardless of what happens.

Being weak in any of these areas doesn't necessarily mean that you shouldn't pray for healing. However, it might require taking a critical look at your current prayer life. Being deficient in any of these areas can indicate that your relationship with God isn't all that it should be. The people who are most effective at praying for others are those who are on solid footing with the Almighty. To help others heal, you may have to heal yourself first. If you're not right with God, it can be real folly to go to Him in prayer for others.

quote

> We are all healers who can reach out and offer health, and we are all patients in constant need of help.
>
> —Henri Nouwen, in *The Wounded Healer*

As much as we might not like to think it true, our own problems can be the cause of unanswered prayers. In *Prayer: Finding the Heart's True Home*, Richard Foster identifies lack of faith or sin on the part of the person doing the praying as two possible roadblocks to the flow of God's grace and mercy. Not being able to align yourself correctly with God can also lead to praying for the wrong things, such as physical instead of emotional healing, or to praying for the right things in the wrong way.

Before praying for healing, it's also important to put your efforts into perspective. Remember that you are just a part of the process.

There is no one set form that healing prayer must take. Certain types of healing prayer, such as that which takes place as part of a church service, often follow a specific order. But they can also be offered up very casually by people praying alone. They can be in the form of a prayerful attitude—a going about life in a compassionate, prayerful state—instead of limited to specific times of prayer. Some research suggests that the most effective prayer reflects the personality of the pray-er. If you prefer a more introverted, inner-directed way of praying, the energetic, emotionally charged atmosphere of a charismatic Christian prayer service might not be for you. If you enjoy the camaraderie and fellowship of praying with a group, however, you might like being part of a prayer group or a prayer circle. Many people believe in the scriptural precept that healing prayer is more effective when it's done ". . . where two or three are gathered together in My name . . ." (Matthew 18:20)

Most important, don't let yourself be intimidated by the enormity of what you're praying for. Prayers for healing are some of the most common prayers offered. So jump in and start praying.

factum

The belief in corporate or communal prayer dates back to biblical times, when it was customary to ask church leaders to pray over people in need of healing. In the New Testament, Jesus tells his disciples that when more than one person prays together, the power of that prayer is greater than the prayer of one person alone.

Where Healing Prayer Takes Place

Healing prayer is done in many different settings and takes a variety of different forms. As previously mentioned, it's a standard part of many church services, but it's by no means the exclusive property of the church. You'll find healing services in synagogues and spiritual centers. Do a search for healing prayer on the Internet and you'll find some Web sites devoted to it as well. You'll find several listed in Appendix B.

Prayer Services

Prayer services generally follow a format similar to a church's regular liturgy. Because of the more intimate nature of a prayer service, however, they're often less formal than a regular service. Many are held in chapels or other small spaces instead of large sanctuaries.

During a prayer service, all participants voice prayers at certain times during the liturgy. Individual prayers, either spoken or silent, are also offered. At some prayer services, lists of people who have asked for prayer are passed around, and each person is prayed for.

A number of services also offer the laying on of hands or anointing with oil. Both are healing practices dating back to ancient times, when they were symbolic of calling upon gods and spirits for supernatural healing. They're also well documented in the Bible. In the Book of James, the writer tells anyone who is suffering to ". . . call for the elders of the church, and let them pray over him, anointing him with oil in the name of the Lord" (James 5:14). In the Book of Acts, a disciple of Jesus named Ananias healed Saul of Tarsus (who later became the apostle Paul) of blindness by putting his hand on him. Special prayers are said for both practices as they are done.

If you're not familiar with these practices, they may seem strange or uncomfortable to you. But they can be a powerful adjunct to prayer. Both signify a special link between the people in need of prayer, those who are praying for them, and God. They make what is already an important act even more important. It may be difficult to see the power in something as simple as a hand laid upon one's body during prayer. But, it can be powerful indeed. Many people who are ill suffer from isolation and rejection. Sometimes, the most basic human contact—touch—is a very welcome gift.

Prayer Groups

Prayer groups are a common fixture in many churches, and are often formed by members of the congregation who feel called to pray in this manner. These groups vary from being very informal to having a pretty specific structure, with prayer leaders and committees and what not. Members might receive specific training in healing prayer as well. Some pray over prayer requests that are submitted to them or that they become aware of in other ways instead of directly over the people in need of healing. Others combine the people requesting prayer with those who wish to pray for them. Laying on of hands may also be done.

Even if you generally prefer to pray alone, participating in a prayer group can be an effective way to practice healing prayer, both for yourself and for others. Not only are you surrounded by a group of people with similar desires, they tend to be a pretty compassionate lot. They're also usually pretty good at what they do. If you're new to prayer, and especially if you're new to healing prayer, there's a lot to be learned from a group of fervent pray-ers who gather together on a regular basis.

Prayer Chains

Another popular type of corporate prayer, prayer chains link together individuals who share the desire to pray for others. Thanks to the Internet, some of these groups extend around the world, which means that a single request for prayer may be prayed over by thousands of individuals. Prayer requests are passed along to members of the circle. Some groups schedule a specific time of day at which prayers are to be offered. Others simply commit to praying daily for the people on the prayer list.

discussion question

Is it better to have a specific goal in mind when praying for healing? Not necessarily. In studies conducted by the Spindrift Organization, directed and nondirected prayers were both proven effective. However, open-ended, or nondirected prayer was shown to be substantially more effective.

Going It Alone

While there is often great strength in numbers when it comes to healing prayer, there's nothing that says you can't do it on your own. If you're praying for someone else, you might find it helpful to have something that reminds you of that person in front of you—a picture, a favorite object, maybe even a letter. Asking the individual for guidance on what you should pray for is also a good idea. Don't assume that you know what's in someone's heart.

Your healing prayer should follow the same or similar pattern you've established for your usual prayer routine. If your emotions overwhelm you and you have a hard time talking to God, simply rest in His presence. He'll understand. You may wish to read scripture that specifically deals with healing. There are numerous examples throughout the Bible. Of them, the Twenty-Third Psalm is one of the best loved.

The very personal nature of the Book of Psalms, and its reflection of just about every human emotion you can think of, makes it a top pick for accompanying healing prayer. Almost every psalm praises God in some way or asks for His help.

At the end of your prayer period, it can be helpful to offer a "thy will be done" prayer. This one by Reinhold Niebuhr may be more familiar to you as the Serenity Prayer, but it is also a good one for this purpose:

God, give us grace to accept with serenity

The things that cannot be changed,

Courage to change the things which should be changed,

And the wisdom to distinguish the one from the other.

—Reinhold Niebuhr

CHAPTER 15

Renewing Your Prayer Life

There will be times in your prayer life when you'll feel stuck. You may feel worn out, in a rut, or simply bored with prayer. You might have hit a dry spell in your prayer practice during which it seems like nothing much is happening, or when it seems like you're moving farther away from God instead of closer. In this chapter, you'll learn about ways in which you can renew your prayer life and keep it moving forward.

Recognizing the Need for Renewal

Just as with any relationship, your relationship with God will have its ups and downs. There are times when you feel like you're racing along so fast that you're out of breath, and times when it feels like it's stalled out. There are good days of prayer when you feel so close to God that you can physically sense His presence. Then there are times when He feels very far away and you're not sure you're connecting at all. You might feel out of sorts with God, either a little or a lot. Or, you're simply not as happy with where things are as you once were. And you're not as excited about spending time with God.

Our time in prayer is supposed to be something that we look forward to. However, just like athletes who get burned out when they work out too often or too hard, it's also possible to get to the point where you feel like you're dragging yourself into prayer instead of welcoming the time you spend talking to God. If this is the case, you're in good company. Everyone has times when they feel like they have to pray instead of wanting to pray. Even the greatest spiritual leaders have had times when prayer became more of a burden than a blessing. In other words, dry spells happen.

It's important to understand these periods and to put them into perspective. They are never indications that our relationship with God is over. Usually, they're signs that we need to take a look at other factors. Some might be physical. Others will be spiritual.

Body Talk

Sometimes the problems we're having in prayer are more related to our bodies instead of our souls. When we're working long hours or working in demanding jobs, our lives outside of prayer can get way out of balance. Being ill can also throw what is usually a very satisfying prayer life out of whack. When our bodies don't feel right, our physical feelings can distract us from focusing on God. When we're done praying, it just doesn't feel like we've connected with Him very well.

If you feel like your prayer problems are more related to your physical being, listen to what your body is trying to tell you. Body and spirit can both be renewed in prayer, but sometimes the body needs to take precedence.

symbolism

When you've hit a dry spot in your prayer life, don't stop praying. This is exactly when you don't want to put the skids on your relationship with God. Continue your prayer practice in some way. As long as you continue to go to God, to talk to Him, to lay your fears and your desires at His feet, your relationship with Him will move forward.

Maybe the half hour that you usually spend praying to God in the morning or at night would be better spent catching up on some much-needed shut-eye, at least for the time being. If so, you can find other times during the day to catch up on your conversations with God. You can pray simply throughout the day. Or, take mini prayer breaks—maybe spend five minutes in the morning reading your Bible, another five minutes at lunch doing an online meditation, and another five minutes before dinner simply sitting in God's presence.

Mind Games

Very often, our problems in prayer are related more to our heads than our hearts. For whatever reason, the prayer life we once found satisfying just isn't cutting it any more. God may seem very far away, and the joy we experience in communicating with Him may be gone as well.

In Psalm 42, the psalmist also talks about his feeling that God is distant, and voices his desire to overcome the chasm between himself and the Almighty:

As the deer pants for the water brooks,

So pants my soul for You, O God.

My soul thirsts for God, for the living God.

When shall I come and appear before God?

My tears have been my food day and night,

While they continually say to me,

Where is your God?

When I remember these things,

I pour out my soul within me.

For I used to go with the multitude;

I went with them to the house of God,

With the voice of joy and praise,

With a multitude that kept a pilgrim feast.

Why are you cast down, O my soul?

And why are you disquieted within me?

Hope in God, for I shall yet praise Him

For the help of his countenance.

O my God, my soul is cast down within me;

Therefore I will remember You from the land of the Jordan,

And from the heights of Hermon,

From the Hill Mizar.

Deep calls unto deep at the noise of Your waterfalls;

All Your waves and billows have gone over me.

The Lord will command His lovingkindness in the daytime,

And in the night His song shall be with me—

A prayer to the God of my life.

I will say to God my Rock,

"Why have You forgotten me?"

Why do I go mourning because of the oppression of the enemy?

As with a breaking of my bones,

My enemies reproach me,

While they say to me all day long,

"Where is your God?"

Why are you cast down, O my soul?

And why are you disquieted within me?

Hope in God;

For I shall yet praise Him,

The help of my countenance and my God.

—Psalm 42

It's also important in times like these to remember that God is willing to listen, and that He will guide us in all circumstances. Even though He may seem beyond our reach at times, He really isn't.

quote

If we neglect prayer and if the branch is not connected with the vine, it will die. That connecting to the branch to the vine is prayer. If that connection is there then love is there, then joy is there, and we will be the sunshine of God's love, the hope of eternal happiness, the flame of burning love.

—Mother Teresa

How can we get back into the swing of things with God? It can be as simple as exchanging your current prayer routine for something new. At other times, you may need to change your attitude about prayer, or readjust your expectations of what you get out of the experience.

In any case, don't let yourself become paralyzed by your feelings. Doing so opens you up for being overcome or defeated by your circumstances. While praying may be the last thing you feel like doing, it's one of the best things you can do. If you're really lacking enthusiasm, make your prayers very simple. The important thing is to keep the lines of communication open. As will be discussed in Chapter 18, all prayer needs to consist of is one word offered up to God with the right intention.

Changing Old for New

If you've been following the same prayer routine for a while, you might simply be bored. It does happen. If you think you're bored, don't stay stuck in your same prayer routine. Try something new. This doesn't necessarily mean completely tossing aside your current prayer practice for something else. Try taking a micro approach first. Consider making small changes such as:

- Praying at a different time of day—If you usually pray at the end of the day, try switching to late afternoon, just before dinner, early morning, or whatever works.
- Praying in a different place—Sometimes a change of scenery can do the trick.
- Praying in a different position—If you always sit in a chair, maybe it's time to try a meditation cushion.

Praying Online

There isn't much you can't do online these days. It might seem a little silly to pray with a computer, but it can be surprisingly effective if you hook up with the right prayer site. If you haven't searched the Internet for sites that offer online prayer experiences, you might be surprised at how many are out there. It may take some time to find one that suits your particular needs, but keep searching as there are sites that offer a truly wonderful experience. Some even have online studies on various facets of spirituality. You'll find a couple of them listed in Appendix B.

Praying with a Group

We're always linked to the community of God when we pray, which means that we're never really alone. However, if your usual prayer practice takes place in physical solitude, you're missing out on the energy that's present when "two or three are gathered."

Prayer groups are often affiliated with houses of worship, and it's usually easiest to find them by checking with local churches and other organizations. Other places where prayer groups meet include monasteries and community centers. While it's usually best to experience group prayer in the physical presence of the people you're praying with, it's also possible to do it through cyberspace. Do an Internet search for prayer sites, and check the site menus to see if they offer group prayer.

Enhancing Your Environment

If you're a "bare-bones" pray-er, maybe it's time to burn some incense or light a candle when you pray. If you already use tools like these in your practice, try something new. It could be as simple as buying a new candle, or treating yourself to that CD of Celtic music that caught your ear the last time you were music shopping. If you don't have a space set aside in your home for prayer and meditation, this might be the time to do it.

Asking God for Help

If making small changes doesn't get you out of your rut, it might be time to make bigger ones. Before you do, it can be helpful to spend some time in discernment with God and see if you can sense the direction He'd like you take.

Ask Him for guidance, either during a scheduled prayer period or informally as you're going about your normal daily routine. It may take some time to get your answers, so be patient.

discussion question

What should I do if God answers my question, but the answers aren't what I wanted to hear?
Sometimes God wants us to move in directions that may initially disturb or trouble us. If the direction you received from Him is of this nature, don't panic or dismiss it out of hand. Continue to go to God in prayer, and stay open to letting His spirit work within you.

Getting a New 'Tude

The early stages of a prayer practice can be pretty exciting. Things are fresh and new to us, and every way in which we encounter the Almighty feels wonderful. After a while, however, the newness wears off. We're no longer carried along by the freshness of the experience. The time we spend with God seems more ordinary, less wonderful, not as special. In other words, the bloom has fallen off the rose.

One of the mistakes that is often made in prayer is thinking of it as being different than any other relationship. We tend to think that our communion with God should always be a profound experience, and when it's less than transforming we feel somehow let down, even disappointed.

Just like a relationship with a spouse or significant other, our relationship with God doesn't remain in one place. As God's spirit moves within us, we move to new places and new ways of experiencing Him. There will be times when things will seem academic and you'll feel like you're merely going through the motions. Then, out of the blue, something will happen that will knock your socks off, and you'll be amazed all over again.

symbolism

> Even when it feels like your prayer life is going nowhere, it always is. It can be difficult at times to sense the small changes that God makes within us, but they always lead to great ones.

Stepping Back to Go Forward

Sometimes the best way to renew your prayer life is to take a step back. In other words, we need to retreat. Most people don't think they can afford the luxury of spending time away from their busy schedules, but it's because we are so busy that we need to withdraw at times. No one can keep going full speed ahead all of the time. Sometimes it's necessary to stop and get your bearings, to gain a new perspective on things. One of the best ways to do this is by stepping back for a time of refreshment and renewal.

A retreat is a time for stopping and resting for the purpose of moving forward with renewed vigor and purpose. It's a time for returning to the basics: basic beliefs, basic attitudes, the basic balance of life. Above all, a retreat is a rest in God.

Many people make prayer retreats a regular part of their spiritual walk, no matter how busy their lives are. Spending time away from normal routines in contemplation and quiet affords singular opportunities for drawing closer to God.

The Tradition of Withdrawing from the World

Retreats are well documented in the Bible. In the Old Testament, the prophet Elijah escaped to the desert to pray after his encounters with Jezebel, the Phoenician princess who threatened to kill him after he deposed her priests.

Jesus began his ministry by retreating into the wilderness for forty days of prayer and fasting. He often went into "a mountain apart to pray," and he invited his disciples to come with him. Paul also practiced the discipline of retreat.

Over the centuries, many men and women have followed these early examples of spiritual discipline and have withdrawn from daily life for various periods of time. The desert fathers and mothers of ancient Christianity took to the desert so they could draw nearer to God, and they recommended the practice, in shortened forms, to all who wished to better direct their lives toward the Almighty. St. Francis of Assisi often traveled to hermitages where he spent time in prayer with his followers. And the prophet Muhammad spent much of his time in retreat, communing with God.

Ignatius's Spiritual Exercises

In the sixteenth century, a young Spaniard named Ignatius experienced a religious conversion, after which he spent nine months in a cave talking to God and discerning His will. After his "desert experience," Ignatius wrote a small book that documented what he had learned. Called *Spiritual Exercises*, it emphasized the importance of retreat in spiritual development, and provided a framework for others who wished to pursue this path of knowledge. In it, he detailed a four-week series of exercises and meditations, along with instructions on various spiritual practices, including prayer. The exercises were meant to be completed on retreat.

Ignatius of Loyola later founded the Society of Jesuits. It was the first religious order that required its followers to go on regular retreats. Before taking their vows, followers also went through the spiritual exercises.

As the practice spread, retreat or "exercise" houses were established across Europe as places where clergy, nobility, and common people alike could go to pray and meditate. Today, thousands of retreat centers around the world offer the opportunity to get away from it all and spend time alone with the Almighty.

Modern-Day Retreats

For some, a retreat might simply mean praying as they take a long walk. Most people, however, find longer retreat experiences of a day or more to be most beneficial for rest and renewal. For the most part, retreats like these mean finding a place away from everyday routines. Many people seek the resources of retreat centers for these times, but it isn't necessary that you do so. What is important is that you find a place where you can meet God alone.

Either way, you'll need to do some advance preparation before you depart and the following three steps are recommended:

1. First, and perhaps most important, schedule your time away—Write it into your calendar, just like you would any appointment. And, consider it as important as any other. Don't start thinking about canceling your retreat or rescheduling it unless you absolutely can't avoid it.
2. Find a place for your retreat—As previously mentioned, you can take a retreat just about anywhere. If you like to camp, find a national park where you can enjoy God's majesty in peace. If the comforts of a bed and a warm meal have more appeal, consider a retreat center or spiritual center. Just about every religious organization has these resources. You might want to stick to ones in your own religious tradition, but there's nothing saying that you have to do so. You might enjoy a week at a Zen retreat center, where you can go on a Zen meditation retreat, or a sesshin. You might like a weekend at a Benedictine monastery where you can get a taste of what the monastic life is all about by praying with and working alongside the monks who live there. You'll find some resources to help you locate these and other places for retreats in Appendix B.
3. Make whatever arrangements are necessary that will make it possible for you to spend your time alone with God—This includes finding someone to watch the kids and pets if you need to.

You probably won't need to bring very much with you. The basics include clothing and perhaps a good pair of walking shoes or hiking boots, your Bible, a notebook for journaling your thoughts, and whatever personal hygiene products you'll need. Many people like to bring a devotional book on prayer or another spiritual discipline to read as well. Leave electronic devices such as cell phones, PDAs, pagers, CD players, radios, and laptop computers behind. Most retreat centers won't allow them. Even if you're spending your retreat time elsewhere, you'll welcome the break from them and the silence that fills their absence. Silence is, of course, when you are most likely to hear the voice of God. You might also consider leaving your watch behind.

Most retreat facilities are pretty sparse, although they're usually far from monastic. Single rooms with shared baths are fairly common. Some may have special accommodations for couples, or hermitages or small cabins where you can have complete solitude. Some separate men and women into different facilities.

For the most part, don't expect luxury, or even most modern conveniences during your retreat experience. You'll have a light for reading, but that will be about it. Forget about such things as phones, televisions, and T1 lines, and even radios. Remember, the focus is on spiritual matters, not affairs of the world.

Retreat centers generally provide things like linens and towels, but it's a good idea to find out for sure ahead of time as you may need to bring your own.

Private Retreats

Many people like to go on retreats where they can call the shots, either at retreat centers or other places of their choosing. On these retreats, what you do and how you use your time is completely up to you. You can get up when you want to and stay up as late as you like. You can keep your schedule very loose and allow God's spirit to lead you to times of prayer, meditation, and rest, or establish specific times for prayer and worship. You can eat regular meals or fast. The choice is up to you.

Regardless of the approach you take, be sure to take time to rest. Your desire to be alone with God might be so consuming that you'll lose track of time if you're not careful. It is very easy to spend hours reading and praying to God when you're away from your normal routines. While there is nothing wrong with this, resting with God is just as important. Take naps. Go for walks.

Sing. Take a break from the Bible and read a devotional book or a book on living spiritually—or take a break from reading altogether.

Directed Retreats

Directed retreats are more structured and are often a good choice for people who are new to the retreat experience. While you can structure your own retreat virtually anywhere, they're best experienced in the context of a retreat center or camp.

The amount of structure in a directed retreat varies greatly. Some retreat centers are very informal. You'll be able to choose how and when you pray and how you want to spend your free time. You might be expected to join others during meal times, or you may be able to take your meals privately. A daily meeting with a retreat director is usually part of the schedule.

Other retreat facilities take a more hands-on approach and offer formal schedules of classes and services. If you go on a retreat at a monastery, you'll have the opportunity to experience the routine that the members of the monastery follow on a daily basis. While you'll be invited to participate in all activities, you usually aren't required to do so.

quote

To pray is to descend with the mind into the heart, and there to stand before the face of the Lord, ever-present, all-seeing, within you.
—Attributed to Russian mystic Theophan the Recluse

The following schedule is typical of one you might be asked to follow at a monastic retreat. Periods of silence alternate with meals and prayer times—Matins, Diurnum, Vespers, and Compline. These are chant-like services that include scripture readings and sung psalms.

Time	Event
6:00 A.M.	Matins
7:00 A.M.	Breakfast
7:30–10:00 A.M.	Free time
10:00 A.M.	Celebration of the Holy Eucharist
11:00 A.M.–12:00 P.M.	Free time
12:00 P.M.	Diurnum
1:00 P.M.	Lunch
2:00–3:30 P.M.	Free time
3:30 P.M.	Vespers
4:30–6:00 P.M.	Free time
6:00–7:00 P.M.	Dinner
7:00–8:30 P.M.	Free time
8:30–9:30 P.M.	Compline

If you are new to retreats, there may be some activities that you'll find strange or that you don't understand. Monastic retreats, in particular, can seem very strange, especially if you're not familiar with the prayer style that they follow. If this is the case, don't hesitate to ask questions of your retreat leader, a member of the monastery, or of others who are attending the retreat. Make sure, however, that you ask your questions at the appropriate time. It's bad manners—not to mention a little embarrassing—to break a period of silence.

CHAPTER 16

Going Deeper into Prayer

At some point along your spiritual journey, you may feel the desire to get to know God in a different way. Your prayer life is going fine, but you're kind of unsettled for some reason. You get a feeling as though there's something more to experience, a mystery door that you haven't yet opened. And it's got you kind of curious.

Understanding Your Feelings

The fact that there is always something else to experience with God is one of the many gifts of a fruitful prayer life. When we open our hearts and minds to God, we go on a journey like no other. We enter into a relationship that knows no boundaries. We might reach points where we are simply dazzled by how far we have come, and we can't imagine going any further. Then we learn that we are just beginning again. We enter into a whole new phase of being with God, walking with God, praying with God. We get to know Him all over again.

Like life itself, a prayer life goes through various stages. Some of these stages are pretty painless, and we move through them relatively quickly. We might not even be aware of going through them until some time afterward. At other times, the transit through the stages of our prayer lives can feel a little uncomfortable. Sometimes it can be a lot uncomfortable. Uncomfortable transits—the ones that hurt because they last too long or they move us too far out of our comfort zones—can, in fact, wreak havoc with our spiritual lives. They can strain our relationships with God, or even dry them up for a certain period of time. This can cause a crisis of faith that can be pretty frightening. John of the Cross, a sixteenth-century monk who had experienced a number of these crises himself, gave them a most fitting description. He called them "dark nights of the soul."

> *At a certain point in the spiritual journey God will draw a person from the beginning stage to a more advanced stage. Such souls will likely experience what is called "the dark night of the soul." The "dark night" is when those persons lose all the pleasure that they once experienced in their devotional life. This happens because God wants to purify them and move them on to greater heights.*

There is nothing fun about a dark night of the soul. When you are in a dark night, you might feel alone and emotionally drained. Prayer brings no relief, and might even make you feel worse. Understanding the dynamics behind times like these, although it won't make them pass any faster, can help you get through them. What these feelings of unrest—these dark nights—often indicate is that you are moving into a new phase of your spiritual journey, or that you are just about to. You are becoming more spiritually mature. As St. John put it, God wants to purify you and move you to greater heights.

Going to those heights, however, does not mean that you are an expert pray-er, or that you'll become one once you reach them. Remember, no one ever is, as there is no such thing as a person who prays perfectly. Perfection is never the goal of prayer. What it does mean is that you are ready for some more serious spiritual work. In other words, you are ready to dig deeper. You may be getting good at praying, but you are not obligated—or even advised—to seek perfection in the way you pray.

What does digging deeper mean? Perhaps it is easier to look at what it does not mean first. Digging deeper does not mean spending more time in prayer, although there is nothing wrong with that if you decide to do so. It does not mean praying more fervently, although there is nothing wrong with this either. What it does mean is spending your time with God in a different way. Instead of talking to and thinking about Him, you are going to put your words, thoughts, and feelings on hold. You are going to be quiet, and you are going to listen.

quote

> . . . And behold, the Lord passed by, and a great and strong wind tore into the mountains and broke the rocks in pieces before the Lord, but the Lord was not in the wind; and after the wind an earthquake, but the Lord was not in the earthquake; and after the earthquake a fire, but the Lord was not in the fire; and after the fire a still small voice.
>
> —1 Kings 20:11–12

Listening Up

We are so good at filling our lives up with sound. We even fill up our time with God with it. Intentionally or not, we often share our prayer time with the background noise created by life. Sometimes it is of our own creation, sometimes we are at the mercy of the people around us. How many times have you prayed with a television set blaring away in the background? How often have you chattered along in simple prayer so long that when you stop it feels like you are surrounded by the void left by the absence of your words? How often have you said, "I can't hear myself think"?

Rational Prayer versus Silent Prayer

So much of the time we spend with God consists of rational, discursive prayer. We talk to Him in words and sentences, either out loud or silently. Either way, these prayers fill our heads with sound. There is nothing wrong with outwardly directed prayer of this nature. It is the prayer style with which many people feel most comfortable. But, it is important to have moments of silence and quiet with God, too.

Prayer can also consist of being quiet in God's presence. It can take the form of simply coming into His presence, sitting down, quieting our minds, and allowing Him to speak to us. When we are quiet, we allow a space to open up inside of us that God can fill without our going through the usual motions of prayer. We don't have to say a word, yet He comes.

As you will soon see, the quiet times you spend with God can be extremely satisfying and an important adjunct to your regular prayer practice. Author and therapist Bruce Davis describes silence and prayer as "two best friends who take each other on all kinds of journeys."

Problems with Silence

If you haven't spent much time in silence with God, it may not be easy for you to do so at first. Many people are so used to the sounds of words that they actually feel uncomfortable when there are no words being spoken. Some people have a fear of silence, and will do everything they possibly can to avoid it. Instead of listening to the voices of their inner selves, they would rather fill their minds and souls with noise.

If you feel uneasy when you are not surrounded by sound, you may have to ease yourself into silence. One of the best ways to do this is to pick a day of the week for taking a break from sound. On this day, you won't turn on any device that makes a noise. No television, no radio, no CD player, no cell phone. You might also try extending the silence to yourself and others. In other words, no talking.

factum

To enhance and protect lifelong health, noted holistic physician and author Andrew Weil suggests taking a weekly "news fast"—a day away from the television, radio, newspapers, and magazines. As he writes in *8 Weeks to Optimum Health,* many people take in too much mental junk food. Taking a break from the news can help you better understand the influence it has over you, and help you decide just how much news you want to let into your life.

Many people regularly take a break from the noise in their lives. Sundays are particularly popular days for this practice as silence fits well with a day of rest.

Taking a break from sound might be incredibly difficult if you are used to having a radio or television turned on to keep you company. If you are, do not force yourself to spend too much time surrounded by silence. Doing so will just make you nervous, and you may resent the experience so much that you won't want to do it again. Turn on the noise before the absence of it starts to bother you too much. The next time you take a sound break, try to extend the silence a bit longer than you did the last time.

Going to the Desert

The desire to experience and understand the unknown through our spirit instead of our rational minds can be found in many religions. It is the basis for Buddhist and Zen meditation. Both Christianity and Judaism also have these spiritual heritages. In the early Christian church, individuals who sought these experiences took to the desert, where they could focus their entire lives on God with no interruptions. In so doing, they developed a spiritual discipline based on solitude, silence, and prayer that enabled them to experience God in a deeply profound and organic manner. You will read more about these early mystics in the following chapters.

Today, it is not necessary to go to the desert (unless, of course, you choose to!) to replicate the experiences of these early spiritual seekers. You can create your own desert—your own solitude—right where you are by drawing on their knowledge and learning how to experience God through a practice called contemplative prayer.

What Is Contemplative Prayer?

Contemplative prayer is a prayer practice that creates interior silence. It is similar to some forms of meditation, but not meditation practices that call for consciously focusing the mind on a specific object or idea and then trying to gain a new understanding of it. Instead, it is similar to meditation styles in which the mind is cleared of thoughts, feelings, and emotions.

factum

Contemplative prayer is also described as resting in God, resting in God's presence, resting the spirit, or gazing lovingly at God. For many people, it is a prayer form that they unconsciously yearn for, and it brings them much joy when they find it.

Contemplative prayer is not a relaxation exercise or self-hypnosis, although it is often compared to or confused with these things. It also is not meant to lead to supernatural experiences of God. It will not knock you to the floor bathed in the Holy Spirit and speaking in tongues. If you are seeking out-of-body experiences, you will not get them through contemplative prayer. Unlike the meditation practices followed by Buddhists and Hindus, contemplative prayer is not a way of learning how to control your mind. Instead, it is meant to still it.

What contemplative prayer will do is put your entire self—your body, mind, and spirit—into a receptive state where God's spirit can inspire your spirit without any interruption or interference caused by your thoughts or actions. In other words, He can enter right in without you doing anything besides being open to Him. To paraphrase the words of the Spanish nun and mystic Theresa of Avila, when you settle yourself in solitude, you will come upon God in yourself.

discussion question

Why is contemplative prayer considered prayer?
Although it is not like the more discursive prayer styles that we're usually more familiar with, we do communicate with God, albeit in a very different way, when we practice contemplative prayer.

This interior silence, or receptive state, is created when we clear our minds of thoughts and feelings and allow ourselves to simply be in God's presence. We will explore how this is done later in this chapter.

Who Does Contemplative Prayer?

At one time, long ago, it was believed that contemplation was a special spiritual gift that only people who had directly experienced God's presence could enter into. Over time, however, it became clear that contemplation was not reserved for only those individuals who had heard God's voice, and heard it in such a way that it transformed them. In fact, it became clear that contemplative prayer is itself a transforming spiritual discipline. It is reserved to no one, and it is open to all who desire it.

As previously mentioned, the discipline of contemplation has deep roots in many world religions. Although we often associate it with Eastern religions, like Hinduism and Buddhism, it is also a part of Jewish and Christian prayer traditions.

In the Christian church, contemplation became a way to fulfill the biblical precept to pray without ceasing. Its best-known form—the "Jesus Prayer"—dates back to the sixth century and was developed by monks and others who were seeking a deeper relationship with God to be able to pray wherever and whenever they could.

Over the centuries, most of the more contemplative prayer styles fell out of favor in Western religions. However, these ancient traditions were revived in the latter part of the twentieth century as people began seeking deeper spiritual experiences. Interest in it continues to grow to this day.

How to Do Contemplative Prayer

Contemplative prayer takes many forms. There is lectio divina, a form of prayer based on the slow, meditative reading of sacred scripture, and centering prayer, which is often done as a prelude to lectio divina or on its own. You can read about these forms of contemplative practices in the chapters that discuss them. Here, we will focus on the most basic contemplative prayer of all—the breath prayer.

factum

The Yoga Sutras of the Hindus, the oldest surviving text on meditation, describe the spiritual discipline of breathing, or pranayama. Pranayama exercises are still an important part of modern yoga practice, and are included in many yoga sequences.

This prayer style is the most organic and intrinsic of all as it taps into the most basic connection we have with God and that which we can't live without. It is said that every breath we take is a prayer of thanks to God.

The "Jesus Prayer" is also a breath prayer, and is probably the best-known form of it. "Lord Jesus Christ" is said (or thought) while breathing in. "Have mercy on me, a sinner" is said while breathing out. As the body relaxes, the words become fewer, dwindling down to just "Lord" and "mercy." They may even slip from consciousness into the heart, where they are said intuitively.

Beginning Breath Prayer

Breath prayer begins with—you guessed it—simply being aware of your breath. The following method is one of many that you can use to learn it:

1. Find a quiet place—Preferably, one in which you won't be disturbed for a while—and have a seat. Sit in any way you like. Some people prefer sitting in a chair with their feet on the ground. Others prefer a prayer or meditation cushion. Allow yourself a few minutes to adjust to the sound of silence.
2. Focus on taking a breath, and letting it out—As you do, note how all you can think of is how you breathe. Keep breathing. In. Out. Slowly. In. Out. If your mind wanders, return your awareness to your breathing.
3. Next, close your eyes and continue to focus on your breath—In. Out. Stay focused on breathing in and out.

Soon, very soon, you should notice a feeling of calmness begin to build inside your body and mind. Keep breathing. In. Out. Let the silence within you continue to build. Keep breathing. As you do, the rhythm of your breathing will change. It will lengthen, and you'll breathe more slowly. You don't have to consciously focus on changing your breathing, nor should you. It will happen on its own.

symbolism

One of the benefits of breath prayer is that you can do it anywhere you happen to be. You can do it while you are standing in line in the grocery store or while you are waiting for someone to come to the phone. In fact, it is a great way to keep yourself from getting impatient in almost every situation that forces you to wait. The breath prayer can also be done when praying with prayer beads or a prayer rope.

As your breaths lengthen, your body will relax and go along with your breathing pattern. Some describe this feeling as sinking into your breathing. You'll be in the flow, or as Sam Keen describes it in *Hymns to an Unknown God*, "After a long while you will feel yourself being breathed. As you surrender to the movement, figure and ground reverse, the gestalt changes. Who you are changes. Where once you were acting, now you seem moved by a power beyond yourself. Your breath tells you that you are of the same substance as the spirit that moves everything."

On the face of it, the breath prayer is a great little relaxation method. In fact, as you practice it you may get drowsy. Some people even fall asleep doing it. However, the breath prayer has a deeper meaning than this. Breath prayer symbolizes God's breath, the breath of life that He gave all living beings. When we breathe in, we are taking in all that is possible in the world. When we breathe out, we give it all back to God.

Breath Prayer, Yoga Style

Another form of the breath prayer is based on a yoga position called Savasana (in Sanskrit), or the Corpse Pose. You do it by lying on the floor on your back with your legs stretched out in front of you. Let your feet fall to the side naturally. Don't try to keep your toes pointing upwards. Also let your arms rest naturally along your sides, slightly away from your torso, with your palms facing upward. Now, actively stretch your arms and legs away from you for a few seconds. Then relax them completely. As you do, close your eyes and turn your attention inward. Note how you are feeling—you should be calm and relaxed.

factum

The Savasana, or Corpse Pose, is deceptively simple but amazingly effective. It is often done at the end of a yoga sequence. It can also be done at any time to soothe the nerves and calm the mind. The state of total relaxation brought out by this pose gives the body renewed energy and determination.

Next, take a few deep, slow breaths. Inhale into your chest while keeping your throat, neck, and diaphragm soft and relaxed. As you exhale, feel your body sink into the floor. Keep your shoulders, neck, and facial muscles relaxed. Try to keep your eyes still as well. As before, focus on your breathing. Become aware of breathing in and out. If your mind wanders, let it return gently to your breathing. Stay in this position for at least five minutes. Ten minutes is even better. As you do, surrender yourself completely to the position. Sink into your breathing.

It is important not to come out of the Savasana pose too quickly. When you are ready to do so, bend your knees and roll slowly to one side. Pause for a moment or two, then gently push yourself up to a seated position.

For an even deeper breath prayer experience, try either of these methods while wearing earplugs. When you close out all external noise, you are left with only the sound of your breath as it enters and exits your body. If you haven't ever listened to this sound, it can be pretty amazing. We tend to take life—and breath—so much for granted. Focusing on it intensely, which is what wearing earplugs will make you do, may help you sense a greater connection to breath prayer and gain a deeper understanding of its role in your prayer practice.

CHAPTER 17

Divine Reading: Lectio Divina

Much of the praying we do takes the form of communications directed from us to God. We go to the Almighty in various ways, and, in so doing, look for answers from Him. Sometimes, however, those answers lie in simply keeping our ears open so that we can hear what He has to say. Lectio divina, the prayer style discussed in this chapter, turns the prayer paradigm around to put us in a better position to hear God's "still, small voice."

What Is Lectio Divina?

Literally meaning "divine reading," lectio divina is a form of prayer based on slow, meditative reading of sacred scripture, and in particular passages from the Bible. It has its roots in Christian monastic practices that were developed as early as the fourth century C.E. It was then that a number of devout Christians, both men and women, left their cities and villages behind and traveled to the desert areas of Egypt, Arabia, Syria, and Palestine, where, away from the distractions of civilization, they could focus on the presence of God in their lives. Some preferred to live completely alone, only emerging from their solitude when approached for spiritual advice, while others established small communities centered around various teachers, known as "abbas."

symbolism

Some of the monks of the desert became so revered that their authority rivaled that of the official leaders of the Christian church. While the two communities stayed separate for a while, by the fifth century C.E. men from the monastic tradition had replaced many of the church's most important bishops.

Lectio Divina in the Desert

These fathers and mothers of the desert, as they're often called, practiced the virtues that have come to define monasticism, including celibacy, fasting, asceticism, hospitality, and charity. Their entire lives revolved around God and being constantly mindful and aware of His presence.

As part of their devotion to the Almighty the desert fathers and mothers followed the scriptural precept to "pray without ceasing." They remained in constant contact with God by reading or hearing short passages from the Bible and memorizing them, choosing a phrase or a short sentence that had spoken to them in some way, and by continually meditating or ruminating on them. They didn't attach any preconceived ideas to the words that they meditated on, nor did they try to analyze them. They just listened to God's word, and reflected on it. As they did, they were led spiritually to new insights into the text, or different understandings of it, and through this to a deeper relationship with God.

quote

> To get the full flavor of an herb, it must be pressed between the fingers, so it is the same with the Scriptures; the more familiar they become, the more they reveal their hidden treasures and yield their indescribable riches.
>
> —St. John Chrysostom, A.D. 347–407

Benedict's Rule

The great fifth-century mystic Benedict, who is often called "the father of western monks," continued the traditions of the fathers and mothers of the desert in the monastic order that he established. After living as a solitary for several years, he led a communal monastery and then founded a number of monasteries. He also developed a code of order, or rule, for the monastics who lived in them. Drawing from the teachings and writings of the desert fathers and mothers, Benedict's rule emphasized obedience to God through intellectual, spiritual, and manual labors.

Liturgy and prayer played a central role in the daily life of the monks who lived by Benedict's rule. So did what Benedict called "prayerful reading"—the same careful, repetitive poring over scripture practiced by the desert fathers and mothers. It was so important, in fact, that Benedict even specified how much time the monks should devote to reading—at least three hours a day—and at what times of the day they should read.

A twelfth-century Carthusian monk named Guigues du Chastel is credited with formalizing the practice of lectio divina. In a letter written to a fellow monk, he described a ladder to heaven, or God, that consisted of four rungs based on his method of reading the Bible:

1. **Lectio (reading or lesson)**—Or "busily looking on Holy Scripture with all one's will and wit."
2. **Meditatio (meditation)**—"A studious insearching with the mind to know what was before concealed through desiring proper skill."
3. **Oratio (prayer)**—"A devout desiring of the heart to get what is good and avoid what is evil."
4. **Contemplatio (contemplation)**—"The lifting up of the heart to God tasting somewhat of the heavenly sweetness and savour."

Du Chastel, who was also known as Guigo de Castro or Guigo II, further described the process as "prayer [rising] to God, and there one finds the treasure one so fervently desires, that is the sweetness and delight of contemplation. And then contemplation comes and yields the harvest of the labor of the other three through a sweet heavenly dew, that the soul drinks in delight and joy."

quote

> Idleness is the enemy of the soul. Therefore the brothers should have specified periods for manual labor as well as for prayerful reading (lectione divina).
>
> —The Rule of Saint Benedict, 48:1

All four stages, or degrees, he wrote, are dependent upon each other, "so bound together," that each was impossible to experience without the other:

What use to spend your time in reading or listening to the deeds of the Holy Fathers, unless we bite and chew on them through meditation, and draw out somewhat and swallow it and send it to the heart, so that we may find, and by this understand, our own defaults, and after such knowing that we set ourselves to work that we may attain those virtues that were in them?

—Guigues du Chastel, from The Ladder of Monks

During the early years of Christianity, lectio divina was widely practiced by both lay people and monks. However, it and other contemplative prayer styles fell out of favor during the Reformation, when religious practices of a mystical nature became suspect. By the nineteenth century, it had all but disappeared except among cloistered Catholic orders like the Benedictines.

symbolism

The Reformation is the term most often used to describe the religious movement that arose in Western Europe during the sixteenth century. Largely led by the German monk Martin Luther, it sought to reform the Catholic church, which had become increasingly powerful and internally corrupt. Instead, it caused a seismic shift in the religious framework of Europe, and split Christianity between Roman Catholicism and Protestantism.

The slow and prayerful reading of scripture and the writings of the church's fathers and mothers is still a cornerstone of the spiritual practices in the Benedictine order and in some other monastic orders. It is also steadily gaining in popularity among Christians and members of other faiths who are seeking ways in which to experience God more deeply and profoundly.

Reading Reverently

At its most basic level, lectio divina is simply praying over the scriptures. While this may make it seem like Bible study, the two are actually quite different. When studying the Bible, we're seekers. We're using God's word as reflected in scripture to learn, to answer questions we might have, or perhaps to encourage or uplift ourselves in some way. And we're actively engaged in the process.

Reading is obviously a part of lectio divina, but it is only a part. In lectio divina, the emphasis is less on reading to gain conscious understanding and more on allowing God's presence to be felt through the words. It is, as M. Basil

Pennington, the Cistercian monk, writer, and revered teacher of contemplative prayer puts it, a way of "letting our Divine Friend speak to us through his inspired and inspiring Word." Instead of actively working at our relationship with God, we instead become receptive to allowing God's spirit to transform us from within.

Unlike most of the reading that we normally do, the emphasis in lectio divina is on quality, not quantity. The goal is to spend time with God through hearing His voice through scripture, not in making it through "x" numbers of Bible passages in "x" amount of time. Instead of racing through the words, we read them slowly—extremely slowly, in fact—and reverently, in order to give each word weight and allow them all to sink into the mind. In this manner, the words can, and often do lead into the other elements of lectio divina— meditation, prayer, and contemplation. They put us in better stead to listen— and hear—the voice of God: a soft voice that is all too often too hard to hear amidst the din of everyday life.

The emphasis on reading slowly and reverently does not mean that lectio divina takes hours to do. In fact, quite the opposite is true. Some who practice it say that instead of prolonging their daily prayer practice, it has instead streamlined it, even cut it in half.

Those who pratice lectio divina regularly also say that it enriches and nourishes their other forms of prayer by making them more aware of their spiritual rhythms, or the natural fluctuation between being spiritually active and spiritually receptive.

quote

Reading seeks, meditation finds, prayer asks, contemplation feels. . . That is to say "Seek and you shall find: knock and the door will be opened for you." That means also, seek through reading, and you will find holy meditation in your thinking; and knock through praying, and the doors shall be opened to you to enter through heavenly contemplation to feel what you desire.

—Guigues du Chastel, in *The Ladder of Monks*

Getting Started with Lectio Divina

One of the aspects of lectio divina that many people find attractive is that it's never experienced the same way twice. It follows no set timelines or rules beyond the forms that one moves through during practice. It can take as little as ten minutes or last as long as two hours—the time spent in the contemplative forms of lectio divina is determined not by us but by God's spirit. You determine what you want to read, when, and where. Like other forms of prayer, however, it does take discipline and a willingness to set aside a certain amount of time for reverent reading during the course of the day. This reading can be done alone or in a small group setting, preferably with no more than a handful of people. Most practitioners, however, prefer to go solo and experience lectio divina on their own, in keeping with the practice's monastic traditions.

Preparing for Practice

Lectio divina can be done virtually anywhere. Just as the desert fathers and mothers remained in constant communication—unceasing prayer—with God by memorizing scripture and meditating upon it wherever they went, so too can modern practitioners take their practice with them wherever they go. However, those who are just learning lectio divina often have a hard time quieting their minds and shutting out distractions when they're praying. For these reasons, beginners often find it easiest to establish their practice in a quiet place before taking it on the road. Practicing at quiet times of the day, such as in the early morning before the rest of the household is awake, can also be helpful.

Many people who practice lectio divina prefer to block out a specific time of day for their practice, and to allow themselves time to move through all of the stages of it during this single period. Another possible way to do lectio divina is to do the sacred reading at night before going to bed, committing to memory the one sentence or word that speaks to you so you can recall it and reflect on it during the next day. If you choose this method, be sure to set aside a specific time for the other parts of lectio divina—prayer and contemplation—each day.

Some people like to enhance their time spent in lectio divina by creating something similar to a monastic environment through closing doors and drawing curtains, lighting candles and burning incense. If you've created a sacred space for your prayer practice, as discussed in Chapter 6, it may be a perfect place for doing lectio divina as well. Be creative with this; use whatever will sweeten the experience for you.

Choosing Your Reading Material

Prior to beginning lectio divina, you'll need to pick a biblical passage as the basis for your prayer. You can use anything that appeals to you; however, it's a good idea to select passages that lend themselves to this prayer style. Popular choices include readings from:

- The Psalms
- The Gospels
- The letters of John
- The Ecclesiastes

Some people use lectio divina to read through the Bible and choose their passages in sequence. Others follow the readings from their church's daily liturgy. The specific words that you choose to read actually matter very little. It is a good idea, however, to select something that's short. Less is more in lectio divina. Remember that the emphasis is on reading reflectively with intention and purpose, not on covering certain amounts of text in prescribed amounts of time. Long-time practitioners of lectio divina have been known to devote months or years meditating on a single sentence. You may find yourself savoring a single word, over and over again, before you're led to move on to the next one. At other times you may find yourself moving through the text more rapidly.

Beginning the Reading

After you've chosen the passage you want to read, find a comfortable posture for reading and praying. Again, there is no right or wrong way to position yourself. If you're most comfortable curled up into a big easy chair, practice lectio divina there. Many practitioners use the same position that they assume for other types of prayer because it's the most comfortable and familiar. You may wish to do the same. Just make sure that the position you choose is conducive to prayer and reading, not for sleep.

discussion question

Can other spiritual writings besides the Bible be used inlectio divina?

While scripture from the Bible is the traditional basis for lectio divina, there's nothing prohibiting the prayerful reading of other sacred texts, including those from other religious traditions. Other possible choices are the works of early Christian writers, such as St. Augustine, St. Theresa of Avila, St. Jerome, and St. Ambrose, or those of modern spiritual authors, such as Thomas Merton, M. Basil Pennington, Kathleen Norris, Thich Nhat Hanh, and others.

Once you're settled into your prayer position, take a few moments to focus on what you're about to do. Allow your mind to become silent. You might find it helpful to use a breath exercise like the ones discussed in Chapter 16. Some people silently recite a special word or phrase, such as "peace," "Lord," "Jesus," "God," "mercy," and so on. Others center their thoughts by focusing on the light of a candle, a cross, or an icon. Do whatever works for you. If you should find your mind wandering off onto other things, simply return your thoughts to the word or object that you have chosen. Continue to focus on your breathing.

After you've enjoyed a few moments of silence, turn to the text that you've chosen and begin reading. Read very, very slowly. Allow your mind to caress the words. Savor them. Read more from the heart than from the head. Try to get a sense of what the writer of the words wished to convey. Allow God's spirit to direct you to a word or phrase for deeper contemplation.

Move forward only when you feel prompted to do so, not when you think you should. If you find yourself merely reading the words, slow down. If you feel like your mind is racing ahead to the next word, slow down. Reading slowly is the part of lectio divina that people find most difficult, but it is essential to this form of prayer.

As you read, you may find a particularly meaningful part of the text that you want to mull over. It could be a sentence, a phrase, or merely a word. Whatever it is, allow it to lead you to the next stage of lectio divina.

Moving into Meditation

Defined in *The Ladder of Monks* as "studious insearching with the mind," the meditative element of lectio divina is where the words move from the mind into the heart. It is a period of reflecting and receiving, of sensing God's presence in the words that have been read. Guigues, the author of *The Ladder of Monks,* notes that this stage should come naturally, with no conscious prompting, and that it may not come right away to those who are new to lectio divina. If it hasn't come for you, don't feel like you've done something wrong, or that you've failed. Don't try to force or will it. God's voice is there; it just might take you more time to learn how to be still enough to hear it. Prayer practice is about many things, but most of all it's about patience.

quote

A spiritual life without discipline is impossible. Discipline is the other side of discipleship. The practice of a spiritual discipline makes us more sensitive to the small, gentle voice of God.
—Henri Nouwen, in *Making All Things New*

If you have moved into the meditative stage of lectio divina, you may feel the need to return to what you have read, and to read it over again, perhaps once, maybe more. As you do, ask yourself why this particular word or phrase is resonating with you. Ponder the significance of the words and why they're reaching out to you. Let your mind touch on the various ways in which they might reflect God's presence in your life, or the message He's speaking to you through them.

The word *love,* for example, might lead to remembering a time when you felt God's presence so clearly that it made you shiver with joy. It might stir up memories of people who have touched your life. From there you might reflect on God's true love. The key here is not to try to guide where your mind goes. Let it travel unfettered. Stay open to the experience.

Prayer

The third form of lectio divina is prayer. Like all prayer, it is a dialogue with the Almighty. Here, however, prayer also takes the form of an offering of self, of what you have learned during meditation, of opening the heart to God and allowing Him to enter in. This prayer can be voiced or spoken with the heart and mind.

Contemplation

The final stage of lectio divina is one of resting in God's presence. It requires nothing more than just staying quietly and simply being in the place you came to through the other three stages, and being open to receiving the grace of God. At times His grace may infuse you, at other times it may not. Those who have experienced God's grace during the contemplative form of lectio divina have described it as "pure love" or as being the most intimate communication with God that is possible in life.

What Comes Next

If you're practicing lectio divina on your own, you can simply rest in silence in God's presence until such time that you feel you're ready to return to your normal routine. In the group practice of lectio divina, it is customary to discuss what was learned at the conclusion of a session.

Over time, as you continue to practice lectio divina, what you gain through your practice will spill over into the other parts of your life.

CHAPTER 18

Centering Prayer

Sometimes the quest to unite with God through prayer becomes too intellectual. We try too hard to use logic and reason to understand the mysteries of faith, and in doing so the understanding we seek becomes even more elusive. Religious mystics of long ago encouraged believers to put their minds on hold and instead use their hearts and souls to connect with the Divine. Centering prayer is an increasingly popular method that uses this approach.

What Is Centering Prayer?

Like lectio divina, which was discussed in Chapter 17, centering prayer is a prayer practice built around centuries-old contemplative traditions in the Christian church and on the teachings of Christian mystics. In some respects, it resembles meditation as it entails sitting quietly for a specified period of time. And, as is done in many forms of meditation, those who practice centering prayer invoke a specific word, similar to a mantra, at various times during a centering prayer session.

The goal of centering prayer is to put aside earthly thoughts in order to create interior silence. It is this silence, when it is accomplished, that allows us to experience God on a very different level than what we're normally accustomed to. As Thomas Keating writes in *Open Mind, Open Heart*, one of the best-known texts on centering prayer, "The root of prayer is interior silence . . . It is the opening of mind and heart, body and feelings—our whole being—to God, the Ultimate Mystery, beyond words, thoughts, and emotions."

Putting aside thoughts during centering prayer, however, doesn't mean resisting or suppressing them. Instead, they are accepted when they arise, and then gently and lovingly released. The goal is to move our awareness beyond them to the ultimate mystery of God.

quote

> Let love alone speak: the simple desire to be one with the Presence, to forget self, and to rest in the Ultimate Mystery.
> —Thomas Keating, in *Open Mind, Open Heart*

Although centering prayer is actually a part of the contemplative prayer tradition, people often use the two terms interchangeably when referring to this prayer style. In this chapter, we'll describe centering prayer as centering prayer, and use the term contemplative prayer when discussing the tradition to which it belongs.

The Basis for Centering Prayer

Like lectio divina, centering prayer is very much a part of the spiritual traditions of the Christian church. It also has strong ties to the meditative practices of other major religions, especially Buddhism. However, unlike lectio divina, centering prayer is a modern practice based on these ancient spiritual traditions. It is similar to the contemplative practices of the mystics of centuries ago, and especially those described in a fourteenth-century book called *The Cloud of Unknowing,* but there are no references to a specific practice called centering prayer in any of the historic writings on Christian mysticism.

Centering prayer as a modern contemplative practice came about largely as the result of the Second Vatican Council in 1965. Among many of the reforms suggested by the council was a call for Catholics to depend less on priests and other church officials and more on themselves when it came to finding ways to enrich their spiritual lives. Learning more about other religious faiths and renewing the age-old practice of contemplative prayer were seen as two ways that would foster this enrichment.

In the years that followed, a number of younger Catholics heeded the Vatican's directive. However, since they knew little of the contemplative traditions in their own church, they generally studied Eastern religions and began to integrate meditative practices related to these religions into their own religious practices.

In the early 1970s, Thomas Keating, a Trappist monk and the head of St. Joseph Abbey in Spencer, Massachusetts, noticed that young visitors to the abbey who had studied with Eastern religious leaders possessed an unusual spiritual maturity for their age. They were, as Keating writes in *Intimacy with God,* ". . . putting in twenty to thirty minutes of meditation twice a day in spite of being in college or professional life . . ." at a time when cloistered monks and nuns were finding it hard to practice one daily session of mental prayer. Intrigued by the practices and experiences of these young people, and their similarities to the ancient forms of Christian contemplation, Keating engaged his fellow monks in a revival. The goal: to bring back prayer forms based on the Christian contemplative tradition, and to come up with a way to make it more attractive—and more available—to anyone wishing to enrich their spiritual lives.

As part of their efforts, Keating and two other monks—William Meninger and M. Basil Pennington—met regularly with teachers from Eastern religions. The three monks also mined the writings of the church's mystics and saints—the fathers and mothers of the desert, St. Theresa of Avila, St. John of the Cross, Gregory of Nyssa, and St. Francis de Sales among them—to put the contemporary practice they were developing into a historical context.

Entering into The Cloud of Unknowing

One of these works—*The Cloud of Unknowing*, a fourteenth-century mystical classic by an unknown author (most likely an English monk)—was the primary inspiration for the format for practicing and teaching contemplative prayer. In it, believers are encouraged to put aside intellectual efforts to understand God, as He cannot be fully and truly known through the human intellect. Contemplation, or allowing oneself to enter into a union with God completely and without reservation, is the only way in which the "cloud of unknowing" that exists between man and God can be transcended.

factum

The Cloud of Unknowing, which first appeared in the second half of the fourteenth century, consists of a number of short letters describing mystical prayer that were sent to a particular monk. The original Middle English text still survives and has also been translated into modern English for ease of reading.

The concept of the "sacred word," which is key to centering prayer, also came from *The Cloud of Unknowing*. The use of a word, preferably "a little word of one syllable," was "powerful enough to pierce the heavens" and was the only prayer that God needed to hear. Unlike a mantra, which is repeatedly chanted throughout a meditation, the sacred word would instead only be invoked when needed.

Centering Prayer Expands

Once the format for centering prayer was established, the monks began teaching it to others through retreats and workshops. As the format was refined, it became known as centering prayer, a phrase used by the contemporary Christian mystic Thomas Merton in his writings.

In the early 1980s, Keating gave a series of talks on prayer at a parish in Aspen, Colorado, where he had relocated after leaving St. Joseph Abbey. Based on the popularity of these talks, Keating helped found Contemplative Outreach, a network of individuals and small faith communities dedicated to practicing centering prayer and teaching others how to do it.

Today, countless individuals around the world practice centering prayer, either by themselves, in small groups, or at retreats. They do so in addition to their other forms of prayer as centering prayer isn't meant to replace them. Instead, the practice is done to enrich other aspects of one's prayer life. But the benefits of centering prayer go beyond this. Those who practice it regularly say that they are more at peace with their life on a day-to-day basis, and that they can more easily discern God's presence in the ordinary. It also makes them more aware of their own spirituality. In fact, most of what is gained during centering prayer is manifested before and after, not during the practice itself.

Learning Centering Prayer

Workshops and retreats are regularly held to introduce the practice of centering prayer to others. Because this prayer style does differ in approach from other forms of prayer, attending a workshop led by someone who is trained in the practice is often the best way to learn its basics. However, it's definitely possible to learn how to do centering prayer on your own. If you plan on taking the latter approach, the following information will help you get started. You will also find some additional resources on centering prayer listed in Appendix B.

Since there is a very specific method of practicing centering prayer, we've based much of the discussion that follows on a brief pamphlet that describes the process, which is also listed in Appendix B.

Practicing Centering Prayer

There are four basic steps to centering prayer:

1. Choosing a sacred word, which "is a symbol of your intention to consent to God's presence and action within."
2. Sitting down, closing your eyes, and silently speaking your sacred word to indicate your desire to enter into God's presence and action within you.
3. Returning to the sacred word to dispel thoughts when they enter your mind and return your focus to God.
4. Ending your prayer time by sitting in silence and with your eyes closed for a few moments.

Most of the time, centering prayer is done privately, or with a spouse or partner. Most people find that private practice is the easiest way to become familiar with the centering experience. If there is a centering prayer group in your area, consider praying with the group on occasion—once a month, maybe more—once you've learned the basics. Many people find these groups to be a great support, and a good way to keep their practice on track.

In keeping with the precepts in *The Cloud of Unknowing*, some who practice centering prayer preface their practice with a short period of lectio divina. Another option is to simply read a short selection of your own choosing from the Bible and go into centering prayer from there. However, the two contemplative practices fit together extremely well. In fact, centering prayer mirrors the contemplative phase of lectio divina, and is an easy way to enter into it.

quote

So I want you to understand clearly that for beginners and those a little advanced in contemplation, reading or hearing the word of God must precede pondering it and without time given to serious reflection there will be no genuine prayer.

—From *The Cloud of Unknowing*

Choosing the Sacred Word

The sacred word, according to the guidelines on centering prayer, "expresses our intention to be in God's presence and to yield to the divine action." In *The Cloud of Unknowing,* it is stressed that the most appropriate word is one that reflects the nature of prayer itself. For this reason, most people pick a word that in some way reflects God, the object of their prayers.

The sacred word can be chosen by praying to God and asking for His guidance. Some people simply ponder various words, rolling them around in their minds, and settle on the one that seems to be the best fit. Possible choices include:

- God
- Peace
- Lord
- Love
- Jesus
- Abba
- Father
- Shalom
- Mother

Whatever approach you take, let the word you choose be your choice. Don't ask for help on this from anyone else but God. Take however much time is necessary to choose it. You want the word to be one that you can stick with for a while. The guidelines for centering prayer state that the sacred word should not be changed during the prayer time, as doing so would engage the mind and require a return to thinking. The same can be said for exchanging one sacred word for another every time you pray. In general, it's better to find a word that resonates with you, one that can accompany you for a good while on your spiritual journey. There is nothing that says you can't change your sacred word to something else somewhere along the line if you feel so inclined. Changing it too often, however, might disrupt your practice.

Beginners of centering prayer often place far too much emphasis on the sacred word. While it is important, it's often not for the reasons they think it is. What the word actually means is of little importance. The intention behind it, which is to open oneself to God, is what's important.

discussion question

Is choosing a sacred word essential to practicing centering prayer? While most people do prefer to use a sacred word, you can also use what is called a sacred gaze, which means turning your focus inward to God, as if you were looking at Him. Some people imagine a visual image to help them let go of their thoughts.

Other things you'll want to determine before you begin your centering prayer practice is when you'll practice and how you'll time it. The standard period of practice for centering prayer is twenty minutes every day, twice a day, preferably in the morning and before supper, although some people go longer than this. Many people start with one twenty-minute session and add the second at a later point, whereas others find they only have the time for one session and they may extend this one session as the spirit moves them. Two sessions, however, are strongly encouraged, and can be especially beneficial in establishing the practice as part of your ongoing prayer practice.

There are a variety of ways to time the minutes spent in centering prayer. Timers are the most popular, and there are also watches that can be set to indicate when prayer time is over. Cassette tapes and CDs are also available to measure the time spent in centering prayer.

Introducing the Sacred Word

The second step in centering prayer details the actual beginning of the practice, as you can choose your sacred word at any time before you begin centering prayer. It entails sitting comfortably, allowing your mind to settle down, and invoking the sacred word "as a symbol of your consent to God's presence and action within."

Finding a Comfortable Position

Finding a comfortable position for centering prayer is just like finding one for any other kind of prayer. The idea is to settle on a prayer posture that you can remain in for the specified time; however, it shouldn't be so comfortable that you find it difficult to stay awake while praying. The guidelines for centering prayer suggest using a chair that helps you keep your back straight and allows your feet to touch the ground. Other possible prayer supports include a meditation cushion, such as those used in Zen practice, or a meditation bench. If you're using a cushion, it's perfectly all right to sit in a lotus or half-lotus position.

Due to the quiet and contemplative nature of centering prayer, it is best not to do it when lying down, as this position makes it too easy to fall asleep. And, because the eyes are to be kept closed during centering prayer, it's definitely not a discipline you'll want to practice while walking or driving a car.

Finally, find a time and place where you can be away from noise and clutter. Don't set yourself up for failure by trying to practice at times when you are likely to be interrupted. If you decide that centering prayer is right for you, and you stick with your practice, you'll become expert at entering into your interior silence even when the world is swirling around you.

Many people like to set the stage for centering prayer by lighting a candle to signify God's presence. Incense is another popular choice. Not only does it enrich the centering experience, the smoke from the incense serves as a symbol of our prayers traveling upward to God.

factum

Centering prayer is best practiced on an empty stomach, as eating a heavy meal can cause drowsiness. If you're hungry, and it's near mealtime, eat a light snack before practice and save your large meal for later. Some people find that centering prayer disrupts their sleep patterns if they practice it before going to bed. For this reason, practicing at other times of the day is encouraged.

Invoking the Sacred Word

Once you've settled into your prayer position, it is time to invoke the sacred word. This is done simply by closing your eyes and saying the sacred word silently and gently in your mind. The guidelines for centering prayer describe this as "laying a feather on a piece of absorbent cotton." Others describe their perception of the sacred word as being just slightly out of focus, floating on a rivulet of water, or being carried on a soft cloud.

In any case, the goal here is not to actively focus on the sacred word as the center point of your prayer, but to allow the word to enter into your subconscious where it can draw your heart and mind toward God. As such, it's not meant to be repeated constantly like a mantra as doing so would make the word, instead of God's presence, the focus of your efforts. It should instead rest lightly in your mind, there when you need it but not as the center of your attention.

quote

Do not use clever logic to examine or explain this word to yourself nor allow yourself to ponder its ramifications as if this sort of thing could possibly increase your love. I do not believe reasoning ever helps in the contemplative work.

—**From** *The Cloud of Unknowing*

Don't meditate on the sacred word, or contemplate it. Just think it silently. As you do, your mind will empty of thoughts. Over time, the sacred word might become vague or completely disappear from your consciousness. This is perfectly all right, and is, in fact, a good thing. Don't actively try to bring it back unless you need it. Let it drift down inside you to where it wants to go.

Returning Gently to the Sacred Word

You will return to the sacred word if you find thoughts rumbling through your head. Thoughts—an umbrella term for the various emotions, images, and sensations that arise during centering prayer—are a normal part of centering prayer, although many people who are just learning this practice feel like they're not doing things right when they have them.

Keep in mind that the goal of centering prayer is not to be free of all thoughts, or to feel like you have to fight with them if they arise. Instead, you want to acknowledge their presence for a second, and then let them go so they can pass right by you. There will be times when you won't be able to clear your head, or when it will take you a long time to do so. At other times you won't be aware of them at all.

When you become aware of thoughts, just bring the sacred word up a little higher into your consciousness. Think it slowly and softly in your mind. Start with one invocation. If the thoughts won't pass by easily, and you need to think it again, by all means do so. But don't start repeating it in your head like a chant. Just use it as often as you need it. It might be a lot at first.

During your practice, expect to come in and out of your interior silence as thoughts arise. When they do, return to the word until you drop back into your silence.

Some people who have practiced centering prayer for a long time no longer have the need to think of the sacred word. They've reached the point where they're capable of moving into interior silence without it.

As you continue to practice centering prayer, you'll find that God's spirit inches in and takes increasingly greater control of your prayer. You can't will this, or wish or hope for it. You can only remain open and receptive to His presence.

quote

The sacred word is only a symbol. It is an arrow pointing in the direction intended by our will. It is a gesture or sign of accepting God as He is. Exactly what that is, we don't know.

—Thomas Keating, in *Open Mind, Open Heart*

Quieting the Chatter

Quieting the mind so it quits chattering away is one of the challenges of centering prayer. It's amazing, in fact, how much centering prayer makes you aware of the stream of things that constantly runs through your head. However, this constant mental chitchat is what stands in the way of our being able to experience God more deeply. For this reason, it's essential to learn how to use the sacred word, or whatever alternative method you've decided on, to put your mental activities on hold and create inner silence. Some practitioners envision putting their thoughts into a little lockbox, to be opened after they're done praying.

What you don't want to do is actively focus on having no thoughts, or on making your mind a blank. Again, keep in mind that thoughts, whatever they might be about, are a natural part of the process.

Other Things You Might Notice While Praying

Some people notice increased awareness of body twitches, or aches and pains. You might, in fact, find it extremely hard to sit still at times, especially if you're coming into centering prayer after a stressful day. These are all signs of your body relaxing and resting in prayer. If possible, try to ignore them. They usually go away. If you absolutely have to scratch an itch, go ahead. But try to stay as still as you can while you're praying. If necessary, rest your mind on them briefly, and then return to the sacred word.

At times you might also notice that your arms and legs feel either very heavy or very light. This is also to be expected and is a sign that you've reached a deep level of spiritual attentiveness.

Sitting in Silence with Your Eyes Closed

When your prayer period has come to a close, simply rest with God for a few minutes with your eyes closed. Don't rush this time—it is important to give yourself a few moments to readjust to the world around you. When you feel ready to return to the outside world, open your eyes slowly. Continue to rest for a bit longer.

Many people like to recite "The Lord's Prayer" during this period. You could also recite a different prayer of your own choosing, or simply remain silent until such time that you're ready to speak.

symbolism

The benefits of a moment of silence are immeasurable. Just take the time to breathe, eyes closed, and let your thoughts drift and gently fall into place. Once done, you will feel reinvigorated and ready to tackle life's stresses.

Challenges of Centering Prayer

One of the biggest problems that people have when practicing centering prayer, and especially when they are new to the practice, is dealing with mental intrusions. As previously noted, it is exceedingly difficult to get our mind to shut down and quit chattering at us, and it always seems like this is an even greater problem when our intention is to become extremely still.

The best way to get through this is to continue your practice. As you do, you will become much more adept at entering into and maintaining your interior silence. The other thing you'll be able to do is learn to accept your thoughts for what they are, which will also help you let them flow past you more easily. As you do, you'll be better able to seek God's inward presence, and to being open to the inflow of God's grace.

CHAPTER 19

Prayer in Motion

Most of the time we spend in prayer consists of staying in one place. We sit or kneel in our spot, often with our heads bowed. Being still is a time-honored way of praying. Even the Bible tells us to "be still, and know that I am God." But it is not the only way to pray. You can also take your prayer practice on the road.

Exercising Body and Spirit

At first blush, prayer and exercise may not seem like a match made in heaven. However, before you dismiss this combo out of hand, take a moment to consider the benefits of talking to God while you're moving your body. It can eliminate the "I don't have the time" syndrome that kicks in all too often when we try to do things that are good for us. Busy schedules can make it difficult for many people to squeeze in both prayer and exercise on a regular basis, but they also take the blame for lax habits in both arenas.

quote

> Above all, do not lose your desire to walk. Every day I walk myself into a state of well-being, and walk away from every illness. I have walked myself into my best thoughts, and I know of no thought so burdensome that one cannot walk away from it.
>
> —Søren Kierkegaard, in a letter to Jette

The twenty minutes a day that health experts say is the minimum amount of exercise we should get also happens to be a great length of time for a prayer session. Instead of choosing between prayer and exercise, why not combine the two? Doing so can go a long way toward freeing up more time in anyone's life.

Mixing prayer and exercise can also bolster your physical and spiritual health in ways that go beyond the benefits of doing each separately. Although they are seemingly disparate activities, prayer and exercise actually share several important qualities. They both require concentration, and they both require work.

Combining the two can create a synergy where each practice enhances the other and lifts it to higher levels. People who pray and exercise on a regular basis often talk about getting so caught up in what they're doing that they don't notice things like time and distance. Because of this, they often spend more time praying and exercising when they do both together than when they do them separately.

Finding Inner Quiet Through Repetitive Motion

Exercise can add an extra dimension to all forms of prayer, including—believe it or not—contemplative prayer. The repetitive motion that is essential to many forms of exercise, such as stroking the oars on a rowing scull, cranking the pedals on a bicycle, or putting one foot in front of the other when walking, helps focus the mind and blocks out outer and inner disturbances. It can also help disperse extra energy that can sometimes interfere with prayer. The rhythm of the repetition, and the attention that we pay to it, can create the same inner stillness that is reached in more stationary forms of contemplative prayer. It elicits what cardiologist Herbert Benson calls "the relaxation response," a feeling of centeredness and calmness that allows the mind to take a break from its usual activities.

factum

Prayer walking is also called spirited walking, or walking meditation. One form is fast; the other is slow. If you walk often enough and at a pace fast enough to raise your heart rate into the working zone, prayer walking can also make a significant contribution to your fitness level and health.

Calming the Jitters

While many people can comfortably sit still and pray, not everyone can. Some people have such high energy levels that just the thought of having to stay in one place makes them nervous. Others simply prefer being active to being still. If you tend to fidget while you pray, or you get bored when you sit still during prayer, you might find the combination of prayer and exercise to be a real boon to your prayer practice.

Prayer Walking

Just about any form of repetitive exercise—bicycling, jogging, walking, rowing, cross-country skiing, even raking the leaves up from your lawn or sweeping your sidewalk—lends itself well to prayer on the go. Of them, walking is a top pick. It is easy and simple. You don't have to wait for leaves to fall to do it. It can be done almost anytime and virtually anywhere—indoors and out, in gymnasiums and shopping centers, in parks and on bridle paths. The equipment needs are simple—a good pair of shoes and some comfortable clothing is about all that is necessary.

Prayer walking is exactly what the words suggest—praying while you are walking. There are various forms of prayer walking. One in particular involves choosing a specific area, walking through it, and praying for everything you see—people, animals, houses, schools, businesses, you name it.

While there is nothing wrong with this type of prayer walking, it emphasizes outwardly directed prayer. And, it has little to do with integrating walking into prayer practice—for the most part, it can be done just as easily in a car. For this reason, this type of walking and praying is not the focus of this chapter. Here, we'll talk about the forms of prayer walking that combine mindful breathing with movement and meditation.

quote

> Walking meditation is really to enjoy the walking—walking not in order to arrive, but just to walk. The purpose is to be in the present moment and, aware of our breathing and our walking, to enjoy each step.
> —Thich Nhat Hanh, in *Peace Is Every Step*

The Mechanics of Prayer Walking

Prayer walking can be done fast or slow. There is no right or wrong speed, only the speed at which you want to go. If you are interested in emphasizing the benefits of exercise during your prayer walks, you'll want to walk fast. If relaxation and meditation are your goals, then walk slowly. Either way, you might find it easier to get into a state of inner stillness. Many people find that the rhythmic motion of walking soothes their minds and allows them to relax better than sitting still and praying.

If you already walk for fitness, you won't have to slow down to prayer walk unless you want to decrease your speed. In fact, praying while you walk might even cause you to pick up your pace.

Some people like to venture out on their own or with their dogs by their sides. Others enjoy the camaraderie of a group prayer walk. Walking alone, however, is usually less distracting and more conducive to praying. It also allows you to be silent, which is essential for a good prayer walk. Many people like to listen to music when they walk. Doing so when prayer walking, however, will keep you from listening to God.

factum

Slow forms of walking prayer are very similar to the Zen practice of kinkin, a walking meditation in which attention is focused on each step, and the breath is measured and controlled. In Zen practice, walking meditation is often done in addition to sitting meditation to keep meditation practice in balance.

The prayerfulness part of prayer walking comes first from walking in silence. Being silent allows you to turn your attention toward God. It also allows you to focus on the other aspects of prayer walking, which are basically the same regardless of how fast or how slow you choose to go:

- **Breathing**—In prayer walking, breathing is deep and cleansing, and it matches the cadence of your stride. As you focus on your breathing, it will guide you into your place of inner quiet.

- **Stepping**—Zen prayer walking almost looks like slow motion, but that slow movement allows those who practice it to be mindful of every part of every step they make: raising the foot, lifting the foot, pushing the foot, dropping the foot, and so on. It isn't necessary to go this slowly during your own prayer walks unless you want to follow the Zen way. Nor do you have to have your attention level set quite that high, but you do want to be mindful of how your feet strike the ground and lift off of it. This awareness is also part of the prayer walking experience.

- **Counting**—Prayer walkers both count the length of their breaths and the number of steps that they take. On the face of it, this sounds confusing, but it isn't when you do it.

- **Praying, or focusing on a sacred word**—Prayer walking is a perfect form for saying short prayers or sacred words. The words of the "Jesus Prayer," "Lord Jesus Christ, Son of God, have mercy upon me, a sinner," are a good match for the cadence of prayer walking. Other possibilities are mantra-like words such as om, peace, love, calm, God, father, and so on. You can use any word you'd like. According to researchers, choosing words with spiritual or personal significance will yield better results as they're more effective in focusing your efforts.

discussion question

What is a good length for a prayer walk?
It is a good idea to measure your time spent praying and walking in minutes, not in miles. Twenty to thirty minutes is about par for the course; walks of longer or shorter duration are perfectly fine as well.

It can be a good idea to decide where you are going to walk before you set out. If you are walking outdoors, it can be nice to be surrounded by beauty and quiet as you stroll. However, the inner focus of prayer walking means you can do it virtually anywhere, even on busy city streets teeming with cars and people. You can even prayer walk in shopping malls. Treadmills work, too.

Gearing Up to Walk

As previously mentioned, prayer walking does not require much in the way of equipment. If you don't have a good pair of walking shoes, however, it is a good idea to do your feet and the rest of your body a favor and get some before you start out. While walking is usually not the most strenuous form of exercise you might do, you also don't want achy feet or sore shins to interfere with your practice.

If you plan to go fast on your walks, you'll need to wear shoes that can take the additional wear and tear that speed can create. There are a number of manufacturers that make athletic shoes that work well for performance or speed walking. Finding the right shoes are especially important for you as ones that fit right will both help you walk fast and help you avoid injuries.

Walking Slow, Walking Fast

All forms of prayer walking begin with simply walking forward. As you walk, keep your body relaxed and calm. Stand tall, but not rigid. Think of your spine as a spring, not a stick. Keep your head aligned with your shoulders and hips—don't walk with your chin thrust forward or down as this will cause upper body fatigue. Keep it roughly perpendicular to the ground. Let your shoulders drop away from your ears. Let your arms and hands move naturally along with your feet. Hold your hands however you feel most comfortable, either at your waist or lower down by your sides. Just let them flow along with you as you walk. To avoid visual distractions, focus your gaze at a point about four feet in front of you.

If you are walking slowly, let your body's natural energy govern your pace. You might feel like walking faster on some days, slower on others. Don't feel like you have to cover a certain distance in a certain amount of time. Many people start out by walking very quickly, like they're in a race. You might do so as well. You might also find it hard to keep your pace steady at first. This will become easier to do over time.

In *Peace Is Every Step*, Thich Nhat Hanh suggests walking a little slower than your normal pace, which will better coordinate your breathing with your steps. In fact, using your breathing to pace yourself is a great way to find the prayer-walking pace that works best for you. Try taking the same number of steps—two, three, or four, whatever works best for you—with each inhalation and exhalation.

quote

Each step we take will create a cool breeze, refreshing our body and mind. Every step makes a flower bloom under our feet. We can do it only if we do not think of the future or the past, if we know that life can only be found in the present moment.

—Thich Nhat Hanh, in *Peace Is Every Step*

Regardless of your pace, it's important to pay attention to your breath. As you do, count their length. In—one, two, three. Out—one, two, three. Once you have this down, start counting your steps. Then start matching your prayer, or your sacred word, to your counts. This does sound a lot like patting your head and rubbing your belly. If you have a hard time keeping it all together, just focus on your breathing. The other parts will come in time.

As you walk, you may want to stop from time to time to admire the beauty of nature. When you do, keep breathing deeply and slowly. When you're ready to start walking again, just pick up where you left off.

At the end of your prayer walk, allow yourself a few minutes to shift your focus back to the world around you. If you've been walking at a pretty good clip, also use this period for a cooldown. Keep moving until your heart rate is fairly close to normal. When it is, treat yourself to about ten minutes of stretching. You should be very relaxed by the time you are done.

Walking in Circles

Walking slowly and meditatively along the coiled, circular paths of a labyrinth is a another very popular type of walking prayer. Tracing the mandala-like patterns of a labyrinth is an ancient spiritual practice dating back some four thousand years. In fact, of all the spiritual tools known to humankind, labyrinths are some of the oldest.

factum

Labyrinths and mazes are often thought of as being similar. They are actually very different. A labyrinth is unicursal, meaning it only has one path in and out. The path never crosses itself or comes to a dead end. Mazes are more like puzzles and contain more than one path. Successfully entering and exiting a maze requires choosing the right paths. Labyrinths require no such choices.

Where and how labyrinths first developed isn't known, but it is believed that some of the earliest labyrinths were created for worshipping female gods and staging fertility rituals. Ancient turf labyrinths—some of them still in use today—have been found in England, Germany, and Scandinavia. There is evidence of labyrinth use at various times in many other countries as well, including India, France, Egypt, Iceland, Peru, and parts of North America.

We also do not know exactly when labyrinths became part of Christian spiritual practice as early records do not contain much mention of their use. However, it is known that they served as a substitute for making pilgrimages to Jerusalem, a practice that was central to early Christianity. When the Crusades made it unsafe to travel to the holy city, Catholic leaders designated seven cathedrals in Europe as pilgrimage destinations, and placed a labyrinth on the floor of each.

factum

In Greek mythology, a labyrinth on the island of Crete was created by Daedalus for King Minos to contain the Minotaur, a monstrous man-headed bull. Archaeologist Sir Arthur Evans, when digging on Crete in the early 1900s, uncovered the ruins of a massive Bronze-age building believed to be the palace of the legendary king, along with enough traces of a labyrinth to prove that the palace was built along the lines of one.

Why a labyrinth? From ancient times, the form's combination of a circle and a spiral was considered symbolic of wholeness. Then, as now, traveling along the labyrinth's path to its center and back out again serves as a metaphor for life's journeys, and for our spiritual journeys with God.

Rather than risk losing their lives to the skirmishes of holy wars, followers of the Christian faith instead could fulfill their sacred vows by traveling to the cathedral cities and walking the cathedral labyrinths.

In the ongoing desire to connect modern spiritual practices to ancient traditions, labyrinth walking has gained new popularity among modern spiritual seekers of all types. Hundreds of labyrinths have been built in the United States since the 1990s when the practice was revitalized, largely through the efforts of Lauren Artress, an Episcopalian priest, who in 1992 installed a replica of the Chartres labyrinth in San Francisco's Grace Cathedral.

In keeping with their traditional use, most labyrinths have been established in spiritual settings—churches, retreat centers, outdoor prayer and meditation gardens and the like. They are also increasingly becoming fixtures in hospitals and rehabilitation centers, where they are used to assist healing, both physically and spiritually. Portable labyrinths are even brought into jails and prisons to help inmates develop their spiritual lives.

The Benefits of Labyrinth Walking

Following the winding path of a labyrinth requires you to focus on what is ahead of you. However, because you know where you are going—to the center of the labyrinth—there are no decisions to be made along the way. Unlike mazes, a labyrinth has only one circular path that winds its way to the center and back out again. All you do is follow the direction of the labyrinth, and allow it to lead you. Doing so puts your logical and rational self on hold, and allows your more intuitive side to come forward. In other words, you shift from right-brain thinking to left-brain thinking.

symbolism

The cathedral in Chartres (outside of Paris, France) contains the only remaining medieval labyrinth. Constructed entirely of pieces of individually carved inlaid marble, it measures 42 feet in diameter. The total length of the path is close to a quarter mile long. According to church legend, the design of the Chartres labyrinth was a part of King Solomon's temple, and was carried by the Knights Templar to France during the Middle Ages.

Because there is no right or wrong direction to take when walking a labyrinth, they are amazingly user friendly. People walk them at whatever pace they choose. Some even skip or crawl. Pausing to reflect on emotions or thoughts that arise along the way is standard practice. Many people walk the labyrinth as a centering exercise. Others enter it with a question or a concern and use the time they spend in it to pray. Still others simply focus on the path ahead of them and enjoy the walk. It can also be an alternative to sitting meditation.

Labyrinths are nondenominational and open to all. They offer the opportunity to reconnect to faith, or experience it in new ways, to everyone who walks them.

The Phases of Labyrinth Walking

The labyrinth experience consists of three phases, or stages:

1. **Traveling to the center of the labyrinth (purgation)**—The first stage of a labyrinth walk is symbolic of leaving everyday life behind. Other words used to describe it are releasing, surrendering, or letting go. Most people start this stage by pausing briefly at the entrance, taking a moment to center and focus. They may say a prayer or voice an intention to guide the spiritual walk they are about to take. Some people acknowledge the experience to come with a bow or a nod. Christians often genuflect or make the sign of the cross before entering.

2. **The time spent in the center of the labyrinth (illumination)**—The center of the labyrinth is a place for prayer and meditation. This is where labyrinth walkers open themselves to God's guidance. There are no specific guidelines governing how much time you spend in the center or what you do there. Many people like to reflect back on the journey they made. Others close their eyes to it and simply rest in God's presence.

3. **Traveling back out of the labyrinth (union)**—The "letting out" phase of labyrinth walking prepares walkers for re-entering the world, taking with them the knowledge they gained in the labyrinth. It is customary to end the experience in much the same way you began it.

quote

> Each step we take will create a cool breeze, refreshing our body and mind. Every step makes a flower bloom under our feet. We can do it only if we do not think of the future or the past, if we know that life can only be found in the present moment.
>
> —Thich Nhat Hanh, in *Peace Is Every Step*

A labyrinth walk is not meant to be a once-in-a-lifetime experience. Although the practice may seem odd or off-putting at first, most people are hooked after their first walk. Many will repeat the experience immediately. Others schedule an annual labyrinth walk as part of their spiritual renewal. Some people walk them every day.

Finding a Labyrinth to Walk

Labyrinths are steadily increasing in popularity, which means that there is a good chance that you'll find one near you to walk. Check with local churches and spiritual centers. If you have trouble finding one, there are several Internet-based locators that can help. You'll find one listed in Appendix B along with several other labyrinth resources, including one that you can use to do a virtual labyrinth walk.

Although it is not much for exercise, you can also walk alabyrinth with your fingers. These personal labyrinths are great for times when walking a full-sized labyrinth isn't possible. Many labyrinth fans use a personal labyrinth every day for prayer, centering activity, or meditation.

CHAPTER 20

Living a Prayerful Life

A prayer life never stands still. We are constantly called to lift our hearts up, to keep moving forward, to learn and relearn from God, to continue seeking His voice and His counsel as we face the joys and challenges of life. On the following pages are some suggestions for continuing your prayer journey, and continuing to move toward God.

Praying with Your Family

Sharing your prayer practice with others—and especially with spouses, partners, and children—can be one of the richest and most gratifying ways you could ever wish for extending your prayer life. As Mother Teresa said, "Among yourselves you can share your own experience of your need to pray, and how you found prayer, and what the fruit of prayer has been in your own lives."

Taking your prayer life beyond its customary boundaries—out of the box, so to speak—can feel a little strange at first. If you're used to praying by yourself, you might be self-conscious about sharing your communications with God where others can hear them. Feeling like you have to be an exemplar at your praying is pretty common when you're asking your family to join in. After all, you want to set a good example, right?

Well, the best example you can set is to expand your prayer practice so it does incorporate your family, and especially your children. In fact, the Bible instructs parents to do so.

quote

Hear O Israel: The Lord our God, the Lord is one. Love the Lord your God with all your heart and with all your soul and with all your strength. These commandments that I give you today are to be upon your hearts. Impress them on your children. Talk about them when you sit at home and when you walk along the road, when you lie down and when you get up. Tie them as symbols on your hands and bind them on your foreheads. Write them on the doorframes of your houses and on your gates.

—Deuteronomy 6:4–9

The most important thing to remember about family prayer is that you don't need to be a prayer expert. What's more, your family won't even expect you to be. Keep the basic precepts of prayer in mind—that it's communicating with God and that we never reach expert level in doing this. There is always more to learn. (That's a lesson, by the way, that you want to make sure your kids understand as well.) When you pray with your family, they'll learn from you and you'll learn from them, too.

symbolism

There's nothing to guarantee that your family will be gung ho about your plans at first. In fact, they may not be. Your children might even look at you funny. But don't let this deter you from making prayer a part of your family's routine.

Getting Started

There's really no magic formula or step-by-step manual for beginning a family prayer practice. However, you can set the stage for success by putting together a little game plan that outlines the basics and establishes your intentions, just like you did when you started your own prayer practice. It should include the following:

- **When you'll pray**—Praying before dinner and nighttime prayers before bed are pretty standard. You may want to add an additional prayer session at another time during the week. Keep things pretty loose.
- **Where you'll pray**—For nighttime prayers, bedrooms are best. Dining-room tables work great for other prayer times. Try to pick a spot where you can gather closely and intimately.
- **How you'll pray**—Choose the format for your prayer time. Remember, simpler is better, especially with small children.

Don't go it alone and assume the sole burden for determining these factors. You want your entire family to pray together, right? Make them a part of the process. Ask your spouse and your children what they would like to accomplish by praying as a family, what their concerns are, and what they would like to pray about. Don't make too big a deal out of this. It doesn't have to be a family meeting. Remember, prayer is a discipline, not regimentation. Keep things light, start simply, and allow God to direct your efforts.

Praying with Young Children

If your children are very young, keep your prayer times short and sweet. Little kids have short attention spans, and they'll get bored and fidgety if prayer time goes on for more than a few minutes or so. If they are already in the habit of reciting nighttime prayers, you might consider adding to their existing practice by gathering the whole family together for a quick prayer at this time. If they're not, one way to start nighttime prayers is with the classic child's prayer (if you've ever wondered where it came from, it first appeared in the *New England Primer,* printed in 1814):

Now I lay me down to sleep,

I pray the Lord my soul to keep.

And if I die before I wake,

I pray the Lord my soul to take.

Other aspects of praying with small children can include:

- Reading scripture from a children's Bible.
- Putting together a short prayer list to help everyone remember whom they want to pray for.
- Reviewing the events of the day, and asking everyone to recall a moment when they saw something that reminded them of God's presence in their life.
- Just talking to them about God and things they could, or would like to pray about.

Praying with Older Children

The same aspects of praying with small children work equally well with older kids. As their curiosity about faith grows, they may especially enjoy having their own Bibles to read and study. Praying at dinnertime or bedtime tends to work fairly well until the teenage years. By then, they're establishing their own lives and are spending more time away from home. They may also—hopefully they will—have prayer lives independent from yours as well. Try not to let their growing independence replace your family prayer times. Find ways to keep them a part of your family's shared experiences. Even if you only get together occasionally, and for just a few minutes or so, they'll be shared moments your children will cherish when they have families of their own.

symbolism

As children grow older, don't hesitate to introduce them to other kinds of spiritual experiences, and especially the ones that mean the most to you. If you enjoy taking annual prayer retreats, for example, you may want to bring the family along (with the facility's permission, of course) on the next one.

Many teenagers are fascinated by spirituality, hungry to try new things, and not shy at all about doing it. You may find their enthusiasm a catalyst for some new experiences of your own. And, at the same time, you might find them willing partners for some of your wildest dreams. Zen meditation might be tough on the knees, but there's nothing like giving it a go when your daughter says she would love to try it with you.

Keeping a Prayer Journal

Many people who pray on a regular basis make little notes to themselves about various aspects of prayer. They may write down certain passages from the Bible they want to pray over, or reminders to pray about certain things or for certain people. Keeping a prayer journal can be a great way to organize all those scraps of paper into one handy resource. Having a written record of the time you spent in prayer can also help you reflect on your efforts. It's proof positive of how much you've grown in your prayer life, and how God has worked through your prayers.

Types of Prayer Journals

Prayer journals are traditionally handwritten, but there's nothing saying you can't make your journal computer based if you find tapping away on a keyboard easier than writing longhand. Some people keep their prayer journals on handheld devices like PDAs. While writing in a beautifully bound journal has a distinctly aesthetic edge over the others, choose the method that works best for you.

If you do decide to go the old-fashioned way, consider making your prayer journaling a spiritual and a sensual experience by picking a beautiful journal in which to write, and maybe even by treating yourself to a good pen. There are blank books specifically designed for journaling available at many bookstores, and ones designed especially for prayer journaling at Christian bookstores. If you prefer a less fancy approach, just use any style of journal or notebook that suits your needs. Some people even use index cards for this purpose. They're great for writing down your thoughts on the fly as you can take them wherever you go. If you want to keep them all in one place, you can paste them into a blank book, or stick them into a recipe box.

quote

All Scripture is given by inspiration of God, and is profitable for doctrine, for reproof, for correction, for instruction in righteousness . . .
—Paul, 2 Timothy 3:16

What to Write About

You can use a prayer journal to:

- Write out your prayers.
- Make a prayer list of everyone you want to pray for.
- Record special prayer requests, both yours and for others.
- Remind yourself to pray for certain things on certain days.
- Record thoughts that come to mind when praying.
- Record the dates when prayers are answered.
- Keep track of key Bible verses.

Everyone who keeps a journal does it in a different way. You might want to write daily, perhaps following a prayer session, or just when the spirit moves you. Your writing could take the form of a log—just brief entries recording the day's events—or a conversation about your thoughts, your dreams, what's on your heart, you name it. Regardless of the approach you take, make the commitment to keep your journal going. Even if it's just a couple of words, make sure you record them on a regular basis. Stay away from writing in your journal for too long, and you'll feel like you have too much catching up to do.

Fasting

Restricting food and drink is a spiritual discipline common in many religions. It has been practiced from the earliest times, sometimes as penance, but more often in conjunction with prayer or an aid to discernment. Muslims, for example, fast from dawn to sunset every day during the ninth month, Ramadan, as a means of underscoring God's importance, to focus on spiritual goals and values, and to help believers identify with and respond to the less fortunate. Some Muslims also fast every Monday and Thursday. The Quran also recommends additional periods of fasting as a way of communing with the Divine.

Jews fast and pray on Yom Kippur, the Day of Atonement, and on five other holidays during the year. Two of them—Yom Kippur and Tishah B'av, which commemorates the destruction of the Temple—are major fasts, which call for refraining from such things as food, water, and sexual intercourse. Less stringent fasts are observed on the other holidays. Followers may also fast privately as a sign of mourning or at any other time when making a special request to God.

factum

In addition to Islam, fasting also plays a role in Hinduism and Buddhism. Hindu ascetics traditionally fasted while on pilgrimage and to prepare for certain festivals; modern adherents fast during festivals and on New Moon days. Modern-day Buddhists commonly fast and profess their sins four times a month as a method of purification.

Fasting in the Christian Church

The practice of fasting varies among the Christian churches. It's been most rigorous in the Orthodox church, where followers traditionally observe four fasting seasons—the Great Lent, the Apostles' Fast, the Dormition Fast, and the Nativity Fast, as well as several single-day fasts. During these fasting periods, Orthodox parishioners eat no meat, dairy products, or eggs. Fish is also restricted at times.

Many Catholics in the United States follow the church's Lenten penance requirements that call for eating only one full meal and two smaller ones on Ash Wednesday and Good Friday. On these days, as well as all the Fridays of Lent, they also abstain from meat, but they can eat eggs, milk products, meat-flavored soups, gravies, and sauces, and condiments made from animal fat.

In Protestant churches, fasting is left to individual choice. Christians who belong to denominations without formal fasting calendars often maintain a partial fast during Lent, giving up a particular food or type of food for this period, and they might fast at other times of the year when they're seeking God's direction.

Fasting in the Bible

References to fasting abound in the Bible. Moses fasted for at least two recorded forty-day periods. Psalm 35 records David's use of fasting in conjunction with prayer when petitioning God for His intervention: "But as for me, when they were sick, My clothing was sackcloth; I humbled myself with fasting; And my prayer would return to my own heart" (Psalm 35:13).

symbolism

In biblical times, abstinence from sleep, marital sex, anointing, and bathing were also considered ways in which people could fast. Other forms of fasting include eating only in moderation, eating only certain kinds of food, or cutting out treats such as junk food or candy.

Many Old Testament prophets—including Daniel, Elijah, Ezra, and Nehemiah—also humbled themselves before God by fasting. The Israelites fasted so often, in fact, that the prophet Isaiah railed about it having become too routine, and said it had lost its true meaning.

There are also numerous references to fasting in the New Testament. Jesus abstained from both food and water for forty days (obviously par for the course for biblical fasting). Early Christians did as well. But there isn't anything in the New Testament that specifically tells believers that they should fast. In fact, fasting didn't become a popular spiritual discipline among Christians until the Middle Ages.

Modern Day Fasting

Many great Christians fasted and spoke to its value. John Wesley, the founder of the Methodist church, fasted every Wednesday and Friday, and required the same of all his clergy. In fact, he wouldn't ordain anyone who didn't follow this schedule. Fasting and praying also played a key role in the spiritual walks of Jonathan Edwards, Martin Luther, and John Calvin.

quote

Of fasting I say this: it is right to fast frequently in order to subdue and control the body. For when the stomach is full, the body does not serve for preaching, for praying, for studying, or doing anything else that is good. Under such circumstances God's Word cannot remain. But one should not fast with a view to meriting something by it as a good work.

—Martin Luther, in *What Luther Says*

More recently, however, fasting has been viewed by many as an outdated spiritual discipline that adds very little to worship and prayer. The central role that food plays in our culture today is often a strong deterrent to the practice. Going without food can be seen as something that damages one's health. But a fast, if done properly, can do good things, both spiritually and physically. Not only can it clear the body of excesses, it can help you reach deeper into prayer, and, through the process, bring you closer to God.

Benefits of Fasting

While fasting clearly has its physical side, the practice's primary purpose is to help us draw closer to God. An occasional short fast helps put physical needs and appetites into better perspective. A fast can also:

- Give us more time to spend with God in prayer.
- Help us better understand, and yield to, God's commands.
- Reveal certain things that play a bigger role in our lives than we'd like them to.

Fasting on a regular basis can also help develop a better sense of discipline in all areas of our lives. Focusing on food can be a great way to avoid dealing with issues that we'd rather avoid. Take that focus away, even for a little while, and there's not much standing between you and your little demons, whatever they may be.

symbolism

> If you have any concerns at all about your health, be sure to talk to your doctor before you begin your fast. If you haven't had a physical in a while, get one. It's a good idea to know if you have any physical problems that would rule out fasting for you.

How to Fast

First, a major, and very serious caveat: Do not even think about fasting—even skipping a meal—if it would in any way compromise your health. If you are pregnant or nursing, or if you have any of the following conditions, do not, repeat, DO NOT fast without professional supervision, preferably a physician's:

- Diabetes or hyperglycemia
- Auto-immune disorders such as HIV and AIDS
- Eating disorders such as anorexia or bulimia
- Anemia
- Chronic diseases, including heart, kidney, or stomach problems, and cancer

Fasts vary in type and duration. The most common are:

- Single-meal fasts, where you skip one meal in a day.
- Twenty-four-hour fasts, where you abstain from food for two meals.
- Extended fasts, which range from a week to the biblical tradition of forty days.

There are also different kinds of fasts, including:

- Water fasts, which should only be followed for several days at the most.
- Water and juice fasts, the most common.
- Partial fasts, during which certain foods are not eaten for a set period of time.
- Complete fasts, which are not recommended due to the obvious medical risks associated with abstaining from all food and liquids. (If you feel called to do a complete fast, definitely consult your physician first.)

There is no single way to do a fast, and no set formula for how long you should fast. In this area, let God lead your efforts. You don't have to follow any particular approach, but it's a good idea to start slowly if you haven't fasted before. Try a partial fast first for one day, maybe from dinner one night to dinner the next, or from lunch to lunch. This means skipping just two meals. Or, start by fasting for one meal a day, or one day a week, or one week a month. In time, you'll be able to fast for longer periods if you so choose.

factum

The Bible records two types of food fasts. There are partial fasts, such as that described in the Book of Daniel, where he only abstained from delicacies, meat, and wine; and absolute or supernatural fasts, during which all food and liquid was off limits The Bible records two types of food fasts. There are partial fasts, such as that described in the Book of Daniel, where he only abstained from delicacies, meat, and wine; and absolute or supernatural fasts, during which all food and liquid was off limits.

What to Expect When Fasting

If you haven't fasted before, be prepared for some negative physical experiences, especially in the beginning. More than anything else, you're going to be hungry. Sometimes unbearably so. Those hunger pangs, though, serve as a reminder as to why you're fasting. During longer fasts, hunger pangs tend to subside, but you'll definitely feel them on shorter ones. Headaches—often due to caffeine withdrawal—are also common during the beginning of a fast.

Fasts of longer than a day will leave you physically weakened. For this reason, it's a good idea to curtail strenuous physical activity while you're fasting. If you're feeling up to it, take short, easy walks. If you're not, don't push it. Remember, the goal in fasting is to gain new spiritual perspectives. Trying to keep an exercise program going during a fast can work against what you're working toward.

What to Do Instead of Eating

The time you'd usually spend eating should instead be spent in prayer or other spiritual pursuits. These may also be good times to catch up on your devotional reading or to journal your thoughts.

How to Break a Fast

If your fast is for a short duration, say you've only skipped one meal, you don't have to do anything special when you return to eating. Try not to overeat, however.

Fasts of longer duration call for easing yourself back into food:

- On the first day after a fast, restrict yourself to foods that are easily digestible, such as clear soup, gelatin, mild fruits such as bananas and melons, and vegetable juice. Keep the portions very small.
- Add solid but bland foods in your second day after fasting. Choose from potatoes, chicken, yogurt, cooked cereals, and cooked vegetables. Continue to keep the portions small.
- As you feel able, continue to move back into your regular eating pattern. Don't be surprised, however, if certain foods aren't as appealing to you as they once were. Remember, fasts redirect the body as well as the spirit.

Guiding the Spirit

Throughout history, many people seeking a better connection to the Almighty have enlisted the help of a trusted adviser to help guide them. In modern times, these learned sages often take the form of spiritual directors or guides.

Spending time with a spiritual director—someone who is committed to helping you grow in your spiritual life—can be immensely rewarding, especially if you're seeking a different perspective on where you're going in your relationship with God. People often misunderstand what spiritual directors do, and feel they should only consult with one when things aren't going well in their spiritual lives. But this isn't the case at all. Spiritual direction can be sought at any time you feel you need a little extra help-in good times and in bad. Individuals wishing to work in some aspect of ministry are often encouraged-and sometimes required-to meet with a spiritual director to determine if their call to ministry is true, and to help them determine what their best area of service would be. But spiritual direction is by no means limited only to matters of discernment.

Spiritual direction is sometimes confused with therapy or pastoral counseling. The practices, however, are very different. Most spiritual directors confine their efforts to helping people sort out their spiritual lives and helping them become more aware of God's presence in their lives, and are generally not qualified as counselors. If you're seeking a more therapeutic relationship, look for someone with the credentials to provide such services.

Finding a Spiritual Director

Sometimes God puts a particular person in our lives to serve as a spiritual guide. Most often, however, you have to go find one. If there is someone you know whose spiritual life you respect, you may want to consider asking that person to work with you. If it's something you both want to do, and it feels right to both of you, you'll know it.

Many people prefer to take a more formal approach to finding a spiritual director, including:

- Asking a church leader—a pastor or minister—for recommendations.
- Asking friends if they know of one or have worked with one.

- Checking with Spiritual Directors International, an association of spiritual directors founded in 1989. You'll find more information in Appendix B.
- Contacting local religious institutions, such as churches or monasteries.

You might have to search a little longer than you'd like to for someone to work with. Spiritual directors usually take a pretty low profile, and they often don't advertise themselves as such, even when talking about what they do. Instead, they rely more on word of mouth and referrals from past and present clients.

Choose your spiritual director carefully. Consider what you're about to embark on as a long-term relationship. It may not end up being one—there is nothing that says you have to keep seeing one spiritual director forever—but you certainly want to approach it that way. You want someone who is capable, and willing, to go the distance with you, however long that distance might be.

Also consider what you want in a spiritual director. Do you want this person to be a member of the same faith as yours? Should he or she be specially trained? Would you feel comfortable working with someone who is a member of your spiritual community? Would you prefer someone outside of your usual circle of friends and acquaintances? Should this person be a member of the clergy, or will a layperson with a compassionate heart be more in keeping with your vision of what you'd like your spiritual direction to be about?

Due to the intimate nature of these relationships, most people prefer to have some distance between them and their spiritual directors. In fact, it's often best to not have any sort of a relationship with the person you choose outside of this. Another fairly standard approach to choosing a spiritual director is to pick one of the same sex—for the obvious reasons. This isn't to say that there aren't any male-female spiritual counseling relationships, as there definitely are. For the most part, though, spiritual relationships work best when there is no sexual tension between the participants.

Once you've found a person or two who are potential candidates for the job, it's a good idea to talk to him or her a little first before making a firm commitment. Think of it as an informal job interview. Ask questions about his or her philosophies, approach, and experience, and what he or she expects of you. Some spiritual directors give their clients assignments or activities to work on between meetings. Find out how often your spiritual director wants to meet, and where you'll meet. Most important, make sure that this is a person you want to work with, someone you feel has the requisite experience and skills to function well in the job you're ready to assign.

What to Expect from Spiritual Direction

Regular meetings, about once a month or so, are about average for spiritual direction. During these meetings, you'll talk about what's been going on in your life. Your spiritual director will listen, for the most part, and will ask you questions when appropriate. He or she might suggest books for you to read, or various spiritual disciplines for you to explore. Most sessions begin and end with prayer, and sometimes a few moments of silent reflection. Unlike counseling sessions, which can sometimes leave you shaky when your time is up, you can look forward to leaving your sessions with your spiritual director feeling uplifted, calm, and peaceful, and perhaps re-energized about your spiritual journey.

discussion question

What is a good length for a prayer walk?
It is a good idea to measure your time spent praying and walking in minutes, not in miles. Twenty to thirty minutes is about par for the course; walks of longer or shorter duration are perfectly fine as well.

A Final Word

We have come to the end of this particular journey in prayer, and we'll now bid you farewell. But we're leaving you in very good hands, in fact, the best hands of all. Use prayer to continue moving toward God. He will never disappoint you.

APPENDIX A

Glossary of Terms

ACTS:

The acronym for a prayer style that includes stands for adoration, confession, thanksgiving, and supplication.

Agni:

The Aryan god of sacrificial fire.

Allah:

"The God" (from Arabic).

Anglican prayer beads:

Prayer ropes of thirty-three beads used by members of the Episcopal church.

apocrypha:

From the Greek for "things hidden away." Refers to Jewish and early Christian writings excluded from the Scriptures.

Baghavad Gita:

Meaning "The Song of the Lord," one of the basic religious scriptures for Hinduism.

Bible:

From the Greek *ta biblia,* meaning "the books."

Book of Common Prayer:

Also known as "BCP," the official prayer book of the Anglican and Episcopal churches.

Brahma:

The Hindu god of the creation.

Buddha:

The "Enlightened One," or the "Awakened One."

canon:

A set of religious writings regarded as authentic and definitive, which form a religion's body of scripture.

Celtic cross:
The cross used by Celtic Christians.

censer:
A vessel, usually suspended from chains, used for burning incense. Also called a thurible.

cherubim:
Supernatural creatures associated with the presence of God. Also thought of as angels.

chotki:
The prayer rope used by members of the Russian Orthodox church.

common prayer:
The regular cycle of services of the Anglican and Episcopal churches, including the Daily Office, the Litany, and the Eucharist.

communal prayer:
Prayer that is done by a group. Also called corporate prayer.

compline:
The last of the seven separate hours that are set aside for prayer each day.

colloquy:
A discussion or conversation.

contemplation:
Concentration of the mind on spiritual matters, such as achieving closer unity with God.

contemplative:
Somebody who practices contemplation as a spiritual exercise, especially a member of a Christian monastic order.

corpus:
The carved figure of the body of Christ attached to a crucifix.

covenant:
A solemn agreement that is binding between all parties.

crucifix:
A cross that bears a representation of the body of Christ.

Daily Office:
The order of service followed by the Anglican and Episcopal churches.

discernment prayers:
Prayers prayed for direction.

Divine Office:
Another name for the Liturgy of the Hours.

doctrine:
A body of ideas taught to people as truthful or correct.

Eastern Orthodox cross:
A cross of early Christianity. Also called the Byzantine cross, the Eastern cross, and the Russian Orthodox cross.

Eucharist:
The religious ceremony that commemorates the last meal of Jesus Christ before his death. Also called Communion, or Holy Communion.

Gospels:
The New Testament books of Matthew, Mark, Luke, and John.

Hanukkah:
The Festival of Light in Judaism, celebrating the rededication of the Temple in Jerusalem in 165 B.C.E.

Havdallah candle:
The candle that closes the Sabbath in the Jewish faith.

Humility:
The quality of being modest or respectful.

Icons:
Depictions of holy figures—often the Holy Trinity, the Holy Family, or Jesus and Mary—and religious events.

Indra:
The Aryan god of the air and the storm.

Intercessory prayers:
Prayers said on someone else's behalf.

Jesus Prayer:
Also called the Breath Prayer or the Prayer of the Heart.

Kinkin:
A Zen walking meditation in which attention is focused on each step and the breath is measured and controlled.

Knights Templar:
Members of a Christian military order founded in 1119 to protect pilgrims after the First Crusade.

Komboskini:
The prayer rope used by members of the Greek Orthodox church.

Krishna:
One of two forms of Vishnu, the Hindu god of sacrifice.

Labyrinth:
A single-path, unicursal tool for personal, psychological, and spiritual transformation.

Lauds:
The first prayers of the day in some churches.

lectio divina:
A form of prayer based on slow, meditative reading of sacred scripture.

litany:
A series of sung or spoken liturgical prayers or requests for the blessing of God.

liturgy:
A form and arrangement of public worship determined by a church or religion.

Liturgy of the Hours:
A Catholic liturgy consisting of prayers, psalms, and meditations for every hour of the day. Also called the Divine Office.

malas:
Prayer counters used by Buddhists and Hindus.

Maltese cross:
A cross with eight points, representing the eight Beatitudes of Matthew.

mantra:
A sacred word, chant, or sound that is repeated during meditation.

Marduk:
The primary Babylonian god.

Mars:
The Roman god of agriculture and war.

meditation:
Emptying one's mind of thoughts, or concentrating on one thing.

monastics:
People who live with others in a monastery and observe religious vows.

mezuzah:
A small case holding a roll of scripture and the name of God, placed on the doorposts of Jewish homes.

mindfulness:
The state of paying attention or being careful.

mystic:
Someone who practices or believes in mysticism.

negative prayer:
Prayer that can affect someone negatively, or have a negative outcome.

officiant:
Someone who conducts a religious ceremony.

order of service:
Another term for liturgy.

Orthodox church:
A Christian church that originated in the Byzantine Empire.

pantheon:
A collection of gods.

petition:
An appeal or request to a higher authority or being.

piety:
Strong, respectful belief in God.

polytheism:
The belief in more than one god or many gods.

prayer:
From the Latin word *precari*, meaning "to entreat."

prayer walking:
Praying while you're walking. Also called spirited walking or walking meditation.

prehistory:
The time before civilization.

private prayer:
Prayer said privately, as opposed to with a group.

prostrate:
To lie flat on the face or bow very low in worship or humility.

Psalter:
A book containing psalms, or the Book of Psalms, used in worship.

Quran:
The holy scripture of the Islamic faith.

Rama:
One of two forms of the Hindu god Vishnu, the god of sacrifice.

rational prayer:
Prayers of the mind, where thoughts are expressed in words and sentences.

Reformation, The:
The religious movement that arose in Western Europe during the sixteenth century.

religion:
The outward expression of spiritual impulses, in the form of a specific religious impulse or practice.

retreat:
A period of quiet rest and contemplation in a secluded place.

osary:

he string of prayer beads used by Catholics. The term comes from the Latin word *rosarius,* which means garland or bouquet of roses.

uach:

he Hebrew word meaning breath or spirit.

acred space:

special place set aside for prayer, decorated with objects to enhance the prayer xperience.

cripture:

acred writings, often used to refer to those from the Bible.

ecular:

ot religious or spiritual in nature, not controlled by a religious body or concerned with eligious or spiritual matters.

hema:

he oldest daily prayer in Judaism.

imple prayer:

rayer in its simplest form, a pouring out of the heart to God. Also called expository prayer, meaning that it sets forth facts.

iddur:

he prayer book used by followers of the Jewish faith. The plural of "siddur" is "siddurim."

iva:

he Hindu god of destruction and reproduction.

oma:

he Aryan god of intoxication.

pirit:

he vital force that characterizes a living being.

spirituality:
An inner sense of something greater than oneself.

St. Andrew's cross:
One of the most ancient crosses, it resembles the letter "X."

supernatural:
That which is not from the observable, tangible, or measurable universe.

supplication:
A humble appeal to someone who has the power to grant a request.

synagogue:
The place of worship and communal center of a Jewish congregation.

Tao-te Ching:
The sacred text that is the basis for Taoism, meaning "The Way and Its Power."

Taoism:
The Chinese religion that seeks harmony and long life.

tefilah:
The Hebrew word for prayer is *tefilah*, which, loosely translated, means "to judge oneself."

tefillin:
The symbols of faith that Jewish men wear on the head, above the eyes.

theology:
The study of religion, a religious theory, school of thought, or system of belief.

transformation:
A complete change, usually into something with an improved appearance or usefulness.

transliterated text:
Foreign words spelled out using the English language to aid in their pronunciation.

Upanishads, The:
One of two sacred texts of Hindu scripture.

Vespers:
An evening church service. Also known as Evening Prayer, or Evensong.

Vishnu:
The Hindu god of sacrifice.

Visualization:
Creating a clear picture of something in the mind, often done to promote a sense of well-being.

Yahweh:
The God of the Hebrews.

Yartzeit candle:
In Judaism, a special candle customarily lit on the anniversary of a family member's death.

Yoga:
The Hindu disciplines that promote the unity of the individual with a supreme being through a system of postures and rituals.

APPENDIX B

Prayer Resources

Books

à Kempis, Thomas. *The Imitation of Christ: How Jesus Wants Us to Live.* A Contemporary Version by William Griffin. New York: HarperCollins Publishers, Inc., 2000. (There are many different translations and versions of this classic work. This is a very modern translation, which makes à Kempis's words extremely easy to read. It may not be for everyone.)

Armstrong, Karen. *A History of God: The 4,000-Year Quest of Judaism, Christianity and Islam.* New York: Ballantine Books, 1993.

Basit, Abdul. *Essence of the Quran: Commentary and Interpretation of Surah Al-Fatihah.* Chicago, IL: KAZI Publications, 1997.

Casey, Michael. *Sacred Reading: The Ancient Art of Lectio Divina.* Liguori, MO: Triumph Books, 1995.

Casey, Michael. *Toward God: The Ancient Wisdom of Western Prayer.* Liguori, MO: Triumph Books, 1996.

Chinmoy, Sri. *Commentaries on the Vedas, the Upanishads and the Bhagavad Gita: The Three Branches of India's Life-Tree.* New York: Aum Publishing, 1997.

Davis, Kenneth C. *Don't Know Much About The Bible: Everything You Need to Know About the Good Book, but Never Learned.* New York: Eagle Brook, An Imprint of William Morrow and Company, Inc., 1998.

Donin, Rabbi Hayim Halevy. *To Pray As a Jew: A Guide to the Prayer Book and the Synagogue Service.* New York: Basic Books, 1980.

Dossey, Larry, M.D. *Be Careful What You Pray For . . . You Just Might Get It: What We Can Do About the Unintentional Effects of Our Thoughts, Prayers, and Wishes.* San Francisco: HarperSanFrancisco, 1997.

Dossey, Larry, M.D. *Healing Words: The Power of Prayer and the Practice of Medicine.* San Francisco: HarperSanFrancisco, 1993.

Easwaran, Eknath (trans.). *The Bhagavad Gita.* Tomales, CA: Nilgiri Press, 1985.

Easwaran, Eknath (trans.). *The Upanishads.* Tomales, CA: Nilgiri Press, 1987.

Fischer, Norman; Goldstein, Joseph; Simmer-Brown, Judith; Yifa. *Benedict's Dharma: Buddhists Reflect on the Rule of Saint Benedict.* New York: Riverhead Books (a member of Penguin Putnam, Inc.), 2001.

Forest, Jim. *Praying with Icons.* Maryknoll, NY: Orbis Books, 1997.

Foster, Richard J. *Celebration of Discipline: The Path to Spiritual Growth.* San Francisco: HarperSanFrancisco, 1998.

Hanh, Thich Nhat. *Peace Is Every Step: The Path of Mindfulness in Everyday Life.* New York: Bantam Books, 1991.

Hall, Thelma. *Too Deep for Words: Rediscovering Lectio Divina.* Mahwah, NJ: Paulist Press, 1988.

nston, William. *The Cloud of Unknowing and the Book of Privy Counseling.* New York: Image Books, Doubleday (division of Random House), 1996.

ting, Thomas. *Open Mind, Open Heart: The Contemplative Dimension of the Gospel.* Warwick, NY: Amity House, 1986.

n, Sam. *Hymns to an Unknown God: Awakening the Spirit in Everyday Life.* New York: Bantam Books, 1994.

ge, Carolyn Scott. *The Spirited Walker: Fitness Walking for Clarity, Balance, and Spiritual Connection.* San Francisco: HarperSanFrancisco, 1998.

hner, Harold S. *When Bad Things Happen to Good People.* New York: Schocken Books, 2001.

n, Patricia S. *Worship Without Words: The Signs and Symbols of Our Faith.* Brewster, MA: Paraclete Press, 2000.

her Teresa. *Everything Starts from Prayer: Mother Teresa's Meditations on Spiritual Life for People of All Faiths.* Ashland, OR: White Cloud Press, 2000.

dy, Linus. *The Complete Guide to Prayer-Walking: A Simple Path to Body-and-Soul Fitness.* New York: The Crossroad Publishing Company, 1997.

nington, Basil M. *Lectio Divina: Reviving the Ancient Practice of Praying the Scriptures.* New York: Crossroad, 1998.

ger, Marcia. *The Path of Blessing: Experiencing the Energy and Abundance of the Divine.* Woodstock, VT: Jewish Lights Publishing, 2003.

lmont, Jane. *When in Doubt, Sing: Prayer in Daily Life.* New York: HarperCollins, 1999.

kle, Phyllis. *The Divine Hours: Prayers for Summertime: A Manual for Prayer.* New York: Doubleday (a division of Random House, Inc.), 2000. This is the first of three prayer manuals compiled by Publishers Weekly religion editor Phyllis Tickle as a contemporary Book of Hours (Liturgy of Hours).

eb Sites

vww.centeringprayer.com—The Web site for Contemplative Outreach, based in Butler, NJ. One of the best Net-based resources for information on centering prayer. This is also the place to go to get a copy of "The Method of Centering Prayer," a short brochure that provides an excellent overview of what centering prayer is all about and how to do it.

vww.faithlinks.org—A Christian Web site sponsored by the Living Church Foundation, which promotes and supports the spiritual growth of members of the Episcopal church in the United States. Rich in content, most of it linked to various facets of the Episcopal church. Sponsors an online prayer center.

vww.gracecathedral.org/labyrinth—A content-rich site sponsored by Grace Cathedral Church in San Francisco, where the ancient practice of labyrinth walking was reintroduced to modern spiritual seekers. Among the offerings here are an online locator for earthly labyrinths and a gift shop with labyrinth-inspired items, including finger labyrinths for meditation.

www.healingscripture.com—A site including prayer chains, discussion about healing, readings, articles, daily devotionals.

www.labyrinthonline.com—Want to walk a labyrinth but don't have one handy? This site lets you experience two different versions—the Cretan Labyrinth, shorter; and the Chartres Labyrinth, a twenty-minute experience.

www.osb.org/lectio—This is part of a Web site run by the Order of St. Benedict. It has links to many classic texts, including some must-reads on lectio divina, such as excerpts from *The Cloud of Unknowing* and Guigo II's epistle that defined the practice of lectio divina.

www.unification.net/ws/—The Web site for World Scripture, a comparative anthology of sacred texts. There are scriptural passages from 268 sacred texts and 55 oral traditions, organized along 164 common religious themes.

www.universalis.com—A resource for praying the Liturgy of the Hours.

www.catholicfirst.com—Cyber home to many great Christian spiritual works, including the writings of St. Catherine of Siena, Thomas à Kempis, St. Ignatius of Loyola, St. Theresa of Avila, and St. Benedict.

www.beliefnet.com—Have questions about faith? Want to network with others walking a spiritual path? This site covers all the bases, offering information on a variety of world faiths, chat rooms, discussions, meditations, and articles by some of the top spiritual thinkers writing today.

www.sacredspace.com—This Web site, run by the Irish Jesuits, is one of the best ones offering online prayer experiences. Making a "Sacred Space" in your day, and spending ten minutes praying with the Jesuits, is a great way to rest with God.

www.fourgates.com—An online retailer of prayer and meditation supplies, including incense, prayer cushions and benches, candles, Tibetan singing bowls, and Tingsha bells.

www.religiousmall.com—Billed as "The Complete Christian Religious Online Mall," this site has an extensive collection of icons and other prayer supplies, including candles, crosses, incense, and incense burners.

www.solitariesofdekoven.org—The Solitaries of DeKoven supports and encourages the solitary religious life within the Episcopal church. They also make prayer beads, which can be viewed and ordered on this Web site.

www.missionstclare.com—An online version of the Daily Office.

www.spiritsite.com—A Web site rich with excerpts from spiritual books, columns, and more. A great place for test-driving books about the spiritual journey before buying them.

www.sdiworld.org—The Web site for Spiritual Directors International.

treat Information and Locators

www.spiritsite.com—Among the offerings on this site is a spiritual retreat center directory. Many popular retreat spots listed, representing a wide range of spiritual traditions.

, Jack and Marcia. *Sanctuaries: The Complete United States—A Guide to Lodgings in Monasteries, Abbeys, and Retreats.* New York: Bell Tower, 1996.

es, Timothy K. *A Place for God: A Guide to Spiritual Retreats and Retreat Centers.* New York: Doubleday, 2000.

albuto, Robert J. *A Guide to Monastic Guest Houses, Fourth Edition.* Harrisburg, PA: Morehouse Publishing, 2000.

er, Jennifer. *Healing Centers & Retreats: Healthy Getaways for Every Body and Budget.* Emeryville, CA: Avalon Travel Publishing, 1998.

ısic

dhist Nuns at Chuchikjall. *Tibetan Prayer Chants.* Sounds of the World, 1999.

ter. *Nada Himalaya.* New Earth Records, 1998.

t, Benjamin. *Seven Metals Singing Bowls of Tibet.* 1999.

su, Thea. *Singing Bowls of Shangri-La.* Inner Peace Music, 1998.

ous artists. *Journey into Light.* New Earth Records, 2001.

fein, Rebecca; Barash, Morris. *Sacred Chants of the Contemporary Synagogue.* Bari Productions, 1998.

iain, Noirin. *The Virgin's Lament (Caoineadhi Na Maighdine).* Sounds True, 1998.

Bingen, Hildegard. *A Feather on the Breath of God.* Hyperion, 1993.

Krishna. *Pilgrim Heart.* Razor & Tie, 2002.

nantsev, Victor; Arkhipova, Irina. *Sacred Treasures III: Choral Masterworks From Russia and Beyond.* Hearts of Space, 2000.

o Contemporary Music for Centering Prayer, 3-Track Meditation Timer. Available from *www.centeringprayer.com*

rgeault, Cynthia. *Singing the Psalms: How to Chant in the Christian Contemplative Tradition.* Three cassettes. Available from Sounds True,1-800-333-9184.